D0146477

Expecting Armageddon

Essential Readings in
Failed Prophecy

Edited by
Jon R. Stone

Routledge
New York and London

Published in 2000 by
Routledge
29 West 35th Street
New York, NY 10001

Published in Great Britain by
Routledge
11 New Fetter Lane
London EC4P 4EE

Library of Congress Cataloging-in-Publication Data is
available from the Library of Congress

#42309476

In Memory of My Grandfather:
Curtis James Stone, Sr.
1909–1999
A kind and generous man

Contents

Preface

The Romans had a saying that captures in a phrase at least one aspect of human nature that contributes to the persistence of millennial expectation: the fear of death is worse than death. Fear of the unknown makes us all a little nervous, especially when that unknown has to do with the end of time. There is perhaps no better example of this than the current obsession over the coming millennium, which may turn into madness by the latter weeks of December. With predictions of computer malfunctions, power failures, nuclear meltdowns, worldwide economic depression, environmental disasters, famine, disease, and the usual social chaos, the end of time might prove a welcome relief.

A question naturally follows: Why all this importance attached to "time," which is, after all, a human invention? While some scholars may think that all the doomsaying and endtime predictions surrounding the mere change from year 1999 to year 2000 reveal modern society at its most neurotic, those of us who remain fascinated by the recurrence of such speculations in the face of centuries upon centuries of prophetic disconfirmation find in these and other most recent doomsday scenarios evidence of the persistent human desire to find meaning in time and events. This search for meaning—or for a discernible pattern to human experience—couples with a deep longing to start anew. The world as it appears and as people experience it seems somehow wrong to them. The problems they face are not so easily solved. As with the ancient Greek dramatists, the modern likewise finds him/herself calling upon a *deus ex machina* to intervene and set things right again.

Admittedly, this particular rendering of endtime expectation brings out some of the more benign and optimistic aspects underlying the desire of most millennial movements to see the old world "go up in flames." As Dick Anthony, Michael Barkun, Thomas Robbins, and Catherine Wessinger have ably pointed out, millennial expectations can sometimes turn violent. Still, one might argue, the emphasis of most endtime predictions is not on cataclysmic destruction for its own sake. Most prophets of doom hold out to their followers the promise of either a heavenly or extraterrestrial world waiting for them beyond this one or a new Eden rising up out of the ashes of the old one.

This present collection of essays takes as its central focus the social-psychological responses of millennial groups to failed prophecy. First asked in 1956 by Leon Festinger and his team of researchers, the question "What happens when prophecy fails?" has spawned a number of subsequent case studies that have sought either to test their original thesis, to elaborate upon their theory of cognitive dissonance, or, in most instances, to offer new theories to account for the differing or seemingly idiosyncratic responses to failed prophecy.

It must be stressed that the case studies included in this anthology represent only a selection of the research that has appeared in print since the publication of Festinger, Riecken, and Schachter. For practical purposes, this collection includes only reprints, in order of date published, what one might call the "essential" readings in failed prophecy. With the exception of typographical and grammatical corrections—and modest spelling and stylistic changes that bring the various texts into conformity with the publisher's own stylistic requirements— all the essays in this present work have been republished *in toto*. Although textual references and quoted passages cited in this volume's introductory essay are keyed to the pages of this volume, for the reader's benefit, the sources of the original articles have been listed in the bibliography at the end of the introduction. It is my hope that the usefulness of this collection to scholars and interested readers will be found in the variety of case studies and theoretical essays it contains, in its interdisciplinary cast, and—in view of the approaching millennium, beginning 2001 C.E.—in its timeliness.

In addition to the many friends and colleagues who have shown interest in my various projects over the years, I would like to express especial appreciation to Phillip Lucas, Eric Mazur, Gordon Melton, and to two anonymous reviewers for their helpful comments on earlier drafts of the introduction, which was first presented in a conference in 1997. William Germano, Jennifer Hirshlag, and Julien Devereux of Routledge deserve special credit for keeping this work focused and on track. I would also like to thank Josh Clifton, Matt Reynolds, and Russell Voth—all three Religious Studies majors at UC Berkeley—for their assistance in proofreading the manuscript despite the tedium and strong temptation to lie back in the summer sunshine.

A final word of appreciation should go to the RS majors who enrolled in my seminar on American Millennialism in Spring '99 and who unsuspectingly "test drove" this anthology. Their interest in this and in the other materials of the course was matched only by their great eagerness to learn. Along with Matt and Josh, they include Sunil Aggarwal, Rich Atalla, Rebecca Birken, Paul Chae, Beth Glick, Sharifa Gulamhussein, Andrew Harper, Colin Holbrook, Louella Jorgensen, Wes Lazara, Jack McHenry, Brian Miller, Julie Mulgrew, Aaron Murdock, Sujata Singhal, and Brad Stoddard. As the line goes: this note of thanks is modest recompense for the difficult but rewarding intellectual journey they were forced to undertake.

Fiat Lux.

Jon R. Stone
Summer 1999
University of California, Berkeley

Introduction

Jon R. Stone

Suppose an individual believes something with his whole heart; suppose further that he has a commitment to this belief, that he has taken irrevocable actions because of it; finally, suppose that he is presented with evidence, unequivocal and undeniable evidence, that his belief is wrong: what will happen? The individual will frequently emerge, not only unshaken, but even more convinced of the truth of his beliefs than ever before. Indeed, he may even show a new fervor about convincing and converting other people to his view.　　—Festinger et al. 1956:3 [31]

The expectation of an end to time and the yearning for an earthly paradise have been enduring themes in Western religious thought. Seemingly every generation from Adam to Madonna has witnessed the emergence of one type of millennialist group or another, each declaring with renewed urgency the imminent destruction of the world and dawn of a new age. "The millennialists you will have with you always," Jesus might well have said. But, then, Jesus was himself a millennialist, the four Gospels being a record not only of his sayings and miracles but of his prophetic warnings as well. "Repent, the Kingdom of God is at hand," he boldly preached to those lining the banks of the River Jordan. Many of those who heard his message believed and followed. As a Galilean prophet, Jesus was perhaps unrivaled, but he was not alone. His radical pronouncements against the religious establishment of his day represented but one of a myriad of "apocalyptic"[1] utterings spoken by prophets before and after his time. Since Jesus' time, many of his followers throughout the world and throughout the ages have eagerly expected his return and, with it, the foretold millennial Kingdom.

There have appeared many differing types of millenarian movements in Western history, and not all of them have been Jewish or Christian.[2] In North America, for example, groups as doctrinally and organizationally diverse as the Shakers, Adventists, Dispensationalists, Pentecostal-Holiness, Rappites, Campbellites, Millerites, Zoarites, Mormons, Ephratans, Oneidans, Jehovah's Witnesses, Nazarenes, Church of God, Children of God, Assemblies of God, Latter Rain, Moonies, Scientologists, British Israelists, Christian Identity, and countless varieties of New Age movements—to name only a handful—have sprouted and thrived in its culturally rich and welcoming climate. All have sought after human perfection and a paradise on or beyond this Earth.

It is therefore no surprise to find millennial expectation everywhere throughout the globe, as its orientation to time and reality has spread beyond the Western world to the remotest places of Africa, Asia, and the Melanesian Islands (see, for example, Worsley 1968; Burridge 1969; and Smith 1976). However, despite the overwhelming varieties of endtime ideologies and movements, what most millenarian (or chiliastic) groups have had in common has been their conviction that their own age was corrupt and their anticipation that a restoration of an earlier, truer, and purer age was on the horizon. Though, to modern sensibilities, such hopefulness in a coming Elysian paradise might appear hopelessly naive, one certainly cannot fault this strong yearning after a peaceful and harmonious world where all things are set right and where the "dwelling place of God is among men."

When we speak of "expectation" of the world's end, we are mindful of the fact that generation after generation of millenarians have been disappointed. Their endtime hopes and prophecies have not come true. Not surprisingly, for some believers, prophetic failure has spelled not only the end of their hopes but the end of their movements as well. Some prophets, to be sure, have taken it upon themselves to fulfill their own predictions. As recent as January 1999, for example, Israeli police arrested fourteen members of a Colorado endtime sect calling itself the Concerned Christians. Their leader, Monte Kim Miller, had prophesied that he would die a bloody death in the streets of the Holy City and be resurrected three days later. This prophesied event, he taught, coming just before millennium's end, would herald Christ's Second Coming in the year 2000. Israeli police have already begun to prepare for similar "endtime" incidents that officials expect will erupt throughout the year. In similar fashion, other endtime groups, both Jewish and Christian, have openly predicted the destruction of the Dome of the Rock, the mosque built over the most sacred site in Jerusalem. This endtime prophecy, whether fulfilled through human agency or divine fiat, is believed by some to be the sign that will usher in the messianic age and, with it, the salvation of the Jews.

As a further example, a number of other groups have armed themselves in the belief that they will be joined by the hosts of angelic armies to fight the endtime battle of Armageddon, prophesied in the Apocalypse of John (the Book of Revelation). In the case of one notorious group, the Branch Davidians, their charismatic leader, David Koresh, taught that Christ would establish his Kingdom, the New Jerusalem, in the dry plains of central Texas. As faithful participants in his Second Coming, the Davidians believed that they had been divinely chosen to aid Christ in bringing his Kingdom to this world. As we know from history, after a long standoff with government agents in early 1993, their millennial dream ended in a fiery hell.

Other sensationalized endtime movements, such as Heaven's Gate, have turned their hatred of the sinful world inward, withdrawing into small, tightly controlled communities. In demonstration of their chosenness and of their determination to reach a heaven beyond the clouds, the thirty-nine members of Heaven's Gate opted for the more drastic and irreversible step of suicide.

No matter their deeply held convictions, when one sees the horrifying images on television of shoot-outs, burning buildings, and then row upon row of pinewood coffins, the questions that naturally come to mind are: How? Why? How could this happen? Why would someone believe this? Such blind convic-tion and its violent consequences baffle the mind. Indeed, all these senseless deaths through violent self-destruction defy human logic and run counter to the human will to survive. If, as Schopenhauer once wrote, man wills to live ultimately and for all time, what is it about religious belief that in embracing it people are willing to cast aside their very lives and the lives of their children? Is the promise of a new life beyond the stars worth the high price of suicide or violent death?

The answer, as most religions teach, lies with the problem of human percep-tion (or misperception) about reality. That is, perhaps the answer lies with the perception—the belief—that the material world is not really *real* and that beyond this world lies a higher and spiritually more satisfying existence. It was St. Paul who wrote in 2 Corinthians: "for the things which are seen are tempo-ral, but the things which are not seen are eternal" (4:18).

This is not to say that to reach it religions extol their adherents to kill them-selves, but most faiths teach that the doorway to that reality *is* physical death. At death, we are told, the material body is either sloughed off or transformed, and the human soul either enters heaven or continues its upward progression along a spiritual plane. With this in mind, then, it is perhaps understandable that to the believer material existence may hold little charm when compared to the eter-nal bliss of a spiritual life that awaits in heaven.

To return, then, to the topic of endtime expectation: while it has sometimes been the case that the anticipation of "Kingdom come" has periodically found its fulfillment through violence, what Sartre might have identified as "bad faith," it is important to stress that historically the turn to violence and self-destruction has been rare. Instead, most human responses to endtime expectation, while no less passionate, have been far more passive and far less dramatic. What is more, despite their lack of sensationalism, these more common and more benign end-time movements have proven no less fascinating to scholars and researchers seek-ing to understand the social and psychological dynamics of religious conviction and its disappointment.

Prophetic Failure and Cognitive Dissonance

Endtime expectation and prophetic failure have presented committed believers with an interesting and persistent cognitive challenge: the problem of disso-nance. Theoretically, cognitive dissonance arises when the beliefs, values, or opinions individuals hold (that is, their cognitions) come into conflict with their experience of reality. When dissonance occurs, there tend to arise countervailing psychological pressures within persons that cause them to seek ways of reducing or eliminating dissonance. In most cases, people respond to dissonance by bringing their thoughts in line with their experiences. In some cases, however, the dissonance between beliefs and experience is not so easily resolved, especially if the conflicting beliefs or opinions have arisen from deeply held religious convictions (see Festinger 1957:9–11).

Perhaps one of the most cited examples of cognitive dissonance is that which arises from prophetic disconfirmation, the failure of a predicted event to come true. How individuals and movements respond to failed prophecy is the focus of this present collection of essays. Taking their cue from the now-classic study, *When Prophecy Fails,* by Leon Festinger, Henry Riecken, and Stanley Schachter (1956), the various case studies that comprise this anthology, all of which have been previously published, address in some specific and theoretical way the social and psychological dynamics of prophecy and its disconfirmation. An interesting aspect of the research that has been conducted into prophecy and dissonance is that, although four decades have passed since Festinger and his colleagues published their seminal study, and despite scathing criticism and determined attempts by some researchers to refute its findings, the central thesis of the Festinger book seems largely to have held true: people tend to respond to failed prophecy in ways that reaffirm their faith.

In this introduction, I will briefly outline the Festinger thesis and then present a lengthy overview of the major subsequent studies collected in this anthology that have sought to test it. From the outset it must be stated that it is not possible to include all research that has appeared in print since the publication of the Festinger text. In fact, given the overlapping and sometimes contradictory observations and analyses these researchers have made, it will not be possible to discuss all the findings of even this sampling. Indeed, to do so would require far too much space and a far greater nimbleness of mind and pen than even the saints and ascended masters possess. Accordingly, the purpose of this introduction will not be to untangle the knots or reconcile the different findings in this growing body of literature but simply to draw out some of the more useful insights these collected studies have offered in their examination of the social and psychological dynamics of failed prophecy. At the same time, this overview will not present these case studies in strictly chronological order but will attempt to weave their findings together into a coherent survey of theoretical research into prophecy and dissonance. This introduction, then, will serve as an invitation to readers not simply to dip into this fascinating body of research but to ponder additional questions that this introduction and these essays leave unanswered.

In addition, since these are essentially theoretical, not historical, works, readers wishing to inform themselves about the history and beliefs of the various millennial movements mentioned in these essays are encouraged to refer to the long list of references found at the end of this introduction. As before, the central focus of this introductory essay, indeed of this collection of essays, is on the social, historical, and psychological question: What happens when prophecy fails?

When Prophecy Fails: The Festinger Thesis

The social and psychological consequences of failed prophecy were first addressed over forty years ago by Leon Festinger, Henry Riecken, and Stanley Schachter in their landmark case study, *When Prophecy Fails* (1956). In its basic formulation, the thesis Festinger and his colleagues advanced stated that an unequivocal disconfirmation of a prophesied event, in this instance the prediction of a destructive flood and the miraculous rescue of believers by flying saucers, creates a crisis of unbelief. This crisis is especially acute for those who have risked their jobs and reputations in the firm conviction that the prophecy will be fulfilled. As Festinger observed: "The fact that the predicted events did not occur is dissonant with continuing to believe both the prediction and the remainder of the ideology of which the prediction was the central item. The failure of the prediction is also dissonant with all the actions that the believer took in preparation for its fulfillment" (1956:27 [48]). Furthermore, according to Festinger, while the best course of action for shaken believers would be to discard their discredited beliefs and return to their former lives, "frequently the behavioral commitment to the belief system is so strong that almost any other course of action is preferable." Indeed, they noted, "It may even be less painful to tolerate the dissonance than to discard the belief and admit that one had been wrong." At the same time, they also noted that "the dissonance would be reduced or eliminated if the members of a movement effectively blind themselves to the fact that the prediction has not been fulfilled" (1956:27 [49]). But, as they then pointed out, most people are rational enough to recognize, and perhaps admit to themselves, that a disconfirmation had in fact occurred.

To Festinger's surprise, however, in the face of obvious prophetic disconfirmation, the group they studied sought to reduce dissonance by actively proselytizing, that is, by telling people that their prediction had in fact been correct. Thus, as their proposition holds, if believers can convince outsiders the truth of their message, perhaps persuading them to become members or supporters, this will reaffirm their beliefs, thereby serving to reduce the dissonance they feel. To quote Festinger at length on this point:

> The dissonance cannot be eliminated completely by denying or rationalizing the disconfirmation. But there is a way in which the remaining dissonance can be reduced. *If more and more people can be persuaded that the system of belief is correct, then clearly it must, after all, be correct.* . . . If the proselytizing proves successful, then by gathering more adherents and effectively surrounding himself with supporters, the believer reduces dissonance to the point where he can live with it. (1956:28 [49])

But while the Festinger thesis placed emphasis on a heightening of evangelistic fervor as the primary means by which shaken believers assuage dissonance, successful conversion of all nonbelievers does not seem to be a necessary component of dissonance reduction. As Festinger and his team seem to imply, whether outsiders actually accept or reject the group's message, it is the proselytizing activity itself—the proclamation of their beliefs to outsiders—that serves to confirm the faith members have in their prophet-leader and in the truth of his or her teachings. Not everyone who hears the message will believe it, of course. Most will reject it out of hand. But, as Festinger stressed, in the minds of believers, rejection itself may become a type of confirmation. The reasoning becomes circular: those who hear and believe will be saved, but those who do not believe are already lost.

In this way, evangelism might be said to hold a greater benefit to the evangelist than to the ones he or she evangelizes. For, as Festinger pointed out, "If the proselytizing proves successful then by gathering more adherents and effectively surrounding himself with supporters, the believer reduces dissonance to the point where he can live with it" (1956:28 [49]). Evangelism, then, as a response to cognitive dissonance, serves a function somewhat akin to a motivational pep rally that a team of athletes (or politicians) holds in the wake of a stunning defeat: it boosts flagging morale and restores confidence in the truth of the message and the messenger. Festinger and his colleagues found this same dynamic to be true of the Lake City flying saucer group they studied. It is to this case study, the story of Mrs. Keech and her group of "Seekers," that this essay will now briefly turn.

Prophecies from Outer Space

The story begins in the late 1940s and early 1950s, when a spiritual seeker, Mrs. Keech (her real name was Dorothy Martin), began receiving messages from higher beings through means of spirit-inspired writing. Long a student of the occult, Mrs. Keech believed that she had been chosen as the medium for a Guardian, called Elder Brother, and for a certain Sananda who in his earthly form had been the historical Jesus.

According to the messages she received, a new age of light had begun, and the Guardians were reaching out to awaken the world and bring it light. In a previous age, they taught, Jesus had appeared on Earth to reclaim humanity from the Prince of Darkness. While many had heard him and responded, spiritual darkness had once again enveloped the Earth. "It is ignorance of the Universal Laws that makes all the misery of the Earth," the Guardians told her. "We see and know that you struggle in darkness and want to bring real light, for yours is the only planet that has war and hatred" (Festinger 1956:45). The Guardians then charged Mrs. Keech to bear witness to the world and to help bring down the light. To testify to the truth of their message, the Guardians told her that flying saucers from Venus would appear in various major cities throughout the world. None did.

Not many months after these first contacts, Mrs. Keech and her small group of followers were warned that a great flood would soon befall the Earth, a flood so strong that it would destroy much of the inhabited areas of Western Europe and North America. But just before the flood would occur, she was told, flying saucers would appear to rescue her and her faithfully waiting followers.

Festinger recounts in some detail the story of the long wait by the "Seekers" in the late December cold and of the disappointment they felt when the spaceships—and the flood—failed to come. Without retelling their entire account, it is enough to say that after a brief period of doubt and confusion, Mrs. Keech received a message from her spirit guide congratulating the group for remaining true to the message. Their faith had saved the world from certain destruction. "Not since the beginning of time upon this Earth," praised the Guardians in their "Christmas Message to the People of the Earth," "has there been such a force of Good and light as now floods this room and that which has been loosed within this room now floods the entire Earth" (1956:169). As Festinger then noted, the Seekers' next action was evangelistic: they told their message to whomever would listen.

The Seekers' evangelistic response to failed prophecy was by no means expected. Logically, as Festinger had stressed, one would expect most people to abandon a disproven cognition in favor of a proven one. Instead, after a brief period of uncertainty, Mrs. Keech and her followers experienced a "recovery of conviction" (1956:10–11 [36–37]): they reaffirmed their belief in the prophecy and became all the more fervent in their faith. Moreover, Mrs. Keech and her Seekers actively, even aggressively, sought out ways to publicize their beliefs through all available media channels. As Festinger reported, the message Mrs. Keech brought to the press was this: "The cataclysm had been called off. The little group, sitting all night long, had spread so much light that God had saved the world from destruction" (1956:169). As before, for Festinger it was not enough for the group to believe that this disconfirmation was instead an affirmation of their faith; to reduce dissonance completely, members felt compelled to convince others that their faith in God had been tested by a divine ordeal *(judicium Dei)*, and that their message was therefore worthy of acceptance.

Recognizing that not all groups experiencing dissonance seek to reduce it through proselytizing, Festinger and his team put forth five conditions under which, in similar cases, their thesis would hold true. These five conditions include the following:

1. A belief must be held with deep conviction and it must have some relevance to action, that is, to what the believer does or how he behaves.
2. The person holding the belief must have committed himself to it; that is, for the sake of his belief, he must have taken some important action that is difficult to undo. . . .
3. The belief must be sufficiently specific and sufficiently concerned with the real world that events may unequivocally refute the belief.
4. Such undeniable disconfirmatory evidence must occur and must be recognized by the individual holding the belief.
5. The individual must have social support. . . . (1956:4 [31–32])

The emphasis that Festinger had placed in these conditions was on the level of a believer's personal commitment to the message, on the believer's recognition that the prophecy failed unequivocally, and on the level of social support available to a believer, the latter condition being perhaps the most critical to dissonance reduction and to group survival.

Not surprisingly, at the time of its publication the Festinger thesis created a stir among researchers, and not simply from those in the behavioral sciences. Festinger's work soon spawned a number of historical, sociological, and psychological as well as religious and literary studies, all of which sought either to test the reliability of Festinger's central thesis or to use its findings to explain the survival, growth, and success of a number of messianic and millenarian movements throughout Western history (see, for example, Holloway 1966; Zenner 1966; Cohn 1970, 1993; Gager 1975; Carroll 1979; and McGinn 1979).

What these and other subsequent studies have shown is that while most end-time groups tend to respond to failed prophecy in ways similar to that of Festinger's test case, not all groups respond by actively proselytizing others. Some have, most have not. Groups that predict catastrophe do experience dissonance in the face of disconfirmation, especially if they have committed themselves to the point where failure would open them up to embarrassment and ridicule. It has also been the case that the level of dissonance, and the corresponding effort by members to reduce it, has varied depending upon the severity and the specificity of the prophesied event. Which failure is more embarrassing, we might ask rhetorically, to predict an earthquake that does not happen or to predict a timely rescue by Venusians before that same predicted earthquake strikes? The former misprediction might be excused by society with a sigh of relief. But no geophysicist, hazarding to predict the latter, would likely escape cognitive dissonance or a straitjacket. In the latter instance, the credibility and sanity of the prophet and of her message is very much at stake. Even so, what the following highlighted studies tend to show is that, as a response to failed prophecy, active proselytizing—the Festinger thesis—is but one of a range of ways by which believers attempt to reduce dissonance, and not the only way.

Testing the Festinger Thesis

Seeking to test the Festinger thesis, Jane Hardyck and Marcia Braden (1962) studied a group of Pentecostal Christians that, like the Seekers, had also predicted imminent destruction of the world and had likewise taken irreversible steps to prepare for it. In this case, however, the threat was a nuclear attack, and the group's salvation would be found in bomb shelters. But while the conditions had been similar to those found in Festinger's case, Hardyck and Braden noted that their group's response to prophetic failure had not been the same. When the 135 members emerged from their shelters after forty-two days together, they showed little sign of dissonance and little inclination to evangelize. In fact, the "True Word" members did not aggressively seek to publicize their beliefs and took some pains to avoid proselytizing, even to the point of ignoring a contingent of tourists.

As Hardyck and Braden speculated, the reason the Festinger model had failed to replicate might have been owing to the high level of social support church members experienced before, during, and after the failed prophecy. To account for the difference between Festinger's test case and theirs, Hardyck and Braden offered two additional conditions to the five proposed by Festinger: "The two suggestions we have made for further conditions are that the group provide only minimal social support for its members and that the group receive ridicule from the outside world" (1962:141 [63]). Both conditions were true for the Seekers but they were not the case for the True Word group, perhaps explaining the need for the Seekers to convince unbelievers that they had been right in their conviction.

Interestingly, one can discern two similarities in the responses of both groups studied that Hardyck and Braden did not notice or mention. In fact, in their findings, neither Festinger nor Hardyck and Braden seem aware of the possible effect these overlooked post-disconfirmation responses might have exerted in reducing dissonance. The first response was to declare that the exercise had served to strengthen group ties and increase personal faith. As Mrs. Shepard, leader of the True Word group, is reported to have said the very morning her people emerged from their shelters: " 'Did you have victory? . . . The Lord has brought the people closer to Him, there is not division, there's a fellowship here and we are the holiness people.' " Then, as Hardyck and Braden related further, "Many other church members gave testimonies as to how their stay in the shelters had both strengthened their Christian fellowship and increased their belief" (1962:138 [59]). The prophecy was a test. Indeed, its fulfillment had never been intended, only its faith-strengthening result. As both Mrs. Keech and Mrs. Shepard had declared to their followers, through this experience their messages and the faith of their respective groups had been affirmed.

The second response relates to the first. The testing of faith through a predicted disaster becomes necessary not simply to affirm personal faith but to impress upon others the truth of the message. The prophecy serves as a warning to nonbelievers. It is meant to open their eyes to the fate that lies ahead for them if they continue in unbelief. This was true for the Seekers and it was also true for Mrs. Shepard's True Word group. As Hardyck and Braden pointed out, members of the True Word church "had discovered by looking back over all of their messages that it had never been stated that an attack was imminent; they had simply misinterpreted God's purposes. Really, God had just been using them to warn a world that was asleep, while at the same time he was testing their faith" (1962:139 [59]).

One important difference between these two case studies that might account for their contrasting analyses is the manner in which the two research teams had collected their data. Festinger's team had participated with the Seekers in the nonevent, while Hardyck and Braden relied on post-disconfirmation interviews and reports. It has been said that the Festinger team's presence during the non-event might have unduly influenced the results of their research (Bainbridge 1997:137). But, at the same time, what Hardyck and Braden might have missed by not being in the shelters and by not remaining with True Word members for the forty-two-day waiting period was the *process* by which group members slowly transformed real or potential doubt (dissonance) into a reaffirmation of faith (cf. Palmer and Finn 1992).

"When the Bombs Drop"

In a much later study, published by Robert Balch, Gwen Farnsworth, and Sue Wilkins (1983), we find a test case whose circumstances are similar to that found in Hardyck and Braden but whose research is conducted in a way similar to Festinger. That is, the group Balch and his colleagues selected to study predicted imminent nuclear holocaust, built bomb shelters, and waited in them on the predicted days; and, when the time came, Balch and his team of researchers entered the shelters and observed firsthand the members' responses to failed prophecy. Given this, we would expect the insights of Balch to complement or perhaps mediate the contradictory findings of these two earlier studies. In fact, they do not. Their findings seem to offer a third possible option.

As early as 1971, a renegade Baha'i teacher, Leland Jensen, had predicted that the prophesied Battle of Armageddon would begin in 1980. Soon after gathering a small group of believers in 1973, Doc, as he was called, began publishing the details of his predictions through his own small printing business. His followers actively spread the message and began building bomb shelters in preparation of the coming event.

According to Doc, the Bible had foretold a coming thermonuclear destruction and that that event would take place on April 29, 1980. What is more, Jensen believed that twenty years after this devastating nuclear holocaust, in the year 2000, Christ would return to Earth to usher in his Kingdom. Between 1980 and the dawning of the Millennium, it would be the task of his group, Baha'i Under the Provisions of the Covenant (or BUPC), to minister to the needs of survivors and prepare the world for Christ's arrival.

As with Hardyck and Braden, whose group held similar beliefs and undertook similar preparations, the responses Balch and his colleagues recorded did not follow Festinger. But neither did they accord with Hardyck and Braden. The Baha'i sect Balch observed had met most of the five conditions put forth by Festinger as well as the two additional conditions offered by Hardyck and Braden. But in the wake of disconfirmation they failed to rally together as a group and did not actively proselytize. The leader's first, but not immediate, response to failure was to reset his prediction. But by the time the new date was circulated among Doc's followers, most of his group's members had already become completely demoralized by the prophecy's failure. In fact, when the second predicted time arrived, few members became as enthusiastic as before and even fewer entered the bomb shelters. A third time was set, but no one, not even Doc, held out hope that the bombs would drop. As a result, a movement of 150 members quickly dwindled down to a core group of about thirty-six. What is more, although after the disconfirmation Doc had encouraged members to renew their publishing activities, few, if any, did so.

But Balch and his colleagues did not leave it there. Something more interesting had taken place. While many members left the group, at the same time little defection took place among the ranks of "genuine believers" (1983:150 [138]). Also, a shift had taken place from talk about "when the bombs drop" to the need for members to be more dedicated to the teachings of their faith. As Balch and his team observed, "most believers had strong *identities* as BUPC that transcended their commitment to Doc's prediction. . . . While most had been attracted to the faith by its apocalyptic orientation, they subsequently acquired a firm grounding in a coherent body of Baha'i teachings dating back over 100 years" (1983:153 [140], emphasis added). This point becomes their most helpful insight. Unlike the Seekers group in Festinger, then, which had been formed around Mrs. Keech's prophecy, the beliefs and the collective identity of BUPC members had not been defined by one specific prophetic event. Though the prediction had energized them and its failure had shocked and saddened them, core members came to see that their faith as members of BUPC was not defined by the fulfillment of one prophesied event. In effect, Doc's prophecy was judged by core members as nonessential to the group's central message. This insight held true in a subsequent study that Balch (1997) and a new team of researchers conducted on Doc's BUPC movement over the next fifteen years.

When the Bombs Still Haven't Dropped

The BUPC's embarrassing 1980 miscalculation would not be the only series of failed predictions its leader (or his successor) would make concerning the end of the world. In fact, as Robert Balch, John Domitrovich, Barbara Lynn Mahnke, and Vanessa Morrison reported in a follow-up study of the BUPC, "Between 1980 and 1995 the group's leader, Dr. Leland Jensen [Doc], set twenty dates for the Battle of Armageddon or lesser disasters that would lead up to the Apocalypse" (1997:74 [269]). What they found true for the first series of predictions before 1980 did not hold true during or after Doc's subsequent predictions. In fact, as time went on and as Jensen continued to utter prediction after prediction, "hardly anyone in the BUPC except for Jensen and a few members of his inner circle met [Festinger's] first condition of deep conviction, and the commitments specified in [Festinger's] second condition were minimal compared to those that members had made in 1980" (1997:75 [270]).

As a modification of the Festinger thesis, Balch and his colleagues suggested that if groups survive the trauma of failed prophecy with their belief in a coming millennial age still intact, in time, the group will develop what they termed an "underground culture of dissonance-reduction" that serves to reduce "the impact of the predictions and subsequent disconfirmations" through "disclaimers and *post facto* rationalizations" and other face-saving strategies. As they put it: "This culture enabled [BUPC] members to dismiss the predictions and move on with their everyday lives while still claiming allegiance to Jensen and the Baha'i faith." In addition, their "goal of preparing for the holocaust ultimately was displaced by more immediate concerns, despite the fact that the group's rhetoric remained as apocalyptic as ever" (1997:75 [270]).

An additional element of the modification Balch and his colleagues offered is their analysis of the differing responses of Jensen and his successor prophet, Neal Chase, and those of their followers. Before and after each prophecy failed, Jensen and Chase had responded in ways consistent with the Festinger thesis, but BUPC lay members had not. For instance, after the failure of Jensen's prediction that on April 29, 1986, Halley's comet would be pulled into the Earth's orbit, break up, and wreak year-long havoc on the planet, "members quietly resumed their lives . . . as if it were just another day" (1997:84 [278]). By August of that year, when it had become patent that Halley's comet would pass by the Earth without incident, members no longer openly talked about when, specifically, the world would end but how to be spiritually ready when the end does come. As Balch and his colleagues observed:

> After each failed prediction, life for the BUPC continued on course. There were few traces of disillusionment among either new or old members. . . . Proselytizing continued unabated, but few members stressed the predictions when teaching the Faith. Instead they focused more on Jensen's mission and the importance of being spiritually prepared when the prophecies of Revelation ultimately would be fulfilled. (1997:85 [279])

Thus, unlike their enthusiastic leaders, who continued to prophesy doom despite repeated failures to predict exact endtime catastrophes, BUPC members had become increasingly desensitized to repeated endtime predictions and preferred instead to continue expecting the end in *theory* while advancing their Baha'i faith in *practice*.

It should be noted that the main themes advanced by Balch in the above studies—the marginalization of prophecy, a developing "culture of dissonance reduction," and the noticeable distinction between leader/member responses to failed prophecy—were not altogether original with him. In fact, a number of earlier case studies, those examining the multiple prophetic failures of the Jehovah's Witnesses, had pointed to responses similar to those in the BUPC. Without too much duplication, it might therefore be helpful to consider the Festinger-related research that has centered on the history of this career prophecy movement, a movement whose founder and his successors have made no fewer than six major and perhaps a dozen or more minor endtime predictions since 1870.

Failed Prophecy as Partial Fulfillment

As Joseph Zygmunt (1970) found in his social-historical study of recurring prophetic failures among the Jehovah's Witnesses over the period of a century, when prophecies fail, disappointed believers tend to adjust their predictions and beliefs both to fit such disconfirmations and to fit changing empirical conditions. Zygmunt referred to this dynamic as the "collective identity change" in career prophecy movements. As Zygmunt argued, a major reason for this change arises when a group derives its self-identity from predictive prophecy and makes endtime expectation central to its success as a movement. As a consequence, the group institutionalizes its prophetic outlook and its membership begins to derive its sense of purpose from endtime expectation.

The Jehovah's Witnesses are perhaps the best example of this interesting social-psychological dynamic. From their founding by Charles Russell in the 1870s, the Jehovah's Witnesses have believed that God has chosen them from among the churches to fill a special role in the consummation of prophetic history. As spiritual elites, they had been given not only insight into the true meaning of the Bible but also the unique ability to discern the signs of the times that would herald Christ's second coming. Interestingly, the advent of his first failed prophecy—that Christ would come in 1878—or even later exact predictions did not shake Russell's or his followers' belief in their chosenness but renewed their sense of urgency and mission. Indeed, as Zygmunt pointed out, to shake off such belief in the face of a momentary or seeming disconfirmation would have spelled an end to the movement. To assuage dissonance, the Jehovah's Witnesses have tended to view prophetic disconfirmation as *delayed* confirmation, or rather, as a temporary reprieve. That is, in one sense, delayed fulfillment has been interpreted as an opportunity for Witnesses to redouble their efforts toward awakening other "saints" to their coming salvation. But in another sense, every nonfulfillment has been understood by Witnesses as an invitation to search the Scriptures and rethink only specific components of prophecy, not their general prophetic outlook. Since chosenness had already been established as part of their *identity*, one would assume that no failed prophecy could be devastating enough to weaken their firmly fixed sense of self.

Accordingly, after every nonfulfillment, Witnesses have discovered retrospectively through a closer reading of the Bible that a fulfillment had in fact occurred, albeit in a spiritual, not a physical, sense (Zygmunt 1970:934 [72]). In this way, the Witnesses have been able to escape the trauma of repeated prophetic failures by reinterpreting empirically stated prophecies into nonempirical fulfillments. In fact, Russell and his successors were able to argue convincingly for the nonempirical fulfillment of their prophecies by pointing out that some significant event in God's endtime calendar had actually taken place (1970:934 [72]).

For instance, though Christ's Second Coming had been predicted to occur in 1878, 1881, 1914, 1918, and 1925 (and later, 1975), for Witnesses, each failure came instead to mark a partial fulfillment of God's plan. Accordingly, the year

1878 "marked the point at which the 'nominal Christian Churches were cast off from God's favor' "; the year 1881 "marked the time when 'death became a blessing' " to the saints; the year 1914, the start of the Great War, marked the " 'End of the Time of the Gentiles [that is, the Christian nations]' "; the year 1918 marked the moment "Christ 'entered the temple for the purpose of judgment' "; and the year 1925 marked the establishment of a "New Nation" with Christ as its head (Zygmunt 1970:934 [72]).

We might add that because the Plan of God was, for Russell and his successors, something similar to a puzzle, its complete picture would be revealed slowly and only as each piece of the puzzle was fitted into place. In a sense, there was not simply one event upon which the entire system hanged but what one might call a "prophetic cluster" of events that formed the endtime picture. In this way, the Witnesses were already prepared for repeated prophetic "failure," since in some spiritual sense every event—every prophetic event—pointed to Christ's Coming. Though no one knew the precise day or hour of the coming Kingdom, it was therefore sufficient for Witnesses simply to know that each passing day would bring them and the world closer to the long-awaited realization of the Millennium.

The Prophecy Failure of 1975

With its well-earned notoriety as an evangelistic movement, one would expect that the Jehovah's Witnesses would provide the best support for the Festinger thesis. But contrary to Festinger, after each failed prophecy, evangelistic activities among Witnesses declined. In fact, as Richard Singelenberg (1989) noted in his study of Dutch Witnesses, most of the movement's evangelistic fervor occurred in anticipation of predicted events, not after their failures. This pattern was most in evidence before and after the prophecy failure of 1975 (cf. Wilson 1978). Moreover, as Mathew Schmalz (1994) has argued, not only did Witnesses fail to proselytize after 1975, but the leaders of the movement first denied that they had ever authorized the prophecy and then, to regain control and stem further losses, removed those discontented individuals who might undermine their authority.

Taken together, the findings offered by Singelenberg and Schmalz, while openly challenging the Festinger thesis, present a fuller picture of the adaptive strategies of the Jehovah's Witnesses. Because of its importance to an understanding of prophecy and dissonance, the failure of 1975 merits further examination.

In 1966, fifty years after the death of Russell, interest among Witnesses in the coming Millennium began to pique once more. It was at this point, Schmalz observed, that the Jehovah's Witnesses, then about three million strong worldwide, experienced a heightening of expectation in the coming millennial kingdom. To quote Schmalz directly: "many Witnesses expected something significant in June of that year because of the association of the date 6/66 with 666, the mark of the beast in Revelation 13:18" (1994:298 [239]). In that same month, *The Watchtower* published a tract which outlined the chronological events that, as it argued, pointed to 1975 as the beginning of the seventh thousand-year period of human history, the Millennium. When 1974 passed into 1975 and Witnesses realized that their hoped-for millennial age had not come, disappointment was widespread. Yet another prediction had failed to come to pass, they collectively sighed.

But, as one might have expected, the result of this prophetic nonevent was disastrous for the Witnesses. As Singelenberg observed, "After 1975 the picture totally reversed: decreasing activities, low recruitment, and high defection" (1989:34). In response, its leaders, who denied that the prophecy had ever taken place, blamed the membership for its failure, quickly instituted a purge of its leadership, and then set about winnowing its membership more generally, especially white-collar professionals and the college-educated (Schmalz 1994:299 [240]; Singelenberg 1989:34 [201–202]; Penton 1985:103–108; cf. Zygmunt 1972:260–261 [97–99]; and van Fossen 1988). This strategy, Schmalz reported, turned attention away from the failure of the 1975 prophecy and essentially saved the organization from certain collapse. As he related, "Watchtower reactions to disconfirmation seem primarily directed toward reestablishing group cohesion through revision, denial, and purge" (Schmalz 1994:304 [246]; cf. Penton 1985:99–126).

While Singelenberg's and Schmalz's intended aims were to show the inadequacies of the Festinger thesis, it should be pointed out that what their papers seem also to have vividly underscored was not only that disconfirmation results in dissonance but that a prediction can sometimes relieve dissonance. This point seems to hold especially true for groups that experience repeated cycles of expectation and disappointment. It is true that Witnesses were certainly eager to accept their leaders' intimations of Christ's soon-coming because such predictions were in keeping with their endtime orientation. But, at the same time, the prediction, such as the one for 1975, also provided momentary relief from the "pent-up" dissonance created by nearly a century of unresolved anticipation. Over time, the Witnesses' watchword, "perhaps today," was threatening to become "perhaps never." Indeed, as the years wore on, Judge Rutherford's oft-quoted refrain, "Millions now living will never die," coined in 1920, was slowly losing its poignancy. The leaders found that they needed some way to renew the immediacy and excitement Witnesses once brought to the task of witnessing. The 1975 prediction served these purposes perfectly.

Thus, as Witnesses worldwide confidently embraced the 1975 prediction, it seemed to have relieved their slowly building dissonance. As Schmalz affirmed: "This prophecy galvanized the movement and proselytism increased substantially" (1994:298 [239]). Even so, though the 1975 prophecy may have provided momentary relief from built-up dissonance, its failure brought with it even greater disappointment, heightened dissonance, inner turmoil, and eventual decline.

Adapting to Failed Prophecy

In trying to account for these differing responses to failed prophecy, subsequent studies have pointed to various strategies that groups have adopted as a means of adapting to empirical disconfirmation. As with the Jehovah's Witnesses discussed above, whose 1975 disconfirmation brought with it denials, finger-pointing, and purges, other movements have responded similarly to failed prophecies. Interestingly, for the Witnesses it was these tactics, plus an existing organizational structure, that helped prevent disintegration of the movement as a whole. Other groups, such as Mrs. Keech's Seekers, were not as creative or enterprising in managing the dissonance of their followers.[3] As Joseph Zygmunt has observed: "The disintegration and collapse of many millenarian movements are traceable to their failure to cope effectively with the strains induced by prophetic disconfirmations or nonconfirmations, generally because they have not developed the requisite organizational resources" (1972:259 [97]). The Witnesses are not unique in their successful use of adaptive strategies.[4]

According to Zygmunt, when movements experience a heightening of dissonance caused by prophetic failure, they tend to draw upon existing organizational resources. These organizational resources include "adaptive patterns of response," or what Zygmunt called three "modes of adaptation" (1972:259–260 [97]; see Prus 1976 on "management of dissonance"). These adaptive strategies underscore the resilience of a group's ideological structure and of the beliefs its members embrace. This seems especially true when those beliefs are largely nonempirical and when a prophet's empirical predictions are ambiguous. Briefly summarized, Zygmunt's three possible modes of adaptation include either: (1) acknowledgment of error and a restructuring of the group along more modified lines of expectation; (2) the assignment of blame, either internal or external, and a redirection of organizational resources toward either purification or revival of the group, greater evangelistic activities, or critique of the nonbelieving social order; or (3) a refusal to accept the failure of the prophecy and the reinterpretation of the group's beliefs along more symbolic and hence more unfalsifiable lines (1972:259–265 [97–100]). Not surprisingly, in subsequent studies on responses to failed prophecy, Zygmunt's pathbreaking approach to addressing the question of prophecy and dissonance has tended to supersede that offered by Festinger. As a result, in a few later cases the Festinger thesis has been relegated to the place of an obligatory footnote (see, for example, Dien 1997).

Zygmunt's third adaptive response—denial of disconfirmation—was developed further in a perceptive essay by J. Gordon Melton (1985). In his article, Melton took issue with the Festinger thesis for its assumption that the entire belief system of a millennial movement hangs on one prophesied event. As Melton put it: "Though one or more prophecies may be important to a group, they will be set within a complex set of beliefs and interpersonal relationships. They may serve as one of several important sources determining group activity, but the prediction is only one support device for the group, not the essential rafter" (1985:19 [147]). To understand this critical element, Melton argued, is to understand a dynamic central to endtime movements: *"prophecy seldom fails"* (1985:20 [147]). Melton challenged the notion that prophecies fail for the group, arguing instead that predictive prophecy is simply part of a larger system of beliefs (what Melton called the "total gestalt" of a movement). As Melton reiterated further, "the denial of failure is not just another option, but the common mode of adaptation of millennial groups following the failure of a prophecy" (1985:21 [149]).

Given this fact, prophetic disconfirmation, while dissonant in itself, will be seen to exert only modest influence over the stability of the group's overall beliefs. As Melton went on to explain: "In the face of dissonance, believers are able to rely upon the broader context of faith, on the unfalsifiable beliefs out of which religious thought-worlds are constructed." Therefore, Melton then noted, alluding to Zygmunt, it is within such a broader context that "believers can engage in a reaffirmation of basic faith and make a reappraisal of their predicament" (1985:20 [148]). In this way, denial of disconfirmation can be seen as an appropriate and expectable cognitive response to failure (cf. Tumminia 1998). As Neil Weiser had stressed a decade earlier, "Prophecies cannot and do not fail *for the committed.*" Core beliefs "will remain intact," he noted, because a group's post-disconfirmation behavior is aimed at reaffirming such beliefs (Weiser 1974:20 [105], emphasis added). But unlike Zygmunt and Melton, Weiser argued that proselytism is itself a mode of adaptation in that it provides believers the means by which "to ascertain social support." Indeed, in his comparative study on dissonance, Weiser pointed to certain rationalizations and diversions that believers use to deny disconfirmation so as to reduce the effects of dissonance. The strategies Weiser offered, many of which are similar to those offered by Zygmunt and Melton, point to the "flexibility and ability of the millennial belief to adapt to new events" that might otherwise undermine a believer's convictions (1974:24 [110]; for an insightful historical example, see Foster 1987).

From Melton's observations one might also add that the social and cultural responses to prophetic failure work in tandem in virtually all successful cases of dissonance reduction. In addition, the spiritualizing of a "failed" prophecy does not take hold or work until there are the necessary social supports upon which disappointed and discouraged members can lean. In the same way, social support, while critical, is not sufficient to assuage disappointment unless the failed prophecy, in turn, can be reinterpreted within the context of the group's overall system of beliefs. The process appears to build upon itself.

What happens when prophecy fails? According to Melton, since the group does not acknowledge empirical disconfirmation in the way an outsider might, the question makes little sense. As before, for endtime movements, whose prophecies are "set within a complex set of beliefs and interpersonal relationships," prophecy as such seldom, if ever, fails (1985:19 [147]). Successful reinterpretation of prophecy and simultaneous reintegration of group members appear to lessen significantly, if not altogether relieve, the sting of a failed prophecy.

Additionally, predictive prophecy might be said to serve purposes beyond simply the fulfillment of the prophecy itself. For instance, a prophecy might be used to motivate group members to achieve certain collective goals (Prus 1976), to relieve dissonance brought about by unresolved expectations (Zygmunt 1970 and Schmalz 1994), or to reassert a prophet's legitimate authority when challenged by a rival (Festinger et al. 1956:92–114). As in the case of Doc and the BUPC (Balch et al. 1997), one might also argue that a series of endtime predictions might simply be a means by which, through trial and error, prophet-leaders slowly work out their cosmologies. In this respect, the prophet is very much like a ship's captain who takes frequent soundings while slowly navigating his vessel through uncharted waters: prophecy becomes a way by which the prophet maps his or her way through a spiritual *terra incognita*, through unknown cosmic time and space.

Ritualizing Prophetic Failure

What these studies tend to assume is the natural receptivity of members to predictive prophecy as well as a willing acceptance by followers of its reinterpretation after failure. While Susan Palmer and Natalie Finn (1992) found some of the same reinterpretive dynamics as Zygmunt and Melton, in comparing the responses of two Canadian groups that had experienced failed prophecy, however, they noted that prophecy can fail if not received within a context already receptive to it. As they found, one group completely disintegrated after the experience of disconfirmation, while the other was strengthened by it. How, they asked, does one account for these differing results? In answering this question, Palmer and Finn looked to the prophesied moment itself and examined how groups pass through what they termed the "rite of apocalypse." What they discovered was that though the leaders of both millennial movements had prophesied an end to the world, the manner in which the groups received the prophecy and then experienced the endtime event differed.

For example, in the case of La Mission de l' Esprit Saint (MES), Emmanuel Robitaille, its young leader, foretold the coming Battle of Armageddon but gave no further instructions to his followers as to how they should prepare for it. Without guidance, the membership eventually scattered in confusion. In the second case, that of the Institute of Applied Metaphysics (IAM), its leader, Winifred Barton, had predicted an extraterrestrial visitation that would change the world "as we know it" (Palmer and Finn 1992:397 [211]). But in contrast to Robitaille, Barton led her followers through a process from preparation to fulfillment much as a priest leads parishioners through the liturgy. As Palmer and Finn explained, "waiting for world's end is a symbolic act . . . and it requires the presence of ritual actors and the organization of sacred time and sacred space" (1992:409 [226–227]). As they went on to note, drawing on Victor Turner's concept of the ritual process, the "rite of apocalypse" is a transformative process, a communal reordering of time and space. Though "improvised," the rite of apocalypse combines elements of initiation, meditation, and purification found in other types of ritual behavior (1992:409 [225]).[5] In effect, the acting out of a predicted event represents a ritualized reaffirmation of belief. Thus, they concluded, as evidenced in the differing results of the MES and IAM movements, to be successful, the process—reception, separation, and fulfillment—must include both the gathering together of members who witness the endtime event and a collective experience of its symbolic fulfillment as mediated by their prophet-leader.

In this way, the ritual dimension of prophetic expectation, a ritual in which members participate in its fulfillment through symbolic acts, aids our understanding of how some millennial groups succeed or fail to pass through the period of crisis that arises following prophetic disconfirmation. As Palmer and Finn skillfully demonstrate, ritual fulfillment seems to provide disappointed members with the necessary social and psychological supports to make such an experience less cognitively distressing.

Regaining Lost Credibility through Prophetic Reinterpretation

In all the studies considered thus far, to a greater or lesser extent the analyses offered by Zygmunt (1970 and 1972) and Melton (1985) have tended to add the most theoretical depth to our understanding. In each of the cases, including Festinger's, when faced with unequivocal disconfirmation, the prophets have offered their followers a spiritualized (nonempirical) reinterpretation of their failed prophecies. In some cases, we might also note, the reinterpretation has been preemptive: it appeared in the form of a qualification given just before or just in case the prediction failed or fails. But in the main, prophets have encouraged their followers to see the apparent nonfulfillment of prophecy through the spiritual eyes of faith. Indeed, it is through eyes of faith that the real meaning and intended purpose of the prophecy come into greater focus. Such is the case in the two final studies to be discussed below, one that examined the spiritualizing activities of the leader of a Japanese sect, the other the spiritualizing activities of the followers of the New York rabbi Menachem Schneerson, the late spiritual leader of Lubavitch Habad.

In the case examined by Takaaki Sanada and Edward Norbeck (1975), that of a small postwar Japanese sect, the focus of failed prophecy shifts from reactions of the followers to the responses of the dishonored prophet. Indeed, for Sanada and Norbeck, dishonor becomes the key to understanding the spiritualizing of disconfirmation. Thus, though certainly presenting a serious challenge to the Festinger thesis, the case presented by Sanada and Norbeck also provides a cross-cultural comparative look at how prophets and their followers respond to and reinterpret prophetic failure.

As they related, Katsuichi Motoki, the prophet-healer of the sect Ichigen-no-Miya, The Shrine of the Fundamental Truth, informed his followers in January 1974 that the Spirit had told him that a devastating earthquake would strike the region sometime the following June. In the past, he claimed to have successfully predicted a range of natural disasters, including a volcanic eruption and a tornado. Motoki also claimed to have foreseen the Vietnam War. On June 10, Motoki related to his followers that the earthquake would strike on June 18, sometime before or after 8:00 A.M. In response, members immediately began making preparations for the disaster, including gathering truckloads of food and medicine, digging a well, and setting up temporary shelters to feed and house potential victims. By June 18, some seventy nonresident members had made their way to the sect's headquarters outside Osaka, joining Motoki and twenty-one resident members in their vigil.

When the appointed hour came and went without so much as a tremor, members remained calm but expectant. Then, at 8:50 A.M., several men began shouting "We are saved!" and made their way to the shrine where their leader had sequestered himself. Earlier that morning, before retiring to the central shrine, Motoki had granted a telephone interview with a local radio station. When asked by a reporter what he would do if his prophecy failed, he candidly replied that he would "take the blame and dissolve the sect" (1975:335 [121]).

Not long after the men had gained entry into the shrine, an ambulance was called to the scene. Motoki had attempted ritual suicide by cutting his belly open with a knife. As Motoki was rushed off to the hospital, a number of members began speculating about the meaning of the day's nonevent and of their leader's attempted suicide. Some thought their leader had misunderstood the Spirit's warning. Others thought that Motoki's sacrifice had averted certain disaster. Still others—again ignoring problems of chronology—believed that their leader had offered his life in gratitude to the Spirit for holding back the earthquake. Motoki himself, after he had recovered sufficiently from his wound to return to his headquarters, told his followers that while he had atoned for his mistake, he would dissolve the sect to spare his followers further dishonor.

But, as Sanada and Norbeck reported, disconfirmation had not shaken the faith of Motoki's followers. Only four of its twenty-one resident members left the sect as a result of the failed prophecy. For the most part, resident members responded by withdrawing themselves from public life and by becoming more contemplative. While they did not actively proselytize, neither did they abandon their leader. In fact, when Motoki called them together for a special ceremony to announce his decision the dissolve the sect, about 180 of his estimated 300 to 400 followers were in attendance. Since Motoki had atoned for his mistake, he had prevented his followers from losing honor. But how did Motoki regain face? Had he not attempted suicide and failed?

In a solo article that extracts nearly verbatim much of the same material from the joint study, Sanada (1979) related in some detail the explanation Motoki gave to his followers for why the prophecy had failed as well as the prophet's own spiritualized account of his attempted suicide experience. In effect, Motoki blamed his followers' fear of being dishonored for the prophecy's failure and reinterpreted his "suicide" as an act of redemption for Japan.

In July 1974, after his return from the hospital, Motoki scolded his followers, saying:

> All of you are failures. Why? You thought that if God's prophecy did not materialize, you would be so scorned and slandered by people that you would fall into total ruin. So you looked with eagerness for a disaster to occur. That was your wish, but it was not the will of God. If you had had the magnanimity to desire that everybody be saved, you could have been content with slander or any treatment you received. (1979:224)

And in October 1974, Motoki gave this account of his attempted suicide:

> After I had cut my abdomen and carotid artery, . . . I lay on my side with my head toward the altar. I could see my own body as if it belonged to somebody else. I thought that I had managed to get out of my body at last, and I was greatly surprised to find that my body had changed itself into the islands of Japan and that a fire had broken out at its center. Then I knew that God had transferred the cataclysm to my own body. I thanked God and felt a bliss I had never experienced before. (1979:227)

Motoki's first comments present an interesting paradox: in response to Motoki's revelation, his followers had prepared themselves for an earthquake; but all their preparations betrayed a desire for the earthquake to come so they would not lose face. In effect, their faith had dishonored them. In his second comments, Motoki explained that he had not failed either to predict the earthquake or to commit suicide. In both cases, he gave his members an accounting of events that served not only to restore their honor—his sacrifice was also for them—but to regain his own credibility as a prophet. As a result, Motoki could reassert his authority as their spiritual leader.

When Prophets Die

But what if the prophet dies before a prophecy is (not) fulfilled? How do groups resolve dissonance produced by an event that does not square with their millennial timetables? If the above observations by Sanada and Norbeck hold true, then we would expect the nonevent to be reinterpreted and then refitted into the belief system. A prophet's death might also serve to strengthen his followers' faith.

Perhaps the best recent example of a group transforming failure into fulfillment is found in the messianic expectations surrounding the famed leader of the New York Lubavitchers, the Rebbe Menachem Schneerson (1902–1994). The responses of the Lubavitchers to their aged leader's paralyzing stroke and subsequent death formed the basis for William Shaffir's (1995) analysis of how members of one messianic movement responded to the dissonance created by an unexpected turn of events (cf. Dien 1997).

In April 1991, the Rebbe Schneerson gave a stirring speech to his followers exhorting them to work diligently to bring the Messiah (Moshiach) and the promised Redemption of the Jews. Then, in September, the Rebbe began to speak of Messianic Redemption as imminent. In response, Lubavitchers worldwide began in earnest a great Moshiach campaign (cf. Dien 1997). But, at the same time they initiated their campaign, many of Schneerson's followers came to believe that their own Rebbe was in fact the long-awaited Messiah. Some, in fact, urged him to reveal himself.

Then, in March 1992, not quite a year after announcing Messiah's coming, the Rebbe suffered a debilitating stroke. Many of his followers believed that their Rebbe would not die, but that a miraculous healing would occur. To their disbelief, their Rebbe's condition progressively worsened. In June 1994, Schneerson died and with him, presumably, their dream of imminent Messianic Redemption.

Scarcely had the news broke of the Rebbe's death when a group of youths began singing and dancing amidst the mourners who had gathered in front of Schneerson's home in Crown Heights. They believed that his death had signaled the beginning of Jewish Redemption and that Schneerson would rise up and guide them to Israel to be exiles no more. Resurrection soon became a subject of speculation among Lubavitchers.

In his analysis, Shaffir (citing C. Wright Mills) spoke of a common "vocabulary of motives" used by Lubavitch men and women as a way "to neutralize any dissonant feelings and to reinforce their faith in the imminent Redemption by their King Messiah" (1995:126 [258]). These verbalized rationalizations helped preserve the legitimacy of their Rebbe's messianic vision and kept alive their own hopes for Redemption. Their dissonance-reducing explanations for why their Rebbe had died and left them orphaned as a movement also helped strengthen member ties by giving individual Lubavitchers reasoned ways to answer their own nagging self-doubts. Their "vocabulary of motives" included such rationalizations as: (1) God alone knows the reasons for this loss; (2) we were mistaken; he never claimed to be the messiah; (3) we are not worthy of Redemption because we lacked sufficient faith to receive it; (4) our Rebbe has chosen instead to place the burden of Redemption on our shoulders; (5) the Rebbe's death does not prove him a false Messiah; the sages themselves had predicted that Messiah would die (1995:126–132 [258–263]; cf. Dien 1997:255–258). The first two rationalizations seem to have been given up in favor of the latter three, with numbers four and five becoming those most often repeated by the Lubavitch faithful.

A week after Schneerson's death, his closest followers convened "Moshiach Day" in Crown Heights. Several hundred Lubavitchers gathered to consider the import of their Rebbe's death. That afternoon, Schneerson's followers reaffirmed their belief in his authority and committed themselves to continue his work. According to Shaffir, the panel of rabbis who convened the meeting assured those gathered that "the Rebbe's prophecy remained as relevant after his death as it had been in his lifetime" (1995:128 [260]). Our Rebbe may not be here physically, they seemed to be saying, but he is still working among us. "'The Rebbe is here. We feel and sense this.'" We know he is watching over us, they continued, for we feel his presence among us. As one woman had put it: " 'The Rebbe told us what to do. The job the Rebbe gave us to do we must continue' " (1995:128–129 [260–261]).

Interestingly, the case of the Crown Heights Lubavitchers comes closest to replicating the thesis proposed by Festinger than any of the other studies considered above. As Shaffir observed, after the death of the Rebbe, the Lubavitchers in the main experienced a renewed sense of mission and greatly increased their level of proselytizing activity among fellow Jews. These "techniques of rationalization" reduced dissonance, helped them recover their flagging faith, and gave them a renewed commitment to the goals of their movement. As Shaffir noted: "The Lubavitchers retained their belief in the Rebbe's assurance that the redemptive process had begun; it was now their task to see that the necessary further steps were taken to fulfill the Messianic prophecy" (1995:131 [263]; cf. Dien 1997:255–258).

One might also point out that in regard to their messianic beliefs and their identity as chosen people, the Lubavitchers see themselves in a way similar to the Jehovah's Witnesses highlighted above. Their community had been built up around the belief that they were chosen by God and that the Messiah would soon appear to usher in the Kingdom, of which they were already citizens. Every event, as refracted through the light of Scripture, gave them renewed hope. In the same way, every failure was read as though it was in fact pointing toward a greater fulfillment yet to come. Nothing dissuaded them. For the Lubavitchers, like the Witnesses, their sense of chosenness, which was affirmed by their traditions, was too much a part of their identity for them simply to discard. They believed too strongly in their Rebbe and in their coming Redemption to let his death disappoint their hopes.[6]

Some Concluding Thoughts

In addressing the question, What happens when prophecy fails?, most of the case studies highlighted above have tended to offer answers that have differed from the findings of Festinger and his colleagues. Were the Festinger thesis to hold true, one would expect that in subsequent cases of prophetic disconfirmation, believers would seek to reduce or relieve dissonance by engaging in some type of proselytizing activity. But in almost all the cases cited above, proselytizing did not occur. What these post-Festinger studies have largely shown is that distressed believers have sought to recover their faltering faith in ways less evangelistic. If anything, later research has tended to suggest that the peculiar evangelistic response of Mrs. Keech's Lake City flying saucer group was indeed *peculiar* to that group: their response was counterintuitive but largely idiosyncratic (cf. Melton 1985:19 [147], 27 [155]).

The strong criticisms leveled at the Festinger study—which has not been unlike an ocean liner that developed leaks soon after its first launch—have all but scuttled its reliability for predicting responses to failed prophecy. Criticisms like those of Gordon Melton (1985), Anthony van Fossen (1988), and William Bainbridge (1997) have called into question not simply its central thesis but the manner in which Festinger and his team gathered and analyzed their data. For instance, Melton has pointed out that the failure of the Festinger thesis to replicate in subsequent cases is owing to "serious conceptual inadequacies" (1985:19 [146]) as well as factual errors in relating the history of the Millerites following the Great Disappointment of 1844.

For his part, van Fossen, who referred to Festinger as "a radically deficient guide" to studying the effects of failed prophecy, has charged Festinger and his colleagues with creating a work of satire, not scholarship. To quote van Fossen's scathing critique at length: for Festinger and his colleagues,

> a prophetic movement is folly, an anomaly butting up against a real world that is solid, immovable, and unable to be dismissed. . . . The leaders or sham oracles of the Seekers are . . . portrayed as bombastic travesties of people of grandeur, whose oratory breaks the prevailing rhythm of simple speech and of the authors' descriptive, realistic, and documentary style, which is undisrupted by the theoretical analysis and jargon confined to the introduction and conclusion of the book. . . . The unstated agreement between Festinger and the reader who smiles is that the movement is undesirable. (1988:195 [176–177])

Not only was Festinger's work tainted by subjectivity and bias, argued van Fossen, but it gave no accounting for why Mrs. Keech's group ultimately failed. (Not long after the disconfirmation, Mrs. Keech disbanded the group and left Minnesota. She eventually resettled in Sedona, Arizona, where she joined a Dianetics center.)

In Bainbridge's assessment, the case evidence Festinger and his colleagues published in support of their thesis did not provide adequate or unequivocal proof for its claims. As he noted:

> Festinger's own book really does not offer unambiguous evidence that Mrs. Martin's [Mrs. Keech's] followers went on a preaching rampage after the world failed to end. Although they issued an upbeat proclamation, the news media were badgering them for some response to their failed prophecy, and there is real doubt how they would have behaved if left to their own devices. Indeed, through the entire period of field observation, Festinger's numerous covert researchers also stimulated the group sufficiently so there is no way of knowing what would have happened without them. (1997:137)

Much of the problem with the Festinger thesis, then, seems to stem from its overemphasis on proselytism as a means of relieving dissonance, an emphasis that has tended to obscure some of its more subtle and insightful observations. Indeed, Festinger and his colleagues did not have to underscore the Seekers' post-disconfirmation proselytizing activity, however contrived it might have been, to impress upon the reader that their response to failed prophecy was not as one might have predicted. It would have been enough for Festinger simply to show that the failure of prophecy does not necessarily spell an end to the group or to group members' faith.

Despite overwhelming evidence to the contrary, individuals will cling tenaciously to their beliefs. As the above case studies have demonstrated, more often than not believers will reaffirm their faith by reinterpretating its substance and meaning. That is, while they may acknowledge empirical disconfirmation, more often than not they will reinterpret the meaning of that disconfirmation nonempirically. Interestingly, this is one of the undeveloped points Festinger and his team had made when first stating their thesis. As they put it, individuals presented with undeniable evidence that their beliefs are wrong "will frequently emerge, not only unshaken, but even more convinced of the truth of [their] beliefs than ever before" (1956:3 [31]). The misstep Festinger and his colleagues made—a mistake that has been rightly criticized—was in assuming that groups will exhibit their "recovery of conviction" primarily through proselytizing activities.

While Festinger's overreaching emphasis on proselytism has undermined the reliability of their research, he and his colleagues had made other, more subtle, observations that later researchers such as Joseph Zygmunt and Gordon Melton have expertly brought to the fore. When presented with unequivocal disconfirmation, Zygmunt observed, prophets are apt to offer their followers reasoned reinterpretations of their prophecies. They might claim that the prophecy was a test of faith or a warning to the world. In an interesting way, members, receptive first to the prophecy and then to its reinterpretation, play a collaborative and corroborative role in prophecy and in dissonance reduction. While the prophet offers a vision for what could be, it is those who embrace that vision who affirm its truth and its value to their lives. When it fails, believers often reaffirm the truth of the message and then recommit themselves to it. As a result, a failed prophecy does not disprove faith but comes instead to reaffirm the very system of beliefs from which it first emerged. We might say, following Roy Wallis (1979:44–50), that prophets carefully cultivate a climate—a prophetic milieu— in which their predictions are not only encouraged but eagerly received by their followers.

But in risking failure prophets likewise risk their reputations. It is therefore understandable why prophecies, as such, never really fail. In defense of their authority, when a prediction fails, most prophets will retreat to more ideologically defensible positions. The empirical elements of a prophecy are quickly discarded in favor of a nonempirical understanding of its meaning and import to the group. In sum, while prophets offer nonempirical evidence that their prophecies have in fact been fulfilled, they do so in ways that renew faith in their message, that give added importance to the group's mission, and that leave the door open for further predictions.

Prophets stand between heaven and earth. They serve as mediums between spiritual and physical worlds. By their very nature, prophetic claims cut across both planes of "reality." For messianic and millennial movements to succeed, their prophet-leaders must successfully negotiate the tensions and contradictions that arise when nonempirical claims come into conflict with empirical realities, and vice versa. The more "spiritual" (nonempirical) the rendering, the more plausible and defensible the system becomes to and for its followers (cf. Stark 1996). But beliefs must still have relevance to "real" life, to the world of experience in which their adherents must live. Thus, in an odd sort of way the most successful prophets have been those able to offer their followers a system of beliefs that gives credence to this intricate interweaving of empirical prediction and nonempirical fulfillment.

But as often becomes the case, group members who are unable to reconcile the disjuncture between what they believe will happen and what in fact does happen often become the first casualties of prophetic disconfirmation. Unable to reconcile a prediction with its apparent failure, they lose faith and quickly fall away. It is these, the faithless, the prophets tell us, who are unable to see through eyes of faith. In contrast, only "true" believers are able by faith to embrace the prophet's vision of a new world to come and then follow that vision no matter where it might logically—or illogically—lead them.

NOTES

1. The terms "apocalypse" and "apocalyptic," from the Greek words for "revelation" and "revelatory" respectively, refer to a genre of literature that first appeared sometime between 200 B.C.E. to 200 C.E. that claimed a heavenly vision or visitor as its source of knowledge (Collins 1984). Perhaps the best-known apocalypse is the Revelation to St. John the Divine (or simply, The Apocalypse), which contains an angelic revelation of imminent world destruction to the Apostle John. In modern parlance, however, these terms have come to connote "cataclysm" and "cataclysmic." Misuse among social and behavioral scientists, most having little grounding in classical languages or biblical literature, is commonplace. Indeed, a more recent (and egregious) example of this is found in an otherwise noteworthy collection of essays edited by Thomas Robbins and Susan Palmer (1997). Given the content of the Revelation to St. John, corruption of these terms is understandable.

2. In simplest terms, millennialism is the belief in the return of Paradise. In both Jewish and Christian mythology, the time allotted to humanity will be 6000 years, patterned after the six days of creation. Each thousand-year period represents a "day" of creation. The Millennium (from the Latin, a thousand years) is the name given to the seventh "day," the day God is said to have rested from his creative activities. The older form of the word, chiliasm, is derived from the Greek word "chilias," a thousand.

3. In an insightful essay on the uses of dissonance in membership recruitment, Robert Prus (1976) argued that the creation of dissonance may be used to motivate members toward achieving the goals of the group. He referred to this and other effective faith-building and faith-maintaining tactics religions employ as the "management of dissonance."

4. Susan Palmer and Natalie Finn (1992) observed a similar result in the Le Mission de l'Esprit Saint movement they studied. The young leader of this small French Canadian adventist group made a similar but unanticipated prediction for 1975. His prediction, perhaps given in an attempt to establish his authority over members after he succeeded his deceased father, disrupted the group's normal social patterns. As Palmer and Finn

noted, the group disintegrated in confusion and the young prophet eventually rejoined the main body of Witnesses.

5. Similarly, Anthony van Fossen argued that such endtime movements will likely endure prophetic disconfirmation if they are able to "translate dissonance into pollution" and establish rules and perform rituals that purge dissonance/pollution from the group (1988:193 [145]). As van Fossen noted further, to survive, such movements must elevate their prophets to near-divine status and restructure themselves along more hierarchical lines (1988:194 [145]).

6. To some interpreters, the most notable being Freud, there is a certain element of wish fulfillment taking place in millennial and messianic movements like those of the Jehovah's Witnesses and the Lubavitchers. As Freud wrote, movements like these "try to re-create the world, to build up in its stead another in which its most unbearable features are eliminated and replaced by others that are in conformity with [their] own wishes" (1961:30). As Freud had speculated, this type of wish fulfillment helps individuals forget their real misery in the world, misery caused by unfulfilled aspirations and desires. If Freud was correct, then it would be difficult not to see the spiritualized reinterpretations of failed prophecies, the rationalizing of disappointment, and other creative strategies for reducing cognitive dissonance as little more than subtle and sophisticated forms of self-deception.

REFERENCES

Bainbridge, William Sims. 1997. *The Sociology of Religious Movements.* New York: Routledge.

Balch, Robert W., John Domitrovich, Barbara Lynn Mahnke, and Vanessa Morrison. 1997. "Fifteen Years of Failed Prophecy: Coping with Cognitive Dissonance in a Baha'i Sect," pp. 73–90 in *Millennium, Messiahs, and Mayhem,* edited by Thomas Robbins and Susan J. Palmer. New York: Routledge.

Balch, Robert W., Gwen Farnsworth, and Sue Wilkins. 1983. "When the Bombs Drop: Reactions to Disconfirmed Prophecy in a Millennial Sect." *Sociological Perspectives* 26, 2 (April):137–158.

Barkun, Michael. 1974. *Disaster and the Millennium.* New Haven: Yale University Press.

———. 1986. *Crucible of the Millennium.* Syracuse: Syracuse University Press.

———, ed. 1996. *Millennialism and Violence.* London and Portland, OR: Frank Cass.

Bloch, Ruth. 1985. *Visionary Republic: Millennial Themes in American Thought, 1756–1800.* New York: Cambridge University Press.

Boyer, Paul. 1992. *When Time Shall Be No More.* Cambridge, MA: Belknap/Harvard.

Burridge, Kenelm. 1969. *New Heaven, New Earth.* Oxford: Basil Blackwell.

Butler, Jonathan M. 1974. "Adventism and the American Experience," pp. 173–206 in *The Rise of Adventism: Religion and Society in Mid-Nineteenth-Century America,* edited by Edwin S. Gaustad. New York: Harper & Row.

Carroll, Robert P. 1979. *When Prophecy Failed: Reactions and Responses to Failures in the Old Testament Prophetic Traditions.* London: SCM Press.

Cohn, Norman. 1970. *The Pursuit of the Millennium* (rev. ed.). New York: Oxford University Press.

———. 1993. *Cosmos, Chaos, and the World to Come.* New Haven: Yale University Press.

Collins, John J. 1984. *The Apocalyptic Imagination.* New York: Crossroad.

Cross, Whitney R. 1965. *The Burned-over District: The Social and Intellectual History of Enthusiastic Religion in Western New York, 1800–1850.* New York: Harper Torchbooks.

Dien, Simon. 1997. "When Prophecy Fails: Messianism amongst Lubavitcher Hasids," pp.

238–260 in *The Coming Deliverer: Millennial Themes in World Religions,* edited by Fiona Bowie. Cardiff: University of Wales Press.

Eliade, Mircea. 1971. *The Myth of the Eternal Return.* (Willard Trask, trans.). Princeton, NJ: Bollinger Series.

Ellwood, Robert S., and Harry B. Partin. 1988. *Religious and Spiritual Groups in Modern America* (2nd ed.). Englewood Cliffs, NJ: Prentice-Hall.

Festinger, Leon. 1957. *A Theory of Cognitive Dissonance.* Stanford: Stanford University Press.

Festinger, Leon, Henry W. Riecken, and Stanley Schachter. 1956 [1964]. *When Prophecy Fails: A Social and Psychological Study of a Modern Group that Predicted the Destruction of the World.* New York: Harper Torchbooks.

Foster, Lawrence. 1987. "Had Prophecy Failed?: Contrasting Perspectives of Millerites and Shakers," pp. 173–188 in *The Disappointed: Millerism and Millenarianism in the Nineteenth Century,* edited by Ronald L. Numbers and Jonathan Butler. Bloomington: University of Indiana Press.

Freud, Sigmund. 1961. *Civilization and its Discontents.* New York: W.W. Norton.

Gager, John G. 1975. *Kingdom and Community: The Social World of Early Christianity.* Englewood Cliffs, NJ: Prentice-Hall.

Gaustad, Edwin S., ed. 1974. *The Rise of Adventism: Religion and Society in Mid-Nineteenth-Century America.* New York: Harper & Row.

Greenwald, Anthony G., and David L. Ronis. 1978. "Twenty Years of Cognitive Dissonance: Case Study of the Evolution of a Theory." *Psychological Review* 85:53–57.

Hardyck, Jane Allyn, and Marcia Braden. 1962. "Prophecy Fails Again: A Report of a Failure to Replicate." *Journal of Abnormal and Social Psychology* 65, 2: 136–141.

Holloway, Mark. 1966. *Heavens on Earth.* New York: Dover Publications.

Kaplan, Jeffrey. 1997. *Radical Religion in America: Millenarian Movements from the Far Right to the Children of Noah.* Syracuse, New York: Syracuse University Press.

Lewis, James R., ed. 1995. *The Gods Have Landed: New Religions from Other Worlds.* Albany, NY: SUNY Press.

McGinn, Bernard. 1979. *Visions of the End: Apocalyptic Traditions in the Middle Ages.* New York: Columbia University Press.

Melton, J. Gordon. 1985. "Spiritualization and Reaffirmation: What Really Happens When Prophecy Fails." *American Studies* 26, 2 (Fall):17–29.

———. 1992. *Encyclopedic Handbook of Cults in America* (2nd ed.). New York: Garland Publishing, Inc.

Melton, J. Gordon, Phillip C. Lucas, and Jon R. Stone. 1997. *Prime-Time Religion: An Encyclopedia of Religious Broadcasting.* Phoenix, AZ: The Oryx Press.

Miller, Timothy L., ed. 1995. *America's Alternative Religions.* Albany, NY: SUNY Press.

Numbers, Ronald L., and Jonathan M. Butler. 1987. *The Disappointed: Millerism and Millenarianism in the Nineteenth Century.* Bloomington, IN: Indiana University Press.

O'Leary, Stephen D. 1994. *Arguing the Apocalypse: A Theory of Millennial Rhetoric.* New York: Oxford University Press.

Palmer, Susan. 1996. "Purity and Danger in the Solar Temple." *Journal of Contemporary Religion* 11, 3:303–318.

Palmer, Susan J., and Natalie Finn. 1992. "Coping with Apocalypse in Canada: Experiences of Endtime in La Mission de l'Esprit Saint and the Institute of Applied Metaphysics." *Sociological Analysis* 53, 4 (Winter):397–415.

Penton, M. James. 1985. *Apocalypse Delayed: The Story of Jehovah's Witnesses.* Toronto: University of Toronto Press.

Prus, Robert C. 1976. "Religious Recruitment and the Management of Dissonance: A Sociological Perspective." *Sociological Inquiry* 46, 2:127–134.

Robbins, Thomas, and Dick Anthony. 1995. "Sects and Violence," pp. 236–259 in

Armageddon in Waco, edited by Stuart Wright. Chicago: The University of Chicago Press.

Robbins, Thomas, and Susan J. Palmer, eds. 1997. *Millennium, Messiahs, and Mayhem*. New York: Routledge.

Sanada, Takaaki. 1979. "After Prophecy Fails: A Reappraisal of a Japanese Case." *Japanese Journal of Religious Studies* 6 (March-June):217–237.

Sanada, Takaaki, and Edward Norbeck. 1975. "Prophecy Continues to Fail: A Japanese Sect." *Journal of Cross-Cultural Psychology* 6 (September):331–345.

Sandeen, Ernest R. 1970. *The Roots of Fundamentalism*. Chicago: The University of Chicago Press.

Schmalz, Mathew N. 1994. "When Festinger Fails: Prophecy and the Watchtower." *Religion* 24, 4 (October):293–308.

Shaffir, William. 1995. "When Prophecy Is Not Validated: Explaining the Unexpected in a Messianic Campaign." *The Jewish Journal of Sociology* 37, 2 (December):119–136.

Singelenberg, Richard. 1989. "'It Separated the Wheat from the Chaff': The '1975' Prophecy and Its Impact among Dutch Jehovah's Witnesses." *Sociological Analysis* 50 (Spring):23–40.

Smith, Jonathan Z. 1976. "A Pearl of Great Price and a Cargo of Yams: A Study in Situational Incongruity." *History of Religions* 16 (August):1–19.

Stark, Rodney. 1996. "Why Religious Movements Succeed or Fail: A Revised General Model." *Journal of Contemporary Religion* 11, 2:133–146.

Stone, Jon R. 1993. *A Guide to the End of the World: Popular Eschatology in America*. New York: Garland Publishing, Inc.

Tumminia, Diana. 1998. "How Prophecy Never Fails: Interpretive Reason in a Flying-Saucer Group." *Sociology of Religion* 59, 2 (Summer):157–170.

Tuveson, Ernest Lee. 1949. *Millennium and Utopia: A Study in the Background of the Idea of Progress*. Berkeley: University of California Press.

van Fossen, Anthony B. 1988. "How Do Movements Survive Failures of Prophecy?" *Research in Social Movements, Conflicts and Change* 10:193–212.

Wallis, Roy. 1979. *Salvation and Protest*. New York: St. Martin's Press.

Weber, Timothy P. 1987. *Living in the Shadow of the Second Coming: American Premillennialism, 1875–1982* (2nd ed.). Chicago: The University of Chicago Press.

Weiser, Neil. 1974. "The Effects of Prophetic Disconfirmation of the Committed." *Review of Religious Research* 16:19–30.

Wessinger, Catherine. 1999. *How the Millennium Comes Violently: From Jonestown to Heaven's Gate*. New York: Seven Bridges Press.

Wilson, Bryan R. 1973. *Magic and the Millennium*. New York: Harper & Row.

———. 1978. "When Prophecy Failed." *New Society* 43 (January 26):183–184.

Worsley, Peter. 1968. *The Trumpet Shall Sound*. New York: Schocken Books.

Wright, Stuart, ed. 1995. *Armageddon in Waco*. Chicago: The University of Chicago Press.

Zenner, Walter P. 1966. "The Case of the Apostate Messiah: A Reconsideration of the 'Failure of Prophecy.' " *Archives de Sociologie des Religions* 21 (Jan.–Juin):111–118.

Zygmunt, Joseph F. 1970. "Prophetic Failure and Chiliastic Identity: The Case of Jehovah's Witnesses." *American Journal of Sociology* 75:926–948.

———. 1972. "When Prophecies Fail: A Theoretical Perspective on the Comparative Evidence." *American Behavioral Scientist* 16, 2 (Nov./Dec.):245–268.

Unfulfilled Prophecies and Disappointed Messiahs

Leon Festinger, Henry W. Riecken, and
Stanley Schachter

A man with a conviction is a hard man to change. Tell him you disagree and he turns away. Show him facts or figures and he questions your sources. Appeal to logic and he fails to see your point.

We have all experienced the futility of trying to change a strong conviction, especially if the convinced person has some investment in his belief. We are familiar with the variety of ingenious defenses with which people protect their convictions, managing to keep them unscathed through the most devastating attacks.

But man's resourcefulness goes beyond simply protecting a belief. Suppose an individual believes something with his whole heart; suppose further that he has a commitment to this belief, that he has taken irrevocable actions because of it; finally, suppose that he is presented with evidence, unequivocal and undeniable evidence, that his belief is wrong: what will happen? The individual will frequently emerge, not only unshaken, but even more convinced of the truth of his beliefs than ever before. Indeed, he may even show a new fervor about convincing and converting other people to his view.

How and why does such a response to contradictory evidence come about? This is the question on which we focus. We hope that we will provide an adequate answer to the question, an answer documented by data.

Let us begin by stating the conditions under which we would expect to observe increased fervor following the disconfirmation of a belief. There are five such conditions.

1. A belief must be held with deep conviction and it must have some relevance to action, that is, to what the believer does or how he behaves.
2. The person holding the belief must have committed himself to it; that is, for the sake of his belief, he must have taken some important action that is difficult to undo. In general, the more important such actions are, and the more difficult they are to undo, the greater is the individual's commitment to the belief.

3. The belief must be sufficiently specific and sufficiently concerned with the real world so that events may unequivocally refute the belief.

4. Such undeniable disconfirmatory evidence must occur and must be recognized by the individual holding the belief.

The first two of these conditions specify the circumstances that will make the belief resistant to change. The third and fourth conditions together, on the other hand, point to factors that would exert powerful pressure on a believer to discard his belief. It is, of course, possible that an individual, even though deeply convinced of a belief, may discard it in the face of unequivocal disconfirmation. We must, therefore, state a fifth condition specifying the circumstances under which the belief will be discarded and those under which it will be maintained with new fervor.

5. The individual believer must have social support. It is unlikely that one isolated believer could withstand the kind of disconfirming evidence we have specified. If, however, the believer is a member of a group of convinced persons who can support one another, we would expect the belief to be maintained and the believers to attempt to proselytize or to persuade nonmembers that the belief is correct.

These five conditions specify the circumstances under which increased proselytizing would be expected to follow disconfirmation. Given this set of hypotheses, our immediate concern is to locate data that will allow a test of the prediction of increased proselytizing. Fortunately, there have been throughout history recurring instances of social movements which do satisfy the conditions adequately. These are the millennial or messianic movements, a contemporary instance of which we shall be examining in detail. Let us see just how such movements do satisfy the five conditions we have specified.

Typically, millennial or messianic movements are organized around the prediction of some future events. Our conditions are satisfied, however, only by those movements that specify a date or an interval of time within which the predicted events will occur as well as detailing exactly what is to happen. Sometimes the predicted event is the Second Coming of Christ and the beginning of Christ's reign on earth; sometimes it is the destruction of the world through a cataclysm (usually with some select group slated for rescue from the disaster); or sometimes the prediction is concerned with particular occurrences that the Messiah or a miracle worker will bring about. Whatever the event predicted, the fact that its nature and the time of its happening are specified satisfies the third point on our list of conditions.

The second condition specifies strong behavioral commitment to the belief. This usually follows almost as a consequence of the situation. If one really believes a prediction (the first condition)—for example, that on a given date the world will be destroyed by fire, with sinners being destroyed and the good being saved—one does things about it and makes certain preparations as a matter of course. These actions may range all the way from simple public declarations to the neglect of worldly things and the disposal of earthly possessions. Through such actions and through the mocking and scoffing of nonbelievers there is usually established a heavy commitment on the part of believers. What they do by way of preparation is difficult to undo, and the jeering of nonbelievers simply makes it far more difficult for the adherents to withdraw from the movement and admit that they were wrong.

Our fourth specification has invariably been provided. The predicted events have not occurred. There is usually no mistaking the fact that they did not occur and the believers know that. In other words, the unequivocal disconfirmation does materialize and makes its impact on the believers.

Finally, our fifth condition is ordinarily satisfied—such movements do attract adherents and disciples, sometimes only a handful, occasionally hundreds of thousands. The reasons why people join such movements are outside the scope of our present discussion, but the fact remains that there are usually one or more groups of believers who can support one another.

History has recorded many such movements. Some are scarcely more than mentioned while others are extensively described, although sometimes the aspects of a movement that concern us most may be sketchily recounted. A number of historical accounts, however, are complete enough to provide an introductory and exploratory answer to our central question. From these we have chosen several relatively clear examples of the phenomena under scrutiny in an endeavor simply to show what has often happened in movements that made a prediction about the future and then saw it disconfirmed. We shall discuss these historical examples before presenting the data from our case study of a modern movement.

Ever since the crucifixion of Jesus, many Christians have hoped for the Second Coming of Christ, and movements predicting specific dates for this event have not been rare. But most of the very early ones were not recorded in such a fashion that we can be sure of the reactions of believers to the disconfirmations they may have experienced. Occasionally historians make passing reference to such reactions, as does Hughes in his description of the Montanists:

> Montanus, who appeared in the second half of the second century, does not appear as an innovator in matters of belief. His one personal contribution to the life of the time was the fixed conviction that the second coming of Our Lord was at hand. The event was to take place at Pepuza—near the modern Angora—and thither all true followers of Our Lord should make their way. His authority for the statement was an alleged private inspiration, and the new prophet's personality and eloquence won him a host of disciples, who flocked in such numbers to the appointed spot that a new town sprang up to house them. *Nor did the delay of the second advent put an end to the movement. On the contrary, it gave it new life and form* as a kind of Christianity of the elite, whom no other authority guided in their new life but the Holy Spirit working directly upon them. . . . [Italics ours.][1]

In this brief statement are all the essential elements of the typical messianic movement. There are convinced followers; they commit themselves by uprooting their lives and going to a new place where they build a new town; the Second Advent does not occur. And, we note, far from halting the movement, this disconfirmation gives it new life.

There is somewhat better documentation of millennial movements in more recent history. For example, the Anabaptists of the early sixteenth century believed that the millennium would occur in 1533. As Heath puts it:

> But these high thoughts were obscured by Hoffmann's prediction that the end of all things was at hand. Strassburg, according to him, had been chosen as the New Jerusalem; there the magistrates would set up the kingdom of righteousness, while the hundred and forty and four thousand would maintain the power of the City, and the true Gospel and the true Baptism would spread over the earth. No man would be able to withstand the power, signs and wonders of the saints; and with them would appear, like two mighty torches, Enoch and Elias, who would consume the earth with the fire proceeding from their mouths. The year 1533 was the time in which, Hoffmann declared, the great fulfillment would begin.[2]

This adventist prediction was apparently proclaimed with vigor and was accepted by many persons who then acted accordingly, that is, they began to prepare for the Second Advent and the end of the temporal world. Heath says, for example:

> The followers of Rothmann [a disciple of Hoffmann], were at this time, as was their leader, distinguished for earnestness and self-sacrificing devotion. They sought to exemplify equality and brotherhood in their lives. Well-to-do Brothers and Sisters gave all their goods to the poor, destroyed their rent-rolls, forgave their debtors, renounced worldly pleasures, studying to live an unworldly life.[3]

Such was the situation in 1533, when the end of the world was due. Many people had accepted this belief and some were even disposing of their worldly goods. What happened as the end of 1533 approached and, indeed, when 1534 arrived, without the Second Coming having materialized?

From all accounts it would seem that instead of dampening the ardor of the Anabaptists, the disconfirmation of the predicted Second Coming increased their enthusiasm and activity. They poured greater energy than ever before into obtaining new converts, and sent out missionaries, something they never had done before. The following excerpts from Heath's study illustrate this increase of enthusiasm and activity following the disconfirmation:

> . . . The year 1533 was almost at an end, the half-year during which it had been prophesied Hoffmann should be imprisoned had nearly elapsed, the two years' cessation from baptism had nearly run out when a new prophet [Matthysz] arose.
>
> The Dutch Baptists felt that a leader had risen up amongst them, and they yielded themselves to his guidance. Matthysz began by sending out apostles . . . These apostles went forth announcing, among other things,

that the promised time had come, that no more Christian blood would be poured out, but that in a short time God would overthrow the tyrants and blood-shedders with all the rest of the wicked. They travelled through many states and visited many cities, going to the gatherings of the faithful, and offering them the kiss of peace. They baptized, and ordained bishops and deacons, committing to the former the duty of ordaining others.

The new tide of enthusiasm rose higher than ever. Jakob van Kampen, who, assisted by Houtzager, worked among the poorer homes in Amsterdam, baptized in February, 1534, in one day, a hundred persons. About two months later it was estimated that two-thirds of the population at Monniaendam were adherents of Jan Matthysz, and it is said to have been the same in the neighbourhood of most of the great cities of Holland.[4]

Another, and rather fascinating, illustration of the reaction to disconfirming evidence is provided by the messianic movement of which Sabbatai Zevi was the central figure.[5] Sabbatai Zevi was born and raised in the city of Smyrna. By 1646 he had acquired considerable prestige through living a highly ascetic life and devoting his whole energy to the study of the cabala. Indeed, though he was only twenty years old, he had already gathered around him a small group of disciples. To these disciples he taught and interpreted the highly mystical writings of the cabala.

Prevalent among Jews at that time was the belief that the Messiah would come in the year 1648. His coming was to be accompanied by all manner of miracles and the era of redemption would dawn. Sometime in 1648 Sabbatai Zevi proclaimed himself as the promised Messiah to his small group of disciples. Needless to say, the year 1648 passed and the era of redemption did not dawn and the expected miracles were not forthcoming.

There is but scant information about immediately subsequent events but apparently the disconfirmation of his messiahship did not daunt Sabbatai or his disciples. Indeed, it seems that after 1648 he made his claim known to the community at large. Graetz writes: "When Zevi's pretensions became known some years later, the college of rabbis, at their head his teacher Joseph Eskapha, laid him and his followers under a ban . . . Finally, he and his disciples were banished from Smyrna [about 1651]."[6] The significant point for our interest is that it was *after* the year 1648 had passed and nothing had happened that Zevi proclaimed his messiahship to people outside his small circle of disciples.

His banishment, however, certainly does not end the story. About this time some segments of the Christian world were expecting the year 1666 to usher in the Millennium, and Sabbatai Zevi appears to have accepted this date. From 1651 until the autumn of 1665 he moved about among the cities of the Near East which had large Jewish communities, making known his claims to be the Messiah and gradually acquiring more and more followers even though the rabbinate continued to oppose him. By 1665 his following was very large and a number of disciples had helped him spread his name and pretensions through-out the Jewish world. The atmosphere in Smyrna had so changed by the autumn of 1665 that when he returned to his native city in that year he was received with great joy. In September or October of 1665 he proclaimed himself the Messiah in a public ceremony in Smyrna:

> The madness of the Jews of Smyrna knew no bounds. Every sign of honor and enthusiastic love was shown him. . . . All prepared for a speedy exodus, the return to the Holy Land. Workmen neglected their business, and thought only of the approaching Kingdom of the Messiah. . . .These events in the Jew's quarter at Smyrna made a great sensation in ever-widening circles. The neighboring communities in Asia Minor, many members of which had betaken themselves to Smyrna, and witnessed the scenes enacted in the town, brought home exaggerated accounts of the Messiah's power of attraction and of working miracles, were swept into the same vortex. Sabbatai's private secretary, Samuel Primo, took care that reports of the fame and doings of the Messiah should reach Jews abroad.[7]

The movement gradually spread to almost the whole of Jewry, and Sabbatai was accepted and heralded everywhere as the Messiah. Furthermore, since this was no idle belief, people took steps to prepare for the promised events. They neglected their work and their businesses, and many prepared for the return to Jerusalem.

Since one of the predicted events was that the Sultan would be deposed (a necessary preliminary to the return of the Jews to the Holy Land), at the very beginning of the year 1666, Sabbatai together with a number of followers set out for Constantinople to accomplish this task. The party landed on the coast of the Dardanelles, where Sabbatai was immediately arrested by Turkish officials and was brought in fetters to a small town in the neighborhood of Constantinople. Graetz writes:

> Informed by a messenger of his arrival . . . his followers [from Constantinople] hastened from the capital to see him, but found him in a pitiable plight and in chains. The money which they brought with them procured him some alleviation, and on the following Sunday [February 1666] he was brought by sea to Constantinople—but in how different a manner to what he and his believers had anticipated! [8]

Clearly, we may regard his arrest as a serious disappointment to the followers of Sabbatai and a disconfirmation of his predictions. Indeed, there were evidences of shock and disappointment. But then there began to emerge the familiar pattern: recovery of conviction, followed by new heights of enthusiasm and proselytizing. Graetz describes the ensuing events very well:

> For some days they kept quietly at home, because the street boys mocked them by shouting, "Is he coming? Is he coming?" But soon they began again to assert that he was the true Messiah, and that the sufferings which

he had encountered were necessary, a condition to his glorification. The prophets continued to proclaim the speedy redemption of Sabbatai and of all Israel. . . . Thousands crowded daily to Sabbatai's place of confinement merely to catch a glimpse of him. . . . The expectations of the Jews were raised to a still higher pitch, and the most exaggerated hopes fostered to a greater degree.[9]

The very fact that Sabbatai was still alive was used by the Jews to argue that he was really the Messiah. When he was moved to another jail and his incarceration became milder (largely through bribery), the argument was complete. A constant procession of adoring followers visited the prison where Sabbatai held court, and a steady stream of propaganda and tales of miracles poured out all over the Near East and Europe. Graetz states:

> What more was needed to confirm the predictions of prophets of ancient and modern times? The Jews accordingly prepared seriously to return to their original home. In Hungary they began to unroof their houses. In large commercial cities, where Jews took the lead in wholesale business, such as Amsterdam, Leghorn and Hamburg, stagnation of trade ensued.[10]

The memoirs of a contemporary European Jewess vividly confirm Graetz's assertions:

> Our joy, when the letters arrived [from Smyrna] is not to be told. Most of them were addressed to the Sephardim who, as fast as they came, took them to their synagogue and read them aloud; young and old, the Germans too hastened to the Sephardic synagogue.
> Many sold their houses and lands and all their possessions, for any day they hoped to be redeemed. My good father-in-law left his home in Hameln, abandoned his house and lands and all his goodly furniture and moved to Hildesheim. He sent on to us in Hamburg two enormous casks packed with linens and with peas, beans, dried meats, shredded prunes and like stuff, every manner of food that would keep. For the old man expected to sail any moment from Hamburg to the Holy Land.[11]

Finally, in an effort to cope with the problem, without making a martyr of Sabbatai, the Sultan attempted to convert him to Islam. Astonishingly enough, the plan succeeded and Sabbatai donned the turban. Many of the Jews of the Near East still kept faith in him. Explanations were invented for his conversion and many continued their proselytizing, usually in places where the movement had not previously been strong. A considerable number of Jews even followed his lead and became Moslems. His conversion proved to be too much for most of his followers in Europe, however, and the movement there soon collapsed.

The Sabbataian movement strikingly illustrates the phenomenon we are concerned with: when people are committed to a belief and a course of action, clear disconfirming evidence may simply result in deepened conviction and increased proselytizing. But there does seem to be a point at which the disconfirming evidence has mounted sufficiently to cause the belief to be rejected.

In the preceding examples many of the facts are not known, others are in dispute, and much is vague. There is, however, a more recent movement about which considerable detail is known—the Millerites, who flourished in mid-nineteenth-century America. Many of the original documents of the Millerite movement have been preserved and there are two fairly lengthy summary accounts available. One, by C. E. Sears,[12] tends to ridicule the Millerites while the other, by F. D. Nichol,[13] is a careful and vigorous defense of them.

William Miller was a New England farmer with a belief in the literal fulfillment of biblical prophecy. In 1818, after a two-year study of the Bible, Miller reached the conclusion that the end of the world would occur in 1843. Nichol's account reads:

> Specifically, he put his first and greatest emphasis on the prophetic declaration, "Unto two thousand and three hundred days; then shall the sanctuary be cleansed." Daniel 8:14. Believing that the "cleansing" of the sanctuary involved the purging of this earth by fire, the "days" in symbolic prophecy stand for years, and that this time prophecy began about 457 B.C., he reached this final conclusion: "I was thus brought, in 1818, at the close of my two years' study of the Scriptures, to the solemn conclusion, that in about twenty-five years from that time all the affairs of our present state would be wound up" (William Miller, *Apology and Defense*, p. 5).[14]

For another five years he continued to study the Bible and to check his calculations before he acquired the confidence to talk much about it to others. Even then he talked only to his neighbors and to a few ministers, none of whom seemed to manifest much interest. He continued talking about his views, however. By 1831 he had evoked enough interest to receive invitations to address various groups. For eight years Miller continued to devote a great deal of his time to giving lectures in which he explained the basis for his prediction of the millennium in 1843. He gradually persuaded more and more people, including a number of ministers, of the correctness of his belief. In 1839 he met and convinced Joshua V. Himes, who helped change the movement from a one-man affair into an organized activity. A newspaper was started, and in 1840, only three years before the Second Coming was due, a general conference of interested ministers was called. Proselytizing activity increased and Miller's views began to spread as the adventist prediction became the focus of a mass movement.

Many of the leading figures in the Millerite movement had still not fully accepted the specific date of 1843 as the time of the Second Coming. In the spring of 1842, a general conference was held in Boston. Nichol states:

> In this conference the significance of the time element in the preaching of the advent came definitely to the front as indicated in this resolution that was passed:
> "*Resolved,* that in the opinion of this conference, there are most seri-

ous and important reasons for believing that God has revealed the time of the end of the world, and that that time is 1843" (*Signs of the Times*, June 1, 1842, p. 69).

The very fact that an increasing emphasis was being placed on the time element meant that all who accepted this phase of the teaching felt an increasing sense of urgency in discharging their responsibility to warn the world. They believed that the time had come to proclaim with vigor what they described as "the midnight cry."[15]

In other words, as the year 1843 approached, belief in the correctness of the predicted date grew stronger. At the same time, activity in spreading the word was on the increase. The general conference had decided to hold a series of camp meetings during the summer of 1842, and these were almost all highly successful. In four months, ending the middle of November, the Millerites held thirty camp meetings at which the attendance was in the thousands. The number of adherents was growing steadily.

In addition to the newspaper *Signs of the Times*, which had been started in Boston in 1840, the Millerite leaders now started another, *The Midnight Cry*, in New York. Many other newspapers were published in various cities for shorter periods of time, usually in connection with a special series of lectures being given locally:

> For example, the *Philadelphia Alarm* was started in 1843, as an adjunct to a series of lectures. Thirteen numbers were issued. Thus a local color could be given to the literature in any city while an initial endeavor was being made there. Afterward the more permanently established publications could be used for promotion and educating the believers in the movement.[16]

While the movement was growing the opposition was also increasing. By the beginning of 1843 many ministers were preaching against the Millerites and newspapers were ridiculing them. Rumors were current and printed widely in the newspapers of the day that Miller's followers were fanatics and that his doctrines drove people insane. A single example should suffice to show the kind of attack directed against the movement:

> The Millerites have very properly been shut out of the buildings in which they have for some time been holding their orgies in Philadelphia, and we are happy to learn that the grand jury of the Boston municipal court has represented the great temple itself as a dangerous structure. After some half-dozen more deaths occur and a few more men and women are sent to madhouses by this miserable fanaticism perhaps some grand jury may think it worth-while to indict the vagabonds who are the cause of so much mischief.[17]

In spite of such opposition, the movement continued to attract believers—so many that it became difficult to find a hall large enough for general meetings. Early in 1843, therefore, the leaders decided to erect a tabernacle in Boston. It was dedicated before an audience of some 3500 people—a capacity crowd that included a number of clergymen of the city. The new building made it possible to speed the word to even larger audiences in the city, while the campaign of pamphlets and newspapers continued unabated.

As one might expect, the beginning of 1843 coincided with an upsurge of interest in the specific date of the Advent. Until the beginning of the year, Miller had usually referred to the Second Coming as taking place "about the year 1843." On January 1, 1843, Miller published a synopsis of his beliefs, and therein stated his expectations about the date:

> I believe the time can be known by all who desire to understand and to be ready for His coming. And I am fully convinced that sometime between March 21st, 1843, and March 21st, 1844, according to the Jewish mode of computation of time, Christ will come, and bring all His Saints with Him; and that then He will reward every man as his work shall be.[18]

Nichol comments:

> Miller set no date or day within this period. The leaders who were associated with him likewise refused to name a specific date. In the first issue of January, 1843, the *Signs of the Times* declared, in refutation of a widely circulated charge that the Millerites had set on a certain day in April: "The fact is, that the believers of the second advent in 1843, *have fixed* NO TIME *in the year* for the event. And Brethren Miller, Himes, Litch, Hale, Fitch, Hawley, and other prominent lecturers, most decidedly protest against . . . fixing the day or hour of the event. This we have done over and over again, in our paper." (*Signs of the Times,* Jan. 4, 1843, p. 121. See also issue of Jan. 18, 1843, p. 141, in which George Storrs, another Millerite minister, protests against the fixing of any day; also issue of April 5, 1843, pp. 33–35, 37.)
>
> It is true that individual preachers or limited groups here and there sought to find a Scriptural analogy or by a certain reading of the prophecy a warrant for predicting the advent on some particular day during the year.[19]

The fact that Miller had specified an interval of time, namely, March 21, 1843, to March 21, 1844, rather than a single day, tended to be temporarily overlooked by many followers. Two predictions of specific days had some currency, although it is impossible to be sure how widely they were believed. Some Millerites expected the Advent to occur on April 23, 1843, although the leaders never endorsed this date. Those who had given credence to the April date reacted to its passing in the following way:

> At first there was evidence of surprise and disappointment among the Millerites, but it quickly gave way to renewed confidence. "After all," they reminded one another, "there is a whole year in which to look for the Coming;—we looked for it too soon, that was all."—and the singing and exhorting took on a new fervor.[20]

Here once again we note the appearance of increased enthusiasm and conviction after a disconfirmation.

In spite of the official position of the leaders, that the end of the period in which the Second Coming was expected was March 21, 1844, many Millerites placed their hopes on the end of 1843. The leaders took note of this specific expectation and, early in 1844, issued statements concerning it. For example, the opening paragraph of a New Year's address by Miller goes as follows:

> "Brethren, The Roman [year] 1843 is past [the Jewish sacred year would end in the spring of 1844] and our hopes are not realized. Shall we give up the ship? No, no . . . We do not yet believe our reckoning has run out. It takes all of 457 and 1843 to make 2300, and must of course run as far into '44 as it began in the year 457 before Christ."[21]

The situation generally at the beginning of 1844 is described by Sears:

> Then a fluttering of doubt and hesitation became apparent in certain communities, but soon those were dispelled when it was recalled that as far back as 1839 Prophet Miller had stated on some occasion, which had been forgotten in the general excitement, that he was not *positive* that the event would take place during the *Christian* year from 1843 to 1844, and that he would claim the whole *Jewish* year which would carry the prophecy over to the 21st of March, 1844. An announcement to this effect was sent broadcast, and by this time the delusion had taken such a firm hold upon the imaginations of his followers that any simple explanation, however crude, seemed sufficient to quiet all doubts and questionings.
>
> Having accepted this lengthening of the allotted time, the brethren who had assumed the responsibility of sounding the alarm entered into their work with renewed energy and outdid themselves in their efforts to terrify the army of unbelievers into a realization of the horrors that awaited them and to strengthen the faith of those already in the ranks.[22]

Again fervor increased; Millerite conferences in New York and Philadelphia were thronged, and, in Washington, there had to be a last-minute change to a larger hall. Popular interest greatly exceeded even the leaders' expectations.

But March 21, 1844, also came and went with no sign of the Second Coming. The reaction of the non-Millerites was strong and unequivocal:

> The world made merry over the old Prophet's predicament. The taunts and jeers of the "scoffers" were well-nigh unbearable. If any of Miller's followers walked abroad, they ran the gauntlet of merciless ridicule.
>
> "What!—not gone up yet?—We thought you'd gone up! Aren't you going up soon?—Wife didn't go up and leave you behind to burn, did she?"
> The rowdy element in the community would not leave them alone.[23]

There was strong and severe disappointment among the believers, but this was of brief duration and soon the energy and enthusiasm were back to where they had been before and even greater:

The year of the end of the world had ended, but Millerism had not. . . .
Though some who had been only lukewarm in the movement fell away
from it, many maintained both their faith and their fervor. They were
ready to attribute the disappointment to some minor error in calculating
chronology.[24]

But in spite of the failure of the prophecy, the fires of fanaticism increased.
The flames of such emotions cannot be quenched at will; like all great confla-
grations they must burn themselves out. And so it was in 1844. Instead of
decreasing, the failure seemed to excite even greater exhibitions of loyalty to the
expectation of the impending Judgment Day.[25]

By the middle of July things were at a new fever pitch and the energy expended
to convert more and more people was greater than ever. Miller and Himes traveled as far as Ohio to make converts, something that had never before been done.
Himes described the general attitude of followers toward the Advent: "I have
never witnessed a stronger, or more active faith. Indeed, the faith and confidence
of the brethren in the prophetic word was never stronger. I find few, if any, who
ever believed on Bible *evidence*, that are at all shaken in the faith; while others
are embracing our views."[26] Following a visit to Philadelphia, Himes, still very
much aware of the disconfirmation in March, showed his elation at the revival
of belief: "The trying crisis is past, and the cause is on the rise in this city. The
calls for lectures in the vicinity were never more pressing than now. The minister in charge of the Ebenezer station, Kensington (Protestant Methodist), has
just come out on the doctrine in full."[27]

As Nichol puts it:

> From Cleveland, Himes wrote early in August of his plan to go to
> England in October, "if time be prolonged," for the purpose of quicken-
> ing the interest already present there. Literature had been sent out.
> Various ministers in other lands had taken up the cry, "Behold, the
> Bridegroom cometh." But Himes thought that now he and others with
> him from America should go forth to strengthen the endeavors abroad.
> Said he:
> "If time be continued for a few months, we shall send the *glad tidings*
> out in a number of different languages, among Protestant and Catholic
> nations. . . .
> "A press shall be established at London, and lecturers will go out in
> every direction, and we trust the Word of the Lord shall have a free course
> and be glorified. What we shall accomplish we can not tell. But we wish
> to do our duty" (*The Advent Herald,* Aug. 21, 1844, p. 20).
> Thus even as Himes and Miller moved westward expanding the work,
> they envisioned a still greater work overseas.[28]

About this time more and more Millerites were accepting a new prediction
first promulgated by one of their number, the Reverend Samuel S. Snow, who
believed that the date of the Second Coming would be October 22, 1844.

Although it might not seem possible for the enthusiasm and fervor to exceed what had already been shown in the first few months of 1844, that is just what happened. The two partial disconfirmations (April 23, 1843, and the end of the calendar year 1843) and one complete and unequivocal disconfirmation (March 21, 1844) served simply to strengthen conviction that the Coming was near at hand and to increase the time and energy that Miller's adherents spent trying to convince others:

> Perhaps not so much from the preaching and writing of Snow, as from a deep conviction that the end of all things could not be far away, some of the believers in northern New Hampshire, even before summer began, failed to plow their fields because the Lord would surely come "before another winter." This conviction grew among others in that area so that even if they had planted their fields they felt it would be inconsistent with their faith to take in their crops. We read:
>
> "Some, on going into their fields to cut their grass, found themselves entirely unable to proceed, and, conforming to their sense of duty, left their crops standing in the field, to show their faith by their works, and thus to condemn the world. This rapidly extended through the north of New England" (*The Advent Herald*, Oct. 20, 1844, p. 93).
>
> Such conviction naturally prepared men to give a sympathetic ear to the proclamation that the day of the Lord would come on October 22. By midsummer a new stimulus had been given to Millerism in New England. Backsliders were reclaimed, and new ardor controlled those Adventists who accepted Snow's reckoning, as they went out to proclaim the cry, "Behold, the Bridegroom cometh, go ye out to meet Him." Indeed, Snow declared that only now was the true midnight cry being given.[29]

It is interesting that it was the insistence of the ordinary members of the Millerite movement that the October date be accepted. The leaders of the movement resisted it and counseled against it for a long time, but to no avail. A Millerite editor, writing in retrospect, commented:

> At first the definite time was generally opposed; but there seemed to be an irresistible power attending its proclamation, which prostrated all before it. It swept over the land with the velocity of a tornado, and it reached hearts in different and distant places almost simultaneously, and in a manner which can be accounted for only on the supposition that God was [in] it. . . .
>
> The lecturers among the Adventists were the last to embrace the views of the time. . . . It was not until within about two weeks of the commencement of the seventh month [about the first of October], that we were particularly impressed with the progress of the movement, when we had such a view of it, that to oppose it, or even to remain silent longer, seemed to us to be opposing the work of the Holy Spirit; and in entering

upon the work with all our souls, we could but exclaim, "What were we, that we should resist God?" It seemed to us to have been so independent of human agency, that we could but regard it as a fulfillment of the "midnight cry."[30]

In the period from mid-August to the predicted new day, October 22, 1844, things reached an incredible pitch of fervor, zeal, and conviction:

> Elder Boutelle describes the period thus: "The 'Advent Herald', 'the Midnight Cry', and other Advent papers, periodicals, pamphlets, tracts, leaflets, voicing the coming glory, were scattered broadcast and everywhere like autumn leaves in the forest. Every house was visited by them.... A mighty effort through the Spirit and the word preached was made to bring sinners to repentance, and to have the wandering ones return."
>
> The camp meetings were now so crowded that they were no longer orderly as they had been. If there had been a time when an undesirable element could be kept out, it was now impossible to do so; and as a matter of fact the world was so near its end, as they claimed, whatever precautions were taken before seemed hardly worth while any longer.[31]

The most active endeavors were made by the Millerites during these closing weeks to broadcast what they believed was the truth concerning the exact time of Christ's advent. Extra issues of *The Midnight Cry* and *The Advent Herald* were published. The editor of *The Midnight Cry* stated that in order to provide the literature needed they were keeping "four steam presses almost constantly in motion."[32]

Further evidence on the extent of the conviction and the drive to persuade and convert others is the fact that now even many of the leaders were advocating partial cessation of normal activities on the part of believers so they would have more time to convert others and spread the word. An editorial in the final issue of *The Midnight Cry* proclaimed:

> Think for eternity! Thousands may be lulled to sleep by hearing your actions say: "This world is worth my whole energies. The world to come is a vain shadow." O, reverse this practical sermon, *instantly!* Break loose from the world as much as possible. If indispensable duty calls you into the world for a moment, go as a man would run to do a piece of work in the rain. Run and hasten through it, and let it be known that you leave it with alacrity for something better. Let your actions preach in the clearest tones: "The Lord is coming"—"The Time is short"—"This world passeth away"—"Prepare to meet thy God." [33]

A news story in *The Midnight Cry* stated:

> Many are leaving all to go out and warn the brethren and the world. In Philadelphia, thirteen volunteered at one meeting (after hearing Brother Storrs) to go out and sound the alarm. . . . In both cities [New York and

Philadelphia], stores are being closed, and they preach in tones the world understands, though they may not heed it.[34]

And Nichol points out:

There were several reasons why the believers in a number of instances sold their possessions in part or in whole. First, they wished to have more money with which to support the cause. It took money to support four presses running constantly, pouring out literature on Millerism. Second, they wished to have all their dealings with their fellow men honorably concluded before the advent, including full payment of all their debts. Third, with the fervent love for others, which true religion certainly ought to generate in the hearts of men, Millerites who owed no debts themselves sought to help others pay their debts. Some Millerites, stimulated by the realization that soon earthly gold would be worthless, and warmed in their hearts with a love for their fellow men, wished to make gifts to the poor, both within and without the faith.[35]

But October 22 came and went, and with it all the hopes of the Millerites. This was the culminating disconfirmation and, at last, conviction was shattered and proselytizing was stilled. The plight of the heavily committed followers was pitiable indeed. They had to bear the taunts and jeers of a hostile world and many were left pauperized. Their cruel disappointment and the hardship are well attested to. Nichol quotes two extracts from the writings of convinced believers that tell the sad story:

Our fondest hopes and expectations were blasted, and such a spirit of weeping came over us as I never experienced before. It seemed that the loss of all earthly friends could have been no comparison. We wept, and wept, till the day dawn. I mused in my own heart, saying, My advent experience has been the richest and brightest of all my Christian experience. If this had proved a failure, what was the rest of my Christian experience worth? Has the Bible proved a failure? Is there no God, no heaven, no golden home city, no paradise? Is all this but a cunningly devised fable? Is there no reality to our fondest hope and expectation of these things? And thus we had something to grieve and weep over, if all our fond hopes were lost. And as I said, we wept till the day dawn.[36]

The 22nd of October passed, making unspeakably sad the faithful and longing ones; but causing the unbelieving and wicked to rejoice. All was still. No *Advent Herald*; no meetings as formerly. Everyone felt lonely, with hardly a desire to speak to anyone. Still in the cold world! No deliverance—the Lord [had] not come! No words can express the feelings of disappointment of a true Adventist then. Those only who experienced it can enter into the subject as it was. It was a humiliating thing and we all felt it alike. . . .[37]

The disconfirmation of October 22 brought about the collapse of Millerism. It had taken three or perhaps four disconfirmations within a period of eighteen months, but this last one was too much. In spite of their overwhelming commitments, Miller's followers gave up their beliefs and the movement quickly disintegrated in dissention, controversy, and discord. By the late spring of 1845 it had virtually disappeared.

The history of the Millerites shows again the phenomenon we have noted in our other examples. Although there is a limit beyond which belief will not withstand disconfirmation, it is clear that the introduction of contrary evidence can serve to increase the conviction and enthusiasm of a believer.

Historical records are replete with further instances of similar movements of a millennial or messianic character. Unfortunately for our purpose, however, in most instances the data which would be relevant to our hypotheses are totally absent. Even in cases where considerable data are available, there will frequently be some crucial point which is equivocal, thus destroying the cogent relevance to our hypotheses. The best instance of such a movement where there is one single controversial point on a crucial issue is the very beginnings of Christianity.[38]

There is quite general agreement among historians that the apostles were both convinced and committed. None would question that the apostles fully believed in the things Jesus stood for and had altered their lives considerably because of this belief. Burkitt, for example, states that Peter, at one point, "exclaimed that he and his companions really had left all to follow Jesus."[39] Thus, we may assert that the first two conditions which we stated early in the chapter are fulfilled.

There is no denying that the apostles provided support for one another and that they went out to proselytize following the crucifixion of Jesus. Thus, we may accept as fact that the fifth condition we mentioned is satisfied, and that there was a point at which proselytizing increased.

But the third and fourth conditions remain in doubt. Was there, in essence, something in the belief system that was amenable to clear and unequivocal disconfirmation and, if so, did such disconfirmation occur? In spite of many things which are not disputed, the major issue is shrouded in disagreement among various historians. There is general agreement that Jesus, in various ways, implied that he was the Messiah or Christ. More importantly, it is also clear that his disciples recognized him as such. For example, Scott states: "When directly challenged by Jesus, Peter speaking for the group of disciples said, 'Thou art the Messiah.' "[40]

It is also clear that, at least so far as other Jewish sects of that day were concerned, the Messiah could not be made to suffer pain. Thus Simpson states: "With equal certainty it may be affirmed that no department of Judaism had ever conceived of a suffering Messiah."[41] If this were all there were to it, then one would assert that the crucifixion and the cry Jesus uttered on the cross were indeed an unequivocal disconfirmation.

But this is not all there is to it. Many authorities assert unequivocally that it is precisely on this question that Jesus introduced new doctrine. Jesus and the apostles, these authorities state, did believe that the Messiah had to suffer, and

Jesus even predicted that he would die in Jerusalem. Burkitt says: ". . . we end with Peter declaring, 'Thou art the Messiah' and with Jesus saying, practically, in reply, 'Yes, and I go now to Jerusalem; but whoever wants to follow Me there must renounce all ambitious hopes and accompany Me—to execution.'"[42] If this view is maintained, then the crucifixion, far from being a disconfirmation, was indeed a confirmation of a prediction, and the subsequent proselytizing of the apostles would stand as a counterexample to our hypotheses. The authorities we have quoted from above accept this latter interpretation and, in fact, they are in the majority.

But not all authorities agree. At the other extreme of interpretation is Graetz, who states:

> When the disciples of Jesus had somewhat recovered from the panic which came upon them at the time he was seized and executed, they re-assembled to mourn together over the death of their beloved Master. . . . Still, the effect that Jesus produced upon the unenlightened masses must have been very powerful; for their faith in him, far from fading away like a dream, became more and more intense, their adoration of Jesus rising to the highest pitch of enthusiasm. The only stumbling-block to their belief lay in the fact that the Messiah who came to deliver Israel and bring to light the glory of the kingdom of heaven, endured a shameful death. How could the Messiah be subject to pain? A suffering Messiah staggered them considerably, and this stumbling-block had to be overcome before a perfect and joyful belief could be reposed in him. It was at that moment probably that some writer relieved his own perplexities and quelled their doubts by referring to a prophecy in Isaiah, that "He will be taken from the land of the living, and will be wounded for the sins of his people." [43]

Was it or was it not a disconfirmation? We do not know and cannot say. But this one unclarity makes the whole episode inconclusive with respect to our hypotheses.

There are many more historical examples we could describe at the risk of becoming repetitive and at the risk of using highly unreliable data. Let the examples we have already given suffice.

We can now turn our attention to the question of why increased proselytizing follows the disconfirmation of a prediction. How can we explain it and what are the factors that will determine whether or not it will occur?

Since our explanation will rest upon one derivation from a general theory, we will first state the bare essentials of the theory which are necessary for this derivation. The full theory has wide implications and a variety of experiments have already been conducted to test derivations concerning such things as the consequences of decisions, the effects of producing forced compliance, and some patterns of voluntary exposure to new information. At this point, we shall draw out in detail only those implications that are relevant to the phenomenon of increased proselytizing following disconfirmation of a prediction. For this purpose we shall introduce the concepts of consonance and dissonance.[44]

Dissonance and consonance are relations among cognitions—that is, among opinions, beliefs, knowledge of the environment, and knowledge of one's own actions and feelings. Two opinions, or beliefs, or items of knowledge are *dissonant* with each other if they do not fit together—that is, if they are inconsistent, or if, considering only the particular two items, one does not follow from the other. For example, a cigarette smoker who believes that smoking is bad for his health has an opinion that is dissonant with the knowledge that he is continuing to smoke. He may have many other opinions, beliefs, or items of knowledge that are consonant with continuing to smoke, but the dissonance nevertheless exists.

Dissonance produces discomfort and, correspondingly, there will arise pressures to reduce or eliminate the dissonance. Attempts to reduce dissonance represent the observable manifestations that dissonance exists. Such attempts may take any or all of three forms. The person may try to change one or more of the beliefs, opinions, or behaviors involved in the dissonance; to acquire new information or beliefs that will increase the existing consonance and thus cause the total dissonance to be reduced; or to forget or reduce the importance of those cognitions that are in a dissonant relationship.

If any of the above attempts are to be successful, they must meet with support from either the physical or the social environment. In the absence of such support, the most determined efforts to reduce dissonance may be unsuccessful.

The foregoing statement of the major ideas about dissonance and its reduction is a very brief one and, for that reason, it may be difficult to follow. We can perhaps make these ideas clearer to the reader by showing how they apply to the kind of social movement we have been discussing, and by pointing out how these ideas help to explain the curious phenomenon we have observed.

Theoretically, what is the situation of the individual believer at the pre-disconfirmation stage of such a movement? He has a strongly held belief in a prediction—for example, that Christ will return—a belief that is supported by the other members of the movement. By way of preparation for the predicted event, he has engaged in many activities that are entirely consistent with his belief. In other words, most of the relations among relevant cognitions are, at this point, consonant.

Now what is the effect of the disconfirmation, of the unequivocal fact that the prediction was wrong, upon the believer? The disconfirmation introduces an important and painful dissonance. The fact that the predicted events did not occur is dissonant with continuing to believe both the prediction and the remainder of the ideology of which the prediction was the central item. The failure of the prediction is also dissonant with all the actions that the believer took in preparation for its fulfillment. The magnitude of the dissonance will, of course, depend on the importance of the belief to the individual and on the magnitude of his preparatory activity.

In the type of movement we have discussed, the central belief and its accompanying ideology are usually of crucial importance in the believers' lives and hence the dissonance is very strong—and very painful to tolerate. Accordingly, we should expect to observe believers making determined efforts to eliminate the dissonance or, at least, to reduce its magnitude. How may they accomplish this end? The dissonance would be largely eliminated if they discarded the belief that had been disconfirmed, ceased the behavior which had been initiated in preparation for the fulfillment of the prediction, and returned to a more usual existence. Indeed, this pattern sometimes occurs, and we have seen that it did happen to the Millerites after the last disconfirmation and to the Sabbataians after Zevi himself was converted to Islam. But frequently the behavioral commitment to the belief system is so strong that almost any other course of action is preferable. It may even be less painful to tolerate the dissonance than to discard the belief and admit one had been wrong. When that is the case, the dissonance cannot be eliminated by giving up the belief.

Alternatively, the dissonance would be reduced or eliminated if the members of a movement effectively blind themselves to the fact that the prediction has not been fulfilled. But most people, including members of such movements, are in touch with reality and cannot simply blot out of their cognition such an unequivocal and undeniable fact. They can try to ignore it, however, and they usually do try. They may convince themselves that the date was wrong but that the prediction will, after all, be shortly confirmed; or they may even set another date, as the Millerites did. Some Millerites, after the last disconfirmation, even ventured the opinion that the Second Coming had occurred, but that it had occurred in heaven and not on the earth itself. Or believers may try to find reasonable explanations, and very often they find ingenious ones. The Sabbataians, for example, convinced themselves when Zevi was jailed that the very fact that he was still alive proved he was the Messiah. Even after his conversion some staunch adherents claimed this, too, was part of the plan. Rationalization can reduce dissonance somewhat. For rationalization to be fully effective, support from others is needed to make the explanation or the revision seem correct. Fortunately, the disappointed believer can usually turn to the others in the same movement, who have the same dissonance and the same pressures to reduce it. Support for the new explanation is, hence, forthcoming and the members of the movement can recover somewhat from the shock of the disconfirmation.

But whatever explanation is made it is still by itself not sufficient. The dissonance is too important and though they may try to hide it, even from themselves, the believers still know that the prediction was false and all their preparations were in vain. The dissonance cannot be eliminated completely by denying or rationalizing the disconfirmation. But there is a way in which the remaining dissonance can be reduced. *If more and more people can be persuaded that the system of belief is correct, then clearly it must, after all, be correct.* Consider the extreme case: if everyone in the whole world believed something, then there would be no question at all as to the validity of this belief. It is for this reason that we observe the increase in proselytizing following disconfirmation. If the proselytizing proves successful, then by gathering more adherents and effectively surrounding himself with supporters, the believer reduces dissonance to the point where he can live with it.

In the light of this explanation of the phenomenon that proselytizing increases as a result of a disconfirmation, let us take another, more critical look at the historical examples we have offered in evidence. There are a number of grounds for feeling unsatisfied with them as proof.

In the first place there is a scarcity of data of the sort required by our analysis. It is an understandable lack, for the people collecting historical records were not concerned with our particular problem, but it is a lack nonetheless. Even our best documented example, the Millerites, contains little evidence on actual proselytizing behavior, especially among the mass members. Statements about proselytizing must be inferred largely from evidence about the number of adherents and the size and frequency of meetings. But such signs as these are dependent not only on the effort made to proselytize—the desire to convince others—but also on the effectiveness of the efforts and on the state of mind of prospective converts.

Even where there is direct evidence about proselytizing attempts, such as the number of speeches made, the fact that Miller and Himes traveled widely, or that the Millerite presses worked twenty-four hours a day, these are activities of the leaders. There is very little concrete evidence of the proselytizing activities of the ordinary members, whose behavior is most significant for our purposes. Leaders of a social movement may, after all, have motives other than simply their conviction that they have the truth. Should the movement disintegrate, they would lose prestige or other rewards.

And if the Millerite case is inadequately documented for our purposes, our other examples are even more poorly supported. On the Sabbataian movement we have virtually no data concerning the initial disconfirmation in 1648, for the very good reason that the movement attracted little attention (and, hence, there were few records of it) until it became very large and important.

A second reason for considering historical data alone as inadequate is the small likelihood that this kind of data could challenge our explanation. Suppose we could find record of a mass movement that had apparently collapsed immediately after disconfirmation. In the absence of adequate measurement, we might well conjecture that the members' commitment to the belief was small—so small that the dissonance introduced by disconfirmation was enough to force the discarding of the belief. Alternatively, if the commitment could be demonstrated to have been heavy, it is still possible that there were attempts to proselytize following disconfirmation, but that these attempts had been unsuccessful. This would be a tenable contention since it is the results of proselytizing efforts that generally find their way into historical records rather than the efforts themselves.

There is a type of occurrence that would indeed disprove our explanation— namely, a movement whose members simply maintained the same conviction after disconfirmation as they had before and neither fell away from the movement nor increased their proselytizing. But it is precisely such an occurrence that might very well go unnoticed by its contemporaries or by historians and never find its way into their annals.

Since the likelihood of disproof through historical data is small, we cannot place much confidence in the supporting evidence from the same sources. The reader can then imagine the enthusiasm with which we seized the opportunity to collect direct observational data about a group who appeared to believe in a prediction of catastrophe to occur in the near future. Direct observations made before, during, and after the disconfirmation would produce at least one case that was fully documented by trustworthy data directly relevant to our purpose.

One day in late September the Lake City *Herald* carried a two-column story on a back page, headlined: PROPHECY FROM PLANET. CLARION CALL TO CITY: FLEE THAT FLOOD. IT'LL SWAMP US ON DEC. 21, OUTER SPACE TELLS SUBURBANITE. The body of the story expanded somewhat on these bare facts:

> Lake City will be destroyed by a flood from Great Lake just before dawn, Dec. 21, according to a suburban housewife. Mrs. Marian Keech, of 847 West School street, says the prophecy is not her own. It is the purport of many messages she has received by automatic writing, she says. . . . The messages, according to Mrs. Keech, are sent to her by superior beings from a planet called "Clarion." These beings have been visiting the earth, she says, in what we call flying saucers. During their visits, she says, they have observed fault lines in the earth's crust that foretoken the deluge. Mrs. Keech reports she was told the flood will spread to form an inland sea stretching from the Arctic Circle to the Gulf of Mexico. At the same time, she says, a cataclysm will submerge the West Coast from Seattle, Wash., to Chile in South America.

The story went on to report briefly the origin of Mrs. Keech's experiences and to quote several messages that seemed to indicate she had been chosen as a person to learn and transmit teachings from the "superior beings." A photograph of Mrs. Keech accompanied the story. She appeared to be about fifty years of age, and she sat poised with pad and pencil in her lap, a slight, wiry woman with dark hair and intense, bright eyes. The story was not derogatory, nor did the reporter comment upon or interpret any of the information he had gathered.

Since Mrs. Keech's pronouncement made a specific prediction of a specific event, since she, at least, was publicly committed to belief in it, and since she apparently was interested to some extent in informing a wider public about it, this seemed to be an opportunity to conduct a "field" test of the theoretical ideas to which the reader has been introduced.

In early October two of the authors called on Mrs. Keech and tried to learn whether there were other convinced persons in her orbit of influence, whether they too believed in the specific prediction, and what commitments of time, energy, reputation, or material possessions they might be making in connection with the prediction. The results of this first visit encouraged us to go on. The three of us and some hired observers joined the group and, as participants, gathered data about the conviction, commitment, and proselytizing activity of the individuals who were actively interested in Mrs. Keech's ideas. We tried to learn as much as possible about the events that had preceded the news story, and, of course, kept records of subsequent developments. The means by which the observers gained entree, maintained rapport, and collected data are fully described in the Appendix. The information collected about events before early October is retrospective. It comes primarily from documents and from conversations with the people concerned in the events. From October to early January almost all the data are firsthand observations, with an occasional report of an event we did not cover directly but heard about later through someone in the group of believers who had been there at the time.

The next three chapters are a narrative of events from the beginning of Mrs. Keech's automatic writing up to the crucial days in December just before the cataclysmic flood was expected.

These chapters provide background material. They will introduce the members of the group, describe their personal histories, their involvement in the movement, and the preparations they made for the flood. We shall also describe the ideology accompanying the prediction and some of the other influences to which the group was exposed. Such background is necessary to make understandable some of the behavior and the events that led up to the night of December 21. Much of this material is not directly relevant to the theoretical theme of the book, but we hope that these details will re-create for the reader some of the vividness of these months.

NOTES

1. P. Hughes, *A Popular History of the Catholic Church* (New York: Doubleday and Company, 1954), p. 10.
2. Richard Heath, *Anabaptism: From Its Rise at Zwickau to Its Fall at Munster, 1521–1536* (London: Alexander and Shepheard, 1895), p. 119. This is one of the *Baptist Manuals: Historical and Biographical*, edited by George P. Gould.
3. *Ibid.,* pp. 147–148.
4. *Ibid.,* pp. 120–121.
5. In describing the Sabbataian movement we shall follow the account given by H. Graetz, *History of the Jews* (Philadelphia: Jewish Publication Society of America, 1895), vol. 5, pp. 118–167. This, in our judgment, is the best single source.
6. Graetz, p. 122.
7. *Ibid.,* pp. 134, 137.
8. *Ibid.,* p. 146.
9. *Ibid.,* pp. 147–148.
10. *Ibid.,* p. 149.
11. *The Memoirs of Gluckel of Hameln,* translated by Marvin Lowenthal (New York: Harper, 1932), pp. 45–46.
12. C. E. Sears, *Days of Delusion — A Strange Bit of History* (Boston and New York: Houghton Mifflin, 1924).
13. Francis D. Nichol, *The Midnight Cry* (Takoma Park, Washington, D.C.: Review and Herald Publishing Company, 1944).

14. *Ibid.*, p. 33.
15. *Ibid.*, p. 101.
16. *Ibid.*, pp. 124–125.
17. *Brother Jonathan,* February 18, 1843, quoted in Nichol, p. 130.
18. *Signs of the Times,* January 25, 1843, p. 147, quoted in Nichol, p. 126.
19. Nichol, p. 126.
20. Sears, p. 119.
21. Nichol, p. 160n.
22. Sears, pp. 140–141.
23. *Ibid.*, p. 144.
24. Nichol, p. 206.
25. Sears, p. 147.
26. *Advent Herald,* July 17, 1844, p. 188, quoted in Nichol, p. 208.
27. *Advent Herald,* July 24, 1844, p. 200, quoted in Nichol, p. 208.
28. Nichol, pp. 209–210.
29. *Ibid.*, p. 213.
30. *Advent Herald,* October 30, 1844, p. 93, quoted in Nichol, p. 216.
31. Sears, pp. 156–157.
32. Nichol, p. 231.
33. *The Midnight Cry,* October 19, 1844, p. 133, quoted in Nichol, p. 236.
34. *The Midnight Cry,* October 3, 1844, p. 104, quoted in Nichol, p. 238.
35. Nichol, pp. 238–239.
36. Hiram Edson, fragment of ms. on his life and experience, pp. 8, 9, quoted in Nichol, pp. 247–248.
37. Luther Boutelle, *Life and Religious Experience,* pp. 67–68, quoted in Nichol, pp. 248–249.
38. Unless otherwise identified, all quotations used in our discussion of Christianity are taken from essays in the collective work *Christianity in the Light of Modern Knowledge* (London and Glasgow: Blackie and Son, 1929). The specific essays from which quotations have been taken are the following: Francis Crawford Burkitt, F.B.A., D.D., "The Life of Jesus," pp. 198–256; Rev. Charles Anderson Scott, D.D., "The Theology of the New Testament," pp. 337–389; Rev. Canon David Capell Simpson, M.A., D.D., "Judaism, the Religion in Which Christ Was Educated," pp. 136–171.
39. P. 335.
40. P. 350.
41. P. 165.
42. P. 226.
43. Graetz, vol. 2, p. 166.
44. The theory of dissonance and its implications are set forth in *A Theory of Cognitive Dissonance* by Leon Festinger, Stanford University Press, 1957.

Prophecy Fails Again
A Report of a Failure to Replicate

Jane Allyn Hardyck and
Marcia Braden

On July 4, 1960, a group of 135 men, women, and children vanished from their homes in a small Southwestern town. Their homes were sealed; the windows were covered with newspapers; the cluster of houses was deserted. The only message they had left was a sign on the door of their church, reading "Gone for two weeks, camp meeting."

The neighbors of the group and the town officials soon discovered where the members of the Church of the True Word[1] had gone. In response to prophecies of a forthcoming nuclear disaster, the group had for many months been building and stocking underground fallout shelters, with as much secrecy as possible. On July 4, one of their prophets received a message, "The Egyptians are coming; get ye to the safe places," and they immediately obeyed what they believed to be a command from God. They were huddled in their shelters, awaiting the nuclear catastrophe. For forty-two days and nights they remained there, in expectation of imminent disaster. While they stubbornly sat underground, the authors walked around the hot, dusty desert town piecing together the history of the group from interviews with townspeople and the few group members who, disillusioned, left the shelters.

The Church of the True Word is an evangelical Christian church associated with the Pentecostal movement. Its members believe in the Bible as the literal word of God and accept as operating today the gifts of the Holy Spirit delineated in First Corinthians of the New Testament, Chapters 12 and 14. These gifts include speaking and interpreting tongues, personal prophecy, and healing by faith. The titular head of the group, a Mrs. Shepard, is their minister and chief prophet, although important decisions are made only after she has consulted with two of the group members, Peter Jameson and David Blake, both of whom are also ordained ministers.

The "colony," as they call themselves, springs from two main sources. Mrs. Shepard established a following about five years ago in the small Southwestern town, and soon began work on the present church building. In this she had the help of Jameson and Blake, who at the time were missionaries to Central America from two congregations in the Midwest. The second source of members of the Church of the True Word was these Midwestern churches.

Even in the early days of her ministry, Mrs. Shepard was preaching preparedness for nuclear attack, and almost four years ago a prophecy was received in the Midwest to the effect that "in fewer years than I have fingers on my right hand" there would be nuclear devastation. The more recent history of the Church of the True Word began with another prophecy. On November 23, eight months before the group finally went underground, a prophet in the Midwest received word that "you have six months to prepare." On receiving this message, Blake, Jameson, and various others packed up and moved to the Southwest and about February began to build fallout shelters and homes.

The shelters were built "through the inspiration of God," according to the specifications of Civil Defense, which is, for these people, "the Noah's Ark of today." They were not designed as bomb shelters, since the group believed that their town would receive only fallout from a direct hit on Desert City, which lay fifty miles to the west. There were probably five large shelters under houses and four smaller ones dug in an open field nearby. The larger ones were quite livable, although far from luxurious, as they lacked modern plumbing and were rather badly ventilated. The shelters were stocked with canned and dehydrated food, large cans of water, and other necessities, and were provided with generators for use when public power failed.

For the group to make such careful and extensive preparations, they must have had a rather clear and specific idea of what was to happen. Indeed they did. From a particular interpretation of portions of the Book of Revelation, they believed that about one third of the population of the earth would be wiped out by nuclear warfare and that injuries and sickness would be widespread among the survivors. The members of the Church of the True Word also expected that after the disaster they would receive special powers from God so that they might perform miracles of healing beyond what they were already able to do, and might be enabled to spread the Gospel to all nations within the short space of about a year. It was the necessity of saving themselves for this purpose that dictated that they must keep their preparations secret. They feared that if the location and nature of their shelters were generally known, they would be unable to prevent others from breaking in at the time of the attack, thus creating a situation in which no one could survive.

From February until the "deadline" of May 23, many more families from the Midwestern congregations arrived to join in the preparations. There were also, of course, several families from the local community who were members of the church and who helped in the work. The shelters were not finished by May 23, and much apprehension arose among the members of the group. In an anxious flurry of preparations they waited until July 4, when they received the message, we believe through Mrs. Shepard, "The Egyptians are coming; get ye to the safe places." They then entered the shelters—29 families, about 135 men, women, and children.

Hypothesis to Be Tested

Our interest in the True Word group arose because of their apparent similarity to the "doomsday groups" discussed by Festinger, Riecken, and Schachter (1956) in *When Prophecy Fails*. The historical accounts of such groups as well as an empirical study of a more recent group, the Lake City group, suggest that the failure of the members to confirm their pessimistic predictions led them to increase in fervor of belief and in proselytizing. Festinger and his colleagues state five conditions that they feel must be met for this to occur:

> 1. A belief must be held with deep conviction and it must have some relevance to action, that is, to what the believer does or how he behaves.
> 2. The person holding the belief must have committed himself to it; that is, for the sake of his belief, he must have taken some important action that is difficult to undo. In general, the more important such actions are, and the more difficult they are to undo, the greater is the individual's commitment to the belief.
> 3. The belief must be sufficiently specific and sufficiently concerned with the real world so that events may unequivocally refute the belief.
> 4. Such undeniable disconfirmatory evidence must occur and must be recognized by the individual holding the belief.
>   The first two of these conditions specify the circumstances that will make the belief resistant to change. The third and fourth conditions together, on the other hand, point to factors that would exert powerful pressure on a believer to discard his belief.
> 5. The individual believer must have social support. It is unlikely that one isolated believer could withstand the kind of disconfirming evidence we have specified. If, however, the believer is a member of a group of convinced persons who can support one another, we would expect the belief to be maintained and the believers to attempt to proselytize or to persuade nonmembers that the belief is correct (p. 4).[2]

These five conditions define a situation in which the believer has two sets of cognitions that clearly do not fit together. That is, he is experiencing a great deal of dissonance between the cognitions corresponding to his belief and the cognitions concerning the failure of the predicted event to occur. This situation, however, is one in which it is almost impossible for the individual to reduce his dissonance. He cannot give up his strongly held beliefs, and he cannot deny that the predicted event has failed to occur. He is also unable either to reduce the importance of his commitment to his beliefs or to make the disconfirmation irrelevant to them. Therefore, the believer who holds to his belief under these conditions has but one recourse if he is to reduce the dissonance; he must seek new information consonant with his beliefs. One of the best sources of new consonant cognitions is the knowledge that others' beliefs are the same. The authors suggest, then, that the need for new supporting cognitions will lead the believer to try to convince others of the validity of his beliefs.

Suitability of the True Word Group
for a Test of the Hypothesis

Our purpose in learning about the history and beliefs of the True Word group
was to determine whether the group met the conditions enumerated in *When
Prophecy Fails* and thus would provide a test of the hypothesis under consideration. The first condition is that the group members must hold their belief with
deep conviction and that the belief have some relevance to action. It is quite clear
that the members held their general religious belief system with deep conviction.
Many were originally ministers or missionaries actively engaged in Christian
work, and most of the members to whom we spoke would refer to "gifts" they
themselves or members of their families possessed. Also, as far as we were able to
discover, Mrs. Shepard was respected by all of the congregation as a truly excep-
tional prophet. Thus, since the prophecy probably came from her and was closely
tied to their belief system, it seems clear that it would be very strongly believed
by the majority of the congregation. The obvious fact that the group members
had acted on their belief by building and entering the shelters is the strongest evidence for their belief in the prophecy and also, of course, proof that the belief
had relevance for action.

The second condition is that the person holding the belief must have committed himself to it by some action difficult to undo. For the Midwestern contingent, the commitment was extreme. They had given up their jobs, had picked
up and moved over a thousand miles, and had invested a great deal of time,
effort, and money in the building and stocking of homes and shelters. Those
from the local area had perhaps given up less, but in several cases they also had
lost jobs and had invested considerable sums of money. The things that they have
done they cannot undo; the money is spent and the jobs are lost. Most important, none of them can deny or take back the fact that he spent forty-two days
in hot, humid, crowded shelters and he did this because of his belief.

The third condition, that the belief must be sufficiently specific and sufficiently concerned with the real world so that events may unequivocally refute it,
is also quite easy to document. At the time that the group went into the shelters,
they believed that a nuclear attack was imminent, and that they would not come
out of the shelters until that attack had occurred. That is, they expected to return
to a world that had been devastated.

The fourth point, that "undeniable disconfirmatory evidence must occur and
must be recognized by the individual holding the belief," is also clearly met. No
nuclear attack occurred while the group was in the shelters, and they did not
return to a devastated world. Thus, we must conclude that the True Word group
suffered the unequivocal disconfirmation of a specific prediction.

The last condition that must be met in order that the True Word group may
provide an adequate test of the hypothesis is that the individual believer have
social support. This was so clearly the case that it hardly needs documentation.
The members of the group had been living together as a separate, rather isolated

community for several months prior to July 4. Indeed, some of the members had known each other for years and many were related by blood or marriage. During the time of the disconfirmation, social support was not only present, it was unavoidable. There were as many as thirty-five people in each shelter; and the shelters provided absolutely no privacy. Furthermore, the shelters were organized in such a way that each contained at least one very strongly convinced member who could hold his group together, and all of the shelters were connected by an intercom system so that the leaders could be consulted in case any members should begin to weaken.

It can be concluded, then, that the five conditions enumerated by Festinger and his colleagues are met by the True Word group. Therefore, if the theory as specified is valid, we should expect to observe an increase in fervor of belief, a greater openness to publicity, and strong attempts to proselytize upon their emergence from their shelters. This, of course, follows from the postulated need for the group members to reduce their dissonance and their inability to do this by any means other than by gaining new cognitions consonant with their belief.

Behavior of the Group Following the Disconfirmation

In the very early morning of August 16, the 103 "faithful" who had remained in the shelters for the full forty-two days received the word to come out. At about 9 A.M. they held a joyous reunion in the church, led by their pastor, in which they were asked, "Did you have victory?" In unison came the reply, "Yes, praise the Lord!!!" Mrs. Shepard spoke of how their faith had not been shaken: "The Lord has brought the people closer to Him, there is not division, there's a fellowship here and we are the holiness people." Many other church members gave testimonies as to how their stay in the shelters had both strengthened their Christian fellowship and increased their belief.

The information concerning this first meeting was obtained from reporters who had been present. During the following week, the authors were able to speak with almost all of the members of the group, to attend their frequent church services, and to interview many of the members, including the leaders, Jameson, Blake, and Mrs. Shepard, quite intensively.

It is clear from our observations that the beliefs of the group remained intact. The group members did have a reinterpretation of the purpose of their stay in the shelters that served as an explanation for the failure of the prediction. They had discovered by looking back over all of their messages that it had never been stated that an attack was imminent; they had simply misinterpreted God's purposes. Really, God had just been using them to warn a world that was asleep, while at the same time He was testing their faith. They passed the test and thus proved themselves even more worthy to be among God's elect. We further discovered that they all continued to believe that an attack would come soon. Thus the group members should be suffering from dissonance; the reinterpretation may have lessened it somewhat, by giving them some reason for having sat so long in the shelters. But their prediction had been shown to be wrong, and they still believed; they should, then, seek publicity and attempt to proselytize.

This did not occur; one must look very hard to uncover even the slightest indication that the members of the Church of the True Word wished to find new converts to their beliefs. The prayer meeting on the morning of August 16 was a golden opportunity if the group wanted to seek new believers. The press was there en masse, including several reporters, cameramen, and TV representatives. One newsman, who had kept in close touch with the group from the beginning of their stay in the shelters, did report that the group was a little more friendly to the press than formerly. Blake asked the press to print certain passages from the Scriptures in their reports, and these passages, which speak of widespread destruction, are clearly intended as a warning to the world. Also, Mrs. Shepard, at this time and later, spoke favorably of all the free publicity they had gained for the Lord by the worldwide coverage of their activities. However, the group members were relatively indifferent to the attempts of Civil Defense officials to contact them and turned away curious tourists who asked to see their shelters. Furthermore, they made no immediate attempts to interest the townspeople in their church services. There is no indication from the behavior of the group when they first emerged or from our observations of them during the following week that they had any intentions of going out to seek new believers on a large scale.

Discussion

The True Word group meets all of the criteria for a test of the theory as set forth in *When Prophecy Fails*, and yet their behavior following the disconfirmation does not conform to the expectations derived from that theory. Clearly, either the theory is wrong,[3] or it is incomplete in the sense that it specifies insufficiently the variables determining the predicted proselytizing. We have two suggestions to make concerning differences between the True Word group and those previously studied that might have affected the differences in behavior that were observed.

The first difference that we wish to consider is that of the amount of social support present within the group. It is stated in *When Prophecy Fails* that one of the conditions necessary for proselytizing to occur is the presence of social support for the believers. That is, a certain minimum amount of support is needed so that the individual believer may maintain his beliefs against the disconfirmation. But what might be the effect of additional amounts of social support? We would like to suggest that the more social support an individual receives above the minimum he needs to maintain his belief, the less need he will have to proselytize.

For this suggestion to be acceptable, it must be assumed, first, that there is some limit to the amount of support that is useful to an individual in his attempts to reduce his dissonance. For example, if only a few of your friends agree with a cherished belief of yours, you may be tempted to seek support by convincing others that you are right. On the other hand, if everyone with whom you associate agrees with you, you will feel very little need to go out and attempt to influence others in order to gain more support for your belief. Second, it must be assumed that a person will choose that means of reducing dissonance that is least likely to introduce new dissonance and most likely to reduce that which already exists. In the situation faced by the True Word group, and by other such groups, talking to other already-convinced group members could not introduce new dissonance. In fact, interacting with others who had survived the same disconfirmation and who had emerged with their beliefs unshaken would be the best sort of support an individual could have. On the other hand, talking to the skeptical would be very likely to introduce new dissonance, since the person approached would probably reject one's attempts at influence and counter with arguments of his own. Thus one would expect that, if at all possible, a person would choose to interact with those who agree with him rather than with the unbelievers.

In a group such as the True Word group with strong social support and a strongly shared belief system, the believer can turn to any other member for confirmation of his beliefs. Following our two assumptions, then, a member of such a group would first choose to talk to other members in his attempts to reduce his dissonance. If in this way he is able to garner new cognitions consonant with his belief up to the limit that he can use, he will then feel no need to seek further support by proselytizing. On the other hand, a believer who is a member of a group such as the Lake City group, in which there is less support and more disagreement with regard to the belief system, would be much less likely to encounter sufficient support from his fellows. Thus he may well have to resort to the otherwise less preferred means of gaining new consonant cognitions, that of proselytizing.

It is easy to document the fact that the Lake City group did not provide social support to a degree that even approached that provided by the True Word group. First of all, the Lake City group was not well under way until about five months prior to the predicted date of the catastrophe; on the other hand, many members of the True Word group had worked together for several years. Further, the Lake City group had never lived as a community separated from the rest of the world, as did the True Word group. This close association present in the True Word group should, one would think, foster a degree of trust in and understanding of the other members that far exceeded that which developed in the Lake City group.

With regard to shared beliefs, there was often disagreement among the members of the Lake City group. For example, the messages received by the two primary leaders of the group often contradicted each other. In contrast, the members of the True Word group were unanimous in their support of Mrs. Shepard, as far as we were able to observe. There was one leader and one coherent set of beliefs shared by all of the group members. In conclusion, the Lake City group seems to have been characterized by only a minimal degree of social support, and we are suggesting that this degree of support was far from sufficient to reduce the dissonance suffered by the members as a result of the disconfirmation. As a result, the members, in search of further support, felt the need to proselytize. In contrast, the True Word group was very close and had a strongly shared belief system. Thus they may well have had as much support within the group as they could utilize to reduce their dissonance and consequently felt no need to proselytize.

An interesting, although almost anecdotal, further piece of support for this suggestion comes from a very short article written by a Dutch psychologist, Van Peype (1960), in a Dutch newspaper. He briefly visited a group called the "Communita," who had gathered together near the top of Mont Blanc in expectation of a flood that would destroy the world on July 14. They had existed as a group for over four years, and many of the members had lived in the lodge on Mont Blanc for several months, separated from the other people living in the area. They had one prophet, one coherent body of beliefs, and, as far as Van Peype reports, a feeling of community and fellowship. When their prediction was disconfirmed, the leader announced to the waiting reporters, "You should be happy that we made that error. Our faith does not waver . . . Amen" (p. 3). He said no more to the assembled crowd and was reluctant to talk to Van Peype. The members had, then, not given up their belief and yet they showed no indications of a desire to proselytize. In the apparent degree of social support that was present, this group resembles the True Word group much more than it does the Lake City group, and their behavior following disconfirmation was essentially the same.

A second difference between the True Word group and the Lake City group that may have affected the amount of proselytizing we observed lies in the amount of ridicule the groups received from the outside world. It would seem reasonable that if a group is receiving considerable ridicule from nonmembers, one way of reducing dissonance that would be apparent to them would be to convince these "unbelievers" that the group is right. If, however, the group is not receiving this sort of treatment from outsiders, this means of reducing dissonance would tend to be a great deal less salient to them. Furthermore, ridicule from others adds more dissonance to that which the group suffers from the disconfirmation. Thus, a very direct way of actually reducing part of the dissonance would be to eliminate the source of ridicule by converting the scoffers.

As far as we were able to determine, the True Word group received very little ridicule from townspeople and the press, considering the unusual step they had taken. The greatest amount of censure the group received seemed to come from other evangelical churches rather than from people in general. In talking to the local townspeople, we often encountered statements such as "Yes, we knew they were building bomb shelters. We believe in doing that, too." The Civil Defense officials in the area even presented the group with an award for "the service which they have performed for the public." After the group had left the shelters, the mayor of the town was quoted in the newspaper as saying, "I sincerely hope no one ridicules them for their beliefs." Newspaper accounts of the group were in general factual and did not make fun of the group.

The treatment the Lake City group received was very differerent. Again, the news stories were generally factual and straightforward. But the headlines were cruel. In response to the announcement of the prediction, one paper headlined, "Tuesday—That Sinking Feeling," and another reported, "World Won't End, but Boy It Sure Will Shake" (Festinger et al. 1956, p. 137). Columnists and editorial writers were equally unkind. Thus, since the Lake City group suffered more ridicule than did the True Word group, it might be supposed that it was easier for the Lake City group to see proselytizing as an effective way of reducing the dissonance they had after the disconfirmation.

Evidence from the Mont Blanc group[4] gives somewhat equivocal support for this second suggestion. Van Peype reported that the Communita was very well thought of by the people in the town near their lodge and was never ridiculed by them. However, they did receive some ridicule at the hands of reporters.

In conclusion, the True Word group, who had suffered a major disconfirmation of an important prediction, held to their beliefs and yet did not proselytize for them. This fact is in clear contradiction to expectation derived from the theory set forth in *When Prophecy Fails*. However, since dissonance theory has received considerable support in laboratory situations, it seems unlikely that it is completely wrong. Thus we have assumed that the specification of the conditions that must obtain in the disconfirmation situation, in order that the predicted proselytizing might occur, was insufficient. The two suggestions we have made for further conditions are that the group provide only minimal social support for its members and that the group receive ridicule from the outside world. It is, of course, impossible to know from the study of one group whether either of these has any relevance to proselytizing. We can only say that there were clear differences in both these factors between the Lake City and True Word groups. We would like to suggest, then, that these two factors be considered and kept in mind by those investigating similar "doomsday groups" in the future.

NOTES

1. This is a fictitious name which, we believe, captures the flavor of the actual name of the group. All other names and places used in this paper have been similarly disguised.
2. From: Leon Festinger, Henry W. Riecken, and Stanley Schachter, *When Prophecy Fails* (University of Minnesota Press, Minneapolis, 1956), p. 4.
3. Leon Festinger, personal communication.
4. W. F. Van Peype, personal communication.

REFERENCES

Festinger, L., H. Riecken, and S. Schachter. 1956. *When Prophecy Fails*. Minneapolis: University of Minnesota Press.

Van Peype, W. F. 1960. "Nu de wereld op 14 Juli niet is vergaan." *Vrij Ned.*, July 30, 3.

Prophetic Failure and Chiliastic Identity
The Case of Jehovah's Witnesses

Joseph F. Zygmunt

Chiliastic movements bid for sociological attention because of the rather distinctive manner in which they express their alienation from the world, justify their rejection of it, and propound their programs of social salvation. Their belief systems represent a curious blend of escapist and quasi-revolutionary orientations, well conveyed in their central convictions: that the prevailing social order is doomed to more or less imminent destruction; that it will be replaced by an ideal system from which all evil will be banished; and that this cataclysmic change will be effected, not by human effort, but by some supernatural agency. Although the eschatological doctrines developed by chiliastic groups vary greatly in their particulars, they tend to induce characteristic social-psychological orientations which unite believers into solidary collectivities and often inspire them to engage in unconventional actions (Case 1918; Cohn 1957; Hobsbawm 1959; Kromminga 1945; Talmon 1965; Thrupp 1962). At the same time, the chiliastic mood and outlook also render such movements vulnerable to organizational crises. These are likely to be especially acute when specific prophecies have been publicly announced and have been phrased in a manner open to disconfirmation. Even in the absence of such specific prophetic failures, the prolonged sustenance of chiliastic fervor is likely to be problematic, and the typically foreshortened time perspectives of such movements may discourage or retard the development of organizational provisions for self-perpetuation.

How chiliastic movements adapt themselves to such exigencies has begun to be explored (Festinger, Riecken, and Schachter 1956; Hardyck and Braden 1962; Lofland 1966). Attention has been focused mainly upon short-term adjustments to specific prophetic failures, with relatively little inquiry into long-term modes of adaptation occasioned by recurrent prophetic failures or by extended delays in prophetic fulfillment. While the historical record does suggest that many such movements turn out to be short-lived because of their incapacity to meet the hazards to which they are peculiarly vulnerable, it also shows that some have managed to surmount them and, indeed, to "institutionalize" their millenarian outlooks.

The present paper deals with one such sectarian movement, Jehovah's Witnesses. During its career of almost a century, this group has assimilated a series of specific prophetic failures, sustained its millennial hopes through decades of "watchful waiting," and resisted secularization with considerable success (Czatt 1933; Salzman 1951; Sprague 1942; Stroup 1945; Zygmunt 1953, 1967). From a small cluster of adherents in Allegheny, Pennsylvania, it has expanded to about a third of a million members in the United States and over a million throughout the world (Watchtower Bible and Tract Society 1966a: 36–43). This paper presents an analysis of the impact of the group's chiliastic commitments upon its career. Inquiry is focused upon the ways in which the sect has adapted its collective identity to sustain these commitments, especially in the face of recurrent prophetic failures and of prolonged delays in the coming of "Armageddon." In this focus, the group provides a striking illustration of the process of "self-fulfilling prophecy," operating at the symbolic-interactional level as an agency not only of collective identity confirmation, but also of collective identity change.[1]

Early Belief System

The millenarian complex which gradually crystallized to form the symbolic core of the movement's belief system was a composite of orthodox and heterodox elements. Theologically, it was intended to reconcile the conflicting strains of Calvinist and Arminian thought which had come to characterize American Protestantism. Sociologically, it was a collective response to the unprecedented currents of change which were beginning to churn the mainstreams of American society in the 1870s.

The group's early ideology centered in the "Divine Plan of Salvation," the biblically derived key to man's history and destiny, believed to be open to fuller understanding in these "last days."[2] The basic creed incorporated a fairly orthodox version of Adam's fall and the entrance of sin and evil into the world. Through willful disobedience to God, Adam forfeited his right to eternal life in Paradise, becoming subject to suffering and eventual death, a fate inherited by all his descendants. The course of humanity since then has been one of steady physical, mental, and moral deterioration. The burgeoning problems of the world were products of man's inherited sinful disposition, intensified by the machinations of Satan. God was not indifferent to man's plight, however. He was permitting worldly affairs to run their ruinous course to teach man the folly of his ways and his need for divine direction. In his loving concern for his creatures, God had, in fact, already set in motion a plan for freeing man from the thralldom of evil, suffering, and death. Its central provision resided in the redemptive role of his son, Christ Jesus. The perfect life and sacrificial death of this "second Adam" served to restore the balance of divine justice disturbed by the first Adam's transgression, providing a basis for reconciliation between God and man.

The work of human redemption, however, was not completed with Jesus' atoning sacrifice. The perfect life of Jesus paid the "ransom price" for humanity, restoring man's spiritual account to its condition before the Fall. Jesus, however, retained custody of this restored "life right" and its application to humanity. The completion of Christ's redemptive mission lay in the near future, and would be accomplished through his establishment of the Kingdom of God on Earth after his Second Coming (Russell 1899, vol. 5).

The inauguration of the millennial Kingdom would pass through two phases, one destructive, the other reconstructive. The first phase, in which earthly institutions would be overturned, was expected to unfold at an accelerated pace in the immediate future. For several decades, the group believed that this world-wide disintegration of the social order would take the form of a bloody struggle between the "wealthy and laboring classes," resulting in pervasive terror and anarchy. While naturally mediated, this revolutionary process was under divine supervision. Members of the group were enjoined to leave this "Battle of Armageddon" to God and to refrain from any overt participation in it (Russell 1897, vol. 4).

An era of grand reconstruction was to begin thereafter. Under the regime of Christ, reforms would be instituted in all sectors of social life, inaugurating a series of just and benevolent arrangements beyond the dreams of the most extravagant utopians. Peace and plenty would prevail; sickness, pain, and even death would go; love and righteousness would at last be triumphant. The survivors of Armageddon, as well as the gradually resurrected dead, would now be given the same opportunity for continued life in this paradise, Earth, as Adam had originally been given, under the condition of continued obedience to divine law (Russell 1891, vol. 3).

In the meantime, between Christ's first Advent and the establishment of the Kingdom after his Second Coming, a superior life offer was being made to a chosen "little flock," restricted to 144,000. Unlike the rest of the earthly creation who were destined to be regenerated and given a second probation under ideal conditions, this select group of "saints" were presently on trial under very difficult conditions. They were destined, if faithful, to undergo "translation" from physical to spiritual form before the earthly Kingdom's establishment, thus achieving the immortality hitherto reserved for God and Jesus (Russell 1904, vol. 6).

The belief system thus propounded a dual doctrine of salvation. In one of its forms, salvation was governed by a modified principle of "election," reserved for a small number of Christians who had responded to God's "special call," had proved their sainthood by steadfastly following the example of Christ, and had thus established their eligibility for the superior prize of "divine nature." This form of salvation was, of course, preempted by the movement for its own members. For the bulk of mankind, on the other hand, salvation would take place on a purely earthly and physical plane, involving a radical change in external conditions of living and a perfection of human nature, but no transcendence of the creatural attributes of materiality and mortality. These two phases of salvation were related, however. The work of millennial reconstruction awaited the completion of the "gospel harvest," the major purpose of which was to complete the ranks of the little flock, who, after their translation, would assist Christ in inaugurating and ruling over the Kingdom.

Early Collective Identity[3]

The movement's collective identity and earthly mission were derived directly from this configuration of beliefs. The group came to conceive of itself as a divinely chosen spiritual elite, selected from the ranks of dedicated Christians to be advanced beneficiaries of God's Plan of Salvation and auxiliary instruments in its fuller execution. They were the "spirit-begotten sons of God," the "justified and sanctified New Creation," the prospective "Bride of Christ," marked for the ruling "Royal Priesthood." The movement regarded its own earthly career as ending with its spiritual metamorphosis in the near future. In the meantime, it had a dual mission: to prepare and perfect itself spiritually for its exalted future role and to act as God's agency for "harvesting" the little flock of saints (Russell 1904, vol. 6).

The manner in which the group proceeded to meet its first mission served to inject elements of pietism and asceticism into its orientation, expressed particularly in its cult of "character development" (Russell 1904, vol. 6). This emphasized the cultivation of the "fruits of the Spirit," prayer and spiritual contemplation, mastery of esoteric biblical knowledge, patient endurance of suffering, and the development of an inoffensive saintly disposition. In undertaking to fulfill its second mission, the movement developed into an actively evangelistic organization, but it rejected the orthodox view of evangelism as an endeavor to convert infidels or to rehabilitate moral derelicts. Evangelism was a temporally limited "call" to "gather out" a small number of already committed Christians to serve as spiritual rulers in the Kingdom. In its preaching, the sect "talked up" rather than "down" to its audiences, seeking not to save them from sin and damnation but rather calling upon those who were already living a Christian life to recognize their still higher role in the scheme of divine purpose. This concept of evangelism led the group to concentrate its early proselytism upon church-affiliated, white, adult Protestants (*Watchtower,* April 15, 1900).

The movement's chiliastic commitments also predisposed it to develop a decidedly negative image of the world and a pessimistic view of the possibilities of improving life conditions through purely human endeavor. The entire social order was irretrievably doomed to destruction in the forthcoming Battle of Armageddon, demonstrating unmistakably that man was incapable of ordering his life without divine guidance. Thus, the movement's general worldview induced not only an "antiworldly" but also an antimeliorist stance.[4]

The early weltanschauung of the movement, however, is perhaps better described as "superworldly" than antiworldly. Despite the revolutionary imagery in which its message was cast, its ideological outlook, though transcendental, remained basically conservative. The saints were to play no direct part in

Armageddon and, in fact, expected to be "snatched away" before its climax (Russell 1886, vol. 1:340 ff.). They were at first enjoined to recognize earthly governments as the "Higher Powers ordained of God" and to cooperate with them in all matters that did not violate divine commands (Russell 1886, vol. 1:249 ff.). The early social ethic of the group generated attitudes of pietistic aloofness and moral superiority rather than militancy, urging the New Creation to "overcome the world" by enduring its sufferings and by practicing spiritual disciplines which perfected Christian character (Russell 1904, vol. 6).

Time Perspective

One feature of the movement's belief system which strongly influenced its development was the time perspective derived from its millenarian views. In attempting to round out its identity, the group formulated a body of historical doctrine, including a mythical self-history, which provided a comprehensive symbolic linkage with the past (Russell 1886, vol. 1; 1891, vol. 3). Such symbolic reconstructions of the past, like the group's constructions of the present, however, were designed to fortify the movement's expectations of things to come. In its basic contours, the group's collective identity was thus really anticipatory in character, anchored mainly in its image of the future.

The general nature of these collective anticipations has been outlined, but one of their important dimensions remains to be considered, namely, the more specific time constructions in terms of which the future was defined. "*When* will the great change come?" was bound to emerge as a pressing question, and the group's answers were to be a very consequential aspect of its orientation. Indeed, in its successive answers the sect begins to reveal some of its long-term patterns of adaptation.

Although the sect had come to espouse millenarian views virtually from its inception in the early 1870s, for several years it ventured no predictions as to when the Second Coming and associated events would occur (Russell 1874). Little more than an independent local congregation at this time, it was predominantly gnostic rather than conversionist in character (Wilson 1959). Crucial in transforming it into the launching ground for a translocal movement were some contacts between the group's founder, Charles Taze Russell, and certain Adventist preachers.[5] The latter, previously involved in the Millerite movement of the 1840s, were now trying to revive some of its prophecies in revised form, expecting Christ to return in the flesh in 1873 or 1874. In an attempt to meet the prophetic failure that followed, some of them advanced the view that Christ had indeed come as predicted, but in the unexpected form of a spirit being. It was not until 1876, however, that Russell adopted their belief that the Second Coming had already occurred and that the gathering of the little flock preliminary to the final climax was already in progress. According to certain biblical calculations, this harvest was to extend only to 1878, at which time the gathered saints were to be translated into spirit form. It was the belated injection of chiliasm of this short-term, date-focused variety that supplied the note of urgency required to launch a broader evangelistic enterprise. This strain of chiliasm, however, also predisposed the group to experience a succession of prophetic failures which were to disturb it periodically during the next fifty years.

The first of these failures in 1878 did not appreciably alter the short-term, date-focused orientation of the movement. A biblical basis for extending the harvest to another proximate date, 1881, was very shortly discovered, and the movement continued its preoccupation with evangelistic ventures, devoting relatively little attention to organizing its following (*Watchtower,* February 1881).

The second prophetic failure in 1881 precipitated a more serious crisis which required a longer period to assimilate. For several years, the group maintained its general posture of watchful waiting for the belated translation to occur. While its chronological doctrine did identify the year 1914 as marking the final end of the "time of trouble," at this point the group found it inconceivable that its earthly departure might be delayed that long (*Watchtower,* October-November 1881, October 1883).

The attitude of tense expectancy was gradually relaxed, and before long the sect began to recast its perspective upon the future. One of the first evidences of reorientation emerged in 1884, when the group applied for a formal charter of incorporation from the state of Pennsylvania. The harvest which had previously been defined as ending in 1881 was eventually redefined to extend to 1914 (*Watchtower,* October 1884). This shift from short-term to long-term chiliasm was to have important bearings upon the movement's subsequent development. Although the sect still conceived of itself as a temporary enterprise, its terminus was now thirty years away, beyond the life span of many members. Heretofore operating on a short-run basis, the movement was now obliged to face the problems of self-perpetuation more squarely. At the same time, in expanding the boundaries of its own future, it provided itself with respite from the crises of prophetic failure.

It was during the next three decades that the movement underwent its first major cycle of institutionalization. The tasks of organization and control began to receive belated attention, resulting in the crystallization of a more formal structure. The sect's doctrinal, cultic, and ethical systems were elaborated and integrated. The identity design previously sketched became more firmly established.

While these institutional forms strengthened the movement's capacity to endure, its commitment to the date-focused form of chiliasm continued to be a source of instability. As 1914 approached, excitement over the prospective "change" mounted and preparations for it began to be made (*Watchtower,* December 1, 1912, November 15, 1913, January 1, 1914). Decades of preaching had by now committed the movement publicly to its prophecies in a firm and extensive way. The third prophetic failure in 1914 accordingly proved to be a major crisis; yet the movement had by now developed the organizational resources needed to meet the new crisis with minimal disruption. Not only did it cling to its chiliastic hopes, it now regressed to its earlier short-term orientation (*Watchtower,* November 1, 1914). A revised set of prophecies were issued, focusing upon 1918 as the new terminus (*Watchtower,* September 1, 1916). After the fourth failure, another round of prophetic revision ensued, focusing upon 1925 (Rutherford 1920). With this fifth failure, the further issuance of dated prophecies was suspended, the movement's millenarian stance assuming a diffusely imminent form detached from any specific point in time (*Watchtower,* March 1, 1925).

The abandonment of date-centered chiliasm, which had prevailed in the movement for half a century and had occasioned its five major prophetic failures, was not the only feature of the group's long-term adaptation. Additional adjustments are discernible in the more specific ways in which the movement sought to meet its prophetic failures and the cumulative impact of these efforts upon its identity and mission.

Responses to Prophetic Failure

The fact that the group's early identity had come to be anchored in specific chiliastic commitments made prophetic fulfillment a vital identity-confirming need and prophetic failure a source of serious identity problems. Potentially, such failures precipitated crises of faith in the broader belief system on the basis of which the prophecies had been ventured. They also occasioned crises of mission, since the movement conceived of its evangelistic operations as temporally limited, its mandate for harvesting saints expiring when the specified prophetic dates were reached. Prophetic failures, furthermore, damaged the movement's public image as well as its self-conception as a divinely directed group.

The sect's responses to the prophetic failures conformed to the following general pattern:[6]

1. The initial reaction was usually a composite of disappointment, puzzlement, and chagrin. This describes the reactions of the leaders as well as of the rank and file.

2. As a secondary adjustment to its dejection and confusion, the group usually regressed for a time to its earlier orientation, maintaining an attitude of watchful waiting for its predictions to materialize. During this interval, the group was likely to adhere to the view that its prior evangelistic mission had been completed, that the harvest had indeed "closed" on the dates previously announced. Proselytism usually declined for a time but did not cease altogether, its continuation being justified as an "educational" rather than a "recruitment" operation. Such incipient redefinitions of group mission were likely to be temporary, however. This was also the phase during which the doctrinal bases for the previously issued prophecies were reexamined and conjectures entertained as to why the events expected might have been "delayed."

3. Sooner or later, the group achieved a fuller resolution of its quandary.

The symbolic strategies through which this was accomplished were substantially the same in all five instances of prophetic failure. The group first asserted the claim that its previously advanced prophecies had been, in fact, partially fulfilled, or that some event of prophetic significance had actually transpired on the dates in question. The conviction that the Plan of God was, indeed, unfolding in the general way indicated by the belief system was thus sustained. The "events" selected to give substance to this claim were supernatural and hence not open to disconfirmation. Thus, in its effort to convert the prophetic failure of 1878 into a partial "success," the group asserted, retrospectively, that the year marked the point at which the "nominal Christian churches were cast off from God's favor" (*Watchtower*, February 1881). The year 1881 was said to mark the time when "death became a blessing," in the sense that any saint who happened to die would henceforth be instantaneously changed into a spirit being at the moment of expiration (*Watchtower*, December 1881). The year 1914 allegedly signified the "end of the Time of the Gentiles," when God's benevolent disposition toward the Christian nations was withdrawn (*Watchtower*, November 1, 1914). The year 1918 was retrospectively defined as the time when Christ "entered the temple for the purpose of judgment" (Rutherford 1920). A further elaboration of the prophetic significance of the latter year was issued on the eve of the prophetic failure of 1925: the year 1918 marked the time when the heavenly portion of the Kingdom was established and when a "New Nation" was born (*Watchtower*, March 1, 1925). Each of the prophetic failures was thus redefined in retrospect in a manner which provided nonempirical confirmation for the group's chiliastic outlook.

4. The supplementary strategy used to revitalize the group's millennial hopes was the projection of unfulfilled portions of prior prophecies into the future through the issuance of redated predictions. As indicated previously, this strategy was used in combination with the strategy of retrospective reinterpretation to meet the first four prophetic failures. A variant of it was used to meet the fifth—the issuance of undated prophecies covering still-unrealized expectations. In addition to renewing the group's chiliastic orientation, this supplementary strategy helped to resolve the crisis in group mission by extending the mandate to proselytize.

5. Beyond the two basic strategies outlined above, the movement employed a variety of other devices to sustain its chiliastic outlook. These have been used not only in conjunction with specific prophetic failures but also more generally to confirm the group's faith in its image of the future. The most frequently used device has been the selective interpretation of emerging historical events as confirming signs of the approaching end (see Russell 1886, vol. 1; Rutherford 1920). The group's negative and pessimistic worldview sensitized it to perceive virtually every major and minor social disturbance and natural

catastrophe as an indicator of the impending collapse of the earthly system. The varied forms of unrest, generated in a society undergoing rapid industrialization, urbanization, secularization, and other changes, were exploited to affirm the hopeless bankruptcy of the prevailing social system and its disastrous downward spiral. The expressions of vexation, alarm, and impending doom voiced by various outside commentators on the passing scene were similarly drawn upon as validating evidence. A related device has been the effort to interpret the experiences and achievements of the movement itself as confirming signs of the approaching climax and as validation of the sect's conception of itself as an agency of prophetic fulfillment (see Watchtower Bible and Tract Society 1959).

Although these several strategies proved to be very helpful in coping with prophetic failures, they also served to introduce some important changes in the movement's general orientation and sectarian style. In these changes are discernible some additional features of the movement's long-term adaptation to the hazards and dilemmas of being a chiliastic group.

Identity Changes

In pursuing the strategy of claiming that some supernatural event of prophetic significance had transpired on the dates previously announced, the group was, in effect, recasting its definition of the present in terms of its symbolic model of the unfolding historical process, thus preparing the context for changes in its own identity. The retrospective claim that 1878 marked the time when "nominal Christian churches were cast off from God's favor," for example, had the effect of stiffening the sect's posture toward other religious organizations. While the movement had from the outset been critical of many features of orthodox theology, its early attitude toward fellow Protestants had been rather benign. As noted previously, Protestant churchgoers were regarded as the most promising candidates for membership in the spiritual elite which was to rule the world. Withdrawal from established churches, though implicitly favored, was at this time not explicitly demanded. After 1878, however, the movement rapidly took on the characteristics of a "come-outer" group, even offering its converts specially prepared "withdrawal letters" to be sent to their former congregations, explaining their reasons for quitting "Babylon."

The claim that the year 1881 marked the time when "death became a blessing" for the saints served to reconcile the idea of translation with the possibility of individual death. Many early believers held the view that the living faithful would never experience a physical death but would be collectively changed into spirit beings "in the twinkling of an eye." The occurrence of deaths among members not only contradicted this belief but was a potential source of strain upon the pivotal idea of translation itself. After 1881, physical death was defined as one of the ways in which some of the saints might undergo their translation, but the idea of miraculous collective flight from the earthly scene by the "remnant" continued to be at the forefront of the group's image of its future for many years.

The prophetically fulfilling claims that exerted the most profound impact upon the movement were those advanced in connection with the failures of 1914 to 1925. In claiming that the "Time of the Gentiles had expired" exactly on schedule in 1914, the group was laying the symbolic ground for its own subsequent radicalization. The full meaning of this claim remained somewhat unclear for a time, but its general implication was that the legitimacy of earthly governments and other institutions had been downgraded in the eyes of God. Although this was not interpreted as calling for abandonment of the previous policy of obeying secular laws which did not violate the laws of God, it did predispose the movement to adopt a more militant stance. The declaration also reduced the symbolic distance between the present and the envisaged "end," discernible in the shift to short-term prophesying at this point, a factor further encouraging the adoption of bolder tactics. In fact, the evangelistic campaigns of 1914 to 1918 proved to be so bold that they precipitated serious difficulties with governmental authorities and resulted in the imprisonment of several of the movement's leaders (Stroup 1945; Watchtower Bible and Tract Society 1959).

The claims advanced later that in 1918 Christ had "entered his temple for the purpose of judgment," that he had assumed his "right to rule," had cast Satan down to Earth, and had, in effect, inaugurated the heavenly portion of the Kingdom, supplied additional grounds for a fundamental change in group identity and mission. In 1925, a short time before the translation was expected, a new revelation was announced regarding the fuller significance of the year 1918: it heralded "the birth of a New Nation." In that year Christ inaugurated a supernatural "government," with himself as "King." Having cast Satan and his hordes from the Earth as well in the Battle of Armageddon, the government's hegemony would be extended over the whole world. While this New Nation was, at the moment, mainly an extramundane establishment, members of the movement were its loyal earthly citizens and "ambassadors." While awaiting their own "crowning," they were to prepare the way for the new government's assumption of universal authority (*Watchtower*, March 1, 1925).

Besides helping to assimilate prior prophetic failures more fully, the 1925 announcement served to offset the prospective failure which faced the movement at this time. It was, in fact, accompanied by the suspension of future date setting, thus eliminating this long-standing source of instability. Cosmic history had moved into its very last stage; the Kingdom had *begun* to be established. The Battle of Armageddon, through which the Kingdom would assume control over the Earth, still lay in the future, but "no man knew the time nor the hour" of its coming.

From this time onward, the image of the New Nation became the main symbolic anchorage for the movement's self-conception. The sect was no longer to conceive of itself merely as the agency for completing the ranks of the 144,000 who were to rule with Christ. This mission had been completed. God had ordained, however, that the "anointed remnant" still on Earth were to play an important role in preparing the way for the Kingdom's fuller triumph. A twofold mission was derived from this view: (1) to recruit and train a "Great Company" of righteously disposed people who, in the safety of the "Lord's Organization," would be "carried through Armageddon" and would be privileged to live in the earthly Kingdom as perfect physical creatures; and (2) to expose the machinations of Satan in trying to obstruct the Kingdom's earthly establishment (Rutherford 1928, 1932).

Evangelistic activity came to be reorganized around these two goals. Although the Great Company recruiting ground was at first identified with the movement's earlier reference group, it underwent extension to include non-Protestants, nonwhites, and those without church affiliation.[7] As an earthly enterprise, the movement no longer conceived of itself as temporary nor inherently limited in ultimate size. Having a role now not only in the heavenly phase of the Kingdom but in the earthly phase as well, its own earthly future was endless and its expected ultimate size infinitely larger than 144,000. While the status of new converts remained ambiguous for several years, by the middle thirties a distinction between two categories of members had emerged: the "Anointed class" (those who joined before the "special harvest call" had ceased and who were destined to become a part of Christ's heavenly government) and the "Jonadab class" (those who joined more recently in response to the "general call" and who were destined to inherit the New Earth as perfect physical creatures) (Rutherford 1932; *Watchtower,* August 1 and 15, 1935).

Even more striking changes occurred in the course of the movement's efforts to discharge its second mission of "exposure." A doctrine of Satanic conspiracy was developed, emphasizing the "unholy alliance" between the "commercial, political, and religious powers" to "exploit the common people" and to oppose Jehovah and his Kingdom. Through identification with the figure of Satan, recently "cast down to Earth," the major institutional spheres thus came to be defined as havens of wickedness, as sources of injustice and oppression, and accordingly as appropriate objects not only of avoidance but of vigorous verbal assault. In the late twenties a doctrinal revision was introduced regarding the meaning of the "Higher Powers" to which the Bible urged subjection (*Watchtower,* June 1, 1929). It was now declared that the phrase did not refer to secular authorities but rather to "Jehovah God and Christ Jesus." This was part of the context in which the group shortly became involved in flag-salute controversies with authorities throughout the country (Manwaring 1962).

The focus of the movement's chiliasm changed from awaiting its collective escape from Earth to waiting for the impending destruction of the present order in the Battle of Armageddon. The image of Armageddon as a class war was changed to that of a war between "Satan's Organization" and the "Lord's Organization" for hegemony over the Earth. The sect continued to adhere to the belief that it would not be a direct combatant in the war, but the anticipatory image of the Battle nevertheless exerted influence upon the movement's operations. The group's evangelistic programs became progressively radical in content and more aggressive in execution.[8] The present was perceived as the preliminary "staging" phase of the Great Battle, during which people were being given an opportunity to "choose sides." The conviction of the Battle's imminence was kept alive, but the chiliastic zeal thus generated was channeled mainly into militant evangelistic forays against Satan's Organization. A concerted drive was now made to enlist every member in these assaults. Evangelism came to be linked to a broader range of supernatural issues, such as the "vindication of Jehovah's name." The enlarged identity salience of preaching was well expressed in the change of the sect's name in 1931 from Bible Students to Jehovah's Witnesses (Watchtower Bible and Tract Society 1931).

In reorganizing the movement's identity around militant preaching and in defining the latter as battling against Satan and witnessing for Jehovah, the major source of identity validation was shifted from prophetic fulfillment to evangelization per se. In its identity-affirming aspects, evangelistic success was to be measured not only in terms of the numbers of converts won, but also in terms of the volume, extensiveness, and vigor of the preaching effort, and even the negative reactions it evoked. This shift also entailed changes in such supplementary sources of internal identity support as the previously institutionalized cult of character development, which had played an important role in sustaining the group's earlier pietistic identity. The latter type of rather introverted cultivation of the fruits of the Spirit had little place in the new identity design and, in fact, came to be eliminated (*Watchtower*, November 1, 1933).

The movement's steady drift in an aggressively antiworldly direction after 1925 was reinforced by the correspondingly aggressive reactions of other groups to its militant and often offensive campaigns. Organized opposition against the movement increased steadily, reaching serious proportions by the early forties. During the year 1940 alone, more than 335 cases of mob violence against the group were reported in forty-four states (American Civil Liberties Union 1941, p. 3). Arrests of group members became widespread. The sect responded with renewed displays of militancy, challenging arrests through vigorous court action and developing tactical innovations to circumvent obstructions to its activities. In all of this, group leaders made adroit use of conflict incidents to bolster the movement's solidarity and to confirm its new identity. Chiliastic sentiment received reinforcement from the same source, particularly in the form of a deepening conviction that Armageddon was nearing.

While functional in affirming the sect's new image of itself and in sustaining its chiliasm, the pattern of militant evangelism turned out to be rather costly. The increasingly serious waves of persecution taxed the movement's resources, resulted in damage to its public image, and retarded its rate of growth. It became clear that still another round of adaptation was called for before the movement achieved stability. This has, in fact, been happening since the middle and late forties.

Recent Adaptations[9]

Proselytism has remained the central preoccupation of the group, but the avowed purposes of preaching have undergone some redefinition, with consequent changes in its content and techniques. Thus, there has been a deemphasis of one aspect of the sect's previous mission, that of "declaring Jehovah's judgment" upon the Satanically dominated world. Recent definitions of the group's mission have dwelt upon its more positive educational and salvational aspects. Evangelism has thus become, in large part, a "warning and rescue" operation, with "deliverance" as one of its major themes (Watchtower Bible and Tract Society 1961). The view of the prevailing order as doomed continues to be held as strongly as ever, but the vituperative attempts at institutional discreditation have been markedly toned down. Members have been urged to exercise "theocratic tact" in their preaching, to avoid direct attacks on other religious groups, and to refrain from making other remarks which might be construed as offensive.

Still another evidence of ideological retrenchment is the recent redefinition of the Higher Powers concept. The Higher Powers (now referred to as "superior authorities") have once again been identified with secular governments, to which the sect now acknowledges "relative subjection" (Watchtower Bible and Tract Society 1966b). The sect has similarly been emphasizing its attributes as a purely religious organization, a "Society of Ministers," politically neutral, peaceable, and law-abiding.

This general pattern of accommodative restraint in the group's public presentations of itself has not only reduced reactive persecution but has also yielded significant returns in organizational growth. During its first forty years under the leadership of its founder, the movement in America had reached the size of about 20,000. During the next twenty-five years under his successor, it grew to about 62,000 (Watchtower Bible and Tract Society 1941). But the most spectacular increases have been realized during the last twenty-five years under the movement's third leader. By 1966, the American sector of the movement reported a "peak" of 318,559 members (Watchtower Bible and Tract Society 1966a: 36).

It needs to be emphasized that this recent decline in militancy has not been at the expense of the group's sectarian rigor. The group has not only maintained its polarity vis-à-vis the world but has continued to cultivate marks of distinctiveness. The publication of its own version of the Bible in the sixties would be only one example of such continued differentiation.

The movement might be described, then, as currently passing through another cycle of change in its sectarian style. It is becoming less antiworldly and more transworldly in its outlook. While its millennial dream still looks to the future for completion, it is cast in terms of earthly renewal rather than earthly escape. In this connection it is interesting to note that questions of an ethical nature have come to receive increasing attention within recent years and that disfellowshipments on moral grounds have become more frequent.[10] This is not to suggest that the group is espousing the view that the Kingdom will be established on

Earth through the group's own spiritual perfection or its moral uplift of human-ity. The triumph of God's Kingdom under Christ is no moral allegory but is, rather, still conceived of as a supernaturally engineered revolution, concrete rather than abstract, cataclysmic rather than peaceful, imminent rather than remote. The sect's refocused chiliasm has been maintained with the aid of the various symbolic techniques previously developed. The resultant feeling in the sect today is not simply that the end has been delayed these many years but rather that the world has been moving steadily closer to it.

Interestingly, after refraining from dated prophesying since 1925, the group has recently begun to revitalize its chiliasm by pinning it once again to a more or less definite time. The year 1975, believed to mark the end of the sixth millen-nium since Adam's creation and the beginning of the seventh, is presently being discussed as a turning point of prophetic significance. This seventh millennium in world history, it is believed, will coincide with Christ's thousand-year reign over the earth, and is expected to usher in the long-awaited "worldwide jubilee" (Watchtower Bible and Tract Society 1966b). While return to this old strategy would seem to expose the sect once again to prophetic failure, the risks are bal-anced by the potent ideological reinforcement accruing from this forthright renewal of faith, which thirty-five years of diffuse watchful waiting seem to have made necessary. Considering the movement's long-term development, the risks of another serious prophetic failure actually appear to be minimal. The new prophecy is being phrased in a manner that lends itself to "confirmation" by the old device of claiming partial supernatural fulfillment, and the group has given itself a thousand years for the remainder of its millennial dream to be realized. If, however, in 1975 the group does advance the claim that the millennial reign of Christ over the Earth has indeed begun, some new developments in its col-lective identity may be forthcoming.

Conclusions

Contemporary sociologists of religion have questioned the generalizations ven-tured by earlier theorists regarding the organizational changes which sectarian movements typically undergo in the course of their institutionalization over time (Pfautz 1955; Wilson 1959, 1961; Yinger 1946, 1957).[11] The career of the Witness movement supports this line of theoretical criticism. Considering the organizational hazards to which millenarian groups would seem to be peculiarly vulnerable, the success of the Witnesses in sustaining their chiliastic fervor over more than nine decades is an instructive example of the capacity of sectarian groups to adapt to crises, to perpetuate themselves, and to grow without appre-ciable capitulation to the "world" in the realm of values. The present case, in fact, indicates that a sectarian group may undergo an intensification of its rigor and militance over time. More interesting still is the demonstration that a sectarian movement may develop successively different collective identities, expressing qualitatively distinctive styles of "antiworldliness," while maintaining its organi-zational continuity (see Wilson 1959).

The major key to the group's success in keeping its millennial hopes alive and in resisting secularization has been its development of an essentially self-confirming and socially isolating symbolic-interactional system which has sustained its basic convictions and reduced its stakes in the present world. Significant portions of the group's symbolic system were designed to define the supernatural realm and did so in a manner that subordinated the "reality status" of the empirical world per se. The supernatural world was assigned psychological priority as an object of concern and as a source of meaning. Empirical events were perceived as occurring within this broader nonempirical context, and an understanding of their "true" significance required viewing them within the frame of reference supplied by the group's symbolic system. The logic of demonstration used to validate reality constructions was quite different from that normally employed by "common sense" or "science" (see Geertz 1957, 1965; Schutz 1955).

The millenarian complex to which the movement developed an early commitment was premised on a teleological, indeed a predestinarian, theory of the historical process. Human history was believed to follow an essentially predetermined course, in conformity with the Divine Plan. The sect's prophetic declarations were public affirmations of faith in the inexorable outworkings of this Plan. The belief system constrained the group to develop an anticipatory orientation that blurred the distinction between the present and the future. In the millenarian perspective, the present tended to be defined projectively, being imbued with meanings derived from the group's expectations regarding the unfolding future. The history of the past century has conveniently provided an objective context favorable to sustaining the group's chiliasm, in the form of an abundant flow of socially disturbing events that lent themselves to selective interpretation as visible signs of the approaching end.

The processes of self-confirmation, however, were anchored in and mediated by the group's organizational structure and interactional dynamics (see Lofland 1966; Merton 1957; Simmons 1964). Ultimately, it was the capacity of this social microcosm to provide internal consensual validation for its beliefs and expectations, to "out-compete" other groups in imposing upon reality its own symbolic constructions, that made it an agency of prophetic self-fulfillment. A detailed examination of this structural and interactional aspect of the process of self-confirmation is beyond the scope of the present paper, but brief mention may be made of a few of its more important features.[12]

One was the movement's provisions for the social-psychological insulation of its membership from other groups whose value orientations were different. The cultivation of social exclusiveness, the discreditation of other groups, the debunking of secular authority, the elevation of internal group roles to a position of dominance in the life organization of members, were among the major ways in which this was accomplished. The sect's belief system led it to develop a decidedly negative and pessimistic worldview which discouraged involvement in social projects of a melioristic sort. The prevailing social order was regarded as irreparably evil and beyond reform. Human salvation was to come, not through moral uplift or gradual institutional renovation, but rather through cataclysmic, supernaturally mediated revolution. The movement's negative worldview and its cataclysmic theory of salvation fostered an estrangement from external reference groups which might have induced outlooks and concerns favorable to secularization. The sect's conception of itself as an exclusive, divinely chosen elite, whose status was not dependent upon external social validation, served as a psychological insulating device. The provision of nonworldly standards and modes of identity validation helped to maintain the group's separateness from the world. The development of a supportive ethical system which encouraged minimal or marginal secular participation and discouraged upward mobility was an additional obstacle to secularization.

The evangelistic campaigns and programs of the movement, a central feature of its organizational life, were likewise of extraordinary significance in occasioning frequent public declarations of faith and defenses of its foundations, which deepened the believer's commitments to the sect. Insofar as it was successful, proselytism broadened the consensual base supporting the belief system. Insofar as it failed, it confirmed the group's conviction that only a select few were spiritually equipped to discern the truth. Insofar as it provoked opposition, it reinforced the group's alienation from the world and confirmed its self-image as a band of moral heroes, who, in Christlike fashion, were persevering through suffering to implement the purposes of Jehovah.

Certain features of the sect's recruitment system deserve mention in this connection also. The liberalization, and presumed secularization, of group standards of membership in the normal process of striving for cross-generational continuity has been emphasized in the theoretical literature as one of the typical sources of denominational drift (Niebuhr 1920; Pope 1942). Some writers have questioned the alleged inevitability of such declining rigor and have pointed to the retention of exacting standards of admission as an important feature of the "institutionalized sect" (Pfautz 1955; Wilson 1961; Yinger 1957). The Witness sect confirms this observation. The evangelistic orientation of the group, furthermore, predisposed it to focus mainly upon external rather than internal sources for its recruits, and its demands upon these recruits have remained quite rigorous.

Despite the symbolic and structural provisions for self-confirmation and despite propitious external events, our analysis also indicates that the group has been obliged to adapt itself to inner and outer exigencies, some of its own making, others beyond its control. In thus struggling to maintain its continuity, it has undergone significant changes.

The most interesting of these is the succession of collective identity patterns which the group developed within the broader framework of its millenarian belief system, each characterized by a more or less distinctive self-concept, orientation toward the world and mission, and expressed in a different "sectarian style." This developmental progression from a superworldly to an antiworldly to a transworldly identity pattern was, to a large degree, occasioned and encouraged by the sect's own prophecies and its need to confirm them in the eyes of believers.

While the public issuance of prophecies was a sustaining affirmation of faith, it was also a test of faith and a source of identity crises in the form of prophetic failures. Within the sect's symbolic-interactional framework, prophecies became essentially self-fulfilling, but their claimed fulfillment also proved to be a source of change in perspective and mission.

Several features of this process of symbolically induced change deserve notice. First, the prophecies were phrased in a manner that made them only partially open to disconfirmation. As already indicated, they were derived from the broader belief system and had both supernatural and empirical reference. Insofar as they pertained to prospective events of a supernatural character, the group's faith in its own belief system provided a basis for the claim of fulfillment, and the selective perception of "objective" events, under the influence of the belief system, furnished supportive "empirical" evidence. In this sense and to this extent, the prophecies could not "fail."

On the other hand, insofar as the prophecies referred to empirical events, the group's private and public commitment to their realization thrust it into a succession of predicaments. Considering the extreme nature of some of the predictions (for example, that the group would vanish from the earthly scene or that the world would undergo extensive cataclysmic changes), prophetic failure was inevitable and could not simply be denied. It could, however, be met by restructuring some of the group's beliefs to reduce cognitive dissonance and to restore chiliastic faith on a revised basis. This was accomplished by conceding error with respect to those empirical predictions which clearly had not been realized, rationalized in terms of the fallibility of human judgment, but welcomed as divinely provided lessons revealing God's purposes more fully. Such admitted errors were merely chronological and not substantive, however. Unfulfilled prophecies, the group believed, would surely come to pass in the proximate future. With the addition of retrospective reinterpretations of the prophetic significance of previously announced dates, prophetic failures were converted into partial successes, sustaining chiliastic sentiment and providing a basis for renewed prophesying and evangelization.

The generalization ventured by Festinger, Riecken, and Schachter (1956) that prophetic failure, under certain conditions, induces a group to increase its proselytization in an effort to resolve cognitive dissonance applies to the Witness sect, but with some qualifications. Its level of evangelistic activity tended to decline immediately after prophetic failure. Proselytization had to be relegitimated before it could be resumed with its former vigor, and this required an intervening process of redefinition. The group's prophecies had, from the outset, been phrased in a manner that was almost certain to precipitate crises in group mission in the face of prophetic failure. They not only predicted the end of the existing earthly order but, in effect, specified the expiration of the group's earthly mission. The decline in proselytization which followed each episode of prophetic failure was, in part, due to this. The revival and expansion of proselytization had to await the fuller resolution of the group's quandary, and a renewal, on this basis, of its mandate to evangelize, generally involving a redefinition of evangelistic goals. But proselytization was, nevertheless, eventually resumed and increased, and its reinstitution was important in sustaining organizational continuity.

Reliance on these strategies to meet the series of prophetic failures, however, had a cumulative impact upon the group's self-conception, its worldview, as well as its mission.[13] Because prophecies were, in effect, prospective definitions of situations, their claimed fulfillments made them a part of the present reality framework within which the group lived and acted. In this fashion, the group's image of the future came to be progressively assimilated into its definition of the present.

While factors endogenous to the sect itself would seem to have been the main elements in activating the self-fulfilling prophecy mechanism in this case, the role of exogenous factors needs to be noted. Thus, for example, the aggressive content and tactics of the sect's evangelization during its militant phase, based on its definition of the world as Satanically dominated and filled with "enemies," triggered formidable opposition, which, in turn, confirmed the sect's initial outlook and reinforced its chiliastic zeal. When such intensified conflict came to be perceived as organizationally costly, the stage was set for another cycle of change, the sect receding from its militant posture to a position of neutrality, aloofness, or marginality. Such tactical moderation has been conducive to rapid membership growth, which, in turn, has sustained the new attitude of neutralism and reinforced the group's self-image as an agency of prophetic fulfillment. Despite rapid expansion and the development of a hierarchical and bureaucratic structure, however, the organization continues to adhere quite strongly to the ideological traits of a "sect."

While undergoing ideological and structural changes, the sect has not only retained its millenarian character but has managed to adapt its millenarian style to the requirements of long-term organizational survival. The expectation of miraculous escape from Earth, an early source of prophetic failure and disappointment, has been abandoned; the previously limited conception of the group's earthly future has been extended; its original image of itself as a little flock of preordained size has been enlarged; its recruiting ground has been expanded; its proselytization has been maintained at a high level and intensified. Date-setting, which had precipitated prophetic failures in the past, was eventually suspended. Its current revival, in connection with a loosely phrased, not easily disconfirmable set of prophecies, embracing an epoch of a thousand years, is not likely to be disorganizing, but seems rather to be having a revitalizing effect. The sect has, thus far, refrained from advancing the claim which has often marked the transformation of millenarian sects into "denominations" and "churches"; namely, that the Kingdom of God has already been established on Earth. In long-term perspective, the sect approximates Zald and Ash's (1966) characterization of the "perfectly stable" movement organization, as "one which over time always seemed to be getting closer to its goal without quite attaining it."

NOTES

1. The analytical perspective of the present study has been drawn from a variety of sources, especially the following: Blumer 1946; Festinger et al. 1956; Geertz 1965; Lofland 1966; Mead 1934; Merton 1957; Parsons 1951; Schutz 1955; Thomas 1929; Wilson 1959, 1961.

2. For a detailed statement of the sect's early doctrine, see Russell 1886–1904. For additional primary sources, see Zygmunt 1967: 949–954. Some useful secondary sources are: Gerstner 1963; Macmillan 1957; Pike 1954; Stroup 1945; Watchtower Bible and Tract Society 1959; Whalen 1962.

3. The term "collective identity" is used here to refer to a collectivity's definition of itself as a distinctive group living within, and meaningfully related to, a symbolically construed existential framework. (For a more elaborate treatment of the concept, see Zygmunt 1967, 32–50. Cf. Durkheim 1947; Geertz 1957, 1965; Kluckhohn 1951.)

4. For representative expressions of these views, see Russell 1886, vol. 1; 1889, vol. 2; and 1897, vol. 4.

5. The early issues of the sect's journal, *Zion's Watch Tower and Herald of Christ's Presence,* contain accounts of some of these contacts (see especially the issues dated October–November 1881; April 1890; April 25, 1894; and July 15, 1906).

6. Data regarding the sect's adjustments to these prophetic failures were gleaned mainly from an intensive study of documentary sources, especially the group's principal journal, the *Watchtower.*

7. See the yearbooks published by the Watchtower Society for the period 1926 to 1932.

8. For examples, see Rutherford 1928, 1937.

9. This portion of the analysis is based upon participant observation, intensive interviews with sect members, as well as an examination of the group's literature.

10. For an example of this renewed moral emphasis, see Watchtower Bible and Tract Society 1967: 170–186.

11. For a broader critique of the standard Weber-Michels model of institutionalization as applied to secular social movement organizations as well, see Zald and Ash 1966.

12. For a more detailed analysis, see Zygmunt 1953, 1967.

13. Crises precipitated by prophetic failures were not the only agencies of organizational change. After the death of Russell in 1916, the sect experienced a serious succession crisis which resulted in considerable disunity and several schisms. Rutherford's efforts to cope with this set of organizational problems were of considerable importance in transforming the group both ideologically and structurally. But the "routinization of charisma" which occurred during Rutherford's regime was accompanied by a radicalization of outlook rather than a conservative retrenchment (see Zygmunt 1967: 735ff.; cf. Zald and Ash 1966).

REFERENCES

American Civil Liberties Union. 1941. *The Persecution of Jehovah's Witnesses.* New York: American Civil Liberties Union.

Blumer, Herbert. 1946. "Collective Behavior," in *New Outline of the Principles of Sociology,* edited by A. M. Lee. New York: Barnes & Noble.

Case, Shirley J. 1918. *The Millennial Hope.* Chicago: University of Chicago Press.

Cohn, Norman. 1957. *The Pursuit of the Millennium.* London: Secker & Warburg.

Czatt, Milton S. 1933. *The International Bible Students, Jehovah's Witnesses.* Scottsdale, PA: Mennonite Press.

Durkheim, Emile. 1947. *The Elementary Forms of the Religious Life.* Translated by J. W. Swain. Glencoe, IL: Free Press.

Festinger, Leon, H. W. Riecken, and S. Schachter. 1956. *When Prophecy Fails.* Minneapolis: University of Minnesota Press.

Geertz, Clifford. 1957. "Ethos, World-View and the Analysis of Sacred Symbols." *Antioch Review* 17 (Winter):421–437.

———. 1965. "Religion as a Cultural System," in *Reader in Comparative Religion,* edited by William A. Lessa and Evon Z. Vogt. New York: Harper & Row.

Gerstner, John H. 1963. *The Theology of the Major Sects.* Grand Rapids, MI: Baker Book House.

Hardyck, J. A., and M. Braden. 1962. "Prophecy Fails Again: A Report of a Failure to Replicate." *Journal of Abnormal and Social Psychology* 65:136–141.

Hobsbawm, Eric J. 1959. *Primitive Rebels.* Manchester: Manchester University Press.

Kluckhohn, Clyde. 1951. "Values and Value Orientations in the Theory of Action," in *Toward a General Theory of Action,* edited by Talcott Parsons and E. A. Shils. Cambridge, MA: Harvard University Press.

Kromminga, D. H. 1945. *The Millennium in the Church.* Grand Rapids, MI: Eerdmans.

Lofland, John. 1966. *Doomsday Cult.* Englewood Cliffs, NJ: Prentice-Hall.

Macmillan, A. H. 1957. *Faith on the March.* Englewood Cliffs, NJ: Prentice-Hall.

Manwaring, David R. 1962. *Render unto Caesar: The Flag-Salute Controversy.* Chicago: University of Chicago Press.

Mead, George H. 1934. *Mind, Self, and Society.* Chicago: University of Chicago Press.

Merton, Robert K. 1957. *Social Theory and Social Structure.* Glencoe, IL: Free Press.

Niebuhr, H. R. 1920. *The Social Sources of Denominationalism.* New York: Holt.

Parsons, Talcott. 1951. *The Social System.* Glencoe, IL: Free Press.

Pfautz, H. W. 1955. "The Sociology of Secularization." *American Journal of Sociology* 61 (September):121–128.

Pike, Royston. 1954. *Jehovah's Witnesses.* London: Watts.

Pope, Liston. 1942. *Millhands and Preachers.* New Haven, CT: Yale University Press.

Russell, Charles Taze. 1874. *The Object and Manner of the Lord's Return.* Allegheny, PA: Published by author.

———. 1886–1904. *Studies in the Scriptures,* vols. 1–6. New York: Watchtower Bible and Tract Society.

Rutherford, Joseph Franklin. 1920. *Millions Now Living Will Never Die.* New York: Watchtower Bible and Tract Society.

———. 1928. *Government.* New York: Watchtower Bible and Tract Society.

———. 1932. *Vindication.* New York: Watchtower Bible and Tract Society.

———. 1937. *Enemies.* New York: Watchtower Bible and Tract Society.

Salzman, Donald M. 1951. "A Study of the Isolation and Immunization of Individuals from the Larger Society in Which They Are Living." Master's thesis, University of Chicago.

Schutz, Alfred. 1955. "Symbol, Reality and Society," in *Symbols and Society,* edited by Lyman Bryson et al. New York: Conference on Science, Philosophy and Religion.

Simmons, J. L. 1964. "On Maintaining Deviant Belief Systems: A Case Study." *Social Problems* 11:250–256.

Sprague, Theodore W. 1942. "Some Problems in the Integration of Social Groups with Special Reference to Jehovah's Witnesses." Doctoral dissertation, Harvard University.

Stroup, Herbert H. 1945. *The Jehovah's Witnesses*. New York: Columbia University Press.

Talmon, Yonina. 1965. "Pursuit of the Millennium: The Relation between Religious and Social Change," in *Reader in Comparative Religion,* edited by William A. Lessa and Evon Z. Vogt. New York: Harper & Row.

Thomas, W. I. 1929. "The Behavior Pattern and the Situation," in *Personality and the Social Group,* edited by E. W. Burgess. Chicago: University of Chicago Press.

Thrupp, Sylvia L., ed. 1962. *Millennial Dreams in Action.* Comparative Studies in Society and History, suppl. 2. The Hague: Mouton.

Watchtower Bible and Tract Society. 1879–. *The Watchtower.* Bimonthly journal. New York: Watchtower Bible and Tract Society.

———. 1931. *1932 Yearbook of the International Bible Students Association.* New York: Watchtower Bible and Tract Society.

———. 1941. *1942 Yearbook of Jehovah's Witnesses.* New York: Watchtower Bible and Tract Society.

———. 1959. *Jehovah's Witnesses in the Divine Purpose.* New York: Watchtower Bible and Tract Society.

———. 1961. *Let Your Name Be Sanctified.* New York: Watchtower Bible and Tract Society.

———. 1966a. *1967 Yearbook of Jehovah's Witnesses.* New York: Watchtower Bible and Tract Society.

———. 1966b. *Life Everlasting in Freedom of the Sons of God.* New York: Watchtower Bible and Tract Society.

———. 1967. *Your Word Is a Lamp to My Foot.* New York: Watchtower Bible and Tract Society.

Whalen, William J. 1962. *Armageddon around the Corner.* New York: John Day.

Wilson, Bryan. 1959. "An Analysis of Sect Development." *American Sociological Review* 24:13–15.

———. 1961. *Sects and Society.* Berkeley: University of California Press.

Worsley, Peter. 1957. *The Trumpet Shall Sound.* London: MacGibbon & Kee.

Yinger, J. M. 1946. *Religion in the Struggle for Power.* Durham, NC: Duke University Press.

———. 1957. *Religion, Society, and the Individual.* New York: Macmillan.

Zald, Mayer N., and Roberta Ash. 1966. "Social Movement Organizations: Growth, Decay and Change." *Social Forces* 44:327–341.

Zygmunt, Joseph F. 1953. "Social Estrangement and the Recruitment Process in a Chiliastic Sectarian Movement." Master's thesis, University of Chicago.

———. 1967. "Jehovah's Witnesses: A Study of Symbolic and Structural Elements in the Development and Institutionalization of a Sectarian Movement." Doctoral dissertation, University of Chicago.

When Prophecies Fail

A Theoretical Perspective on the
Comparative Evidence

Joseph F. Zygmunt

While differing greatly in their ideological and structural particulars, millenarian movements share one important social-psychological property: a collective conviction that a drastic transformation of the existing social order will occur in the proximate future through the intervention of some supernatural agency (Cohn 1962; Talmon 1962, 1968). The development and diffusion of such beliefs create symbolic contexts for the emergence of novel forms of collective behavior and culturally marginal groups, which raise many provocative theoretical questions. One such question of generic import concerns the manner in which collectivities sustain deviant belief systems in the face of challenging or disconfirming empirical evidence. The reconciliation of conflicting claims about the nature and meaning of "reality" is, of course, a problem not peculiar to millenarian movements. Yet movements of this type, by virtue of their reliance upon prophecy to mobilize and sustain collective action, experience this problem quite regularly and often in its most pressing forms (Festinger et al. 1956). Ideological crisis born of prophetic failure is a virtually universal feature of the careers of millenarian groups. Comparative study of the patterns of collective response to such crises and of the processes mediating their differentiation may contribute to our understanding of the broader question. This paper outlines an analytical framework designed to expedite this line of research and to suggest some theoretical directions which it might fruitfully follow. Derived in part from the comparative literature on millenarian movements, the scheme of analysis also draws upon several bodies of theory which it attempts to apply to this problem in an integrated way.

Preliminary Refinements

Viewed from a comparative perspective, prophetic failure turns out to be a highly variable phenomenon, about which generalizations must be ventured with caution and only after a discerning analysis of the varying degrees and types of exigency which it may pose for the groups involved. Global treatment of the phenomenon in such abstract psychological terms as "cognitive dissonance" may divert attention from such qualitative variations as well as some of their important collective-interactional dimensions. A critical reexamination of the concept of "prophetic failure" itself and especially a fuller explication of the exigency dimensions of this phenomenon are preliminary requirements for a more extended comparative analysis.

Psychologically considered, the essential feature of prophetic failure, of course, is the occurrence of perceived discrepancies between expected and actual events (Festinger et al. 1956). The collective expectations about the future which are generated within millenarian groups vary greatly in their specific contents, constituent imageries, affective and motivational overtones, supportive ideologies, the nature of the actions which they inspire—all of which contribute to defining the kinds of exigencies which subsequent prophetic failures are likely to precipitate, as well as the alternatives available for trying to cope with them.

While millenarian prophecies are typically phrased in a manner that makes them amenable to some kind of empirical confirmation or disconfirmation, this is not completely or uniformly so. References to supernatural personages, agencies, or events are quite commonly included in prophetic pronouncements, insulating them, at least in part, from empirically based logics of proof and disproof. Elements of ambiguity or uncertainty concerning the exact nature of expected events and especially about the manner in which they will be brought about are also quite common, making empirical invalidation more difficult to perceive and creating a context favorable to "prophecy-validating" selective interpretations. Especially important are variations in the degree of temporal specificity incorporated in the predictions ventured. Some millenarian groups conceive of prophetic fulfillment as a prescheduled process and tie their predictions to definite points in time (Case 1918; Froom 1946–1954; Zygmunt 1970). Others refrain from making specifically dated predictions, engendering expectancies of a more diffuse, temporally unfocused form. While the latter may be charged with imminence, the problem of sustaining such still nonvalidated prophecies poses exigencies which are somewhat different from those that emerge when prophecies are clearly invalidated. It would, therefore, seem desirable to refine the concept of prophetic failure by drawing a distinction between "prophetic disconfirmation" and "prophetic nonconfirmation."

This distinction is still premised on the assumption that reality-testing is the sole, the main, or the ultimate basis upon which prophecies and associated beliefs are either sustained or challenged. There are several difficulties with this assumption. The first stems from the fact that empirical evidence—the evidence of the senses—and even the testimony of common sense are often quite ambiguous and subject to alternative interpretations. The difficulty is likely to be compounded when the prophecies issued are elaborate but stated in imprecise terms. Still another limitation of the assumption is its failure to recognize other types of confirming evidence or other sources of validation. Consensual validation stemming from the believing group itself is one such supplementary source of support. Another is the symbolic anchorage of specific millenarian expectations in a more comprehensive ideology. It is particularly in the latter two connections that variations in millenarian group structures and in the relationships of such groups to nonbelieving groups become important parts of the context in which collective responses to crises of faith are forged. These observations suggest the importance of inquiring into alternative modes or channels of belief-reinforcement in any comparative analysis of group adjustments to prophetic disconfirmation in the empirical sense (cf. Bittner 1963; Lofland 1966; Simmons 1964). The exigencies posed by the latter will be, in part, a function of the relative availability of provisions for alternative or supplementary sources of validation and support.

It is at this point that one becomes more explicitly aware that the problem of prophetic disconfirmation merges with the broader problem of millenarian group formation. The convictions and expectations which constitute the psychological substance of millennial dreams are, of course, products of collective interaction. The role of individual prophets in triggering, directing, and sustaining such collective interaction must certainly be examined, but always with due recognition of the fact that we are dealing here with a group phenomenon and not merely with an individual psychological phenomenon. We must at least be open to the possibility that the psychodynamics of collectively derived and collectively sustained expectations may turn out to be a little or a lot different from the psychodynamics of individuals considered in abstraction from one another. Many of the theoretical disputes about the psychological nature and origins of millenarianism actually revolve around this more basic issue (cf. Cohn 1957; Talmon 1962; Worsley 1957). The points that are directly germane to the present discussion, however, are simply these: millenarian expectancies are collective in nature; the collectivities involved in the formation and diffusion of such expectancies vary greatly from case to case and, in particular instances, over time; and such variations in the sociological character of these collectivities have vital bearings upon their patterns of action, including their modes of response to prophetic disconfirmations. These theoretical observations become quite central to any meaningful comparative inquiry into the problem at hand.

Collective Dimensions

Although available data regarding the interactional and structural properties of millenarian collectivities are in many instances incomplete or otherwise deficient, they do quite clearly establish the fact that rather wide variations occur in these dimensions (Lanternari 1963; Mühlmann 1961; Talmon 1962; Thrupp 1962; Worsley 1957). Some of these collectivities assume the form of rather rudimentary, loosely organized groupings, whose interactional dynamics approximate those commonly associated with the "crowd." Such mechanisms as circular interaction, emotional contagion, rumor creation, and the like appear to be prominently involved in disseminating the intensifying excitement, fanning expectations, inflating enthusiasm, and triggering episodes of collective action. While such collectivities may, in a context of social unrest, erupt suddenly, spread quickly, and even achieve high degrees of solidarity, they tend to be short-lived because they fail to develop the organizational resources required to sustain themselves over time. For collectivities of this sort, prophetic disconfirmation or nonconfirmation pose exigencies which tend to be seriously disorganizing. Their collective enthusiasm is easily deflated, their solidarity readily fragmented, their sanguine expectations quickly converted into disappointments. Faith may run high at the peaks of excitement and inspire extreme actions, but it may just as rapidly undergo dissipation, leading to disillusion and despair (Cohn 1957; Worsley 1957).

But the sharing of millenarian expectations may also give rise to more orga-nized collectivities, characterized by more stable leaderships and internal struc-tures, more fully developed ideologies, rituals, and the like, approximating the general specifications of more enduring social movements or movement organi-zations (Barnett 1957; Essien-Udom 1962; Killian 1964; O'Dea 1957; Wilson 1961). Within this general mold, furthermore, the process of group formation may follow a variety of alternative organizational-ideological paths: communi-tarian withdrawal, cultic escape, sectarian redefinition and reevaluation of secu-lar existence, quasi-revolutionary assertiveness and rebellion, and so on. While the long-term survival of such movements is by no means automatically assured, they are, in general, structurally better equipped to sustain involvement and to renew commitment over longer periods of time. Particularly crucial in meeting the special crises precipitated by prophetic disconfirmations or delays in prophetic fulfillments is the development of ideological, cultic, and organizational provi-sions for maintaining faith and revitalizing hope.

The formulation of an ideology which supplies believers with a more or less comprehensive and shared worldview consistent with and supportive of their basic faith, which defines the movement's collective identity, and legitimizes its mission, is an exceedingly potent addition to a movement's organizational resources. The anchorage of specific beliefs, attitudes, and expectations in such broader symbolic systems gives them some new dimensions which have impor-tant implications for how they operate as psychological variables. The constituent elements of ideologies tend to be interlinked into mutually supportive symbolic patterns. If successfully implanted, they predispose converts to perceive, evaluate, and respond to situations and events in selective ways, which tend to be consis-tent with ideological premises (Bittner 1963; Schwartz 1970; Shils and Johnson 1968; Wallace 1956). Insofar as specific prophecies are ideologically derived and bulwarked by commitments to such broader structures of faith, their empirical disconfirmation is not likely to be seriously or lastingly damaging to the continu-ity of the movement in question. Millenarian movements with well-developed ideologies are in a position to meet such crises by drawing upon their own ideo-logical resources. Prophetic failures may thus be ideologically rationalized, explained, reinterpreted, or denied, leaving millennial hopes intact.

The generation and maintenance of commitment to an ideology, particularly when it deviates markedly from conventional styles of thinking, require additional provisions, however. Especially important are cultic and other means for the induction and revitalization of group solidarity, the social reinforcement of basic beliefs, the formation and sustenance of in-group identifications, and the fortification of believers against competing out-group influences (Blumer 1951; Hardyck and Braden 1962; Wilson 1961, 1959). The demise of millenarian movements in the face of prophetic failures and delays is perhaps most frequently attributable to inadequate provisions along these lines.

Patterns of Action

Comparative analysis of millenarian groups must consider not only the beliefs they develop but also the actions which these beliefs inspire. Collective anticipation of radical changes in prevailing arrangements may come to be translated into many different patterns of private and public activity. These chiliastically inspired actions and the reactions which they evoke are integral parts of the process through which millenarian collectivities emerge and become vital sources of contingency affecting their careers. The variable degrees and types of exigency posed by prophetic failures derive, in significant measure, from variations in such action patterns. Their pointed significance in this respect stems from several facts. First, such actions represent overt expressions and public affirmations of faith in the movement's prophecies, contributing to strengthening commitments to them. Second, they commonly entail changes in the social roles previously performed by the actors in question, in their former interests, values, and concerns, as well as in their relationships to other actors. Such changes may be both difficult to sustain and difficult to reverse when prophecies do not materialize. Third, such actions may have broader objective consequences which directly or indirectly affect the movement's capacities to endure.

By way of preliminary systematization, the collective actions of millenarian collectivities may be classified into several types on the basis of their functional characteristics: (1) expressive, (2) agitational, (3) preparatory, and (4) interventional (cf. Wilson 1963).

Expressive Activities

Collective activity of an expressive sort seems to be a virtually universal feature of the early stages of development of millenarian movements. The reference here is to various forms of emotionally provocative and releasing collective behavior which commonly emerges within assemblies of restless and excited people under conditions of stress and in the absence of clearly defined goals or alternative channels of action (Blumer 1951). The literature on millenarian movements is sprinkled with accounts of episodes of expressive crowd behavior and waves of emotional contagion aroused by prophetic messages and rumors of impending radical change (Cohn 1957; Lawrence 1964; Sears 1924; Thrupp 1962). The "milling" process is built up and sustained through such mechanisms as excited conversations, collective chanting and dancing, group feasting, improvised rituals, emotionally expressive and provocative prayer, ecstatic utterances, glossolalia, and the like. Such circular interaction is a potent source of reinforcement, converting germinal beliefs into convictions, restructuring concerns about the present, arousing expectations, charging them with emotion, and providing group support for the new images of the future. While such collectively induced currents of passion serve to solidify and anchor convictions, they also increase the potential for serious disappointment, disillusion, and defection when such inflated expectations are not realized.

Agitational Activities

The crystallization of millenarian convictions is usually accompanied by the emergence of agitational activity. The reference here is to various efforts by leaders and converts to disseminate the prophetic message among people who remain unacquainted with it or unresponsive to it. The impulse to proselytize and to seek new conversions is both an expression and an affirmation of faith on the part of those already convinced. Translated into action, it becomes, in effect, a public demonstration of faith, deepening commitments further. While the encounter of resistances to conversional endeavor may contribute to dampening the zeal of proselytizers, or may at least pose challenges to their ardor, the effort to overcome such resistances through persuasion, exhortation, debate, and so on may equally well leave the proselytizing convert more fully converted than before. The winning of new converts, of course, serves even more directly as a source of validation for the beliefs being disseminated.

Like expressive behavior, however, agitational activity embodies a "double-edged" potential significance for millenarian movements as far as crises of prophetic failure are concerned. In deepening faith and broadening the social base for its consensual validation, proselytization is certainly a positive resource. In exposing the faith to public scrutiny and in making predictions a part of the informal and formal "public record," proselytization may prove to be a source of embarrassment, ridicule, discreditation, and attack in the face of prophetic failures. It would seem to be more freely available as an organizationally sustaining resource in the face of prophetic nonconfirmation than of empirical disconfirmation. Yet, as the study by Festinger and his colleagues (1956) has pointed out, proselytization may continue and even be resumed with extra vigor under the latter conditions as well. Such resumption, however, is usually preceded by some kind of rationale for the failure and some revision in the prophecies to be purveyed in the new round of missionary endeavor.

Preparatory Activities

In addition to expressive and agitational activity, millenarian expectations generally give rise to some forms of preparatory behaviors. The reference here is to various kinds of individual and collective actions undertaken publicly or privately in anticipation of the changes that have been prophesied, and envisaged as, in some sense, preparing or qualifying believers to meet the new future. Included also are various modifications in conventional roles, previously performed in accordance with different sets of expectations and concerns. The attitudinal and behavioral impact of millenarian convictions becomes dramatically visible in this sphere. Here too are commitments forged and psychological investments broadened, again with a dual set of potential implications for the believing group's actual future.

The specific kinds of preparatory actions in which the believing group is likely to engage, as one would expect, reflect the particular prophetically-based definitions of the future that have gained currency and the ideological elaborations of them which have emerged. Where, for example, the millenarian vision includes the idea of disaster as a stage or phase of the establishment of the new order, preparatory activity may take the form of precautionary measures designed to ensure the safety and survival of believers. Thus, for instance, food supplies may be stocked and other advance measures taken to assure the physical well-being of believers during the expected time of trouble. Or the group may seek protection by withdrawing to some place regarded as safe. The requirements for survival may also come to be defined in spiritual terms and thus inspire penitential behavior, praying, and various types of cultic activities designed to achieve and maintain candidacy for salvation (Cohn 1957; Hardyck and Braden 1962; Lofland 1966; Sears 1924; Zygmunt 1970).

On the other hand, future expectations may be so structured as to induce sharply contrasting attitudes and behaviors. Where the immediate future has come to be defined in glowingly optimistic terms as an era of material plenty, utopian bliss, and so on, present consumption patterns may be radically altered in the direction of using up surpluses, depleting scarce resources, and even destroying some of them. Productive activities and work roles in general may be neglected or abandoned in favor of cultic activities or proselytizing endeavor. Crops may be prematurely harvested or destroyed, livestock slaughtered, land left uncultivated (Lawrence 1964; Thrupp 1962; Worsley 1957).

The refocusing of collective attention from the problematic present to the millennial future typically encourages more comprehensive shifts in value-orientations, interests, and attitudes, which may prompt other forms of novel behavior. Millenarian ideologies generally embody implicit or explicit critiques of prevailing arrangements and practices. Under their influence, various dimensions and spheres of traditional cultural life may come to be redefined. Previously supportive attitudes toward established authorities and institutions may undergo erosion and be replaced by more critical and even hostile postures. Norms previously respected may be violated. Where sectarian groups have crystallized, they may develop their own styles of antiworldliness and enforce norms of conduct among their own members which may be at variance with the broader society's conventions (Balandier 1963; Barkun 1971; Essien-Udom 1962; Köbben 1960; Talmon 1968, 1962; Thrupp 1962).

The emergence of such deviant behaviors may deepen and enlarge the alienation of believers from other persons and groups in society, creating grounds for misunderstanding, conflict, ridicule, persecution, and the like. The fate of millenarian collectivities depends crucially on their capacities to manage such contingencies. Insofar as such problems arise, they add to the stringency of the prophetic failure situation.

Interventional Activities

The conflict potential of millenarian groups is revealed more directly in the type of collective action identified previously as interventional. This is meant to refer to acts undertaken by believers to implement the millenarian vision or to facilitate its realization. The probability that such actions will occur and the specific form which they are likely to take depend largely upon the kind of collective identity pattern which has emerged within the millenarian group and particularly the manner in which the group has come to define its mission. All millenarians conceive of themselves as prospective beneficiaries of the new system which they envisage, expecting to share in its material rewards and to occupy privileged positions in its revised social arrangements. They do not ordinarily, or at least initially, conceive of themselves as agents of prophetic fulfillment, however. Millenarian ideologies tend to be somewhat vague about the manner in which the new order is to be established (Talmon 1962). Insofar as some mediating agent or agency is identified, this tends to be conceived of in supernatural terms. The transition from the old system to the new one is, in effect, expected to occur miraculously, without the active intervention of believers themselves. Prophets may, in fact, explicitly enjoin their followers to refrain from any kind of direct action that might be construed as revolutionary.

Yet acts of prophecy-fulfilling intervention have by no means been rare among millenarian groups. Some have developed definitions of themselves and of their collective missions which prompt them to try to play more active roles in ushering in the new order. Conceiving of themselves as the earthly instruments of supernatural forces, entrusted with special mandates to act as liquidators of the old system or as vanguards for the establishment of the new, some movements have engaged in acts of rebellion, warfare, pillage, and the like (Balandier 1963; Cohn 1957; Lanternari 1963; Mühlmann 1961; Price and Shepperson 1958; Rogers 1966; Smithson 1935; Thrupp 1962; Werner 1960). Fairly frequent also have been movements whose supernaturally legitimated sense of active mission has been expressed through physical withdrawal and attempts to create separate communities envisaged as "spiritual beachheads" or "capitols" of the coming new order (Holloway 1951; Nordhoff 1966). Endeavors to hasten the inauguration of the new system may also assume the form of ritualistic acts, conceived of as fulfilling some set of supernatural prerequisites for the change. The Ghost Dance among the Plains Indians would be an example (Linton 1943; Mooney 1965).

Interventional actions of the aggressive or revolutionary type are obviously hazardous and pose serious threats to the continuity of the movements undertaking them. While a few militant millenarian groups have been known to train and maintain armed reserves, these have hardly been sufficient to launch and sustain a full-scale revolution. The record shows this route to prophetic fulfillment to be, in the long run, disastrous. It is likely to dissipate organizational resources and to elicit retaliatory and repressive action from authorities, whose power is usually overwhelming. The movement may still try to operate in underground fashion, but its continuity is likely to be sustained on a revised ideological basis. The deflation of the mood of invincibility with which such actions are commonly undertaken, born of feelings of special supernatural support, precipitates serious problems of relegitimation, calling for basic ideological reformulation.

The route of collective withdrawal and communitarianism, while somewhat safer, is also beset with serious problems. The creation of a viable subsociety is a formidable undertaking, fraught with its own peculiar hazards (Kanter 1968). The survival of millenarian communities depends upon their success in meeting these. Recurrent organizational problems are likely to have an erosive effect on the group's conception of itself as an agency of prophetic fulfillment.

Although the route of cultic intervention, like that of withdrawal, may have some value in delaying the crises of prophetic failure, it cannot avoid them completely. It may contribute to the sustenance of solidarity and hope by inducing short-term states of excitement and collective euphoria. But the efficacy of rituals in helping to bring about the real changes expected is sooner or later likely to be questioned. If, however, the collectivity can work out appropriate redefinitions of its identity and ideology, such rituals may be reincorporated and put in the service of supporting the new symbolic and structural design.

Prophetic Failure and Organizational Dissonance

The frustration of millenarian expectations, particularly when they have been charged with great emotional significance, is likely to be an acutely disorganizing experience for both individual believers and the millenarian collectivity. For persons who have developed strong commitments to the prophecies and deep investments in their realization, who may, furthermore, have reorganized their lives in confident anticipation that they would be fulfilled, disconfirmation may precipitate cognitive and motivational quandaries of a rather perplexing sort. Surprise, shock, disappointment, disbelief, dismay, bewilderment, disorientation are common initial reactions. In relation to nonbelievers, before whom declarations about the expected events had been previously made with passionate conviction, feelings of chagrin, embarrassment, or defensive uneasiness are now likely to arise (Festinger et al. 1956; Sears 1924; Zygmunt 1970).

It needs to be emphasized, however, that individual believers do not ordinarily cope with such quandaries in isolation from one another. They confront them together. Indeed, as solidifying as their original sharing of certainties had been, so now their sharing of uncertainties induces a sense of common plight and occasions new rounds of collective interaction. The issues at stake are as vital for the collectivity as they are for believers considered singly. If any resolutions of the predicament are arrived at, they are almost certain to be, first and foremost, collective and not merely individual. It is necessary, therefore, to examine the process of collective interaction among the affected individuals if one is to understand the dynamics of response to prophetic failure. In fact, the processes involved in meeting prophetic failures and in sustaining millenarian dreams do not seem to be altogether different from the processes mediating the generation and diffusion of prophecies in the first place.

The empirical disconfirmation of specific prophecies is, of course, a potential threat to the continuity of a movement, inducing organizational strains of several sorts. It may invalidate the charismatic status of the movement's leadership and thus contribute to group discoordination and the attrition of membership support. It may foster the rise of new leaders, whose competition with each other and with existing leaders contributes to organizational fragmentation in the form of factionalism or schism. Insofar as the prophecies in question were derived from, or were linked to, a broader body of doctrine, their disconfirmation may undermine faith in the latter, thus precipitating more comprehensive ideological crises. Preparatory actions taken in anticipation of prophetic fulfillment may have depleted the resources of individual members and of the movement, leaving them in a stringent predicament. Agitational, preparatory, or interventional actions previously undertaken may have alienated other groups, who now heap abuse and ridicule upon the movement for its delusions and rash behaviors. Discreditation of the movement in the eyes of marginal or potential supporters may seriously reduce the movement's recruiting ground and the effectiveness of its proselytization.

Although prophetic nonconfirmation (delay in prophetic fulfillment) creates somewhat less immediately pressing problems for millenarian collectivities, it nevertheless poses exigencies which have equally important bearings on the careers of such groups. In fact, during the earlier stages of millenarian group formation, which tend to be characterized by tense immediacy, the exigencies posed by the two types of prophetic failure may be quite similar. The general problem confronting the group is to prevent nonconfirmation from being interpreted as disconfirmation. This requires the social and ideological reinforcement of beliefs, a restructuring of expectations in a direction that makes them more easily "confirmable" or "renewable" by the group itself. In effect, this means the establishment and maintenance of a self-confirming symbolic-interactional system, typically accomplished through the gradual institutionalization of the movement.

Modes of Adaptation

The disintegration and collapse of many millenarian movements are traceable to their failure to cope effectively with the strains induced by prophetic disconfirmations or nonconfirmations, generally because they have not developed the requisite organizational resources. A variety of adaptive patterns of response may, however, be elicited by such crises, serving to mitigate their disturbing impact.[1]

Acknowledgment of Error and Organizational Recycling

The group may acknowledge that it was in error in expecting its prophecies to be fulfilled at a particular time but cling to the belief that they will materialize in the proximate future. It may remain for a period in a state of vigilance and suspenseful waiting, drawing upon its cultic and ideological resources to keep its faith alive. More specific definitions of "error" tend to be made, along such lines as admitted misinterpretations of supernaturally supplied evidence, misreadings of signs and omens, misdirection by evil forces, miscalculation of the supernatural schedule of impending change, and so on. As corrections to such errors are worked out, the orientation of the group is restored, with a minimal restructuring of its basic belief system. The group, in effect, reaffirms its faith in its prophetic vision and merely revises its expectation as to when it will be actualized.

Where this mode of adjustment is adopted, the movement is recycled around essentially the same framework of prophecies, reprojected into the future. A time of expected fulfillment may again be specified, or it may remain undefined. If left undefined, the expectation of imminent fulfillment is likely to prevail for some time, and exhortation and ideological elaboration designed to sustain this kind of expectation become a prominent part of the movement's internal life. If the time of expected fulfillment is specified, it is usually, at this stage, a date in the not-too-distant future, generally within the life span of most of the believers. Having thus been recycled, the movement can relive the earlier part of its career. If it is solidly organized, it may be able to survive through several such revivalistic cycles before making more fundamental readjustments.

Assignments of Blame and Organizational Redirection

An alternative pattern of collective response, which may likewise occur as part of the above-mentioned recycling sequence, involves the construction of "explanations" for the acknowledged fact that previously declared prophecies have not been actualized at the time expected. In this instance, specific prophetic disconfirmations are not attributed to the fallibility of human judgment in discerning the unfolding cosmic process, but rather to natural or supernatural agencies which are believed to be responsible for deflecting, retarding, or obstructing the process.

The manner in which such interpretations are phrased assumes special importance not only in sustaining the millenarian orientation of the group but also in conditioning the nature and direction of its subsequent rounds of collective action. Thus, for example, if the causes of prophetic failures are identified as internal to the movement itself, being construed, for instance, as reflecting the incomplete spiritual readiness of believers to inherit the new earth, a cycle of collective self-purification, spiritual regeneration, and moral upbuilding may ensue. The same context may encourage rounds of "purging" activity within the movement, in the course of which marginal or dissident members, cliques, and factions are eliminated, leaving behind a smaller but more uniformly zealous and tightly knit remnant, capable of generating more potent consensual validation for the movement's belief system. The movement may, in fact, become more or less permanently reorganized around such goals of spiritual edification and perfection, seeing their pursuit as being in the service of prophetic fulfillment. Millennial hopes remain intact but they come to be drawn upon to sustain motivation for more enduring patterns of preparatory action. As they undergo institutionalization, the latter patterns take on the properties of anticipatory socialization, providing regular occasions and opportunities for the rehearsal and ritualistic dramatization of roles which believers expect to play in the millennial arrangement. They thus become vital symbolic elements in the group's apparatus for self-validation and self-maintenance.

If, on the other hand, the causes of prophetic failure are interpreted as residing outside the movement itself, rather different patterns of collective action may emerge, their more specific character depending upon the particular type of explanation ventured. If, for example, the prophetic failure is construed to be a delay due to the lack of preparedness of those who have remained outside the movement but who are defined as potential candidates for salvation, the movement may resume its proselytization, possibly with greater vigor and extensiveness than before. Missionary activity, undertaken to expand the salvationary scope of the coming millennial upheaval, may thus emerge as the central mission of the group, becoming a key element in its collective identity as well as its organizational structure. Here again the millennial dream is not surrendered but is kept alive through public preaching and other types of conversional endeavor. As noted previously, reinforcement of the group's basic convictions may derive from such interactional sources even under conditions of limited success in making converts. When proselytizing activity has come to be defined as a key agency of prophetic fulfillment, it tends to take on a self-validating character. Even negative reactions can be assimilated as supporting evidence that a real struggle for the new world's establishment is going on and that the group must persevere in its missionary efforts as part of this struggle.

The attribution of prophetic failures to external agencies construed as acting malevolently to obstruct the working out of the millennial process is likely to encourage waves of more militant collective action. Such assessments of blame may undergo ideological elaboration in the form of conspiratorial doctrines, which then furnish the symbolic ground for new rounds of defensive or offensive activity. Like the previously considered style of explanation, this one may stimulate more intense proselytization, but it tends also to alter its purpose and content. Proselytizing endeavor is likely to become more genuinely agitational in character, seeking not only to make direct conversions but also to expose, criticize, and discredit those persons and groups who have become the major targets of blame for the delay in the actualization of prophecies. Other forms of aggressive action against established authorities and groups may be undertaken in the same context, often triggering open conflict between them. Temporary or lasting changes in the millenarian group's identity and mission may result from such interactional processes. While continuing to adhere to its basic millenarian convictions, it now sees itself more than before as an active agency of prophetic fulfillment, whose present mission includes some kinds of interventional roles. Its collective outlook becomes more forthrightly antiworldly and its self-conception more militant. Thus structured, the interactional process again takes on a self-confirming character, reinforcing the beliefs which initiated them in the first place. Although it may, of course, have organizationally damaging consequences in such forms as persecution and suppression, it may also be a source of renewed solidarity and may serve to insulate members from outside influences which might otherwise weaken group attachment.

Assertion of Prophecy-Fulfilling Claims and Organizational Transformation

Instead of, or in addition to, attempting to meet prophetic failures by attributing them to errors of human interpretation or by assigning blame for them onto internal or external agencies, millenarian movements may follow still another course. The modes of adaptation thus far considered are all premised on the recognition and acknowledgment of prophetic failure. Quite often, however, millenarian movements fail to recognize or refuse to concede that a genuine failure has occurred. They may advance the assertion that the prophecies previously announced have, in fact, been fulfilled, either partially or substantially.

To an unbeliever who has not shared in the life of the movement prior to the point of crisis, such claims may appear to be irrationally wrought delusions or crassly face-saving tricks of propaganda. But why such claims should so frequently appear credible to a believing group becomes more understandable when viewed in the context of their prior interactional history and their crisis-born predicament. The latter do not merely predispose believers in a diffuse way to accept uncritically any assertion that is offered. To win acceptance, the assertion must be meaningful and credible within the symbolic-interactional framework that has come to be developed by the believing group. The credibility of a claim is not merely a function of its empirically demonstrable "truth" but also a function of its symbolic compatibility with previously developed convictions. As noted earlier, when such convictions are shared, consensually validated, and ideologically anchored, they become an important source of "autonomous" influence upon group responses to prophetic failures.

Viewed in this way, recourse to this symbolic strategy is not merely a denial of reality, but a novel interpretation of reality from an ideologically structured and socially insulated perspective. Encouraging and facilitating such claims, as previously pointed out, would be the inclusion of ambiguous or empirically unverifiable statements in the original prophetic declarations. It is these portions of prophecy which are especially likely to furnish the base or content for such claims. Previous ambiguities may thus be clarified in the very course of advancing and elaborating such claims, creating the appearance of fulfillment in the eyes of believers. Selective interpretation of objective events may similarly be resorted to as a supplementary way of mobilizing "empirical evidence" in support of the claims, being pointed to, for example, as indices or reflections of supernatural events in keeping with the group's prophecies.

Such prophecy-validating claims may be advanced with varying degrees and kinds of qualification. They typically assert that prophesied events, or developments relating to them, have indeed occurred, but on the supernatural level, their earthly materialization being more imminent than ever. Still unrealized expectations are projected again into the future, occasioning new rounds of collective action. These may essentially repeat previous patterns of activity or they may lead to innovations in group programs and new forms of group integration. Specific prophecies relating to yet unfulfilled expectations may be reissued, precipitating new crises, which may be met in the same way. But prophetic successes repeatedly claimed in this fashion may have a cumulative impact upon the orientation of the group which, sooner or later, induces changes in collective identity and its supporting organizational structure.

As with the modes of adaptation previously considered, long-term viability, if achieved, is a gradually evolved product of institutionalization, which provides internal means for belief-reinforcement, making consensual validation, ideologically stylized psychological transactions, cultic activities, and patterned in-group/out-group interaction the main sources of confirmation. The basic structure of the millenarian belief system may thus be perpetuated. Periodic crises, previously precipitated by specific short-term predictions, may be avoided as the completion of prophetic fulfillment is projected into a more distant or indefinite future. Rather than seeing itself as a movement having a temporary mission, the millenarian group comes to conceive of itself as the organizational link between the supernatural and earthly phases of the millennial drama, the bridgehead to the new future, entrusted with the responsibility of maintaining and spreading the faith until the time for complete fulfillment finally arrives.

Conclusion

This line of interpretation of the comparative evidence leads to a paradoxical conclusion: prophetic disconfirmation and nonconfirmation are among the most important causes of millenarian movement disintegration, but they are also an extremely important part of the process through which such movements undergo institutionalization. The directions in which the process of institutionalization carries the movement and transforms it depend upon the specific exigencies posed by crises of prophetic failure and the manner in which these crises are defined and adapted to by the believing collectivity in its broader societal context.

NOTE

1. Examples of the modes of adaptation discussed below may be found in the sources previously cited; see also Burridge 1961, 1969; Cochrane 1970; Sandeen 1970; and Shaw 1946.

REFERENCES

Balandier, G. 1963. *Sociologie actuelle de l'Afrique noire: Dynamique sociale en Afrique centrale.* Paris: Presses Universitaires de France.

Barkun, M. 1971. "Law and Social Revolution: Millenarianism and the Legal System." *Law and Society Review* 6:113–141.

Barnett, H. G. 1957. *Indian Shakers: A Messianic Cult of the Pacific Northwest.* Carbondale: Southern Illinois University Press.

Bittner, E. 1963. "Radicalism and the Organization of Radical Movements." *American Sociological Review* 28:928–940.

Blumer, H. 1951. "Collective Behavior," in *Principles of Sociology,* edited by A.M. Lee. New York: Barnes & Noble.

Burridge, K. 1961. *Mambu: A Melanesian Millenium.* London: Methuen.

———. 1969. *New Heaven, New Earth: A Study of Millenarian Activities.* New York: Schocken.

Case, S. J. 1918. *The Millennial Hope.* Chicago: University of Chicago Press.

Cochrane, G. 1970. *Big Men and Cargo Cults.* Oxford, UK: Clarendon.

Cohn, N. 1957. *The Pursuit of the Millennium: Revolutionary Messianism in Medieval and Reformation Europe and Its Bearing on Modern Totalitarian Movements.* New York: Harper.

———. 1962. "Medieval Millenarism: Its Bearing on the Comparative Study of Millenarian Movements," in *Millennial Dreams in Action: Essays in Comparative Study,* edited by S. L. Thrupp. The Hague: Mouton.

Essien-Udom, E. U. 1962. *Black Nationalism: A Search for an Identity in America.* Chicago: University of Chicago Press.

Festinger, L., H. W. Riecken, and S. Schachter. 1956. *When Prophecy Fails.* Minneapolis: University of Minnesota Press.

Froom, L. 1946–1954. *The Prophetic Faith of Our Fathers: The Historical Development of Prophetic Interpretation,* vols. 1–4. Washington, D.C.: Review & Herald.

Hardyck, J. A., and M. Braden 1962. "Prophecy Fails Again: A Report of a Failure to Replicate." *Journal of Abnormal and Social Psychology* 65:136–141.

Holloway, M. 1951. *Heavens on Earth.* New York: Turnstile.

Kanter, R. M. 1968. "Commitment and Social Organization: A Study of Commitment Mechanisms in Utopian Communities." *American Sociological Review* 33:499–517.

Killian, L. M. 1964. "Social Movements," in *Handbook of Modern Sociology,* edited by R. E. L. Farris. Chicago: Rand McNally.

Köbben, A. J. F. 1960 "Prophetic Movements as an Expression of Social Unrest." *Internationales Archiv für Ethnologie* 49:117–164.

Lanternari, V. 1963. *The Religions of the Oppressed: A Study of Modern Messianic Cults.* New York: Alfred A. Knopf.

Lawrence, P. 1964. *Road Belong Cargo.* Manchester, UK: Manchester University Press.

Linton, R. 1943. "Nativistic Movements." *American Anthropologist* 45:230–240.

Lofland, J. 1966. *Doomsday Cult.* Englewood Cliffs, NJ: Prentice-Hall.

Mooney, J. 1965. *The Ghost-Dance Religion and the Sioux Outbreak of 1890.* Chicago: University of Chicago Press.

Mühlmann, W. E. 1961. *Chiliasmus und Nativismus: Studen zur Psychologie, Soziologie und Historischen Kasuistik der Unsturzbewegungen.* Berlin: Reimer.

Nordhoff, C. 1966. *The Communistic Societies of the United States.* New York: Dover.

O'Dea, T. F. 1957. *The Mormons.* Chicago: University of Chicago Press.

Price, T., and G. Shepperson. 1958. *Independent African: John Chilembwe and the Origins, Setting and Significance of the Nyasaland Native Rising of 1915.* Edinburgh, UK: Edinburgh University Press.

Rogers, P. G. 1966. *The Fifth Monarchy Men.* London and New York: Oxford University Press.

Sandeen, E. R. 1970. *The Roots of Fundamentalism: British and American Millenarianism.* Chicago: University of Chicago Press.

Schwartz, G. 1970. *Sect Ideologies and Social Status.* Chicago: University of Chicago Press.

Sears, C. E. 1924. *Days of Delusion: A Strange Bit of History.* Boston and New York: Houghton Mifflin.

Shaw, P. E. 1946. *The Catholic Apostolic Church, Sometimes Called Irvingite: A Historical Study.* New York: King's Crown.

Shils, E., and H. M. Johnson. 1968. "Ideology," pp. 66–85 of vol. 7, *International Encyclopedia of the Social Sciences.* New York: Macmillan and Free Press.

Simmons, J. L. 1964. "On Maintaining Deviant Belief Systems: A Case Study." *Social Problems* 11:250–256.

Smithson, R. J. 1935. *The Anabaptists: Their Contribution to Our Protestant Heritage.* London: Clarke.

Talmon, Y. 1962. "Pursuit of the Millennium: The Relation between Religious and Social Change." *Archives Européenes de Sociologie* 3:125–148.

———. 1968. "Millenarism," pp. 349–362 of vol. 10, *International Encyclopedia of the Social Sciences.* New York: Macmillan and Free Press.

Thrupp, S. L., ed. 1962. *Millennial Dreams in Action: Essays in Comparative Study.* The Hague: Mouton.

Wallace, A. F. C. 1956. "Revitalization Movements." *American Anthropologist* 58:264–281.

Werner, E. 1960. "Popular Ideologies in Late Medieval Europe: Taborite Chiliasm and its Antecedents." *Comparative Studies in Society and History* 2:344–363.

Wilson, B. R. 1959. "An Analysis of Sect Development." *American Sociological Review* 24:3–15.

———. 1961. *Sects and Society: A Sociological Study of the Elim Tabernacle, Christian Science, and Christadelphians.* Berkeley: University of California Press.

———. 1963. "Millennialism in Comparative Perspective." *Comparative Studies in Society and History* 6:93–114.

Worsley, P. 1957. *The Trumpet Shall Sound: A Study of "Cargo" Cults in Melanesia.* London: MacGibbon & Kee.

Zygmunt, J. F. 1970. "Prophetic Failure and Chiliastic Identity." *American Journal of Sociology* 75:926–948.

The Effects of Prophetic Disconfirmation of the Committed

Neil Weiser

The student of religion has encountered an imponderable number of prophetic episodes, all of which will continue to stretch history to its seams as long as misfortune exists. Members of all societies who consider themselves troubled and oppressed have welcomed deliverance cults designed around such events as the Second Coming of Jesus, the Advent of the Jewish Messiah, or world destruction through a cataclysm.[1] Nevertheless, such a prophetic cult will often bear witness to prophetic disconfirmation, an objectively apparent falsification of a belief by the occurrence or lack of occurrence of some prophetic prediction. Does the disconfirmation in fact cause the belief to be abandoned?

Why did the failure of the Second Advent give new life and form to the Montanist movement and to the Anabaptists of 1534 rather than cause these groups' immediate end? What was the explanation for the increased energy and enthusiasm held by the American Millerites for an extended period after the 1843 falsification of their belief in the Millennium's advent (Festinger et al. 1956:6–17)? In Samoa, in approximately 1863, a healing prophetess of the Sisu Alaisa pagan-Christian cult announced the immediate arrival of the Son of God on the crest of a wave, bringing from heaven all the food that the natives needed. Having neglected their occupations with the expectation that the Messiah would care for them, many natives hastened to the shore to see the event (Lanternari 1963:198). Why and how did the cult survive for some time despite disillusionment after the disconfirmation?

Disconfirmation Hypothesis

By examining the behavioral patterns of the committed after a falsification of their millennial beliefs, this author wishes to propose that the core of such beliefs, almost without exception, will remain intact for a period of time subsequent to the disconfirmation event. Prophecies cannot and do not fail for the committed. Any post-prophetic disconfirmation behavior will be an attempt to diminish the dissonance created by the believed act's failure to occur, an act inherent to the religious belief and for which great sacrifice has been taken. It will be shown that such behavior will include the conscious and/or subconscious rationalization of the event, aided by (1) an eventual displacement of the goal with marginal goal modification; (2) the welcoming of imitator-prophets; and (3) increased proselytizing activity in order to ascertain social support. "Endogenous" movements undergo greater strain subsequent to prophetic disproof than the two "external" movements differentiated by Wallis (1918). As an extension of Bowra's study (1959) of prophetic poetry, it will be noted that "good" prophets lead to greater post-disconfirmation dissonance and subsequently greater rationalization and proselytizing activity than do "bad" prophets. Whatever the nature of the movement, the prophet, the messianic cult, and the entire religious system are created for a specific individual and social objective. The latter in itself leads to the necessary survival of the core messianic belief subsequent to disconfirmation.

Falsification and Dissonance

In an examination of the social and psychological occurrences following a prophetic falsification, one must introduce the concept of dissonance. The latter will arise in view of an "attempt" by the disconfirmatory act to nullify both the follower's messianic beliefs and the great sacrifices that the believer has suffered in preparation for the messianic fulfillment. The magnitude of the dissonance will depend on the importance of the belief to the individual and on the magnitude of his preparatory activity. The two are actually united in that only those firmly committed to the belief will take important actions difficult to undo (Lanternari 1963:28). Some may uproot their lives in order to build a new town in another area. Some may neglect worldly things and dispose of their earthly possessions in their preparation. The Millerites, like many other messianic groups, sold their possessions in order to have more money to support the cause and to conclude honorably their dealings with their fellow men prior to the advent. "With fervent love of others, the Millerites who owed no debts themselves also sought to pay those of others" (Lanternari 1963:7). Thus what is done by way of preparation for the prophetic event is difficult to undo, and the jeering of nonbelievers makes the dissonance even greater (Lanternari 1963:5). Firth (1951:113) has noted that such elaborate work performed by the committed, be it mass crop cultivation or destruction, or the construction of new villages, is an expression of the great desire for the goal and a mitigation of the highly charged emotionalism involved. The latter, in turn, accompanied by various psychological phenomena (for example, twitching, mass possession, and trances) is the product of the inability to satisfy such "enormously inflated" desires.

> Feelings of deprivation and frustration are heightened by the apparent irrationality of [the oppressor] society whose incomprehensible economic

and political changes the natives vainly strive to understand and manipulate in their own interest. (Worsley 1957:247)

Such feelings are further magnified by the dissonance created by the desire's disconfirmation.

The individual must thus reduce the painful dissonance created by the prophetic failure. Those not so strongly committed to the belief may discard it. They may cease the behavior that had been initiated in preparation for the prediction's fulfillment and return to a more usual existence (Festinger et al. 1956:3). Nevertheless, if the behavioral commitment is so strong as a result of powerful beliefs in the prediction and great sacrifice for these beliefs, it may be less painful to continue the belief than to discard it.

The messianic prophecy may be incorporated into the type of revitalization process which aims to reduce the dissonance not by manipulation of the prophecy itself but by manipulation of the real world (Schindler 1886:72). The movement organized around such a culture-conflict process is termed by Wallis as external nativistic, in contrast to the endogenous movement which seeks salvation solely through spiritual, cultural, or ethical channels. Here, salvation implies a methodical advance toward life in the hereafter, a place where the individual may attain liberation. Thus the aspiration of delivery is focused on the end of the world, which may take on positive meaning through the renunciation of earthly goods and the escape from society. The latter is accomplished in order to establish a society of one's own beyond history, reality, and the need to bring about change and improvement. Such endogenous movements include the sixteenth-century migratory cults of the Tupi-Guarani tribes of Brazil and the anti-sorcery societies of Africa, such as that established in 1904 by Epikilipikili in the Congo (Wallis 1918:247).

Endogenous movements suffer greater strain following a prophetic disconfirmation than do external movements.[2] Although both have arisen from somewhat similar causes—the experiencing of a life of misery—external groups have given vent to their persecution and frustrations by the creation of an often militant struggle. Thus, the latter cult not only expresses religiously a yearning for liberty and a fuller life but implements this expression by immediate military and political action in opposition to the oppressing forces (Lanternari 1963:20). Dissonance created by a prophetic failure will be minimized because the external group can "take action into their own hands." Even if their own attempt flounders, theirs is still a sentiment of attempt rather than one of helplessness. The endogenous movement, however, relies solely on spiritual salvation. Prayer and a spiritual state by the cult member may offer some feeling of impetus toward salvation, but helplessness and insecurity follow equally. Quite obviously, a prophetic disconfirmation for these individuals would create, according to Freudian theory, disastrous psychological pain.

Examples of external movements, emerging in reaction to intensified imperialistic efforts and the growing awareness by the natives of an economic and cultural lag in their society, include the Taiping nativistic movement (which arose in order to overcome Chinese feudalism and missionary Christianity) as well as the Kugu Sorta and the Burkhan in reaction to czarist rule (Wallis 1918:241). Several external movements have emerged in response to internal oppression, such as those in twentieth-century Japan, where they were motivated by political, social, and cultural problems generated by war. Mostly of Shinto derivation, many of these minor middle-class sects are often linked with powerful financial interests which use religion as a front for their own ends (Wallis 1918:243).

Extending Bowra's discussion of prophetic poetry (1959) with his implication that the "good" prophetic poet is sincere in his beliefs and predictions, in contrast to the "bad" poet, one may assume that the statements of the "good" prophet led to a greater magnitude of post-disconfirmation dissonance among believers than those of his rival. The prophet's attitude toward his prediction must be comparable to that of the poet toward his art:

> Such an art demands the highest degree of seriousness, self-knowledge and truth to vision. . . . Their failure was that they did not look seriously enough, that their concern was parochial and short-sighted, that they deluded themselves into beliefs which they did not really hold. They assumed all the airs of prophecy and sought to speak with the voice of thunder from Sinai, but they failed because they tried to say more than they really meant. (Bowra 1959:17)

The "good" prophet finds more devoted followers than the "bad" prophet because of his greater candor and sincerity by which he is judged (Bowra 1959:19). Thus such sincerity may lead to a firmer belief by his followers and subsequently greater dissonance after a prophetic disconfirmation. As the tendency toward imitation is great, especially when the circumstances foster it, so often arises the existence of such a "bad" prophet or "imitator." Berokia Zevi, Miguel Cardo, and Mordecai Mokiah—three "imitators" of Sabbatai Zevi, the European self-proclaimed Jewish Messiah of the seventeenth century—arose only to meet with far less faith, acceptance, and post-prophecy dissonance on the part of their followers (Wallis 1918:64).

Problems of Miscalculation and Rationalization

Pain may exist in varying degrees in the individual of both external and endogenous movements. Although one can blind himself to the fact that the prediction simply has not been fulfilled, he more often seeks to rationalize the disconfirmation. The human mind seeks to order the unordered; otherwise anxiety is produced. Similarly, the mind seeks to rationalize the irrational, also with the purpose of quelling anxiety. Freudian theory notes a second objective, the defense of the ego. Thus, with the occurrence of a prophetic disproof, an irrationalization for those who are firmly committed to the particular messianic belief and who have sacrificed greatly in preparation for the event, rationalization must follow in order to assuage present and prevent future anxiety created by this disconfirmation. Such reasoning will aid in reducing the believer's dissonance, permitting him to continue his messianic belief.

The rationalization may take the form of a miscalculation of the date of the prophecy. William Miller, a New England farmer, predicted the world's termination to occur in 1843, basing his belief on a prophetic declaration in the Book of Daniel (8:14). By 1839, his belief had substantially dispersed so as to form a national organization of exuberant followers. The Millerite leaders announced only a period of time during which the advent would occur, not a specific date. However, various dates were set by disciples, and after each disconfirmation, greater fanaticism arose. Believers first maintained that the Millennium would arrive on April 23, 1843, and later maintained its arrival on March 21, 1844 (Wallis 1918:84). Soon, most Millerites were accepting a new prediction first proposed by a member, Rev. Samuel S. Snow, who believed that the date would be October 22, 1844. Members neglected their occupations and sold their possessions to prepare for the Advent. Although leaders first counseled against this date, they later generally accepted it. Though again doomed to disappointment, they formulated their faith in a near coming in the flesh of the Son of God with the formation of the Second Adventists (Festinger et al. 1956:9).

The underlying principle of the Sioux nativistic movement, the Ghost Dance, was that the time would arrive when the Indian race, living and dead, would be reunited in a life of happiness. This was to be accomplished by an overruling spiritual power with the human assistance of the ceremonial Dance. Though certain individuals were disposed to anticipate the Indian Millennium by preaching resistance to the whites' encroachments, such teachings formed no part of the true doctrine. Different dates had been assigned at various times for the fulfillment of the prophecy; and the Messiah himself, Wovoka, set several dates as one prediction after another failed to materialize. In his message to the Cheyenne and Arapaho in August 1891, his indecisiveness is apparent (Eliade 1967:406): "You will receive good words again from me some time. . . . No man knoweth the time, not even the angels." However, the millennial date universally recognized among all the tribes was the spring of 1891, immediately prior to the Sioux outbreak. As winter passed without realization of their hopes, their beliefs gradually assumed their present form.

> Some time in the future, the Indian will be united with his companions who have gone before to be forever happy and that this happiness may be anticipated in dreams, if not actually hastened in reality by earnest and frequent attendance of the sacred dance. (Eliade 1967:409)

Thus, dissonance had been created after each disconfirmation prior to 1891 but rationalization by the prophet, God's spokesman, helped to ease group member anxiety and permit them to continue their messianic beliefs. The people themselves rationalized the disastrous failure of the messianic Advent of 1891 which nevertheless did not quell such credence.

In this way, the idea of "prophetic imminence" may be replaced by a more general promise of a distant Millennium. However, as Worsley (1957:xx) notes, the basic belief constructed around the prophetic notion still remains. In fact, such a core belief will always be inherently general in order to withstand any "stretching" by new developments. So one sees the lack of specificity of both the first Millerite leaders and the Sioux prophet in their respective announcements of religious principle. With regard to Melanesian cargo cult theory, Jarvie brings to light the idea that the committed may examine their various beliefs and modify and restructure them if necessary, but those more basic will be considered "unbreachable" and will not be tested (Worsley 1957:lxviii).[3]

Rationalization and the Millennium

The flexibility and ability of the millennial belief to adapt to new events may permit its more marginal concepts to be interwoven into the political framework of the society. Citing the assumption of passivism by the Anabaptists (later to become the American Mennonite Community) and by the Jehovah's Witnesses movement, Worsley (1957:xlii–xlvii) notes that political hopes tend to be expressed politically rather than religiously with the defeat of the millennial cult: "Millenarianism always gives way to secularized forms, and thenceforward becomes marginal, and usually more pacific and other-worldly" (xliii). Postponement of prophecy will occur for the reasons outlined above, but the maintenance of the religiosity of the marginally based cult should by any means not be underscored. The Mennonite and Jehovah's Witnesses movements are fully alive religiously and, in fact, their secular facets very much complement their religious ones. Cult pressure groups of such a political nature may also arise, as witnessed by the Kimbangu movement and its effective political role allied to the Bakongo nationalist party.

The unworthiness, unsacredness, and consequent need for greater spiritual preparation by the believers and possibly the rest of the world have served quite often as post-disconfirmation rationalizations. The Afghan Mohammedans believed that once the Holy War had been proclaimed the numerous infidel battalions would become powerless against a handful of soldiers of the Faith. Their belief paved the way for the Mad Mullah who led the attack against the British in Malakand in 1897. When the tribesmen returned without a quarter of their number after the fighting, the faith of the survivors was unshaken. According to the Mullah, only those who had doubted had perished (Wallis 1918:140). Failure of the cargo's arrival for the Central Highland cult of New Guinea did not cause the believers' faith to be diminished. It was explained as being due to human deficiencies or the interference of foreigners but not in terms of the spirits themselves (Worsley 1957:202). In 1889, a Bannock spokesman of the Fort Hall Reservation in Idaho informed the Shoshoni of Wind River Reservation in Wyoming concerning the Ghost Dance and the return of the followers' dead friends and relatives. The Shoshoni danced and, with the obscuring of the area by dense smoke from a nearby fire in the fall of 1890, they interpreted the event as an indication of the predicted Advent. In spite of the smoke's waning, the dance was fervently maintained for another year until the predicted date passed, at which time the Shoshoni concluded that they were wickedly deceived by the informant (Mooney 1893).

In 1920 Alexander Bedward, a Jamaican regarded as prophet and Messiah, forecast that subsequent to his Second Advent the earth would be destroyed by fire. When his ascent to heaven failed to occur on his predicted date, he announced that God had delayed the event so that more may become worthy of reward. Although he was soon arrested and declared insane, his followers continued to revere him as prophet (Simpson 1956:334). In 1941 a Brazilian Tukina prophet, obeying a vision and message of God, told his people to construct on a jungle clearing a temple where rituals were to be performed. He later reported a subsequent vision that God no longer protected the Tukinas because of a member's violation of the marriage taboo. Thus the prophecy was disconfirmed by the prophet, but religious rites are still practiced (Lanternari 1963:142).

The prophetic failure can be further rationalized with a symbolic theme. One may have questioned Jesus' role as Messiah "since he had endured a shameful death," creating a "disconfirmation" in the minds of his followers. However, any doubts (Festinger et al. 1956:24) are quelled by referring to a prophecy in Isaiah: "He will be taken from the land of the living and will be wounded for the sins of his people." In such a way, any dissonance is rationalized symbolically. In Russia, with the announcement of an anathema against the old faith in 1666, the Rascolniks, adherents of the old orthodoxy, announced the arrival of the reign of Antichrist. They believed that since his reign would last over three years, the world's end would come in 1669. After the prediction failed, the Rascolnik leader explained that Antichrist had not come in the flesh, as he reigned spiritually in the contaminated Church. At first sight, one may think that the leader's rationalization may not have been sufficient for his disappointed followers. However, similar Antichrist ideas rearose during the reign of Peter the Great (Wallis 1918:191).

Therefore, both conscious and at times unconscious deceptions are carried out by believers to renew both their own and their neighbors' faith, thereby quelling any doubt and dissonance preceding or subsequent to the prophetic disproof. Any event may be manipulated as a sign of the success of the prophecy. Faith was bolstered among members of the Central Highland cargo cult of New Guinea following the failure to receive predicted cargo by such "concrete 'evidence' of success [as] cartridges from wrecked planes, newspaper, calico and other trade-goods . . . shown as magical first-fruits of the harvest to come" (Worsley 1957:203). The failure of certain events to occur according to the predictions of the Sioux Messiah in September 1890, caused a temporary loss of faith on the part of the Cheyenne. Yet shortly afterward, with the report by several visiting Shoshoni and Arapaho from Wyoming that they had encountered a group of Indians resurrected from the dead, the Cheyenne returned to the dance with renewed fervor (Grinnell 1891:61–69).

Quite often, post-disconfirmation dissonance will be diminished if a diversion occurs, taking the believers' minds off the former incident until the anxiety has greatly lessened. The advent of Judgment Day in the year 1186, in accord with astrological beliefs, oppressed Europe like a nightmare. Shelters were built, windows boarded up, and fasts of atonement were begun. The prophecy failed; but an astronomical part of the prediction did occur, leaving little lasting disillusionment (Lewinsohn 1961:78). Festinger and his colleagues point out that, after suffering the strong disconfirmation of not being met with flying saucers on the predicted date of a cataclysm (which itself failed to materialize), the Lake City group, a recent American millennial cult, experienced a diversion in the expected death and resurrection of the leader's husband: "If the attention of the group could focus on so spectacular a matter as the promised miracle, they could forget at least temporarily the terrible disappointment they had suffered" (1956:169). The miracle's failure was rationalized; it was clearly either a spiritual matter, a misinterpretation of the prophetic message, or a delay to allow others to prepare for salvation.

At times, after the failure of a prophecy, the deaths of the prophet and/or of the cult members occur, either because of their being quelled by opposition or as a result of natural means. The death of a prophet in itself may disconfirm his role as Messiah. This may lead to the cult's termination. In the fifth century A.D. in Crete, one Moses, declaring himself the Messiah, ordered his followers to throw themselves into the ocean as the waters would surely part. Many drowned and the cult ended (Wallis 1918:68). In 1819, the Kickapoo Indians, attempting to awaken their dead Messiah's soul, contracted his fatal disease. The cult's extinction followed (Lanternari 1963:40).

However, it is more commonplace to witness the martyrization of these dead by any cult survivors or by those suffering under similar misfortunes. Thus, a disaster-causing disconfirmation, including the death of the presumed messiah, may lead to inspiration and continuation of the messianic belief with possibly greater fervor than formerly may have been held by those who perished for it. The sermons of Conselheiro, a Brazilian prophet who identified the advent of the Millennium with the restoration of the monarchy, failed in their prediction. He and his followers were "suppressed by the Antichrist institution, the Republic of Brazil," since they were considered a threat to the political authorities. Many, having martyrized these deaths, still await the Second Coming (Lanternari 1963:33). With the deaths of countless Jews throughout history—often while awaiting the advent of the Messiah—has been incorporated the idea of their martyrization. Great messianic excitement preceded the Jewish revolt led by Bar-Kochbah against Rome's Titus (Wallis 1918:67).

Dissonance and Disconfirmation

Dissonance in the minds of the believers, created by a prophetic disconfirmation, cannot be lessened without social support. Festinger and his colleagues remark that:

> Dissonance created by an unequivocal disconfirmation cannot be appreciably reduced unless one is in the constant presence of supporting members who can provide for one another the kind of social reality that will make the rationalization of the disconfirmation acceptable. (1956:207)

The believer must receive support from others in order to make both his rationalization following prophetic disproof and the belief itself seem correct. Man necessitates the approval of others so as to continue functioning effectively in his psycho-social world. Disappointed believers can turn to fellow movement members to seek such support. Remaining dissonance will be even further reduced if a greater number of people can be persuaded that the system of belief is correct. Clearly, it must be correct if others find it true. Thus increased proselytizing by the committed is a primary aspect of post-disconfirmation behavior.

The Lake City group, prior to its disconfirmations, preached antiproselytizing admonitions and assembled almost in complete secrecy. Lessons supposedly received from the supernatural were burned and passwords were exchanged. With the failure of the prophecy came indiscriminate acceptance of all who were interested in the group. Their admission and very warm reception, in contrast to preconfirmation behavior, were attributed in part to their need for guidance by supernatural messengers and also to their subconscious exigency for social approval. The post-disconfirmation dissonance suffered by less committed Collegeville members, a subgroup of the Lake City organization, was diminished by discarding their belief. Yet the important difference between the two groups lay in commitment strength and social support. Lake City members held fast and tried to create a supportive circle of believers, while Collegeville members possessed neither the commitment nor the group support that the majority of Lake City members possessed. In the presence of nonbelievers, the doubts of the Collegeville members far surpassed their belief commitment (Festinger et al. 1956:208–209). Even those who did not face active opposition and who were alone in their belief could not obtain the social support necessary for their acceptance of any rationalization as correct—a necessary condition for the dissonance reduction to commence. Lake City members conversely were able to accept their own rationalizations in view of the existence of such support; they reduced dissonance and regained confidence in their original beliefs. Thus, the presence of supporting cobelievers, achieved greatly by proselytizing, is an essential requirement for recovery from such extreme disconfirmations. Nevertheless, such support—whatever the form—will ultimately come to those firmly committed to the prophetic belief, and their faith will continue. Strong believers will rationalize any event that has any favorable relation to their reception of social acceptance, as illustrated by the Lake City members.

Whatever the path's direction (that is, rationalization to provide social support or social support of a rationalization subsequent to the disconfirmation), the strongly committed will reduce the created anxiety in order to continue belief. Festinger and his colleagues (1956:214–230) record the final effect of the falsification on the Lake City group members. Two lightly committed members dismissed their beliefs; five, who entered the pre-disconfirmation period strongly convinced and heavily committed, passed through the disconfirmation period and its aftermath with their faith mostly unshaken and lasting.

Conclusions

In an attempt to predict post-disconfirmation action and behavior, it has been observed in each illustration that, subsequent to the reduction of dissonance by rationalization and a search for social advocacy, the committed tend to continue their messianic belief with similar or increased fervor. Explanations for such a phenomenon may be derived from those of the existence of messianism itself. Briefly, these include a continued need for a source of hope by the oppressed individual and his society, the necessity for the two to be molded into a common goal, and the human and social demand for survival.

The prophet and his messianic belief are a necessity to the individual believer living with misfortune, offering to him the only remaining hope of obliterating the social and/or psychological malaise to which he has been subjected. It is the oppressed, though, who more often manipulates the prophet, calling on the latter only when he is most needed, continuing to utilize him as long as he (the believer) desires. As Wallis states, "The multitude must be receptive to the zealot and his creed, otherwise he will be zealous in vain. On the other hand, if it longs to be saved and there is no zealot at hand, a zealous people will stir up one" (1918:92). Worsley (1957:xvi) therefore claims that the following of a prophet is the result of his individual personality or "mystical quality." The relationship between his followers and him is socially derived. The former's ideas embody an effectively relevant message, one in which his movement maintains an interest. In this way, leadership will be primarily symbolic and socially relational, and only secondarily personal. The prophet and creed, though, continue to mold the sufferers into a common purpose, whether it be the comforting hope of future spiritual salvation or the group as an organized center of resistance (Worsley 1957:47). Maintenance of belief in the millennial cult may issue from the desire to continue the political and social integration of smaller and sometimes hostile groups in opposition to a common ruling society (Worsley 1957:228).

As religion in general, messianism represents the acceptance of certain values whose internalization is necessary for the integration of different parts of the society. Durkheim thus proposed that the true object of religious veneration was not a god but society itself and that the mission of religion was to inculcate those sentiments necessary to society's survival (Wallace 1966:25). Therefore, he would presumably add that messianism is the hope for salvation or survival of the social group involved.

Apparently, millennial beliefs and their continuation subsequent to a prophetic disconfirmation must be dealt with in terms of psycho-social explanation. Both the individual and the encompassing society require and apply these beliefs in a complementary fashion. Man possesses certain psychological exigencies which, in turn, must receive social support so that he may continue to function effectively. These necessitate even greater approval if they are dealt a crushing blow. The society, in turn, requires the existence of man and his supporting beliefs in order for it functionally to survive against foreign or inherent opposition.

The committed will rationalize and seek social approval for their beliefs in order to reduce the dissonance created by a prophecy's failure. Such dissonance will be greater in endogenous movements as well as in those movements led by "good" prophets. Marginal beliefs may be extended. Most fascinating is the fact that the committed will never fail to continue their messianic beliefs as long as the need arises. Thus, prophecies cannot and do not fail for those committed believers; the core messianic beliefs remain intact.[4]

NOTES

1. Worsley (1957:xx) differentiates these movements into prophetic and millennial, and the latter into mass and microsects. For the purposes outlined, these terms will be used interchangeably. The author selected those early cults that are presently described for their diversity in form and location in order to illustrate the universality of the case in question among groups less current than that of Lake City. References are made to the latter for the purpose of clarification. Exploration of post-prophetic disconfirmation behavior among other present-day believers is a formidable but necessary task.

2. In the second century, Montanus, founder of the Montanist movement, allegedly received a private inspiration and predicted the Second Coming of Jesus to occur at Pepuza, present-day Angora. His disciples (Festinger et al. 1956) flocked to the prophesied site, building a new town, forming a sect of the Christian elite "whom no other authority guided in their new life but the Holy Spirit working directly upon them."

   The Dutch Anabaptists of the early sixteenth century believed that the Millennium would occur in 1533. According to Hoffman, their leader, the city of Strassburg had been selected as the New Jerusalem and the "true Gospel and the true Baptism would spread over the earth." Followers were distinguished by their revolutionary earnestness and they renounced material pleasures. The movement acquired greater fervor after the disconfirmation of 1533. Subsequent to their rule of Münster and their defeat in 1535, there arose a new emphasis on peacefulness. By 1826 the group received toleration in the Netherlands. It survives today as the U.S. Mennonite community (Festinger et al. 1956; Worsley 1957).

   The Samoan Pagan-Christian cult of 1863 was established by Sio-vili, a local preacher, who prophesied world termination and the Advent of the Messiah Sisu Alaisa (a native adaptation of the name of Jesus Christ). The sect's promoters believed in a single God and in His son, Sisu Alaisa, but also restored polygamy and ritual religious rites banned by Christian rule (Pritchard 1866).

   The Second Adventists, formed as an extension of the Millerites after their fourth disconfirmation on October 22, 1844, believed in the Second Coming of Jesus. The four disconfirmations of Christ's Advent throughout the Millerites' history had served simply to strengthen the conviction that the coming was near at hand. The Second Adventists later divided into six sects, the largest of which, the Seventh-Day Adventists, was formed in 1860. This group also maintains a belief in the Millennium and in their principal creed of Heaven for the righteous and Hell for the evil (Festinger et al. 1956).

The sect founded by Epikilipikili in 1904 was dedicated to the worship of the *bwanga* fetish, effective against all evil (including sorcery), and capable of rendering the native immune to the white man's bullets. The first great prophetic movement in the Congo, this secret sect spread from the Congo to other regions, gaining the support of numerous tribal chiefs, and established a pattern for other secret societies throughout Central and West Africa. Although stemming from the traditional association of tribes for mutual protection from sorcery, they were basically anti-Western in intent (Lanternari 1963).

Chinese isolation ended with the treaty of Nanking of 1842 and the commercial and military penetration of the European powers. The Taiping nativistic movement, organized in 1850, preached opposition to Manchu despotism, mandarin feudalism, and foreign intervention in China. Confronting the Manchu dynasty for fourteen years with a constant threat, the movement combined pagan and Christian elements in its ritual and revolutionary ideology. The movement was suppressed by the Emperor's forces in 1864 with their recapture of Nanking (Lanternari 1963).

The Kugu-Sorta cult was established in 1870 among the Cheremis, a Finnish people inhabiting the Upper Volga and Kama regions. The cult, under the leadership of the Jakmanovs, had a strong anti-Czarist emphasis, as they had been conquered by Ivan the Terrible, persecuted, and forcibly converted to Christianity (Lanternari 1963).

The Burkhan cult, established in the Altai Mountains in 1904 by the prophet Chot Chelpan, advocated the restoration of the ancient Mongolian Empire. Its followers were mostly hunters and shepherds who were compelled to pay taxes to both China and Russia, the latter loosely controlling the area since 1866. Their doctrine was composed of Lamaist, Buddhist, and Christian teachings (Lanternari 1963).

Paralleling the early twentieth-century messianic cults that were being fostered in the Congo and Equatorial Africa by native revolts, the Kitawala or Kitower cult was introduced in 1925 by Romo Nyirenda into the mining regions of Katanga, where bitter clashes between natives and whites were occurring. Nyirenda proclaimed himself to be Muana Lesa, the Son of God. The Kitawala was an indigenous interpretation of the doctrines of Charles Russell, the 1874 founder of the American Watchtower movement or Jehovah's Witnesses. The Witnesses believe in the advent of the Millennium after the final battle between God and the Devil; denial of the Trinity, the divinity of Jesus, the immortality of the soul, and eternal damnation; and condemnation of the state and the organized church. Kitawala preachers advocated the practice of polygamy and accused Christian missionaries of distorting the Bible. The movement received wide support in South and Central Africa, but Muana Lesa was soon imprisoned by colonial authorities, accused of killing white Christians, and hanged in 1926. The Kitawala movement in recent times has preached the imminent end of all foreign religious and political bodies and thought in Africa and a Pan-African ideology based on justice (Lanternari 1963).

In 1921 Simon Kimbangu, answering a psychic call to evangelism, went forth as a prophet among his Congolese nation. Although his evangelism was Christian and baptism and confession were adopted by his followers, his tone of preaching was extremely nationalistic. Kimbangu prophesied the imminent ousting of foreign rule, a new African way of life, the return of the dead, and the coming of a Golden Age. Strongly opposed by the local authorities, he was arrested and deported; he died behind bars in 1950 (Lanternari 1963).

An astrologer, John of Toledo, predicted that a terrible catastrophe would occur in 1186 when all the planets would unite under the "stormy" sign of Virgo. A storm followed by an earthquake would occur in September 1186, Judgment Day. Although the planetary conjunction did occur, the prophecy failed to materialize. John's prophecy was later interpreted to be purely symbolic, a prediction of the Hunnish invasion (Lewinsohn 1961).

The Federation of Northwestern Tribes dissolved after the death of their founder, Tecumseh, and the Kickapoo Indians, ceding Illinois in return for a reserve on Missouri's Osage River, signed the treaty of Edwardsville in 1819. However, the Kickapoos refused to enter the land of their enemy, the Osages. Those who remained in their villages despite the white man's warnings were persuaded to do so by their prophet Kanakuk. He assured them that they should be permitted to remain on their land until they "found greener pastures in which to settle in peace and security" if they renounced liquor, and magical healing rites, and obeyed several principal commandments. However, Kanakuk's people were compelled by the Americans to migrate to Kansas. Kanakuk contracted smallpox and died in 1852. Believing that on the third day he would rise again, his followers insisted upon waking his body; and most of them died of the same disease (Lanternari 1963).

The American Lake City group (studied and reported by Leon Festinger et al. in 1956) evolved around a prophetess, Mrs. Keech, who claimed to have received messages foretelling the world's end from an intelligent source in the universe. The group, later to split into a less devoted Collegeville sect, suffered severe disconfirmations, both in terms of their failure to be transported to the "new world" and the failure of the Millennium to materialize.

3. The following sources describe the American Indian Ghost Dance movement: Mooney 1893 and Spier 1935. The Melanesian cargo cult movements are discussed in Worsley 1957.

4. The above concepts may serve as a useful guideline to the study of contemporary prophetic and millennial movements. In his examination of the Jehovah's Witnesses, Joseph F. Zygmunt (1970:926) has focused attention on the long-term modes of adjustment to recurrent prophetic failures. Ways in which the sect has adapted its collective identity to meet these crises are noted. In the Mormon Church, a conflict has arisen between the popular and official religion—between the needs of the people and those of the society on one hand, and the action required by the clerical hierarchy on the other. In this way, the belief system may be evolving into Lanternari's (1963:245) endogenous movement model. Exploring the Jewish-Christian Adventist movement which arose from the German persecution and massacre of European Jews, Stephen Sharot (1968:1) states that their belief system is a response to conditions which no longer exist. Yet subsequent world events are explained in terms of it.

The researcher of prophetic disconfirmations may wish to draw on conceptual schemes other than that of cognitive dissonance (e.g., Merton's reactions to anomic situations).

REFERENCES

Alves, Ruben A. 1969. *A Theology of Human Hope.* Washington, DC: Corpus Books.

Bowra, Maurice. 1959. "The Prophetic Element," in *The English Association.* London, UK: Oxford University Press.

Conant, William C. 1958. *Narratives of Remarkable Conversions and Revival Incidents.* New York: Derby and Jackson.

Eliade, Mircea. 1967. *From Primitives to Zen.* New York: Harper and Row.

———. 1969. *The Quest.* Chicago, IL: University of Chicago Press.

Etzioni, Amitai. 1964. *Modern Organization.* Englewood Cliffs, NJ: Prentice-Hall.

Festinger, Leon, et al. 1956. *When Prophecy Fails.* Minneapolis: University of Minnesota Press.

Firth, Raymond. 1951. *Elements of Social Organization.* London, UK: C. A. Watts.

Grinnell, G. B. 1891. "Account of the Northern Cheyennes Concerning the Messiah Superstition." *Journal of American Folklore* 4:61–69.

Lanternari, Vittorio. 1963. *The Religions of the Oppressed.* New York: Knopf.

Lewinsohn, Richard. 1961. *Science, Prophecy and Prediction.* New York: Harper Brothers.

Mooney, James. 1893. *Ghost-Dance Religion and the Sioux Outbreak of 1890.* Washington, DC: Government Printing Office.

Phelan, John L. 1970. *The Millennial Kingdom of the Franciscans in the New World.* Berkeley, CA: University of California Press.

Pritchard, W. T. 1866. *Polynesian Reminiscences; or Life in the South Pacific Islands.* London, UK: Chapman and Hall.

Ray, V. 1936. "The Kolaskin Cult." *American Anthropologist* 38:67–75.

Schindler, Solomon. 1886. *Messianic Expectations of Modern Judaism.* Boston, MA: Cassino.

Sharot, Stephen. 1968. "A Jewish Christian Advent Movement." *Jewish Journal of Sociology* 10:1.

Simpson, G. E. 1956. "Jamaican Revivalistic Cults." *Social and Economic Studies* 5:334.

Spier, Leslie. 1935. "The Prophet Dance of the Northwest and its Derivatives: The Source of the Ghost Dance." *General Series in Anthropology* 1.

Wallace, Anthony F. C. 1966. *Religion: An Anthropological View.* New York: Random House.

Wallis, Wilson D. 1918. *Messiahs: Christian and Pagan.* Boston, MA: Gornam Press.

Worsley, Peter. 1957. *The Trumpet Shall Sound: A Study of Cargo Cults in Melanesia.* London, UK: MacGibbon and Kee.

Zygmunt, Joseph. 1970. "Prophetic Failure and Chiliastic Identity: The Case of Jehovah's Witnesses." *American Journal of Sociology* 75:926–948.

Prophecy Continues to Fail

A Japanese Sect

Takaaki Sanada and
Edward Norbeck

On June 14, 1974, Japanese newspapers reported that the leader of a new religious sect in Osaka had prophesied that an earthquake would occur on June 18 at 8:00 A.M. Members of his sect were reported to have distributed among the citizens of Osaka 100,000 copies of each of two leaflets concerning the prophesied disaster. The prophecy failed to come true and shortly thereafter the prophet attempted to commit suicide, an event that was given much attention by Japanese news media.

Reactions to prophecies that fail have been a topic of interest in social psychology for some years. This paper pursues the subject by comparing a Japanese example with earlier U.S. studies offering interpretations based on a theory of cognitive dissonance (Festinger et al. 1956; Hardyck and Braden 1962). Descriptive data presented herein are based largely on personal observation by the senior author of the activities of the Japanese sect at its headquarters in Osaka before and after the date of the prophesied earthquake. During this time Sanada lived at the headquarters, participated in the sect activities, and was able to have lengthy personal conversations with the prophet.

The Prophet and His Sect

Ichigen-no-Miya, "The Shrine of the Fundamental Truth," is one of many small sects that have arisen in Japan since the end of World War II. Known collectively as *shinkō shūkyō*, "newly risen religions," these sects tend to be looked upon by nonmembers as lowly refuges of the misguided. It is useful to note that the majority of the Japanese population, perhaps 70 percent, disclaims affiliation with any organized religious sect. Thus, although Ichigen-no-Miya is a common type of modern sect, it cannot be regarded as typical of the nation as a whole.

Ichigen-no-Miya was formed in 1950 on the basis of a revelation. Its founder and leader, Katsuichi Motoki, was born in 1905 and, before his retirement from secular life, had served for several years as vice-president of a small firm in Osaka that manufactured simple metal products. The teachings of the sect are an eclectic mixture of traditional ideas drawn principally from Shinto and Buddhism. Motoki has the divine ability to cure illnesses by blowing his breath on undergarments and sleeping garments that are brought to him. He is also able to prophesy, which he performs by glossolalia that he later translates into Japanese. According to his own claims, his accurate prophecies include the eruption of a volcano in Japan, the Vietnam War, and a recent tornado in the United States.

The headquarters of Ichigen-no-Miya is a group of structures and gardens covering about eighty acres that lie atop a hill called Takayasu-yama in Yao-shi, Osaka. The principal buildings are a religious center (which, as a matter of convenience, will hereafter be called the shrine), business office, kitchen-dining room, and dormitory. The parklike grounds are extensively planted with azaleas and contain many cages holding birds from various parts of the world and several carp ponds. Maintenance of the headquarters is done by a group of male and female members of the sect who reside there and who, at the time of the prophesied earthquake, numbered twenty-one persons. These people receive no salaries, although small allowances for personal expenses are given to young members who have no other income. A number of outside members spend weekends working without remuneration at the headquarters.

Ichigen-no-Miya claims a membership of 1500 persons, but, as is usual for claims of sect membership in Japan, the actual figure is undoubtedly much smaller, probably not exceeding several hundred people. About seventy outside members had taken refuge at the headquarters on June 18. Outside members who were unable to go to the headquarters were instructed by the prophet to proceed to certain other areas as temporary refuges, at which they were to await further instructions. It was not possible to observe the behavior of these people and, for this reason, they are omitted from further consideration here.

The men and women residing at the headquarters lead a simple, ascetic life that includes much physical labor. According to their own statements, which appear to be reliable, they work from 7:30 A.M. to 6:00 P.M. maintaining the grounds and buildings and raising vegetables for their own consumption. As a group, these devout members may be identified socially as coming from the lower or lower middle classes of the nation. Their membership in the sect is a matter of commitment by self-choice and not a means of providing a livelihood, which, for these industrious people, could be gained more easily and richly elsewhere. One member formerly owned and operated a retail store, which he sold in order to move to the sect headquarters, and two young men are college graduates, presumably well qualified for gainful employment. Meals are very simple, consisting of agricultural products raised by the members and purchased staples limited principally to rice and inexpensive kinds of fish.

Regular ceremonies of the sect consist of one rite that is conducted daily from 7:30 to 8:30 P.M. in the shrine. During this rite, called *jorei*, "purification of the spirit [of the members]," the prophet addresses the convocation by talking in tongues, which he later "translates." These glossolalic utterances, which appear to consist of meaningless syllables with a rhythmic pattern, are referred to by the prophet as *gengo*, "the original language." According to him, gengo is a "cosmic" language spoken by highly civilized beings from outer space who have fallen onto the Earth.

The Prophecy

The prophet states that he first started to receive warnings twenty years earlier of a disaster that would occur in 1974. On January 1, 1974, the holy spirit informed him that the disaster would be an earthquake and that it would happen in June 1974. However, the spirit would not at that time reveal the day or hour, because doing so "would cause people to worry excessively." On June 10 the holy spirit informed the prophet that the quake would occur "before or after" 8:00 A.M. on June 18. On June 13, following instructions of the prophet, sect members at the headquarters began to construct shelters for refugees from the more densely settled urban areas of Osaka. The digging of a well to provide drinking water also began on this date, after the prophet had determined its site by dowsing.

Distribution of the warning leaflets began on the same day and was done mostly by members of the headquarters group, several of whom were arrested for disturbing the peace and were briefly taken into police custody. On June 16 refugees began to arrive at the headquarters. Some were family groups with children, of whom those of school age, of course, were committing truancy. Several tons of rice and a truckload of medications for later dispensation to the needy were purchased by the headquarters group. One refugee stated that he had sold his furniture because it would be destroyed by the earthquake. Another stated that he had used over ¥200,000 (about $700) of his own money to purchase food for the refugees.

The Day of the Prophesied Earthquake

Following their prophet's instructions, the ninety persons at the headquarters ate an early, hurried breakfast on June 18 and gathered at 7:00 A.M. at a square near the shrine. There they heard on a transistor radio a telephone interview with their leader then being conducted by a newscaster at an Osaka radio station. In response to a question of what he would do if his prophecy failed, the prophet replied, "I shall take the blame and dissolve the sect." When the interview ended, the prophet emerged from the shrine and joined the group in the square. As if in preparation for many days of unsettled life, he wore boots and trousers instead of his usual clothing of traditional Japanese style. The prophet addressed the assembled people, urging them to be unselfish and to aid as many people as the facilities at the headquarters could accommodate. After his address ended, over forty people remained in the square and the others went to places on the sect grounds which the prophet had designated as being safe. Before 8:00 the prophet left the group and entered the shrine, going in alone and closing the door behind him.

The catastrophic hour of 8:00 A.M. arrived, and nothing happened. The assembled people remained calm and continued to wait. At about 8:30 a number of people went to the foot of the steps leading to the shrine and began anxiously to look upward, as if expecting some action by the prophet. At 8:50 several men shouted, "We are saved!," and ran to the shrine entrance. Only a few gained admittance. At 9:15 an ambulance arrived, and the men who had entered the shrine soon carried the prophet to the vehicle on a stretcher. The information spread that the prophet had attempted to kill himself by cutting his abdomen with a knife. At 9:30 two police cars arrived and the police began their investigations.

Soon thereafter about ten refugees left, stating that they had work to do elsewhere. The thirty people remaining in the square seemed to expect an explanation of the reason why no earthquake had occurred and speculated among themselves. One young woman stated that the earthquake might come on the following day because the prophet had said the time would be "before or after" 8:00 A.M. Whether the prophet was dead or alive was unclear. All of the males in the headquarters group had by this time gone by car to the hospital. Around 11:00, females residing at the headquarters returned to their routines of feeding the caged birds and other tasks, including the preparation of lunch. After lunch, the remaining outside members began to leave, and nearly all had gone by 5:00 P.M. The headquarters group remained.

The Aftermath

While the prophet was recovering under medical care, some information about attitudes of the sect members was provided by reports in newspapers and weekly magazines of interviews of three men of the headquarters group. Ignoring the fact that the attempted suicide occurred about thirty minutes after the predicted time of the quake, one man surmised that the prophet had prevented the earthquake by offering himself in sacrifice. Another man reasoned that their leader attempted to commit suicide because he had failed as a prophet and that the failure was caused by his misunderstanding the message in the original language. The third interviewee held that the suicidal attempt was an expression of gratitude to the holy spirit for withholding the earthquake.

The prophet returned to the sect headquarters on July 18 and resumed conduct of the sect ritual on July 19. His first performance again included a glossolalic message, which he translated. The message was a reproach. The prophet stated that all members had improperly wished for at least a moment that the earthquake in fact had occurred. He stated also that the warning of the earthquake was a matter of the supernatural world, of which mortal beings, as mere puppets, have little knowledge and no control.

The prophet continued to perform his old role in the weeks that followed and he, as well as sect members, speculated about the reasons for the failure of the prophecy. A letter from the headquarters of a small sect in Tokyo asked if the problem did not lie in the distinction between the Gregorian calendar, the official calendar of modern Japan, and the ancient lunar calendar. June 18 by the lunar calendar corresponds with August 5 by the modern calendar. On August 4 an earthquake did occur in Japan, in a region about 300 miles from Osaka. The group at the headquarters then became uneasy, speculating that the earthquake might strike Osaka on the following day, August 5, but the prophet gave them no instructions to prepare for such an event and, accordingly, they did nothing. When the quake failed to materialize on August 5, they reasoned that it had already been prevented by the prophet's sacrificial attempt to commit suicide.

On August 6, the fifteenth anniversary of the date when the prophet first came to the site of the present sect headquarters, a special ceremony was called by him. Members were notified well beforehand that he would at this time make an important announcement. About 180 members gathered at the appointed time in the small shrine and on its steps. The prophet announced he had decided to dissolve the sect, because he had so committed himself if his prophecy failed. He explained that this course of action would make him and his sect seem reasonable to other people. Referring to his attempted suicide, he stated that he had already vindicated himself before his holy spirit and that his life had been given to that holy spirit. He informed his audience that he would sell his own property in order to return to them the money which they had donated for sect use, but that the return might be as little as one-fourth of the amount given. He stated that he was attempting to persuade the prefectural government of Osaka and a private business firm to accept the headquarters property as a gift and to maintain it as a public park. He stated also that he would find employment for the members at the headquarters. Concluding his address, he said that he would in the future practice palm-reading in the streets, and thereby he would continue to help people. All members of the audience appeared to remain calm. Those who lived elsewhere soon left, but the headquarters group remained. In the days that followed, the customary rites were conducted daily by the prophet. On October 15, the time of Sanada's last visit to the headquarters, it appeared that the offer to donate the property for public use would soon be accepted. Four of the twenty-one headquarters members had recently left, but the remaining seventeen gave no indication of doing so. Rather, their zeal appeared to have increased, and they seriously discussed various plans for the future that would keep them under the guidance of the prophet.

Discussion

Basing their interpretation on historical data on several U.S. doomsday cults and one modern case study, Festinger and his colleagues (1956) held that among these sects failed prophecies led to deeper faith and more enthusiastic proselytizing by sect members. In a later case study, Hardyck and Braden (1962) similarly report greater faith in the sect beliefs after the prophecy failed to materialize, but no signs of fervor in proselytizing. Festinger and his colleagues (1956: 4) formulated five conditions under which their interpretive theory of cognitive dissonance is applicable. These are presented in abbreviated form:

1. A belief must be held with deep conviction, and it must have some relevance to action, that is, to what the believer does or how he behaves.
2. The person holding the belief must have committed himself to it; that is, for the sake of his belief he must have taken some important action that is difficult to undo.
3. The belief must be sufficiently specific and sufficiently concerned with the real world so that events may unequivocally refute the belief.
4. Such undeniable disconfirmatory evidence must occur and must be recognized by the individual holding the belief.
5. The individual believer must have social support.

In other words, if someone holds a firm belief, he cannot discard it despite the failure of a prophecy based on it, although he cannot ignore the fact that his belief has been disconfirmed. He cannot resolve this dissonance himself, and he must seek a cognition that is consonant with his faith. Under such circumstances, the most convenient cognition conceivable for him is the fact that others share his belief. On this basis, he tries to make his belief known to others and to convert them to it.

The fact that the Japanese sect was dissolved by its leader does not eliminate it from consideration in connection with the American cases. Rather, it presents for consideration an alternate course of action, a subject which we shall later consider. It is useful first, however, to examine the Japanese example in the same manner as the American cases were considered; that is, to examine the reactions of the prophet's followers until the time when the forthcoming dissolution of the sect was announced by him.

A review of the preceding descriptive data on the Japanese sect shows that the first four conditions listed above were met by the headquarters group. These people gave clear evidence of deep conviction that had relevance to their own actions and of commitment to their belief. This evidence includes ascetic, self-sacrificing devotion to the prophet and to his instructions. The beliefs of this group clearly concerned mortal existence; earthquakes, hunger, thirst, injury, illness, and death are all events of the "real world," as are unemployment, humanitarianism, and aesthetic appreciation of flower gardens. The followers did indeed commit themselves to their belief in ways that are difficult to undo, as is evident in such behavior as working at the headquarters without salary, distributing the leaflets, and making preparations for the earthquake that included the expenditure of much money and physical effort. The prophecy in question was highly specific, as were the instructions contained in the leaflets. Similarly, there is no doubt of the existence of "disconfirmatory evidence"; no earthquake occurred, a matter that was clearly recognized by everyone.

Circumstances pertaining to the fifth condition, that the individual follower must have social support, are somewhat less clear. If the later probable dissolution of the sect is set aside from consideration, however, this condition was also met by the headquarters group. These men and women continued to live at the headquarters and to perform their customary roles. They sought among themselves explanations consonant with their faith and were successful in finding them. Their explanations of the failure of the prophecy to materialize expressed no lack of faith in the reliability of their prophet. The newspaper interviews of the followers were in this respect mutually supportive, presenting different surmises but a single line of thought. As people who had long lived in close association, they had previously given mutual social support and they continued to do so. Although the sect members showed no signs of increased zeal in proselytizing, their roles as headquarters workers had never called for or allowed much active proselytizing. Moreover, their prophet was hospitalized much of this time so that they lacked leadership.

Hardyck and Braden (1962) report that although members of the American group they had observed clung to their belief when the prophecy failed and even seemed to increase in their fervor, the members of this sect similarly did not attempt to proselytize for their belief. This difference from the findings of Festinger and his colleagues, they suggest, is attributable to two factors: the degree of social support available within the group, and the amount of ridicule the group received. These suggestions appear to be worthwhile. The anticlimax after the Japanese prophecy failed to materialize was perhaps particularly strong because of the great publicity the newspapers and other news media had given to it, publicity that the nation as a whole generally looked on as more or less amusing accounts of the bizarre. However, the headquarters members were apparently able to withstand this ridicule, a matter which will be discussed later.

The U.S. studies referred to here centered their attention on the followers rather than on the prophets, a procedure that seems reasonable since the self-faith of the U.S. prophets appears to have been unshaken by the unfulfilled prophecies. The reaction of the Japanese prophet differed from that of his followers, however, and he merits separate consideration. The first four of the five conditions described earlier appear to apply more strongly to him than to his followers. Suicide is certainly an irreversible act, for example. The circumstances of the prophet with reference to the fifth condition differed from those of his followers, and his response also differed. He had assumed responsibility for his actions and he had committed himself to dissolve the sect if the earthquake did not occur. His attempt to commit suicide might be regarded as the result of loss of faith in himself, a matter to which the views of Hardyck and Braden concerning social support and ridicule seem relevant.

If Japanese values are considered, the leader's suicidal act seems to be an attempt to vindicate impugned honor, which, in turn, relates to social support and ridicule as well as to internalized sanctions. The truly devoted followers of the prophet had always been few and they stood far below him in social prestige.

Perhaps especially in Japan, where social hierarchy is more pronounced than in the United States, the status of the social supporters of the prophet—that is, their inferior status as followers—lacked the necessary force to provide assurance. Such support might more effectively be given by peers and superiors, but none existed. The question of the effects of ridicule on the prophet are closely related, of course, to the matter of social support. The prophet was thoroughly aware of the publicity given to him by the news media, but the extent to which he might have regarded this publicity as ridicule is uncertain. It is certain, however, that he regarded himself as having failed, and it is equally certain that he failed to give social support to his followers, a matter of the utmost importance for the continuance of their faith. Nevertheless, it is noteworthy that the prophet's announcement of dissolution of the group ended with a statement expressing faith in himself, that is, his declared intention to use his gifts in another way by practicing palmistry.

The dissolution of the Japanese sect seemingly puts an end to all discussion of continued and increasingly zealous belief of the entire sect. This denouement does not cast, however, any serious doubt on the validity of the interpretations offered for the U.S. cases. In our opinion, the ideas of the U.S. researchers continue to have merit and to have heuristic value. The Japanese circumstances closely resemble in many ways those reported for the U.S. cases. The Japanese example differs, of course, in its final events, and thereby presents an instance of an alternative outcome. At the same time it points to a group of conditioning variables which the American researchers have not considered.

Although neither of the earlier U.S. studies explicitly so stated, they implied that their interpretations are applicable in their entirety to other and perhaps to all societies. The Japanese case clearly points to the influence of a complex group of cultural factors unique to Japan in their particular form which, for the sake of brevity, we shall call social values. If certain of these values and the customs associated with them are examined, the Japanese case becomes more readily comprehensible. An intricate web of several such values appears to be involved. These include the importance in Japan of hierarchic social status, the deeply internalized value placed on meeting commitments, the importance of ridicule as a social sanction, and the strong affective dependency of the Japanese on other members of their society (see De Vos 1973; Norbeck and Parman 1970). Among the faithful at the headquarters, for example, it appears that ridicule was ineffective in putting an end to their faith in the prophet. Faith involves commitment and honor, and among these sect members, it also involved social ties with great emotional importance which are not easily or willingly broken. Attitudes and values surrounding suicide in Japan seem particularly relevant. Suicide is a traditional and honorable way to solve otherwise insoluble dilemmas involving commitment and honor. Although uncommon today in this context, it has an honored modern counterpart in the custom—in politics, industry, civil service, and elsewhere—of leaders resigning or committing occupational suicide when matters under their jurisdiction go irremediably awry. Unsuccessful in his attempt to vindicate himself by traditional suicide, Prophet Motoki followed a second and similar course of resigning, a course that was perhaps equally appropriate for a traditionally-minded man who had formerly been a businessman.

The preceding discussion may be summarized briefly in a way that calls attention to the suggestions, sometimes implicit, that it contains. The Japanese circumstances are essentially congruent with those described by Hardyck and Braden, except in their final events. As modified by Hardyck and Braden, the theory of cognitive dissonance presented by Festinger and his colleagues seems generally applicable until the time of the announcement of the dissolution of the sect and perhaps for a longer period. To gain a fuller understanding of the events surrounding prophecies that fail, however, and to understand alternative reactions such as those reported here, factors which the U.S. researchers have not considered must be taken into account. As a means of avoiding ethnocentrism, it is urged that comparative study be undertaken insofar as possible and that attention be given in each society to cultural factors of the kinds that we have called social values which might condition the human behavior in question. We also recommend that attention be given to the extent to which the circumstances of the prophet as well as those of his followers meet the conditions on which the interpretation of cognitive dissonance is based.

REFERENCES

De Vos, G. A. 1973. *Socialization for Achievement.* Berkeley: University of California Press.

Festinger, L., H. W. Riecken, and S. Schachter. 1956. *When Prophecy Fails.* Minneapolis: University of Minnesota Press.

Hardyck, J. A., and M. Braden. 1962. "Prophecy Fails Again: A Report of a Failure to Replicate." *Journal of Abnormal and Social Psychology* 65, 2:136–141.

Norbeck, E., and S. Parman, eds. 1970. *The Study of Japan in the Behavioral Sciences.* Rice University Studies 56, 4 (whole number).

When the Bombs Drop
Reactions to Disconfirmed Prophecy in a Millennial Sect

Robert W. Balch, Gwen Farnsworth, and Sue Wilkins

On April 29, 1980, members of a small Baha'i sect[1] entered fallout shelters to await a thermonuclear war that would fulfill the prophecies of Revelation. In exactly one hour they believed one-third of mankind would perish in the holocaust. During the next twenty years they expected the world to be further ravaged by starvation and disease, worldwide revolution, and natural disasters caused by the Earth's shifting crust. Finally, in the year 2000, God's Kingdom would be established on Earth and a thousand years of peace would ensue.

About one month before April 29 we began a participant-observer study of this group. Although the project has become an ongoing affair, our original intent was to replicate the classic study by Festinger, Riecken, and Schachter (1956) of the reactions to disconfirmed prophecy. Festinger and his colleagues infiltrated a millennial flying saucer cult to test the hypothesis that disconfirmation of the leader's prophecy would result in increased conviction and heightened efforts to recruit new believers. They argued that members of apocalyptic groups experience severe cognitive dissonance when their prophecies fail. If believers have made strong commitments based on their faith, they cannot easily abandon their beliefs. Instead, their only recourse is to seek consonant information, including the social support of fellow believers, and that should entail increased efforts to persuade nonbelievers to accept the faith.

Festinger and his colleagues tested their hypothesis by observing the reactions of a millennial cult (the Lake City group) when the expected catastrophe failed to happen. The group's leader, a woman they called Marian Keech, had received several messages from a space being named Sananda warning her about a devastating flood that would inundate much of North America on a particular date. Even after her prophecy failed, the most committed members maintained their beliefs. Mrs. Keech claimed that the world had been saved by their faith, and she pointed to earthquakes in other parts of the globe to prove that disastrous upheavals had really occurred, although not in the manner she expected. She also made several more predictions in rapid succession, all disconfirmed, in what appeared to be a desperate attempt to save face. Most important, she and her followers began to proselytize almost immediately—a finding that is especially remarkable in view of the fact that Mrs. Keech had been relatively unconcerned about spreading Sananda's messages prior to the disconfirmation.

However, a subsequent study of a millennial Christian sect called the Church of the True Word failed to support the proselytizing hypothesis. Hardyck and Braden (1962) found that church members did not attempt to win new converts after an expected nuclear attack failed to occur. Out of 135 believers who entered fallout shelters, 103 remained underground for forty-two days until Mrs. Shepard, their prophet, told them to come out. Testimonies and follow-up interviews indicated that they remained firm in their beliefs. Members claimed that God had merely been testing their faith and using them as an example to warn an apathetic world. Mrs. Shepard's followers continued to believe that war was imminent, but they made no efforts to proselytize after they emerged from their shelters, even though they had numerous opportunities to do so.

Consequently, the evidence concerning the urge to proselytize after prophetic failure is contradictory. Hardyck and Braden suggested that Festinger and his colleagues failed to specify all the conditions under which proselytizing will occur. Here we attempt to build on their conclusion by arguing that reactions to disconfirmed prophecy depend on the social context in which disconfirmation is experienced. Because adaptation to prophetic failure is a collective process (Zygmunt 1972), any theory that neglects the role of interactional variables will have limited value in explaining how millennial movements react when their prophecies fail.

Data Collection

Unfortunately, most accounts of millennial movements do not provide much information about group dynamics at the moment of disconfirmation. The best way to get this information is to be on the scene when prophetic failure occurs, but outsiders rarely have that opportunity. They must rely on after-the-fact interviews, as Hardyck and Braden did, or historical records, which are often unreliable or incomplete. Like Festinger and his colleagues, however, we were lucky enough to witness firsthand the moment of truth.

We first heard about the apocalyptic sect known as the Baha'is Under the Provisions of the Covenant (BUPC) about two months before the impending cataclysm.[2] The little-known sect, based in Missoula, Montana, was catapulted into the headlines when the local paper exposed a nuclear preparedness group as a BUPC organization. Known as SAFE, standing for Shelter and Fall-Out Education, the group had been organized by the BUPC to upgrade Missoula's fallout shelters and educate Missoulians about nuclear survival.

With the permission of the sect's leader, Dr. Leland Jensen (known as "Doc" to his followers), we began participating in all manner of BUPC activities. These included "feasts" held every nineteen days according to the Baha'i calendar, "firesides" where the BUPC leaders teach the faith to "prospective members," and "deepenings," intended to explore Baha'i writings in greater depth. In the hectic days before April 29, we spent long hours collating pages for Doc's latest manuscript (Jensen 1980) and helping members prepare their fallout shelters. When the fateful day finally arrived, we joined believers in three different underground shelters, and we returned on May 7 after Doc reset the date for the catastrophe. During the next six months we interviewed forty-one of Doc's followers, including believers in Wyoming, Colorado, and Arkansas. In addition to these formal contacts, we have spent a considerable amount of time with the BUPC in more casual settings.

A Closer Look at the Baha'is under the Provisions of the Covenant

Any discussion of the BUPC must begin with Doc, the jovial sixty-seven-year-old chiropractor who predicted the cataclysm for April 29. Once an internationally known Baha'i teacher, Doc was expelled from Baha'i faith in 1960 for aligning himself with a schismatic leader named Mason Remey. Believing that a catastrophic flood was about to inundate much of the United States, Mason urged his followers to move to high ground in the Rocky Mountains, and in 1964 Doc opened a chiropractic office in Missoula. Because of opposition within Mason's following stemming from a 1963 doctrinal dispute, Doc became discouraged with the human side of the faith and stopped teaching altogether shortly after moving to Montana.

In 1969 Doc was convicted of performing a "lewd and lascivious act" on a fifteen-year-old patient, and despite his claims of a frame-up, he was sentenced to twenty years in the state penitentiary. Not long after his arrival, Doc says he was visited in his cell by an angel who informed him of his spiritual identity. Drawing on a remarkable set of parallels between events in his life and certain biblical prophecies, Doc issued a proclamation in 1971 claiming to be Joshua, the high priest prophesied in Zechariah 3. According to Doc, Joshua is the return of Jesus who will establish the Kingdom after the holocaust. Eventually Doc claimed several other Biblical identities, including the Lamb and the Seventh Angel described in Revelation.

Once the angel lifted the veil from his eyes, Doc was able to comprehend the symbolism of the Scriptures. He began tying together diverse strands of biblical prophecy, Baha'i teachings, and pyramidology, a fascination dating from his childhood. All the evidence pointed to the same inescapable conclusion—that nuclear catastrophe was imminent. As early as 1971 Doc predicted that the war would begin in 1980, caused by a conflict between the superpowers over Middle East oil. After the four waves of destruction (Revelation 7:1) had cleansed the world of evil and apostasy, Doc believed that the remainder of mankind would embrace the BUPC faith, and peace and harmony would prevail for the next thousand years.

Shortly after his visitation, Doc began holding firesides for his fellow inmates. Twice a week, twenty to thirty people attended his meetings, and by the time he was paroled in 1973 Doc had recruited a small group of highly committed believers. Some of his converts became effective teachers in their own right. One of Doc's first recruits was largely responsible for establishing a branch of the faith in Sheridan, Wyoming, where about fifteen people eventually became followers.

After his release Doc began spreading his message outside the prison walls. In 1978 he took an extended trip throughout the Midwestern and Rocky Mountain states trying to convert many of Mason Remey's followers, and his efforts led to the establishment of small BUPC groups in Durango, Colorado, and Ft. Smith, Arkansas. It is impossible to say how many believers there were on the eve of April 29, 1980, but roughly 150 people in Montana, Wyoming, Colorado, and Arkansas made plans to enter fallout shelters "when the bombs dropped" (one of Doc's favorite expressions).[3]

Prior to April 29 the BUPC was a recruitment-oriented group whose members' lives revolved around teaching the faith. Teaching was expected, and Doc claimed that proselytizing would be rewarded with a high station in God's Kingdom. To that end, the BUPC organized the Communications Club, a group modeled after Toastmasters, to improve public speaking skills and compiled a "teacher's manual" explaining how to teach the faith to nonbelievers. Recruitment proceeded almost entirely through friendship networks and family ties (Stark and Bainbridge 1980). Persons interested in learning about the faith were invited to a series of firesides, usually held in a member's home, where they were systematically introduced to Doc's teachings as well as the basic principles of the Baha'i faith. Although we have no reliable figures, it appears that most of those who completed the fireside sequence became believers.

In 1979 Doc determined that the bombs would drop at precisely 5:55 P.M. Mountain Daylight Time. As the date approached, his followers stepped up their efforts to prepare for the holocaust. Their most ambitious undertaking was SAFE. Recognizing that the organization might be discredited if it became identified with a group of "religious fanatics," they preferred to keep its connection with Doc a secret. Under the auspices of SAFE, members taught classes on shelter management and radiological monitoring, and they printed thousands of leaflets explaining what to do in the event of a nuclear attack.

SAFE disbanded after it was exposed as a BUPC project, and because of lack of public support, its members abandoned their plans to improve the community's shelters. With the date less than two months away, even teaching the faith diminished as Doc's followers turned their energies to building and stocking their private shelters. There were eight in the Missoula area, including a "community shelter" for members who could not afford their own. The major focus of group activity during the last month was the print shop. Doc owned a small printing business that printed commercial work by day and Doc's manuscripts by night. Day after day the BUPC assembled pages until 2:00 or 3:00 A.M. in a frantic effort to publish 10,000 copies of Doc's latest book before April 29.

Meanwhile, the public was at least vaguely aware that the Baha'is were preparing for Armageddon. Doc received considerable local newspaper and TV coverage, and the Associated Press carried several stories about his predictions. Although members occasionally complained about media bias, they generally believed the coverage was fair. In Missoula there was some ridicule in the form of jokes on the radio, impromptu doomsday parties, and a few crank calls to believers, but overall the atmosphere could best be described as indifferent.

Finally, on the night of April 28, about eighty believers met at a potluck feast in Missoula for the last time before Armageddon. They joked and laughed and enjoyed their meal as if nothing unusual were about to happen. Were it not for the speeches that followed, an outsider would not have guessed that these cheerful people were expecting nuclear warheads to strike within twenty-four hours. The festivities concluded around 10:00 P.M., and then the faithful dispersed to their respective shelters to await the missiles that would usher in the New Age.

Suitability of the Baha'i Sect for Testing the Festinger Hypothesis

Festinger and his colleagues specified five conditions that must be met before prophetic failure can be expected to be followed by increased conviction and vigorous proselytizing. According to the first, a belief must be held with deep conviction and it must have some relevance for action. Although the BUPC included many fringe members who were skeptical about Doc's prediction, the vast majority took it very seriously. Only a few expressed doubts to any of us, and interviews with ex-members who left the group before April 29 confirm our impression that the level of belief was very high. Doc's prediction obviously had direct implications for their behavior. Even true believers would perish if they did not prepare for the holocaust, and the fact that they made extensive preparations is strong evidence that members expected the bombs to drop on April 29.

The second condition is closely tied to the first. Believers must make irreversible commitments based on their conviction. Doc was so confident that he staked the validity of all his teachings on the accuracy of his prediction. For example, in a small book entitled *The Most Mighty Document* (1979:61–62) he posed the following question:

> Does your religion (sect or denomination) tell you the "Day and the Hour" for the oncoming *thermo-nuclear holocaust* in which *a third of mankind are to be killed,* so that you can be 100 miles from a thermonuclear blast (Rev. 14:20)? If it doesn't it lacks Divine Guidance to save you. [Italics in original.]

There is no doubt that most believers made enormous commitments. They organized SAFE to alert the community to the dangers of radioactive fallout, and they built their own shelters at great expense, often running up huge bills which they had trouble paying after April 29. Virtually all of them attempted to persuade friends and relatives to accept the faith or at least take precautions. Some wrote to the local paper explaining their beliefs; a few wrote pamphlets about the faith, which Doc printed and distributed along with his own manuscripts. Many believers had moved to Missoula, in some cases from almost 2000 miles away, just to be near Doc when the war began.

The third condition is that the prediction must be sufficiently specific to be refuted unequivocally. By specifying that the bombs would drop at precisely 5:55 P.M. Mountain Daylight Time on April 29, 1980, Doc clearly left no room for hedging.

The fourth condition requires undeniable evidence that the predicted events did not occur. This, too, was quite clear. No bombs fell on April 29; Doc's followers were well aware that the day passed without incident.

Finally, there must be social support for the apocalyptic belief. Festinger and his colleagues added this provision because they felt that believers would be unable to withstand the devasting impact of disconfirmation if they did not have at least some degree of support from others. The BUPC met this condition as well. They were a close-knit group, bound by a single undisputed leader, a shared set of beliefs, family and friendship ties, and regular social interaction. The believers referred to themselves as "the friends" or "the community," and some compared themselves to an extended family, an analogy that we found quite appropriate. The sect constituted a relatively exclusive social world where close ties with nonbelievers were unusual.

In short, the BUPC met all five conditions specified by Festinger and his colleagues. How well, then, did their behavior following April 29 conform to the hypothesis that conviction and recruitment efforts would increase after disconfirmation?

Reactions to Disconfirmation

Contrary to the hypothesis, the failure of Doc's prediction did not strengthen the believers' convictions, nor did it produce an increase in proselytizing. In fact, just the opposite occurred. It took several months before some members would admit to us just how badly shaken they had been when the bombs did not drop on April 29.

Although reactions varied from shelter to shelter, most believers at first appeared relatively unconcerned, as if the 29th had not been an important event. Events in the community shelter provide a good example. The appointed time appeared to pass unnoticed, even though there had been a high degree of tension earlier in the day. Members continued to work on last-minute projects, but the atmosphere became increasingly subdued as 5:55 approached and passed without incident. Since the shelter door still was not securely in place, it was easy for believers to slip out quietly, and many took advantage of the opportunity. Those who remained said little. Around 8:30 P.M. a large group, including the senior author, went out for dinner at a nearby restaurant. No one seemed concerned about the possibility that Doc's prediction might have been off by a few hours. In fact, no one said anything about the bombs. Much of the meal was spent in silence broken only by occasional small talk. Back in the shelter they watched television or read quietly, saying almost nothing until 12:15 A.M., when the shelter manager casually asked a small group of believers what they thought about the unexpected turn of events. However, there was little discussion, and by 1:00 A.M. the lights were out and the shelter was completely silent.

The next few days were undoubtedly the most anomic the BUPC had ever experienced. The situation could best be described as an informational vacuum. Doc's followers were scattered over four states, and even in the Missoula area there were several shelters, three of them about thirty miles out of town. Members were even more widely dispersed than this implies because many stayed at home on the assumption that they would have about eight hours to seek shelter before the fallout arrived from West Coast target areas like Portland and Seattle. Although their shelters were equipped with CB radios, Doc had not bothered to make specific plans for keeping in contact with his followers, nor had he specified any particular length of time that members should remain underground. He merely assumed that they would need to stay there about two weeks. In Missoula some of the believers stayed for as long as three days, but most had come out by the evening of April 30. In the community shelter about two-thirds of those who had been there before 5:55 P.M. on the 29th had left by midnight.

Doc's first response to disconfirmation was to reset the time for 6:11 A.M. on May 7. Citing a passage in Revelation, he claimed the reason for the delay was "to give the peoples of the world a chance to hear the voice of their savior and be saved, or to condemn him and go into the fire." However, word of the new prediction circulated informally by word of mouth because Doc made no systematic effort to get the message out. In fact, the BUPC did not meet again as a group until May 16.

During this period group activities stopped almost completely. We never saw more than two or three people at the print shop, and work on the community shelter was halfhearted at best. The shelter committee met at least twice, but most of the enthusiastic volunteers we had observed before April 29 had disappeared. The group became decidedly less visible as believers withdrew into their private spaces, and observation suddenly became very difficult. Members who had once been extremely open to us cooled noticeably. For example, on the senior author's first visit to the community shelter after the 29th, most of the believers avoided eye contact, gave brief, businesslike replies to questions, and generally acted as if he were not there. Although Doc remained friendly and open, we generally felt like intruders.

By May 4 Doc had added a four-page addendum, printed in red, to his manuscript explaining what really happened on April 29. Citing numerous phone calls from reporters as far away as Australia, he claimed to have fulfilled the prophecy of Revelation 16:17–18 in which the Seventh Angel pours his "bowl of wrath" into the air. This, he said, refers to the worldwide media coverage his message received on April 29. In this addendum Doc also drew a parallel between himself and Noah, claiming that the Old Testament prophet had been similarly mistaken the first time he predicted the deluge. He cited the Koran, which says that Noah made three predictions before the flood finally occurred, and Matthew 24:37, which prophesies that "The coming of the Son of Man will repeat what happened in Noah's time." This explanation quickly became the most widely cited reason for the disconfirmation.

While the red pages were being added to the book, Doc received a phone call that provided him with still another explanation for April 29. The caller, a former naval officer, claimed that the Soviet Union had launched a spy satellite armed with nuclear warheads at the precise moment Doc had predicted.[4] Believing that the United States considered this an act of war, Doc announced that this action would set in motion a chain of events that would culminate in the holocaust, now set for May 7.

In spite of Doc's explanation, the BUPC appeared very demoralized. Most members we interviewed expressed skepticism about Doc's account of the spy satellite, although none would rule it out entirely, and we rarely heard anyone mention it in casual conversations. The parallel with Noah continued to be the most popular explanation for the disconfirmation, but some members who had once presented themselves to us as true believers now insisted that they had always been skeptical about Doc's prediction. Many of them cited Matthew 25:13, which says that no man knows the day or the hour when the Son of Man will return.

The May 7 date failed to rekindle enthusiasm. Most members told us they did not believe the bombs would drop then, and hardly anyone volunteered to work in the print shop or community shelter. Fewer people made plans to reenter a shelter, and the community shelter was almost empty when the date arrived. After May 7 also passed uneventfully, Doc tried one last time, suggesting that the bombs might drop on either May 22 or 23, but by then no one (to our knowledge) believed him, and even Doc later admitted to us that he had been "grasping at straws."

Within a few days after April 29 we began hearing comments about increasing quarrels and family problems in the group, including a brief fight between two members of the shelter committee. We witnessed several flare-ups ourselves. Most were triggered by minor incidents like borrowing a tool without permission, not returning something to its proper place, or leaving a shelter door open.

On May 16 the Missoula group finally gathered for its first feast since April 29. Normally the responsibility for feasts fell to Doc's followers, but this time no one volunteered, so Doc organized the gathering himself. Thirty-six believers attended, not counting Doc and his wife, and almost all of them were core members who had been extremely active in the faith prior to April 29. Superficially there was no evidence of the tension and demoralization we have described. The atmosphere was friendly and cheerful, and not once did we hear anyone mention

April 29 or the thermonuclear war, even though the third date was only one week away.

After a few prayers about persecution, suffering, and standing fast in the faith, Doc addressed the group. Besides explaining what happened on April 29, he criticized his followers for bickering and shirking their responsibilities. Using himself as an example of courage in the face of adversity, he exhorted them to remain true to the faith, but we failed to observe any signs of enthusiasm during his talk. Of particular significance were Doc's comments on proselytizing. As if even he did not think the bombs would drop on May 22 or 23, he declared that the war would not begin until the BUPC had recruited the 144,000 prophesied in Revelation. To help spread the message, he had brought a box of his books and urged members to distribute copies all over town. Doc was more forceful about proselytizing than we had ever seen him. In some of his strongest language he exhorted them to "Rise and shine! Establish the Kingdom! Teach as you never have before!"

Despite Doc's pep talk, no one took any books and hardly any teaching occurred throughout the summer. To our knowledge none of Doc's followers was ever approached by the press, and none of them sought media attention. Firesides were discontinued, and most believers kept a low profile in town. Usually they told us that they did not mention the faith to anyone unless someone asked them about it. Even Doc's efforts at spreading the faith were subdued. He issued a press release, composed a lengthy letter to the local paper which was never published, and answered questions from dozens of reporters who called after April 29; but otherwise he did nothing to get his message out to the world.

Attendance at feasts continued to drop over the summer until it hit an all-time low of eleven on September 27. The BUPC even missed two feast dates because, again, no one volunteered. There were three major reasons for the small attendance figures. First, some of the eighty who attended the April 29 feast were not committed believers, but friends and relatives who knew relatively little about Doc and his teachings. None of these people ever returned. Second, several members moved out of town, ostensibly to find work, but often to escape what they described as an oppressive atmosphere within the group, poisoned by internal conflict. Even though the BUPC strongly condemned the practice of backbiting, the amount of malicious gossip that circulated after April 29 was considerable. Doc himself contributed to the problem. For example, during a feast we attended, he openly questioned his followers about alleged drug use by three members who were rumored to have joined a rival sect. The third reason for poor attendance at feasts is what some members characterized as "burnout." They had worked feverishly and exhausted their resources preparing for the 29th, and now with the date postponed indefinitely, they preferred to return to some semblance of normalcy.

However, the poor turnout at feasts did not reflect widespread defection from the faith. For our purposes, defection can be defined as rejection of the formerly held belief that Doc is the "promised one" prophesied in Zechariah. Since some of those who made plans to enter a shelter did not even know much about Doc, they could hardly be classified as defectors when they failed to attend the feasts after April 29. If we restrict our attention to those who genuinely believed in Doc, two patterns become apparent. In the Missoula group we found only four members who could be classified as defectors six months after April 29. Three of them had been central figures, and their defection came as a shock to the rest of the group. While the defectors refused to reject the possibility that Doc might ultimately be right, each of them expressed serious reservations about his messianic claims. Otherwise, everyone in the Missoula group continued to profess belief in Doc, although many admitted that they occasionally entertained doubts. It appears that even those who failed to attend feasts over the summer continued to believe. On the other hand, almost all the believers outside Montana eventually rejected Doc's teachings. Everyone in the Arkansas group defected, as did most of the believers in Colorado and Wyoming. To our knowledge, only three members of the Colorado group remained steadfast by the end of the summer, and possibly two in Wyoming.[5]

During the summer we began to hear a new theme in both formal interviews and casual conversations with believers. The BUPC explained that the community had been so preoccupied with preparations for the war before April 29 that they had neglected the basic Baha'i teachings. They spoke less and less about Doc and his predictions and increasingly about the need to live their lives according to Baha'i principles. The best way to teach the faith, they claimed, was to become a living example for others. As one woman explained, "I think we all made a mistake. We got too caught up in the physical. We weren't ready for the war because spiritually none of us were strong enough." As early as May 14 we noticed that hardly anyone still used the familiar expression, "when the bombs drop." Although they all continued to believe that war was inevitable, their personal predictions varied from "within a year" to "the turn of the century."

We also detected a new fatalistic trend. Once obsessed with preparedness, many believers adopted the attitude that they would survive if God meant them to. They lost the community shelter when they could no longer pay the rent on the warehouse basement where it was located, and most of the group's private shelters, including Doc's, were at least partly dismantled. Only two BUPC in Wyoming remained active in Civil Defense work, but one of them claimed she no longer believed in Doc.

For his part, Doc continued to revise his explanations for the failure of the April 29 prediction, and in a lengthy new introduction to his book he declared that the seven-year Tribulation described in Revelation had commenced on the predicted date. Although he continued to insist that war was imminent, Doc claimed that the four winds of destruction (Revelation 7:1) were being held back until the 144,000 had been recruited. However, he set no new date for the catastrophe and refused to be pinned down even to an approximate time.

Despite Doc's concern for teaching the faith, he dismissed his followers' inactivity as a temporary period of "quiescence," and subsequent observations of the group in 1982 have borne out his assessment. Teaching has gradually resumed, and a few of Doc's new generation of believers have become energetic proselytizers. Nevertheless, the size of Doc's active following remains small, and the new members generally appear far more enthusiastic about teaching than do those who accepted the faith prior to April 29.

Discussion

Contrary to the theory advanced by Festinger and his colleagues, we found no evidence of increased conviction or proselytizing in the first six months after disconfirmation. Instead, there is considerable evidence that the BUPC's faith was badly shaken by the failure of Doc's prediction. Defection was widespread in the out-of-state groups; and even in Missoula, where virtually everyone continued to profess belief, members resisted Doc's efforts to resume proselytizing. This finding is especially devastating for the Festinger hypothesis because the Missoula group had a long tradition of active recruitment before April 29.

In an attempt to explain why members of the True Word sect did not proselytize after Mrs. Shepard's prophecy was disconfirmed, Hardyck and Braden suggested that two additional variables need to be considered in order to understand a group's reaction to prophetic failure. The first is the degree of public ridicule. According to Hardyck and Braden, the more a group is berated for its beliefs by outsiders, the more its members should feel the need to justify their position by proselytizing. Compared with the Lake City group, which was ridiculed unmercifully by pranksters and the local papers, the BUPC and True Word group had an easy time with nonbelievers. In both cases the press was generally fair and the public seemed indifferent to the episode.

The second variable is the level of social support enjoyed by believers. While Festinger and his colleagues argued that some degree of support is essential to prevent defection, Hardyck and Braden contended that the consensual validation provided by a strong community of believers could reduce dissonance to the point where it would be unnecessary to recruit additional members. That is, the urge to proselytize following disconfirmation should be greater in groups providing weak support than in groups that are highly supportive. Marian Keech's Lake City cult was a relatively new, loose-knit group that lacked a well-integrated set of beliefs. For awhile Mrs. Keech even had to vie for leadership with another member who claimed to receive messages from none other than the Creator Himself. By contrast, the True Word sect was a highly cohesive group with undisputed leaders and a coherent belief system, so it should have provided greater social support in the face of disconfirmation.

The BUPC case is less clear-cut but still consistent with Hardyck and Braden's hypothesis. Although the Missoula group had been relatively "tight" before April 29, it was quickly splintered by gossip and hostility, and most members withdrew from organized group activities. Is it accurate to say, then, that the BUPC enjoyed a high degree of mutual support? We think it is, but only with some clarification. First, despite the quarreling, most members had formed strong ties with other believers that were not affected by the group's internal disputes. Second, and perhaps more important, most believers had strong identities as BUPC that transcended their commitment to Doc's prediction. For them the faith offered both an all-embracing theodicy and an eminently desirable plan for living. While most had been attracted to the faith by its apocalyptic orientation, they subsequently acquired a firm grounding in a coherent body of Baha'i teachings dating back over 100 years. As a result, Doc's followers were able to cope with disconfirmation by shifting the focus of their lives away from Doc and placing greater emphasis on the fundamentals of the BUPC faith. Members of the Lake City group lacked this option because their belief in Mrs. Keech's prediction was the sole basis for their identity as members.

Thus Hardyck and Braden's *post facto* hypotheses appear to explain why both the True Word group and the BUPC failed to proselytize after disconfirmation. Yet there remains a puzzling anomaly in our finding. Doc's followers were severely demoralized by disconfirmation, while members of the other two groups proclaimed great victories for their faith. In both the Lake City and True Word groups, testimonies and follow-up interviews indicated that disconfirmation may have even strengthened belief.[6] What accounts for the difference? Comparison of the three groups suggests that the social context in which disconfirmation is experienced might be the critical factor determining the reaction to prophetic failure.

In the Festinger study, Mrs. Keech and most of her followers were together in the same house when disconfirmation occurred. Within hours after her prophecy failed, Mrs. Keech offered what became the group's "official" explanation. The world had been spared from destruction because of their faith. The next day members confronted numerous reporters and other visitors who came to the house to hear how Mrs. Keech would explain the failure of her prediction.

The situation was very similar in the True Word group. Although there were several shelters, each group had a strong leader and the shelters were connected by an intercom system that allowed the leaders to deal with questions, doubts, and dissent as soon as they appeared. We are not told how long it took Mrs. Shepard to rationalize the failure of her prophecy, but her explanation obviously could have been communicated to all of her followers very rapidly. When members of the True Word sect finally emerged from their shelters, they also confronted the press as a group, and the leaders held an impromptu news conference to explain why the attack had not occurred.

On the other hand, the BUPC experienced disconfirmation as a widely dispersed collection of small groups that lacked a well-thought-out plan for staying in contact with each other. Doc made no systematic effort to communicate with his followers immediately after disconfirmation, and his explanations—suggested and revised over a period of months—were disseminated haphazardly by word of mouth. Members never confronted representatives of the outside world as a group; even in Missoula they did not meet again for over two weeks after April 29.

What we have here are three groups with enormous material and psychological investments in millennial dreams which suddenly collapsed. It is hard to imagine a more ambiguous situation than the first uneasy moments after disconfirmation. It is a well-established principle that the more ambiguous the situation, the greater the demand for information in the form of rational explanations and guidelines for behavior, especially when the situation has important implications for action (Allport and Postman 1947; Festinger 1954; Shibutani 1966; Turner and Killian 1972). In his early theory of social comparison, Festinger (1954) postulated that there is a basic drive in human beings to evaluate their opinions and beliefs. When objective reality checks are unavailable, people tend to rely on others as points of reference. Since Doc was the undisputed spiritual authority for the BUPC, his followers naturally turned to him for guidance, but he did little to fill the void.

Doc's failure to act decisively and the group's lack of organized communication channels conspired to perpetuate the ambiguity caused by prophetic failure. Without the imminence of catastrophe to focus their lives, the goal of establishing God's Kingdom suddenly seemed remote and the means for achieving it unclear. Under those circumstances it is not surprising that the membership became demoralized. Small-group studies (for example, Cohen 1959; Raven and Rietsema 1957) have demonstrated that ambiguous goals and uncertainty about how to achieve them are related to personal insecurity, emotional tension, weakened attraction to the group, loss of motivation to accomplish collective tasks, and declining conformity to group norms. Compared to the Lake City and True Word groups, the BUPC experienced the ambiguity of disconfirmation for a longer period, and also appeared far more discouraged by the failure of their prophecy. Significantly, the Lake City believers who were most likely to defect were those who experienced disconfirmation alone. Much like Doc's followers, they had to endure the ambiguity of prophetic failure longer than the believers who were in the company of Mrs. Keech.

When Doc finally made a strong pitch for proselytizing seventeen days after April 29, his followers were already demoralized and a pattern of resignation, withdrawal, and internal conflict had been established, so it is easy to understand why they failed to respond. Mrs. Keech, on the other hand, immediately provided a clear example for the others by calling a reporter to explain what had happened. Given the susceptibility to social influence of people caught in highly ambiguous situations, it is possible that the leader's initial reaction to disconfirmation could determine whether or not the group engaged in proselytizing regardless of social support or public ridicule.

Not only did the BUPC endure more uncertainty, but they never had to confront the press as a group. This is a significant difference, because this kind of public meeting is likely to elicit a strong reaffirmation of faith. Members are, in effect, on stage in the company of fellow believers before an audience of skeptics, and in that situation they are likely to play the role of believer regardless of their real feelings (Balch 1980). By enacting the role, especially before reporters, press photographers, and TV cameramen, they are recommitting themselves to their beliefs. Except for Doc, none of the BUPC was ever induced to recommit himself or herself in this manner.

In conclusion, we believe the data discussed here suggest that reactions to disconfirmed prophecy depend on the nature of the social situation in which prophetic failure occurs. The example of the BUPC reveals the inadequacy of the psychological model used by Festinger and his colleagues. The theory of cognitive dissonance is simply unable to account for the complexities we observed in the wake of disconfirmation.

Although our conclusions are tentative, three hypotheses appear to be warranted by the data. First, the more central the prediction is to one's identity as a believer, the greater the need to convince others after disconfirmation. Second, members are most likely to suffer severe demoralization when their leader fails to provide a quick explanation for their predicament and take decisive steps to restore the group's integrity. Third, believers who are forced to explain the failure of their prediction to nonbelievers in public settings are more likely to profess strong convictions and attempt to persuade others after disconfirmation. As these hypotheses suggest, future research on disconfirmed prophecy should explore the nature of the believer's identity as a member, the reactions of the group's leadership to prophetic failure, and the kind of contact the group has with outsiders immediately after disconfirmation.

NOTES

1. In this article we follow the definitions of "cult" and "sect" offered by Stark and Bainbridge (1979). A sect has a prior tie with another religious organization, while a cult is a nonschismatic group that lies outside established religious traditions. A millennial movement may be either a cult or a sect. It is a religious group that promises imminent collective salvation for the faithful in an earthly paradise that will rise in the wake of apocalyptic destruction brought about by supernatural means (Cohn 1970:15).

2. This is the group's real name, and members refer to themselves as Baha'is despite the fact that the Baha'i faith disavows any connection with the sect and objects to its use of the Baha'i name. At the request of a spokesman for the Baha'i faith, we have used the abbreviation BUPC to prevent confusion. The Baha'i name has been used only in connection with the international Baha'i faith or Baha'i writings that are fundamental to both groups.

3. With few exceptions, Doc's followers are young working-class adults. Typical occupations in the Missoula group include gardener, mechanic, tree thinner, mill worker, bus driver, electrician, printer, and welder. Although a few members hold white-collar positions, only two in Missoula could be classified as professionals. Doc's wife, an elder in the faith, is also a chiropractor, and another woman is a speech therapist. Overall their living standards are quite modest. Most own relatively few material possessions and hardly any of them are homeowners. All but a few are in their twenties, and roughly a third of the active believers are married.

4. In fact, the local paper reported that the Soviets did launch a spy satellite on April 29, but we have been unable to verify the time of day. The caller claimed to have received his information "from the Holy Spirit."

5. Unfortunately, our knowledge of the out-of-state groups is based on just eight interviews. While we have no doubts about the overall direction of the results in these groups, the exact numbers are open to question.

6. We are not entirely convinced by Hardyck and Braden's data. Rather than observing the True Word group directly, they relied entirely on after-the-fact interviews, which are highly subject to retrospective interpretation and social desirability effects. Members of deviant religious groups often misrepresent their true feelings to outsiders (e.g., Balch 1980), and without built-in validity checks, especially direct observation, these distortions can easily pass unnoticed. In our study of the BUPC we found numerous instances where members' recollections of their reactions to disconfirmation did not jibe with our observations or the reports of others. Unfortunately, there is no evidence that Hardyck and Braden attempted to verify the accuracy of their findings.

REFERENCES

Allport, G. W., and L. Postman. 1947. *The Psychology of Rumor.* New York: Henry Holt.

Balch, R. W. 1980. "Looking Behind the Scenes in a Religious Cult: Implications for the Study of Conversion." *Sociological Analysis* 41:137–143.

Cohen, A. R. 1959. "Situational Structure, Self-Esteem, and Threat-Oriented Reactions to Power," in *Studies in Social Power,* edited by D. Cartwright. Ann Arbor: Institute for Social Research, University of Michigan.

Cohn, N. 1970. *The Pursuit of the Millennium.* New York: Oxford University Press.

Festinger, L. 1954. "A Theory of Social Comparison Processes." *Human Relations* 5: 117–140.

Festinger, L., H. W. Riecken, and S. Schachter. 1956. *When Prophecy Fails.* Minneapolis: University of Minnesota Press.

Hardyck, J. A., and M. Braden. 1962. "Prophecy Fails Again." *Journal of Abnormal and Social Psychology* 65:136–141.

Jensen, L. 1979. *The Most Mighty Document.* Private printing, available from Box 4003, Missoula, MT, 59806.

———. 1980. *The Seventh Angel Sounded: Jeane Dixon Was Right.* Private printing: Box 4003, Missoula, MT, 59806.

Raven, B. H., and J. Rietsema. 1957. "The Effects of Varied Clarity of Group Goal and Group Path upon the Individual and His Relation to His Group." *Human Relations* 10: 29–45.

Shibutani, T. 1966. *Improvised News: A Sociological Study of Rumor.* Indianapolis: Bobbs-Merrill.

Stark, R., and W. S. Bainbridge. 1979. "Of Churches, Sects, and Cults: Preliminary Concepts for a Theory of Religious Movements." *Journal for the Scientific Study of Religion* 18: 117–133.

———. 1980. " 'Networks of Faith': Interpersonal Bonds and Recruitment to Cults and Sects." *American Journal of Sociology* 85: 1376–1395.

Turner, R. N., and L. M. Killian. 1972. *Collective Behavior.* Englewood Cliffs, NJ: Prentice-Hall.

Zygmunt, J. F. 1972. "When Prophecies Fail: A Theoretical Perspective on the Comparative Evidence." *American Behavioral Scientist* 16:245–268.

Spiritualization and Reaffirmation
What Really Happens when Prophecy Fails

J. Gordon Melton

Sori Sori—there shall be greater winds and fires shall rage and floods shall be as raging torrents and they shall be as ones swept before them—give unto them this warning that they be prepared.

While we are about it let it be known that there shall come no harm unto Mine Servants which obey Mine Will.   —Mrs. Keech, 1985

Characteristically, millennial religious groups possess a deep conviction of being in touch with cosmic history. Within that cosmic history they have attained a status as key individuals in the flow of human history. They view that history as either reaching its culmination or, at the very least, taking a decisive turn in the immediate future. Typically such groups may develop an apocalyptic worldview and see the world progressively disintegrating with no hope for salvation. As the elect and faithful remnant, they will survive and transcend the situation by being taken from it by a transhistorical force. In popular Protestant fundamentalism, Jesus will come to "rapture" his saints before the terrible Battle of Armegeddon.

Within a scheme of cosmic history, millennialists are tempted to write future history as if it were in the past. Millennialists have frequently sketched pictures of the future course of human events based upon their understanding of the ultimate goals of universal forces. Within American millennialism such schemes have been constructed through the elaborate manipulation of Biblical chronology and have imposed upon history an element of numerical symmetry based upon the completion of thousand-year cycles (thus the label millennial) or the repetition of previous eras of history.

Once a cosmic scheme is established, many millennial groups go further than merely predicting the future. They offer, as part of their claim to veracity, the accuracy with which they can have prior knowledge of particular future events. However, once groups commit themselves to a specific and definite prophecy, they run the risk that the prophecy will not come true. The failure of predicted events to occur within the expected timetable of the group creates a major problem, a problem threatening the very life of the group itself. How groups handle that problem illuminates some basic religious dynamics.

When Prophecy Fails

The fact that millennial groups hold a worldview quite at variance, at least on matters of eschatology, with that of their surrounding, dominant cultures, has made them one of several types of religious groups which have been of interest to social scientists and religious historians. Questions of how such a different and seemingly fragile belief system is created and sustained over a period of time, especially in the face of social antagonism and the events surrounding a disconfirmation of a prophecy, offer the possibility of providing a variety of new insights into human religious interaction.

This article examines one small aspect of the life of millennial groups: their response to the failure of prophecy. It derives from the examination of reports of numerous examples in the life of American religious groups (though the specific event may have occurred in another country), in which common patterns of adaptation to failed prophecy in groups with widely varying theologies were isolated. These patterns reported by observers in older groups are easily transposed into examples of behavior for which researchers might look in future research on similar groups.

The most famous study of the problem created by "failed" prophecy within a religious group, *When Prophecy Fails* by Leon Festinger, Henry W. Riecken, and Stanley Schachter, examined various millennial groups throughout history and surveyed in depth one small millennial group, led by an individual identified only by the pseudonym Mrs. Keech, to see how behavior was affected by the non-occurrence of predicted events.[1] The study concluded that believers rarely followed the "logical" course of action when faced with the failure of a prophecy (that is, to discard their belief system as inadequate). Instead, they attempted to reduce the dissonance created by the failure with intensified efforts at proselytization. The survey summarized their thinking: "If more people can be persuaded that the system of belief is correct, then clearly, it must, after all, be correct."[2]

The main thesis of the *Prophecy* study has retained strong support among social scientists, for some reason, despite the failure of several attempts over the last three decades by other scholars to replicate the study and thus confirm its findings.[3] They failed because of serious conceptual inadequacies in the study which infringe on the ability of its central theses to explain the behavior of millennial groups in the face of the non-occurrence of predicted events. For example, the thesis of the study hinges upon a number of errors in the historical section, not the least important being its assertion that after the Great Disappointment of 1844, William "Miller's followers gave up their beliefs and the movement quickly disintegrated in dissention, controversy and discord. By spring of 1845 it had virtually disappeared."[4] The several million present-day Millerites were not informed of this fact. The failure of other observers to replicate the finding of the study, coupled with errors in the reporting of the historical examples cited, also suggests that many of the phenomena observed may have been idiosyncratic to that group and peculiar to that moment in time, and therefore of little relevance in understanding millennial groups or the general failure of prophecy.

The more significant problems of the study derive from two basic conceptual errors. First, *Prophecy* approaches millennial groups from the position that "Typically, millennial or messianic movements are organized around the prediction of some future events." Such is rarely, if ever, the case. Millennial movements must possess a comprehensive thought-world, such as fundamentalist Christianity or, as was the case with Mrs. Keech, the elaborate occult cosmology underlying belief in contact with extraterrestrial superbeings. The movement must also develop a group life within which ritual can be performed and individual interaction occur. Though one or more prophecies may be important to a group, they will be set within a complex set of beliefs and interpersonal relationships. They may serve as one of several important sources determining group activity, but the prediction is only one support device for the group, not the essential rafter.

The belief that prophecy is the organizing or determining principle for millennial groups is common among media representatives, nonmillennial religious rivals, and scholars. In their eagerness to isolate what they see as a decisive or interesting fact, they ignore or pay only passing attention to the larger belief structure of the group and the role that structure plays in the life of believers. Unfulfilled millennial expectations failed to invalidate Apostolic Christianity, which gradually reinterpreted the apocalyptic elements of its emerging theology; similarly, unrealized expectations failed to invalidate the faith of other groups.

Understanding that millennial groups are not organized around a single or single set of prophecies makes a significant difference in one's observation of them. If a prediction is the organizing principle of a group, its failure logically would be fatal to the group. But observation does not suggest that groups generally disintegrate after an error of prediction. If a prediction comes within a context of broad belief and group interaction, then its nonfulfillment provides a test for the system and for the personal ties previously built within the group. Times of testing tend to strengthen, not destroy, religious groups.

Second, the 1964 study, lacking a broad view of millennial groups, fails to understand that *within religious groups, prophecy seldom fails*. Within Christian groups, particularly, failure could be devastating since God's integrity is at issue. If the prophet's words do not come true, then the prophecy was not of God, and the prophet spoke falsely (Deut. 18:21–22). Religious groups, unlike the psychics in the weekly tabloids, are not in the prediction business. Instead of trying to score a high percentage of accuracy, they try to discern cosmic truths which they conceive in very tangible terms consistent with their perceived closeness to spiritual reality. For the "outsider" who does not share the total belief system and/or participate in the group life, the specific prophecy is often the only item of concern, but members perceive a broader perspective.

An outsider (or peripheral member) may view the failure of a major predicted event to occur as a sign of the obvious inadequacy of the group itself. However, the outsider had already decided that the group's worldview was wrong, which is why s/he is an outsider. The peripheral member who is still trying to decide upon the validity of the group's beliefs is still in the process of establishing strong social ties with other members. Among the committed believers, the failure of the prophecy to occur establishes a situation of dissonance, a situation in which the validity of the belief system which one has accepted is contradicted by the strong feelings of dejection and disappointment of the moment. The event challenges faith and threatens social ties within the group.

Confronted with an event that creates a high level of dissonance, one must dispel that dissonance. The nonbeliever, the person who has already concluded that the group's religion is personally inadequate, sees one logical course: abandon the group and its worldview. The believer, on the other hand, possesses a strong motivation to resolve the dissonance and so works with group members to provide various alternatives for bridging the gap between belief and reality.

In the face of dissonance, believers are able to rely upon the broader context of faith, on the unfalsifiable beliefs out of which religious thought-worlds are constructed. Within that context, believers can engage in a reaffirmation of basic faith and make a reappraisal of their predicament. For Christian bodies, such a reaffirmation may include focusing upon God's sovereignty and control of the course of history. At that moment obvious theological truths, such as human fallibility at understanding God's plan and revelation, can take on a new clarity. The non-occurrence of a predicted event provides a time to discover human limitation. Groups also search for means to reaffirm group life. They will gather for verbal affirmation and ritual activity. They may sing familiar hymns, exhort each other with admonitions to stand firm in the faith, and look to their leader(s) for guidance.

In a more satisfying but less heralded treatment of the problem than that provided in *When Prophecy Fails,* Joseph F. Zygmunt proposed three modes of adaptation, of reaffirmation and reappraisal, by groups after a prophetic failure.[5] First, groups may acknowledge an error of dating. Following the failure, they may designate a new date for the projected event or establish a new but less definite time frame, and then return to the mode of expectancy they enjoyed before the crisis event. Second, groups may shift the blame for the failure to some force, either within or outside the group, which has interfered with the cosmic timetable. As with the first instance, the group can then construct a new time frame for the prophesied events and return to a mood of expectancy.

Zygmunt, however, has taken the first steps in acknowledging the integration of the specific prophecies into the group's overall theology. Thus he poses a third alternative: that a group may, by reference to its broader theological worldview, deny the failure of the prophecy and assert its fulfillment, if not completely then at least partially. Beginning from the point at which Zygmunt concluded his observations, it will be argued below that the denial of failure is not just another option, but the common mode of adaptation of millennial groups following the failure of a prophecy, and that the process of adaptation follows two common patterns which for convenience may be labeled cultural (spiritualization) and social (reaffirmation) responses.

Cultural Response

Whenever a prophecy fails, groups consistently engage in one activity—they reconceptualize the prophecy in such a way that the element of "failure," particularly the failure of the Divine to perform as promised, is removed. While a group may, temporarily, assume an error in timing, *the ultimate and more permanent reconceptualization is most frequently accomplished through a process of "spiritualization."* The prophesied event is reinterpreted in such a way that what was supposed to have been a visible, verifiable occurrence is seen to have been in reality an invisible, spiritual occurrence. The event occurred as predicted, only on a spiritual level. The process of spiritualization can be illustrated in the activity of a recent millennial group, the Universal Link.[6]

The Universal Link groups began with the visionary experiences of Richard Grave of Worthing, England. On April 11, 1961, while fixing up a newly rented house, he encountered "a bearded Christlike figure" who blocked his way. On this occasion the figure did not speak; he merely pointed to a framed picture of the Annunciation. The glass covering the picture exploded and fragments lodged in the image of the angel. The apparition then disappeared in a blaze of orange light. The picture which had been the object of the strange visitor's attention soon gained renown. Salty drops formed on its surface and people began to designate it "the Weeping Angel of Worthing."

The strange visitor returned to Grave on a number of subsequent occasions. He called himself "Truth," and told Grave of the imminent Second Coming of Christ in the wake of humanity's disastrous condition. Grave's story was picked up in a May 4, 1961, article in *Psychic News,* England's most widely circulated Spiritualist newspaper. Liebie Pugh, an artist in southern England, read of Grave and contacted him. During their meeting, Grave realized that, independently of him, Pugh had sculptured a representation of his visitor whom she called "Limitless Love."

Out of their convergence the Universal Link concept was forged. It welded together a number of individuals and groups who were being linked to the Highest and to each other as instruments of bringing in revelations of the cosmic operation which was ushering in the New Age. Universal Link groups formed around the world, as individual channels (mediums) of the cosmic message emerged. For them the period 1961 to 1967 became crucial. Truth told Grave: "No one can know the day nor the hour of MY COMING, or when the great

Universal Revelation will be enacted; however by Christmas morning 1967, I will have revealed myself through the medium of nuclear evolution. This is MY PLAN which is absolute."

Thus Grave passed on to the Universal Link a specific prediction. While vague in some respects, those within the movement understood it as a plain statement that before December 25, 1967, an event visible to all involving some kind of atomic activity would occur. During the next six years members engaged in a zealous effort to spread the message and to tie together channels and groups around the world. Anthony Brooke, former ruler of Sarawak, aided the process greatly by touring Europe and America, lecturing and promoting the Universal Link cause. With Monica Parish, a close associate, he formed the Universal Foundation in England.

As December 1967 approached, a great expectancy grew within the movement. Members hoped and looked for an objective event, a spectacular occurrence which would signal the coming New Age. No event resembling what anyone of them had imagined occurred. Thus by the morning of December 26 the situation of dissonance was firmly established.

Being scattered around Europe and the United States as they were, members could do little to provide direct support to each other. They put no noticeable increase of energy into proselytizing. However, attempts began almost immediately to deal with the dissonance. Typical of those faced with the non-appearance of the expected event, Nellie Cain of the Spiritual Research Society in Grand Rapids, Michigan, reflected upon the disappointment:

> Many people who had read, or heard of the prophecy the Cosmic Being, "TRUTH," had given Richard Grave, that He would reveal Himself to the Universe through the medium of nuclear evolution, on or before Christmas morning, 1967, anticipated an outer, or physical manifestation. Of course they were disappointed, since they had given no thought beyond the *literal* meaning of the words, yet past experience concerning most prophecies indicates that one should ponder them deeply to extract the "esoteric" or inner meaning.

A year later she observed:

> There has been ample evidence during the past twelve month period of the great Cosmic outpouring of spiritual energies. As people feel the tremendous acceleration of these vibratory energies, they do not understand what is transpiring, and they are unable to adjust to the new frequencies. This is actually a very scientific process, which is unfolding. . . .

Having saved the prophecy, she went on to explain the atomic reaction that the world is undergoing:

> The atom has its balance of positive and negative charges working in complete and total harmony with each other, and when this balance is disturbed, as in the detonation of an atomic bomb, let us say, this creates an imbalance or a maladjustment of the subatomic and the atomic ele-

ments, or the ratio of positive and negative charges one to another, and consequently an explosion develops.[7]

Violet Barton seconded the statements of Nellie Cain. She reported that a vision of Christ framed in light had appeared to her around midnight on Christmas Eve.[8] Anthony Brooke reported his faith that Monica Parish, who had died a year prior to the prophesied day and whom he had begun to see as an extension of Liebie Pugh's "Limitless Love," was spreading her influence, and "Limitless Love" was appearing with ever greater frequency in the actions of and to the visions of more and more people.

Thus by spiritualization the members of the Universal Link were able to take the discomfiting experience—failure—and turn it into a cause for affirmation. By Christmas 1968 they could join with Nellie Cain in asserting: "A great Cosmic release is taking place in which the building of vibrational levels and frequencies is being developed in which the New Man will operate."[9]

The process observed in the Universal Link appears repeatedly in millennial movements. Typically, during a movement's first generation, a prophecy of a specific visible event is presented and integrated into the belief system of a group over a period that may range from a few weeks to a few years to many years (in one case, a century). The prophecy possesses a certain appeal because of its specific content, and potential converts recognize the risk incurred if they place their faith in the prophecy. It is falsifiable. When the moment predicted for the prophecy to be fulfilled passes, little doubt remains to either believer or nonbeliever of its occurrence or non-occurence.

The believer, however, does not react to the non-occurrence of the event by admitting failure. To do so would call into question the total experience of the group. Instead the believer begins a process of reinterpretation. The believer begins to see not that the prophecy was incorrect, but that the group merely misunderstood it in a material, earthly manner. Its truth came at a spiritual level, invisible except to the eye of faith. Thus from the original prophesied event, the believers create an "invisible," "spiritual," and, more importantly, unfalsifiable event.

By doing so, the group saves the prophecy from failure, retains its close connection with cosmic history, and provides the condition under which its work can continue. Individuals, even thoughtful leaders, might depart, but the group survives. The payment for such a spiritualization of its prophecy is low, the mere admission of a slight error in perception, a readily acceptable human failure. The price is small compared with the loss of both face in the community and the intimate relationship with the cosmos implied in admitting that the prophecy might have failed. For the group, *prophecy does not fail*—it is merely misunderstood.

The examination of other millennial, adventist, and prophetic movements throughout history reveals numerous examples of the attempt to spiritualize prophecies. The case of Joanna Southcott, an English prophet of the 1770s, provides a vivid example.[10] As visions began to appear before her, the young woman recorded them. After the publication of her message, followers gathered around her, convinced that she was a prophetess.

A crucial element in Southcott's message, the prediction of the imminent return of Christ, stirred many who flocked to her. As the peculiar revelation developed, she speculated on the crucial role of the "woman clothed with the sun" mentioned in the Book of Revelation (12:1). According to the Bible, this woman would bring forth a male child who would rule the nations with a rod of iron. Southcott identified the woman of Revelation 12 with the Bride of the Lamb (Rev. 19:7) and then accepted both roles for herself.

She attracted followers for over a decade and "sealed" them (confirmed them in their faith) with small pieces of paper she personally distributed. Then in 1814 she revealed the climactic word. She was to become the woman clothed with the sun in physical reality and bear a son who would be named Shiloh (Gen. 49:10). Though sixty-four years old, she began to show signs of pregnancy, and several doctors confirmed that she was indeed with child. With her followers preparing for a new virgin birth, Southcott was experiencing a false pregnancy. She failed to produce a baby, and after some months all the symptoms of pregnancy left. Within a few weeks of the departure of the symptoms, she weakened and died. Some of the followers left the movement, but not the majority.

George Turner, a former disciple of prophet Richard Brothers, arose to save Southcott's prophecy. Turner reaffirmed the reports of the doctors who had attended her; she had indeed been pregnant. Then returning to the source of her vision (Rev. 12), he reminded the believers that the child of the woman was to be taken up into heaven. Shiloh lives! He was taken into heaven directly from the womb. He will in due time reappear.

Thus Turner catalyzed the transition for the Southcottites by turning what was to be a visible, if miraculous, birth of a child into a cosmic event witnessed only in the empty womb of Joanna Southcott. He failed at one point, however, in that he proposed a new prophecy. He predicted Shiloh's return in 1820. The failure of the six-year-old Shiloh to return destroyed Turner's credibility and elevated John Wroe, who effectively argued that Shiloh's return awaited an indefinite period of testing for God's people. Wroe's followers, in the form of the Christian Israelites and the House of David, are still presumably in that period of testing.[11]

Social Response

The failure of a predicted event to happen generally shocks believers to some extent. Disappointment is real, as is the threat to the group's survival. The non-occurrence of the expected event cannot be denied. Life cannot return immediately to the norm enjoyed prior to the non-event. Some means must be found to reaffirm the validity of the group and the truth of its beliefs. Some action must be taken to repair the social fabric torn in the prophecy's failure. At such moments groups tend to turn inward, as much as their environment will allow them, and engage in processes of group building.

The response by members of that most famous of American millennial movements, the Millerites, amply illustrates the process. Bible student William Miller projected the end of the world for October 1843, and twice revised the time to dates in 1844. The non-occurrence of Christ's return, known as the Great Disappointment, finally led Miller to tell his fellow believers, "I confess my error and acknowledge my disappointment." Miller took an extreme minority position. The majority of the estimated 50,000 Millerites were not ready to give up either their belief in the imminent Second Coming of Christ or the inside knowledge of the cosmic secrets that Miller's chronological speculations implied. Nevertheless Jesus had failed to appear as scheduled.

Some followers revised chronological schemes, including new projected dates for Christ's return; one such date was 1854.[12] As it and successive projected dates came and went, each proved a disappointment. After each disappointment, the number of believers who would accept a new date diminished.

Eventually the believers had to reach a more satisfactory solution to the dissonance created by the Great Disappointment. Some moved slowly to a position that the chronology was wrong but not far wrong. Jesus would return soon. They easily transformed that position into a general faith in the Second Coming at an unknown date. Thus later generations of Millerites could laud the first generation for recovering faith in the Second Coming while ignoring their date-setting errors.

The means to vindicate the Millerite claims, however, by spiritualizing Miller's prophecy, was discovered by Hiram Edson, the Adventist leader in Port Gibson, New York.[13] But his solution, which gradually was embraced by most Millerites, was found only in the process of the reaffirmation of the group and its beliefs. The Adventist group at Port Gibson gathered at their meeting place (Edson's barn) on October 22, 1844, to await in a prayerful atmosphere the expected return of Christ. They waited all day, until the midnight hour signaled the end of the calendar day. At dawn on the 23rd some believers, stung by disappointment, departed for their homes.

Their departure induced Edson to reflect upon his joyful months as an Adventist. He called those remaining to prayer and led them in a cathartic vocalization of their confusion and disappointment. Their questioning soon turned to affirmation. God did hear their cries. His word was true and sure. They convinced each other that God would reveal the nature of their error and offer new leading. Immediately, however, they had to attend to the more important task before them—mending the group's wounds. The small band left the barn to visit and encourage the other Adventists with the affirmations that had resulted from their prayers. They left the meeting not to proselytize the public but to encourage their disappointed brothers and sisters.

The spiritualized reinterpretation of the prophetic event came to Edson while on his mission of mercy after the prayer meeting. He pondered one image used by Millerites to describe Christ's Second Coming: his role as high priest. At His coming, Christ would step out of the heavenly temple in which He had been ministering and greet His followers on Earth. There, Edson found the mistake. Reading chapters 8 through 10 of the Book of Hebrews, he saw Christ as high priest following the pattern of the Day of Atonement. Christ did not leave the heavenly sanctuary on October 22, 1844; on that day He had just entered it:

> [I]nstead of our High Priest coming out of the Most Holy of the heavenly sanctuary to come to this earth on the tenth day of the seventh month, at the end of the 2300 days, he for the first time entered on that day the second apartment of that sanctuary and that he had a work to perform in the Most Holy before coming to this earth.[14]

As Adventist historian Leroy Edwin Froom observed, this new truth illuminated the whole question, clarified the disappointment, and dispelled the confusion. It cut through the dissonance and eventually spread as a principle around which eschatological doctrine would be worked. Those who agreed with Edson became what are known today as the Seventh-Day Adventists. By spiritualizing, following Edson's teaching, they were able to keep their faith in Miller's chronology; in their minds, Miller's failed prophecy of 1844, the prophecy which had called them together, proved true. However, the reinterpretation of the prophecy worked in tandem with the activity of the group in reaffirming its faith and life.

A more recent example of the group-building process was observed and recorded by Jane Allyn Hardyck and Marcia Braden in a study published in 1962 which aimed at testing the *Prophecy* hypothesis. The unnamed Pentecostal group they studied was led by "Mrs. Shepard," who occasionally uttered prophecies believed to be from God. These were recorded and seemed to predict an imminent nuclear holocaust. The group responded. Fifty miles from an urban center which they believed would receive a direct hit with a nuclear bomb, they built fallout shelters, stocking them with food and supplies.

The group believed, as a result of their study of the Bible, that one third of the earth would be killed in the war and that sickness would afflict the survivors. They as the remnant would be given miraculous powers of healing and would spearhead a worldwide evangelism campaign.

On July 4, approximately 135 people entered the shelters, which were linked via an intercom system. They stayed underground for forty-two days. A few hours after emerging from the shelter, the group gathered at its church building. Mrs. Shepard commenced the process of reaffirmation and reinterpretation immediately with the question: "Did you have victory?" The unison reply was: "Yes, praise the Lord!" She then addressed the group on how their stay had not weakened but had strengthened their faith and fellowship. Testimonies of the members confirmed their leader's initial reaffirming remarks.

Though observed by the press during the entire period from the construction of the shelters through the weeks after their emergence from them, the group showed no evidence of increased attempts to proselytize, putting their entire concentration instead on understanding their experience. They reexamined the recorded prophecies and discovered that no actual prediction of an imminent attack had been made. They had made an error of interpretation. They finally concluded that God had been testing their faith and using them to warn a world fallen asleep.[15]

Conclusion

In this essay I have attempted to reevaluate one very popular thesis within the social sciences concerning the response of religious groups when faced with the failure of a predicted event to occur on schedule. That thesis, that in the face of the failure of prophecy, groups tend to reduce the experienced dissonance by increasing efforts at proselytization, has found no confirmation in subsequent studies and, in the case of Mrs. Keech's group, can best be explained as an idiosyncrasy of Mrs. Keech intensified by the high level of attention focused upon the group in the local press. The reaction to the press, the bedrock of the claim of increased proselytizing activity, is best understood in the context of the group's earlier attempts to gain the attention of the press prior to the prophesied event. In the light of such failure to confirm the thesis over three decades, and our ability to understand all that Festinger, Riecken, and Schachter observed without recourse to their thesis, I suggest that it be discarded, at least until some observable incidents replicating its finding appear.

I also suggested that the *Prophecy* study was weakened by a lack of appreciation of the manner in which beliefs and actions with a particular focus (in this case prophecy) are integrated as but a single gestalt, though an important one, into the total religious life of a group. Thus behavior which seems logical to an outside observer is not followed by group members, who operate within a completely different intellectual and social reality. Future studies of groups experiencing a prophetic failure should look for the effects of the more comprehensive religious faith and life upon the group at each stage of its evolution. As scholars, we should approach religious groups as phenomena to be observed and understood in their own complexity, with at least as much respect for the complexity and integrity of our subject matter as a biologist or physicist has for the phenomena of nature.

As an alternative, I proposed beginning with Zygmunt's suggestion that prophecies, which to outsiders appear to have failed, may not have failed for the millennial group as a whole, though individual members may go through varying levels of doubt after the predicted event fails to happen. The denial within the group—of what to outside observers is obvious failure of a prophecy—is accomplished through the two processes of spiritualization of the prophecy and reaffirmation of the group's faith and life by reference to the larger context of group belief and experience. This reaction is not just one among many but is, in fact, the most common mode of adaptation used by millennial groups. Thus failure is transformed into success and disappointment into an occasion for celebration. Both processes have been explained and illustrated, and while only four examples were cited here, numerous others can be found in the recent history of the Jehovah's Witnesses, the Worldwide Church of God, the Children of God, and other occult and Christian millennial bodies.

Finally, it should be noted that this article focused upon only *one* issue raised by failed prophecies: the common process by which prophetic failure is integrated into the total group experience. A host of issues concerning prophecy and prediction within religious groups awaits future consideration. For instance, millennial groups vary widely in their thought-worlds and lifestyles. Some are tightly structured, communally organized, and separatist; others are the opposite. Some are small, informal, and intimate while others are relatively large, well-organized, and composed of members unacquainted with each other. Some are more successful than others both before and after the failed prophecy. (Mrs. Keech, now settled in Northern California, is still looked upon as a significant leader in the flying saucer contactee movement.) Some have a worldview largely adopted from their surrounding culture while others have assumed a completely alternative cosmology. Some theologies are more sophisticated (having integrated the wisdom of a religious community over a period of years) and elaborate (having dealt with a wider range of issues) than others, especially more recently developed theologies, and group leaders have a varying command of the resources available from their own religious tradition. Each of these factors, along with the individual tendencies in a charismatic leader, will affect the nature of a group's response to failed prophecy. Now, one hopes, knowledge of the processes of adaptation described above can serve as a beginning point for the examination of these additional factors, thus leading to a more complete understanding of the processes which determine millennial group behavior.

NOTES

1. (New York, 1964). The person known as Mrs. Keech was in fact a well-known figure in the UFO contactee community, and, as the opening quote demonstrates, is still an active group leader.
2. *Ibid.*, 28.
3. For example, see: Jane Allyn Hardyck and Marcia Braden, "Prophecy Fails Again: A Report of a Failure to Replicate," *Journal of Abnormal and Social Psychology* 65 (1962): 136–141; and Robert W. Balch, Gwen Farnsworth, and Sue Wilkins, "When the Bombs Drop," *Sociological Perspectives* 26 (April 1983):137–158.
4. Festinger, Riecken, and Schachter, 22–23.
5. "When Prophecies Fail," *American Behavior Scientist* 16 (November-December, 1972): 245–267.
6. Cf. Brother Francis, *The Universal Link Concept* (Los Angeles, 1968); and Anthony Brook, "The Universal Link Revelation" (London, 1967).
7. Brother Francis, 22–24.
8. *Ibid.*, 29.
9. *Ibid.*, 23.
10. On the Southcott movement, see G. R. Balleine, *Past Finding Out* (New York, 1956), or the more recent biography of Southcott by James K. Hopkins, *A Woman to Deliver Her People* (Austin, Texas, 1982).
11. It is interesting to note that the Interdenominational Order of Twin Falls, Idaho, relived this identical prophecy in the 1930s. They are currently awaiting the return of the child snatched from the womb of their leader, Frances Sande. See *Reincarnation Presents the*

Christ Again (Boulder, Colorado, 1960) and *"A Little Child Shall Lead Them"* (Twin Falls, Idaho, 1960).

12. The Christian Advent Church grew out of the believers in the 1854 date.

13. On the history of Adventism in general and Hiram Edson in particular, see Leroy Edwin Froom, *The Prophetic Faith of Our Fathers* (Washington, D.C., 1954), 4 vols.

14. *Ibid.,* 881.

15. Hardyck and Braden, 138–139.

Had Prophecy Failed?
Contrasting Perspectives of the Millerites and Shakers

Lawrence Foster

The career of the Midwestern Adventist leader Enoch Jacobs highlights the complex interrelationship between the Millerite and Shaker movements during the 1840s. Serving initially as editor of *The Western Midnight Cry!!!*—a newspaper started in Cincinnati, Ohio, in 1841, with Joshua V. Himes as its publisher—Jacobs tirelessly sought to spread William Miller's message that Christians must repent and prepare for Christ's literal return to earth in 1843. Following the failure of the 1843 predictions and of the prediction of October 1844 as well, Jacobs, like many others who experienced the Great Disappointment, struggled to understand what had gone wrong. The number of exclamation points in the title of *The Western Midnight Cry!* was reduced from three to one, and on February 18, 1845, the newspaper's title was changed to *The Day-Star*, with Jacobs as the sole editor and publisher. The name change reflected a significant change of emphasis: "The day-star must arise *before* the Sun of Righteousness: The Resurrection must take place before Christ can come with '*all* his saints.' "[1]

Jacobs increasingly found himself attracted to the United Society of Believers in Christ's Second Appearing, better-known as Shakers, who were convinced that the Second Coming of Christ's spirit had already taken place in 1770 through the person of their foundress, Ann Lee. Shakers argued that the kingdom of heaven was now literally being realized on earth in their closely knit communities, which shared all things in common, like the primitive Christian church, and practiced celibacy as a sign of their participation in the resurrected state in which "they neither marry nor are given in marriage." Jacobs opened the columns of *The Day-Star* to spirited letters for and against Shaker claims. An editorial observed: "None should think that the 'Day-Star' is the instrument of a sect or party: it is God's instrument; and God's children ALL have a right to talk through it to each other, and speak aloud the praises of God in the language of Christ."[2]

By May 23, 1846, Jacobs had converted to Shakerism. He began publishing extracts from Shaker doctrinal works, as well as lengthy argumentation on the necessity of celibacy as tangible proof of the overcoming of carnal propensities separating humankind from God. Jacobs repeatedly visited and reported on his visits to the Shaker villages at Whitewater and at Union Village in Ohio. That latter community, near Lebanon, Ohio, was the first and largest Shaker settlement in the Midwest, with some 400 members in the 1840s. Jacobs worked closely with prominent Shaker leaders seeking to convert disaffected Millerites, and he was instrumental in eventually attracting more than 200 persons to Shakerism in the Midwest.[3] In the summer of 1846, Jacobs traveled throughout the Northeastern United States on a proselytizing mission. During that time, *The Day-Star* appeared irregularly, with two issues from New York City and one from the Shaker village at Canterbury, New Hampshire, where on September 19, 1846, thirteen hundred copies were issued, the Shakers assisting with typesetting and press work and also contributing $20.00 toward expenses.[4] A large and inconclusive meeting between Millerites and Shakers near Enfield, Connecticut, was thoroughly reported in *The Day-Star*.[5] Following Jacobs's return to Ohio, he and his wife, Electa, and family lived at Union Village, Ohio, publishing *The Day-Star* from that community beginning on November 7, 1846. In all probability, the press used was that of Richard McNemar, an influential figure in the founding of Shaker communities in the Midwest and author of *The Kentucky Revival*, the first published Shaker book.[6] Articles from Union Village increasingly reflected Shaker concerns. Jacobs took vigorous exception to the Millerites who criticized his conversion to Shakerism in a short-lived Adventist publication, *The Day-Dawn*, which was self-consciously modeled on Jacobs's newspaper.[7] Publication of Jacobs's own *The Day-Star* ceased abruptly and without explanation following the issue of July 1, 1847, about the time that Jacobs left the Shakers. A letter from Jacobs published many years later in the Shaker newspaper, *The Manifesto*, in November 1891, showed that he had subsequently been influenced by the Spiritualist movement and that he still retained fond memories of the Shakers.[8]

Enoch Jacobs's curious odyssey raises a host of complex questions. How and to what extent were his experiences representative of those of other Millerites following the Great Disappointment? Why did Shakerism come to have special appeal for some of these distraught Millerites? What was the impact of the sudden infusion of Millerites into the Shaker communities, which had themselves already been suffering great disruption as a result of the "spiritual manifestations" which had begun in 1837? Why did Jacobs, like so many other Millerites who briefly joined the Shakers in the late 1840s, eventually become dissatisfied with the group and move on to continue searching for other, more appealing ways of interpreting his experiences? And from a larger perspective, can the experiences of individuals in these two highly unconventional movements shed light on more general questions of religious development, especially how millenarian movements may be able most effectively to deal with the apparent failure of prophecy?

This article will address these and other questions relating to how millenarian movements handle problems of apparent failure or disconfirmation of their claims. First, I shall analyze Shaker theological beliefs, especially their symbolic understanding of Christ's Second Advent, and raise the question of the degree to which the Shakers by the 1830s and 1840s had found their beliefs confirmed and their social practices satisfying. Second, I shall focus on the reasons that some Millerites joined, and often subsequently left, the Shakers. In conclusion, I shall briefly suggest that the experiences of these Millerites-turned-Shakers may shed light on the eventual success of the Seventh-Day Adventist movement, which emerged out of the ashes of the failure of Millerite prophecy.

Shaker Theological Beliefs and Social Practices

Both the theological and social aspects of early Shakerism show a remarkable degree of sophistication which would later help account for the appeal of the Shaker movement to disaffected Millerites. Although Shaker and Millerite views of the nature of Christ's Second Advent were initially in sharp opposition, individuals attracted to both groups shared many common dissatisfactions with established religious and social practice. Shaker unorthodoxy and theological liberalism is suggested by the story that Thomas Jefferson was sent a copy of *The Testimony of Christ's Second Appearing* (1808), the first published Shaker doctrinal treatise, and that this freethinker and devotee of "natural religion" pronounced it the best ecclesiastical history he had ever encountered, declaring he had read it through "three times three."[9] Jefferson's letter has not survived and the entire story may well be apocryphal, yet in all probability he would have been impressed by Shaker theology had he read it. The brilliant nineteenth-century freethinker and social reformer Frederick W. Evans was only the most noteworthy of the liberal religious figures who were attracted to Shakerism and rose to prominence within the movement. Such figures were counterbalanced by equally articulate theological conservatives such as Hervey L. Eads, who spent much of the nineteenth century debating Shaker theology with Evans. Within Shakerism, with its emphasis on continuing revelation, there was much room for religious seekers of all varieties.

Looking back, the scholar of American cultural history Constance Rourke notes in her sensitive appreciation "The Shakers" that Shaker theology, breaking with Calvinism, had a remarkably "modern" cast, with its emphasis on secular progress, functionalism, and equality for women. Indeed, she asserts, Shaker views would have been quite appealing to the likes of Thomas Paine.[10] Another scholar of the early Shakers, Stephen Marini, links their appeal following the American Revolution to that of groups such as the Free Will Baptists and Universalists.[11] And Whitney Cross, dean of scholars of the Burned-over District and enthusiastic religion in western New York State from 1800 to 1850, sees Shakerism throughout this period as "a kind of ultimate among enthusiastic movements." It incorporated many ideas which would become characteristic of the other major enthusiasms of the area and provided a temporal as well as a spiritual refuge for the most earnest seekers who became disturbed by the vagaries of revivalistic religion.[12]

Shaker theology used a spiritualized rather than a literalistic approach to biblical interpretation from a very early date, perhaps from the very beginning of the movement. Three themes are worthy of special emphasis here. First was the call for repentance and confession of sin, specifically the demand that celibacy be practiced as a tangible sign of the realization of the kingdom of heaven on earth. This emphasis grew primarily out of the traumatic sexual experiences of Ann Lee, an illiterate but highly intelligent factory worker from Manchester, England, who would eventually bring the Shakers to America and prepare the foundations for the group's subsequent expansion in the United States. During nine turbulent years in England following her marriage in 1761, Lee bore four children, all of whom died in infancy or early childhood. Her last delivery was exceptionally difficult, and for hours afterwards she lay near death. In 1770, following a powerful visionary experience in Manchester, Lee concluded that lustful sexual intercourse was the original sin in the Garden of Eden, the specific act of disobedience committed by Adam and Eve which had resulted in the fall of man and the entry of sin into the world. Only by giving up all carnal propensities and devoting oneself wholly to God could humankind ultimately achieve salvation.[13]

Later Shaker theological writers, such as Calvin Green and Seth Y. Wells in *A Summary View of the Millennial Church* (1823), greatly elaborated on this symbolic rather than literal interpretation of the Garden of Eden story. They declared that although disobedience to a specific command of God was the *cause* of man's fall, the specific *act* of disobedience was one of carnal intercourse engaged in out of its proper time and season. The specific curse pronounced upon the woman, sorrow in her conception and childbearing, was a response to sexual transgression:

> This same curse has been more or less felt by the fallen daughters of Eve to this day. . . . Thus the woman is not only subjected to the pains and sorrows of childbirth, but even in her conception, she becomes subject to the libidinous passions of her husband. . . . This slavish subjection is often carried to such a shocking extent, that many females have suffered an unnatural and premature death, in consequence of the unseasonable and excessive indulgence of this passion in the man. Thousands there are, no doubt, who are able to bear sorrowful testimony to the truth of this remark.[14]

A second theme in Shaker theology related to the role of Ann Lee and the nature of the millennium. In her vision in Manchester in 1770, Ann Lee not only became convinced that lustful carnal intercourse was the root of all evil, but she also felt herself infused by the spirit of Christ and became convinced that she had a special calling to spread her message to the world. Later Shaker theological writers argued that at this time Ann Lee had been infused by God's spirit in the same way that Jesus had previously been infused by God's spirit. Ann Lee was, therefore, Christ's Second Appearing—using the term "Christ" not to refer to the man Jesus but rather the Divine spirit which had similarly animated Jesus. With this second coming of Christ's spirit to earth, realization of the millennium, the kingdom of heaven on earth, was now underway. Christ's Second Advent had not occurred instantly in literal "clouds of glory," as so many expected it would, but was rather "gradual and progressive like the rising of the Sun." The first coming had been through a male; the second, in order to maintain balance, was through a female. Reflected in this notion of restoring a true balance between the sexes was the Shaker rejection of the Trinity, which they took to be an exclusively male conception of God. Instead, the Shakers argued that God, like the whole of creation, was dual, a combination of male and female elements harmoniously related to each other.[15]

The extent to which this complex theology was developed and articulated by Ann Lee and her followers prior to her death in 1784 is open to question. Available evidence, however, suggests that much of this theology had indeed become established, at least in embryonic form, while Lee was still alive. In the first published apostate attack on the Shakers, written in 1780, Valentine Rathbun notes: "Some of them say, that the woman called the mother [Ann Lee], has the fulness of the God Head, bodily dwelling in her, and that she is the queen of heaven, Christ's wife: And that all God's elect must be born through her; yea, that Christ through her is born the second time."[16] Whatever Ann Lee herself may have believed, her followers came to express their love and affection for her by viewing her as a distinctive embodiment of the Divine spirit in human history.

A third element in Shaker theology was their restorationist effort to return to the spirit of early Christianity, the "primitive Christian church," in which believers truly loved each other and held "all things common," sharing not only their spiritual commitment but all aspects of life. As in their dealings with other issues, the Shakers did not slavishly attempt simply to copy the specific forms which had been used by early Christians. Instead, believing that a progressive revelation and elaboration of truth was going on in their own as well as in biblical days, they sought to infuse the spirit of early Christianity into new forms appropriate for their time. All aspects of life would ultimately come to form a unified spiritual and temporal whole within a distinctive community devoting itself, like a monastery, to the service of God. Shaker success in linking spiritual and temporal life would ultimately prove a key factor in their appeal to dissatisfied individuals seeking a secure spiritual home which would free them from the emotional roller coaster of revivalistic religion.[17]

Although Shaker restorationism was present from the very beginning of the movement, the precise forms that Shaker communal life would take did not become established until after Ann Lee's death. The first "gathered" Shaker community was established in 1787 at New Lebanon, New York, and by the close of the 1790s, eleven communal centers, each composed of numerous smaller "families" of thirty to ninety individuals, had been established in New York State and in New England and were thriving with 1600 members.[18] A distinctive dual governmental organization, with parallel and equal leadership roles for both men and women at all levels of the group, was institutionalized. All possessions except the most personal were held in common, and the group attempted continually to focus its attention and loyalty on God, both through frequent religious services and through daily living. As early as 1803, two Shaker communities were sufficiently well established that they could give away thousands of dollars of specie, livestock, and produce to help feed the starving poor who were suffering from cholera in New York City.[19] A second wave of expansion in the Midwest, growing out of the Kentucky Revival of the early 1800s, and a lesser revival in 1827, brought the Shakers to eighteen communal centers across New England, New York, and the Midwest, with more than 4000 members by 1830, the date at which the Shakers felt they had reached the peak of their spiritual and temporal strength.[20]

Visitors to Shaker communities during the period were struck by the order, serenity, and simplicity of Shaker life, and the impressive degree of fellow feeling which was manifested. One observer noted: "The people are like their village . . . soft in speech, demure in bearing, gentle in face; a people seeming to be at peace not only with themselves, but with nature and with heaven."[21] John Humphrey Noyes, founder of the Oneida Community and commentator on the nineteenth-century communitarian movements, was another individual who found much of Shaker spiritual and temporal life appealing. He praised the Shakers for providing the "specie basis" which counteracted the failures of numerous other experimenters of the period, proving that a thoroughgoing cooperative and communistic system was not simply an impractical pipe dream but a form of organization that could successfully be established throughout the world.[22]

In summary, the Shakers had numerous strengths, both theologically and socially. Theologically, the Shakers began with a sophisticated and largely spiritualized understanding of the basis for their movement, which could easily be modified to deal with changing circumstances. Socially, the Shakers had achieved recognized excellence in communal living, and even their critics were forced to admit that the fruits of Shaker spirituality appeared to be good. Although celibacy and communal living were demanding practices, they also called forth a high degree of commitment which initially strengthened the group. The Shakers might have been expected to look toward the future with confidence.

Yet by the late 1830s, the Shakers clearly were experiencing a decline. In 1837, exactly fifty years after the formal gathering of the first Shaker community in 1787, most of the believers who had known Ann Lee and the other early leaders personally had died or grown old and feeble. A serious gap existed between the old and young in many communities. Discipline was becoming lax. Curious visitors would come in to stare with uncomprehending amusement at the strange Shaker worship services. The leadership had a sense that they were gradually and ever-so-subtly beginning to lose control over their communities. Even though Shaker theological beliefs were remarkably flexible, the loss of spiritual dynamism in the group was calling into question whether the Shakers would be able to continue to see themselves as key movers in setting up the kingdom of heaven on earth.[23]

In response to the growing Shaker internal tensions and loss of nerve—which coincided with the Panic of 1837 and ensuing depression in the outer world—a remarkable decade of "spiritual manifestations" began among the Shakers in 1837 and rapidly spread throughout all the Shaker communities. The extraordinary revivalistic effusions included everything from deep trance and possession phenomena to speaking in tongues, ecstatic dancing, and thousands of reports of messages supposedly coming from deceased Shaker leaders and others. The details of this upwelling of fervor and its impact on the group have been discussed elsewhere and need not be recounted here.[24] Suffice it to note that the manifestations helped to revitalize the spiritual commitment of some believers but they also provided an opportunity for others—specially young female mediums—to challenge the authority of Shaker leadership. Many Shaker leaders initially were cautiously supportive of the phenomena, seeing them as a means of strengthening the group by encouraging young Shakers and other flagging believers to undergo a powerful direct experience of the truth of the Shaker message. Eventually, however, the anarchic potential implicit in individual revelation coming from all members of the group forced the leadership to restrict the "spiritual manifestations" and reassert full control over the societies.[25]

The dramatic Shaker spiritual phenomena peaked at approximately the same time during the early 1840s when Millerite tensions were also beginning to rise to a crescendo. By the time that the Millerite Great Disappointment took place in October 1844, the Shakers had largely reestablished order in their communities and were able to supply a seemingly secure and appealing alternative for some Millerites who were seeking further light to help them understand their difficult experiences. In curious and very different ways, both groups during this period were struggling to come to terms with an apparent failure of prophecy. Alert Shakers could sense that their communities, the visible sign of Christ's Second Appearance on Earth, were beginning to experience a temporal decline, while dedicated Millerites were painfully aware that Christ had not returned to Earth a second time when they had expected him.

Millerite Relations with the Shakers

The reasons why some Millerites became converted to Shakerism and why many of those same converts eventually left the movement can clearly be seen by looking at the heated argumentation that took place in the pages of *The Day-Star* between 1845 and 1847. The final failure of the Millerite prediction of the specific date for Christ's literal Second Coming was emotionally shattering to many in the movement. Shock, grief, and perplexity were widespread. Derided by outsiders and unsure themselves of what had gone wrong, Second Advent believers desperately sought to salvage something out of the commitment which they had so sincerely devoted to the cause. Some individuals fell apart emotionally, at least for a time, due to the "tribulations deep" which they experienced, or else became completely cynical about all religion and morality. Some continued, though in ever-decreasing numbers and with less and less enthusiasm or success, to set new dates for Christ's Second Advent, each of which eventually would prove false. And some returned to orthodoxy.[26]

But for those who had been thoroughly convinced, a return to orthodoxy offered no solution. Rather than "go back," they felt that they must "go on" to a new and fuller understanding of God's will and plan for their lives. The Shakers had much to offer these more committed believers. In the first place, the Shakers, too, were devout Second Adventists who, it seemed, had already gone through many of the same thought processes that disappointed Millerites were now experiencing. Enoch Jacobs spoke approvingly of how the Shakers, unlike so many others, took his Second Advent concerns seriously. He was astonished to discover that Shaker accounts going back to the Kentucky Revival of the early 1800s were almost uncanny in the degree to which they seemed to illustrate emotional and thought processes which he was experiencing, as though for the first time, many years later.[27] Jacobs was impressed to discover that a Shaker poem composed in 1807 or 1808, "The Midnight Cry," could speak so clearly to his present condition.[28] Articulate Shaker leaders worked with him as an individual, encouraging him to "go on" to develop a deeper spiritual insight. Given these circumstances, Jacobs was at least open to considering that the Shakers might have something to teach him.

The most appealing aspect of Shakerism for Jacobs and other Millerites like him was not so much theological as social. The Shakers really seemed to be living their faith successfully, unlike so many Millerites. Even Millerites who were most critical of the Shakers in the columns of *The Day-Star* could not restrain their grudging admiration for the well-ordered, loving communities that the Shakers appeared to have created.[29] Jacobs commented how impressed he was by the Shakers' stress on works, not on mere talk. Though Jacobs initially had difficulty accepting the Shaker contention that their organization was the true representative of the "body" of Christ on earth, he noted that "the spirit of the Shakers is much more like Christ, than the spirit that opposes them."[30] If the test by which one was to know truth was by its fruits, then the Shakers scored high marks, especially for those individuals who had been so badly burned by the revival fires and were seeking true religious security.

Henry B. Bear, a Millerite who joined the Shakers and wrote a reflective account of his Advent experience, exhorted his brethren: "O come and be gathered . . . I know there can be no happiness in being thus scattered."[31] Even more eloquent was Enoch Jacobs's peroration:

> O what an ocean of contradictory theories is that upon which the multitudes have been floating for the last 18 months. Do you not long for rest from these conflicting elements? Do you want to find a place where Advent *work* takes the place of Advent *talk*,—where "I" is no longer the

prominent *idea* in any theory—where the purity of wives and husbands is the purity of heaven, and where your little children are protected from the poisonous influence of the world.[32]

The Shaker symbolic rather than literal interpretation of Christ's Second Advent was in sharp opposition to Millerite literalism, yet a symbolic approach appeared much more appealing following the Great Disappointment. Shaker doctrinal works going back to *The Testimony of Christ's Second Appearing* in 1808 presented an extremely persuasive case for seeing Christ's Second Advent as an inner, not an external, phenomenon. In the wake of Christ's failure to make a literal return as they had anticipated, Millerites searching the Scriptures for guidance could come to the conclusion that the error had been in their *own* understanding and not in the Lord's word.

Enoch Jacobs again articulated the Shaker alternative to Millerite literalism:

> Have you found salvation? It was that for which we looked in 1843, and in the autumn of 1844. On the 10th day of the 7th month of the last named year, we were all placed in a situation to receive it, if it had come in *our way*. George Storrs told me that he felt just as completely dead to the world as though he had been laid in his coffin—buried under ground and waiting for a resurrection. This was the feeling of thousands. It was mine. Earthly ties were as completely sundered, for the time being, as though they had never been known. Thus we waited, but Salvation did not come: We thought the fault was all without—sad mistake!! It was *within*. This out of doors salvation has always been a precarious thing.[33]

And a stanza from a poem by the Shaker Charles Main also made the same point:

> So stand no longer waiting, ye men of Galilee,
> Into the literal heavens, your Savior there to see;
> But listen to his teaching, and cleanse your soul from sin,
> The everlasting kingdom must be set up within.[34]

There were problems, of course, with the specifics of Shaker adventist theology. Why, for example, should Christ's Second Advent have been through a woman? And, even if one were to accept such a possibility, why should one conclude that Ann Lee was that woman? Yet in the face of great need for a new understanding of their experience, even the unorthodoxy of Shaker theology was not an insurmountable stumbling block to devout Millerites who found the Shakers otherwise attractive.[35]

The great stumbling block, instead, was celibacy. This, not Shaker theology per se, had always been the ultimate limiting factor in the growth of the group. Not only did celibacy make Shakerism entirely dependent upon a continuing supply of converts from the outer world for its survival and growth, but celibacy was also a powerful test of whether the dedication of new converts was sufficiently great that they were prepared to give up "all" for Christ. By demanding an extreme degree of loyalty and the severing of normal earthly relationships,

Shaker celibacy could have considerable appeal to the most devoted believers in the great revivals who sought to commit their lives wholly to God without any carnal distractions. Millerites who had been eagerly awaiting Christ's Second Advent, living with husbands or wives, following St. Paul's advice, as though they had none, could understand the need for such sacrifice, at least for a time.[36]

Yet when Christ did not literally appear in clouds of glory in 1844, even devout Millerites must have reassessed the desirability of continued celibacy. As a lifelong practice rather than a prelude to eternal glory, the demands must have seemed excessive to most. Enoch Jacobs himself struggled with his impulses and with those of his wife, who initially opposed Shakerism because of that demand.[37] Again and again, Jacobs emphasized how difficult the commitment to celibacy was:

> I now ask if there is one Advent believer in the land, who would not gladly share the peaceful home they [the Shakers] enjoy, were it not for the cross [celibacy]? Excuse after excuse is brought forward, while the real one is hidden. You wish to reserve the privilege of gratifying the lusts of the flesh, which you know you cannot do under any circumstances, in the dispensation in which we live, appealing to God that you do it for his glory.[38]

Some Millerite converts to Shakerism accepted the Shaker celibate cross permanently. Henry B. Bear and his family, for example, remained committed members of the group throughout the remainder of their lives. Yet far more Millerite converts to Shakerism appear to have "turned off" from the movement than remained. Although Shaker membership figures still have not been completely analyzed, the work done to date is suggestive. The membership records of the New Lebanon Second Family between 1830 and the dissolution of the community in 1896 show, for example, that only slightly more than 10 percent of all converts during the entire period remained in that community for the rest of their lives.[39] The percentage of converts who stayed faithful dropped precipitously in the 1830s and 1840s.[40] The fluidity of membership was even greater in the Sodus Bay, New York, community from 1826 to 1838, where more than 50 percent of the group changed in some years.[41] While we do not yet know the reasons that Millerites who joined the Shakers in the 1840s often subsequently failed to stay, celibacy must have been an important factor. The story is that Enoch Jacobs himself left the Shakers declaring that he would "rather go to hell with Electa his wife than live among the Shakers without her."[42]

If some Millerites were influenced for a time by Shakerism, then how, correspondingly, were Shakers influenced by Millerites? Only a few hypotheses can be raised here. The impact of significant numbers of Millerite converts joining some Shaker communities, particularly in the Midwest, and then subsequently leaving the group must have been considerable. In the first case, the Shakers surely were enthusiastic at the infusion of new converts and may well have modified the emphasis of their group in order to retain the Millerites. In the extreme case of the Shaker village at Whitewater, Ohio, in 1845, for example, eighty out of a total of 144 members were former Millerites, and their influence on the direction of the group must have been considerable.[43] At Union Village, Ohio, the largest and one of the most internally troubled Shaker communities during the 1830s and 1840s, thirty Millerites were added to one family alone in the course of six months.[44] Even if no direct changes in Shaker theology or practice were made, such an infusion of converts must have had an impact on what aspects of Shakerism were emphasized at the time.

Direct Millerite influence on the Shakers is difficult to establish, based on available evidence, but experimentation with new forms of ritual may have been one activity stimulated by the Millerite influx. One of the most colorful of the new forms of group worship which the Shakers introduced during the 1840s, for example, was called the "Midnight Cry." A platoon of Shaker mediums—six male and six female, with two elders in the lead carrying lighted lamps in their right hands—marched through all the community buildings at midnight every night for a period of two weeks. "Every medium wore upon the right wrist, a scrap of scarlet flannel, some two and one half inches wide, and attached to this a written inscription as follows—'War hath been declared by the God of heaven, against all sin, and with the help of the Saints on earth, it shall be slain.' "[45] These activities were interpreted as the actualization of the "searching as with candles" foretold at the beginning of the manifestations. At midnight on one of the nights, the brothers and sisters were awakened with singing:

> Awake from your slumbers, for the Lord of Hosts
> is going through the land,
> He will sweep, he will clean his holy sanctuary.
> Search ye your Camps, yea read and understand
> For the Lord of Hosts holds the Lamps in his hand.[46]

All the believers dressed quickly and hurried out to join in the marching and singing before repairing to the meeting house for an hour of active worship. "This strange alarm had a wonderful effect on the minds of those thus suddenly aroused."[47]

If a new spirit and enthusiasm was imparted to Shakerism by the Millerite influx, then the subsequent departure of many of those same Millerite converts a few years to a decade later must have undercut Shaker morale, contributing to the deep pessimism apparent in so much of the Shaker writings of the 1850s and 1860s. While difficulty in retaining converts can be traced to the decade of the 1830s, before the Millerite infusion, the length of time that the Shakers were able to keep their converts became progressively shorter with individuals who entered during the 1840s, 1850s, and 1860s. Thoughtful Shakers must have wondered if their own efforts had also "failed," not theologically but socially.

Ultimately the most appealing answer to the apparent failure of Millerite prophecy of the 1840s was provided not by the spiritualized Second Advent beliefs and practices of the Shakers, but by the beliefs and practices introduced by Ellen G. White and others, who argued that, on October 22, 1844, Christ had entered the most holy compartment of the heavenly sanctuary to begin the "investigative judgment" preliminary to the Second Coming. In effect, belief in a heavenly event which could not immediately be confirmed or disconfirmed was substituted for Millerite belief in an earthly event which had not occurred as anticipated. On the foundation of this new belief, as well as other distinctive beliefs and practices, would rise the Seventh-Day Adventist movement, a classic example of a successful group which developed out of the ashes of an apparently failed prophecy.[48]

NOTES

1. *The Day-Star,* February 18, 1845, 5:3. For bibliographical details on *The Western Midnight Cry* and *The Day-Star,* see Mary L. Richmond, *Shaker Literature: A Bibliography,* 2 vols. (Hanover, NH: University Press of New England, 1977), vol. 1, p. 69. Although Jacobs's newspaper was published in thirteen volumes between 1841 and July 1, 1847, the version available on microfiche at the Western Reserve Historical Society in Cleveland, Ohio, and at the Library of Congress in Washington, D.C., begins with volume 2, number 1, on December 9, 1843, and appears to be complete thereafter. The interpretation of the Shakers presented throughout this paper is an outgrowth of the work reported in Lawrence Foster, *Religion and Sexuality: Three American Communal Experiments of the Nineteenth Century* (New York: Oxford University Press, 1981), and reprinted in a paperbound version, with identical pagination, as *Religion and Sexuality: The Shakers, the Mormons, and the Oneida Community* (Urbana: University of Illinois Press, 1984), pp. 21–71, 226–247.

2. *The Day-Star,* May 9, 1846, 10:44.

3. Richmond, *Shaker Literature,* vol. 1, p. 69. Shaker membership figures are often fuzzy, but there is no question that numerous Millerites were attracted, for varying periods of time, to the Shakers.

4. *Ibid.,* p. 69.

5. A detailed summary of the proceedings at Enfield was provided in *The Day-Star* on August 25, 1846, and in subsequent issues.

6. John P. MacLean, *Sketch of the Life and Labors of Richard McNemar* (Franklin, OH: Franklin Chronicle, 1905), p. 61n.

7. *The Day-Star,* August 8, 1846, 11:18.

8. *The Manifesto,* November 1891, 21:250–251, prints Jacobs's letter to Elder Hervey L. Eads and Elder Henry C. Blinn's favorable comment.

9. Benjamin Seth Youngs's *The Testimony of Christ's Second Appearing* was first printed at Lebanon, Ohio, by John McClean in 1808. For the Jefferson story, see John P. MacLean, *A Bibliography of Shaker Literature* (Columbus, OH: F. J. Heer, 1905), p. 6.

10. Rourke's fine essay "The Shakers" appeared in her *The Roots of American Culture and Other Essays,* ed. Van Wyck Brooks (New York: Harcourt Brace, 1942), pp. 195–237.

11. Stephen A. Marini, *Radical Sects of Revolutionary New England* (Cambridge, MA: Harvard University Press, 1982).

12. Whitney R. Cross, *The Burned-over District: The Social and Intellectual History of Enthusiastic Religion in Western New York, 1800–1850* (New York: Harper & Row, 1965; originally published by Cornell University Press in 1950), p. 32. One reason for Cross's

great appeal to scholars is that at one point or another through his book he refers to virtually every one of the many groups that he analyzes as the key to understanding the Burned-over District. As only a few examples, if the Shakers are "a kind of ultimate among enthusiastic movements," the Millerites are, quoting Ludlum, "the summation of all the reforms of the age" (p. 317), and Noyes's Oneida Community is "veritably the keystone in the arch of Burned-over District history, demonstrating the connection between enthusiasms of the right and those of the left" (p. 333). Scholars who must justify their work by pointing to the centrality of the particular group they have chosen to understand an age can use Cross to give credibility to the study of almost any group in the Burned-over District.

Among the most insightful of the discussions of Shakerism as a refuge from the vagaries of revivalism, see Stow Persons, "Christian Communitarianism in America," in *Socialism and American Life,* eds. Donald Drew Egbert and Stow Persons, 2 vols. (Princeton, NJ: Princeton University Press, 1952), vol. 1, pp. 127–151.

13. For the most authoritative primary source on Ann Lee's life, see the rare *Testimonies of the Life, Character, Revelations, and Doctrines of Our Ever Blessed Mother Ann Lee and the Elders with Her* (Hancock, MA: J. Talcott and J. Deming, Junrs., 1816). Also see the treatments in Calvin Green and Seth Y. Wells, *A Summary View of the Millennial Church or United Society of Believers (Commonly Called Shakers)* (Albany, NY: Packard and Van Benthuysen, 1823), and Edward Deming Andrews, *The People Called Shakers,* new enl. ed. (New York: Dover, 1963). The treatment of the Shakers given here is condensed from Foster, *Religion and Sexuality,* pp. 21–71.

14. Green and Wells, *Millennial Church,* pp. 132–133.

15. See Youngs, *Testimony of Christ's Second Appearing,* and Green and Wells, *Millennial Church.* A revealing secondary analysis of Shaker theology is Rourke, "The Shakers." Normative Shaker christological beliefs of the early nineteenth century are succinctly presented in the following affirmation: "Christ first appeared in Jesus of Nazareth, by which he was constituted the head of the new spiritual creation of God. . . . [The human tabernacle of Ann Lee] was a chosen vessel, occupied as an instrument, by the spirit of Christ, the Lord from Heaven, in which the second appearance of that Divine spirit was ushered into the world." Green and Wells, *Millennial Church,* pp. 216, 219.

16. Valentine Rathbun, *An Account of the Matter, Form, and Manner of a New and Strange Religion* (Providence, RI: Bennett Wheeler, 1781). Rathbun dated his account December 5, 1780.

17. See Persons, "Christian Communitarianism in America," and Cross, *Burned-over District.*

18. "Introduction to Records of Sacred Communications" (New Lebanon, NY: ca. 1843), p. 10. This is a manuscript in the Western Reserve Historical Society Library in Cleveland, Ohio, which provides the best contemporary Shaker analysis of the factors which led to the unusual outbreak of "spiritual manifestation" which began in 1837. It also provides a brief summary of earlier Shaker membership growth.

19. Thomas Brown, *An Account of the People Called Shakers* (Troy, NY: Parker and Bliss, 1812), p. 343.

20. "Introduction to Records of Sacred Communications," p. 10.

21. William Hepworth Dixon, *New America,* 6th ed., 2 vols. (London: Hurst and Blackett, 1867), vol. 2, p. 86.

22. John Humphrey Noyes, *History of American Socialisms* (Philadelphia: J. B. Lippincott, 1870), p. 670.

23. "Introduction to Records of Sacred Communications."

24. An overview of the phenomena is provided in Foster, *Religion and Sexuality,* pp. 62–71. Also see Lawrence Foster, "Shaker Spiritualism and Salem Witchcraft: Social Perspectives

on Trance and Possession Phenomena" (paper presented at the annual meeting of the National Historic Communal Societies Association in New Harmony, Indiana, on October 15, 1983).

25. One of the most disruptive phenomena occurred, for example, in 1839 when three leading Shakers, including the venerable Richard McNemar, a key figure in the founding of the Midwestern Shaker communities, were expelled from the Union Village, Ohio, community at the behest of a young medium. Only belatedly were McNemar and his associates reinstated by a directive from the central office at New Lebanon, New York. Following this episode, rules began to be formulated to test the validity of spiritual communications.

26. For a summary of reactions, see Cross, *Burned-over District*, pp. 307–321, and David T. Arthur, "Millerism," in *The Rise of Adventism: Religion and Society in Mid-Nineteenth-Century America*, ed. Edwin S. Gaustad (New York: Harper & Row, 1974), pp. 154–172.

27. Jacobs prints extracts from a letter of John Dunlavy to Barton W. Stone in 1805 during the Kentucky Revival, *The Day-Star*, June 13, 1846, 11:6–9.

28. *Ibid.*, May 23, 1846, 10:56.

29. See O. L. Crosier's "Visit to the Shakers," printed in its entirety, *ibid.*, August 8, 1846, 11:18–19.

30. *Ibid.*, May 9, 1846, 10:44.

31. Letter of April 24, 1846, from Henry B. Bear, *ibid.*, May 9, 1846, 10:44. Bear's pamphlet, *Henry B. Bear's Advent Experience* (Whitewater, Ohio, n.d.), is one of the finest summations of the emotional and intellectual processes through which a thoughtful Millerite went during the 1840s.

32. *The Day-Star*, May 23, 1846, 10:51.

33. *Ibid.*, June 13, 1846, 11:9.

34. *Ibid.*, June 13, 1846, 11:5.

35. Numerous discussions by Enoch Jacobs show that Shaker theology was sometimes difficult to justify to Millerites, but Jacobs continually stressed the importance of considering the whole achievement of the Shakers rather than individual bits of theology in isolation.

36. For example, see the letter from Sister E. S. Willard approving of celibacy prior to Christ's Second Advent, *ibid.*, May 9, 1846, 10:42.

37. *Ibid.*, May 9, 1846, 10:42.

38. *Ibid.*, June 13, 1846, 11:12.

39. See the analysis in Foster, *Religion and Sexuality*, pp. 54–58. Approximately 20 percent of converts either remained in the Second Family or transferred to another Shaker group.

40. *Ibid.*, p. 56. Further analysis would be necessary to determine how many of the individuals who left the Shakers after joining in the late 1840s were former Millerites, but it seems certain that a significant proportion had been associated with the Millerite movement.

41. *Ibid.*, pp. 56–58.

42. MacLean, *Bibliography of Shaker Literature*, pp. 19–20.

43. *The Day-Star*, August 8, 1846, 11:18.

44. *Ibid.*, November 7, 1846, 11:36.

45. Henry C. Blinn, *The Manifestation of Spiritualism Among the Shakers, 1837–1847* (East Canterbury, NH: 1899), p. 49.

46. Andrews, *People Called Shakers*, pp. 160–161.

47. Anna White and Leila S. Taylor, *Shakerism: Its Meaning and Message* (Columbus, OH: Fred J. Heer, 1904), p. 235.

48. For a provocative analysis of the transformation of the Adventist movement after the Great Disappointment, see Jonathan M. Butler, "Adventism and the American Experience," in *The Rise of Adventism,* ed. Gaustad, pp. 173–206. Discussions of the early development of Adventist sanctuary theology are found in LeRoy Edwin Froom, *The Prophetic Faith of our Fathers: The Historical Development of Prophetic Interpretation,* 4 vols. (Washington, DC: Review and Herald, 1954), vol. 4, pp. 877–905; M. Ellsworth Olsen, *A History of the Origin and Progress of the Seventh-Day Adventists* (Washington, DC: Review and Herald, 1925), pp. 177–197; and Ingemar Lindén, *The Last Trump: An Historico-Genetical Study of Some Important Chapters in the Making and Development of the Seventh-Day Adventist Church* (Frankfurt-am-Main: Peter Lang, 1978), pp. 129–131.

One of the best theoretical discussions of the larger issue of how groups adapt to an apparently failed prophecy is provided in J. Gordon Melton's "What Really Happens When Prophecy Fails?" (paper presented at the Conference on American Millennialism held at the Unification Theological Seminary, Barrytown, New York, October 24–26, 1980). Melton criticizes the approach adopted in the classic study by Leon Festinger, Henry W. Riecken, and Stanley Schachter, *When Prophecy Fails: A Social and Psychological Study of a Modern Group that Predicted the Destruction of the World* (New York: Harper & Row, 1964; originally published by the University of Minnesota Press in 1956). Melton argues that millenarian groups are not primarily organized around the prediction of some future event. Instead, prediction in a well-organized millenarian movement is only one of many important elements in the group's belief system. When a specific prophecy does not occur, millenarian movements typically reinterpret or "spiritualize" the prediction. It is decided that "the prophecy was not incorrect, the group merely misunderstood it. The group understood it in a material earthly manner. Its truth comes as a spiritual, invisible (except to the eye of faith) level. Thus from the original prophesied event, the believers create an 'invisible,' 'spiritual' and more importantly unfalsifiable event" (p. 5). An incisive analysis of the development of early Christianity from a similar perspective is found in John G. Gager, *Kingdom and Community: The Social World of Early Christianity* (Englewood Cliffs, NJ: Prentice-Hall, 1975).

How Do Movements Survive Failures of Prophecy?

Anthony B. van Fossen

This paper confronts the issue of how a movement survives prophetic failures and how contradictory events are denied, forgotten, or reinterpreted. The contemporary French messianic movement of Georges Roux is examined in relation to three influential models of prophetism: those of Festinger, Douglas, and Burridge. By comparing these models and the movement[1] that each of these investigators studied firsthand with the history of Rouxism, new hypotheses are generated. It is suggested that a movement is more likely to survive if, soon after the failure of its prophecies, it creates rules that translate dissonance into pollution, locates it in some offending organ of the member's body, and then proposes a ritual of purification for relief. A second hypothesis is that a credible expansion of the claims and identity of the prophet will help to contain the disruption of a significant prophetic failure. The third and major hypothesis is that to survive the failure of an important specific prophecy, a movement must become more hierarchical—demoting the unreliable and consigning nonbelievers to insignificance but, most importantly, elevating the prophet and his original and most trusted apostles and disciples by introducing new roles and statuses for them near the summit of the hierarchy. The implications of this hypothesis and how it differs from conventional views of new religions and their "routinization" are explored.

The movement of Georges Roux (The Universal Christian Church, *L'Eglise chrétienne universelle*) has never before been investigated by a social scientist (see Alliez et al. 1955). This is unfortunate, because it has been a relatively isolated, integral, and self-defining phenomenon, and an intensive study of it may suggest new ideas about the origins, development, and decline of social movements in general. Moreover, Rouxism constitutes a particular problem, since it arose in the West at a time when impersonal rationality has been seen as triumphing and discrediting charismatic claims—especially those that are not derived from marginal ethnic groups or from alien societies (Wilson 1975:113–114). Although I propose a general model, I have attempted to demonstrate it only within the single context of Rouxism. A *leitmotif* of this paper, then, is the relationship between the failure of prophecy and Rouxism's progressive revelations that its faithful apostles would become healers, visionaries, immortals, and artists (see van Fossen 1984 for a more detailed history).

When Prophecy Fails

My investigation concerns how hope and faith are maintained after prophecies fail, and yet I find *When Prophecy Fails,* the influential and widely acclaimed book by Festinger, Riecken, and Schachter (1956), a radically deficient guide. Festinger and coworkers (hereafter referred to simply as Festinger) investigated a movement called the Seekers that began in the Midwestern United States in the 1950s when its middle-aged leader claimed to have received messages from outer space predicting the end of the world. She was joined by about thirty others, five of whom were investigators posing as believers. The Seekers left their jobs, neglected their studies, failed to make repairs, and otherwise readied themselves for the arrival of a spaceship that was supposed to take them to a safe planet. With the conclusive failure of the prophecy, the group reversed its attitude. Instead of rebuffing persistent journalists, members began zealously seeking publicity. But they seemed lost, exhausted, searching in every direction for guidance, and mixing incompatible and half-hearted denial, excuse, and reaffirmation. The movement attracted no new converts and soon disintegrated, rising and falling exceedingly rapidly, like the vast majority of prophetic movements—even those that have lasted long enough to be recorded.

Festinger assumes that there is a real world against which prophecies are measured, so his attitude as an author can be easily withheld from disclosure and a prophecy labeled as clearly confirmed or unconfirmed. For him a prophetic movement is a folly, an anomaly butting up against a real world that is solid, immovable, and unable to be dismissed. He implicitly advises caution and the avoidance of extreme positions, fantasy, and obsessional behavior. What is subtly recommended is the ordinary life, which seems, if not at the level of his deepest conviction, a conventional, commonsensical level to which the Seekers have not been raised, making discussion of higher standards pointless.

This inconspicuous pragmatism unites Festinger with most of his readers and subtly satirizes any prophetic theory of behavior. The authors and the two hired investigators posing as believers are presented as plain, commonsensical foils for the Seekers. They are retiring, reserved, and unnoticeable, and agree politely with all, revealing their perspicacity only to the reader. The leaders or sham oracles of the Seekers are, on the other hand, portrayed as bombastic travesties of people of grandeur, whose oratory breaks the prevailing rhythm of simple speech and of the authors' descriptive, realistic, and documentary style, which is undisrupted by the theoretical analysis and jargon confined to the introduction and conclusion of the book. The knowing smiles of the prophet, Mrs. Keech, when she confronts a stranger she believes to be a spaceman, the blubbering, frustrated sexuality, and illiterate trance messages of her sometime rival, Bertha, and the dumb confidence of the chief proselytizer, Dr. Armstrong, make them recognizable fools. We break into a smile when Mrs. Keech assumes that one of the authors must have his own channel of communication with the "Guardians" (since she is ignorant of his conspiratorial network of communication with the other observers). Indeed, the Seekers often seem to be unconsciously satirizing themselves, as when the informal Dr. Armstrong refers to his redeemers as "the boys upstairs" (Festinger et al. 1956:97).

The unstated agreement between Festinger and the reader who smiles is that the movement is undesirable. And this conclusion depends largely upon it being presented as based on an absurd prediction rather than on the deep spiritual, moral, political, and cultural dimensions that are crucial to the prophetic movement. The humor of the situation might be diluted if we knew what attracted people to the group, but Festinger bars this deeper intellectual inquiry as irrelevant (Festinger et al. 1956:6).

Yet in the last analysis the reader does not escape simply by smiling at the Seekers' dogmas. For conventional wisdom also entertains unwarranted assumptions, notably, that when a prophecy fails, its believers will doubt the prophet more than before and do less for the movement. Festinger shows that this is not true. But he does not open a dark and fertile field of objections to common sense in general; he merely slightly modifies the conventional viewpoint while extending its plausibility. People who have an unusual and strong commitment and meet certain other conditions will believe more firmly and proselytize more fervently after than before a prophecy fails.

This brings Festinger's reduction to absurdity of the Seekers to its logical conclusion. And yet serious inadequacies exist in this model. He fails to explain the quick demise of the movement and is forced into facile speculations that it was caused by accidents of personal situation, legal action, and the fact that its members were poor proselytes—none of which are convincing explanations to the book's most eminent reviewer (Hughes 1958:437). And Festinger also fails to answer the question implicitly put to himself in the first chapter: why some prophetic movements survive and even recruit new members after prophetic failure.

Cosmology, Pollution Rules, and the Prophet

For a more profound approach, we turn to Mary Douglas (1966) and to Kenelm Burridge (1960). Although they never mention *When Prophecy Fails*, and Festinger shows no awareness of Douglas's and Burridge's works, the latter offer evocative hints that I will interpret to provide a more satisfactory model of how movements survive failure of prophecy. Douglas and Burridge view prophetic movements as indicating the members' concern for the world in which they live and move—a concern best described as cosmological. For these cosmologists, the whole is part of every event, and every event occurs only within the structure of the whole. For them, Festinger's definition of a specific prophecy as either a success or a failure (encouraging a leap of faith) would seem extreme and arbitrarily conceived, since their universe is denser than his. It is a continuum which makes it more difficult to isolate and distinguish the crucial event, to separate it from its antecedents and contexts. Their works have fewer emphatic moments than Festinger's and are devoted to close interconnections, uninterrupted impressions, multiple approaches.

For our purposes Douglas's most significant insight is that the cosmology is a world pattern and totality that is able to embrace and contain contradiction. Douglas regards the narrow preoccupation with belief and the efficacy of rites and prophecies (so dear to Festinger) as an emotional and prejudiced approach that leads to a barren perspective. For her, the basic pattern of the cosmology, the collective conscience, the common commitment to common values, is to unite contrary realities and statements harmoniously (Douglas 1966:31–32). This shifts attention from inconsistencies between belief and reality to the intrinsic logic and metaphysics of a society's cosmology. Whereas Festinger implicitly defines religion in terms of a dichotomy between supernature and nature and focuses attention on the absurd actions and acts of faith that attempt to reconcile them, for Douglas religion is defined by ritual models of purity and pollution. Prophecies of purity through new rituals are more acts whose justification rests in themselves, part of a logical and coherent cosmological system in which belief, faith, and material disconfirmation are relatively minor aspects.

Whereas Festinger treats the prophecy as a concept (systematically formulated, translated into rational terms, and specifically acting on the intelligence), Douglas sees it as a symbol—speaking to the whole human being, emphasizing people's social nature, and forming a social memory (Douglas 1966:48–49, 79–80). Symbols are common property of society and they emerge in ritual, when people perform as a group. Concepts, on the other hand, stress abstraction and the lone individual's isolated reflection.

The basic pattern underlying Douglas's concept of cosmology, symbol, and prophetic movement involves the body and its symbolic relation to pollution. She brilliantly demonstrates that modern people have lost the religious sense of bodily functions. Her organic metaphors contrast sharply with the electromechanical metaphors of Festinger, which accord so well with the seemingly irresible diffusion of techniques and ideologies from industrialized nations. For him the Seekers' minds, nervous systems, and modes of communication are akin to electrical mechanisms. The prophecy is written automatically and communicated by telephone, television, newspapers, and radio. The primary emotions are excitement and tension. And the failure of prophecy is a kind of short circuit (like the malfunctioning of a switch at a crucial test), producing a jolting shock and intolerable strain. Festinger's model presents a schematic diagram that shows how a secondary transfer supplies added energy and effectively denies the significance of the original failure. Electromechanical metaphors accord well with the Seekers' attempt to relate their science and technology meaningfully to the rest of human existence using the cultural and religious conventions of America. But they would seriously distort the meaning of prophetic movements in many non-literate societies as well as in the Rouxist movement, where members periodically attempt to discover the pristine purity of organic experience in an earthly Arcadia, not a mechanized utopia on another planet.

For Douglas prophetic movements propose new taboos and rituals that aim at the redemption of the world. Conversion, or "drinking the medicine," in the Zaïrois Lele cult she studied is a sort of organic epiphany: the meeting with a new system of purity and pollution revolutionizing how and what one eats and drinks, how and with whom one has sex, whom one visits, and how one's time and work are organized (Douglas 1963b:249–250). And if the prophetic movement fails, it is for organic and not technical reasons. The truth she communicates is that there is a direct relation between humanity and natural law (that which is and must be), that the body and organic society build frontiers and constrain human self-creation. Prophetic movements, in categorically suppressing existing taboos, rules, and rituals, passing into spirit communication, and proposing an open horizon of almost limitless possibility, cross this limit at the cost of self-violation (Douglas 1963a; 1963b; 1973:72–73, 166). The prophetic movement denies the balance of the natural order, a balance that must inevitably be restored. And the righting of the balance, like the Mosaic law with which Douglas is so concerned, occurs impersonally. She leaves us with a sense of the restricted powers of human beings to transform their lives.

She defines the failure of prophecy in terms far more complicated than Festinger concedes—since he assumes that there is a real world which may unequivocally refute belief (Festinger et al. 1956:4). Douglas points out that events refuted belief when they violated commonsense standards within the group (Douglas 1963a:141). Second, she implies that the failures of prophecy were less decisive for the survival of the movement than the members' observance of its strict rules of pollution (1963a:135–141). Each Lele prophetic movement had its set of rules and prohibitions on food and behavior, whose breach accounted for any failure of the movement to fulfill its promises (Douglas 1963b:245).

It is possible that Festinger's Seekers did not survive as a movement because they failed to create or enforce effective rules that would translate dissonance into pollution, locate it in some offending organ of the body, and then propose a ritual of purification for relief, which would attain permanence by being grafted onto the body (their most solid personal manifestation of existence). The Seekers' prophet proposed vegetarian rules of dietary purity, but they were never compulsory, permanent, or fully ritualized (Festinger et al. 1956:74, 96, 101, 111, 114, 131). The tedium of waiting for fulfillment was their discipline (1956:95), and the failure of the prophecy was their drill (1956:147–148). The movement appeared to be extremely individualistic and lacking cohesion, since it had no significant basis or center other than prophecy. When prophecy failed, the Seekers were initially paralyzed. Then aimlessly they searched for guidance.

And finally, they feared a threat that seemed to emanate from no one direction, a threat with no shape, from which their leaders soon escaped to places where myth could flow again (the prophet joined a Dianetics center in Arizona, and her chief disciple became an occult proselytizer; 1956:231–232).

This hypothesis of the centrality of rules of purification for solving prophetic failure could be sufficiently supported only through an exhaustive study of a number of movements. My investigation proposes merely to specify the terms of the hypothesis. In Roux's movement, each successive rule of purification emerged immediately after a failure of prophecy disturbed members. In 1950 Roux revealed to his disciples that all must adopt a special diet after they discovered that he had not healed himself of cerebral meningitis. In 1953 they began to close their eyes to recite purifying messages from spirits after the first of three children of disciples died for want of medical care. In June 1968 Roux commanded that they abstain from sexual intercourse until 1980 after French students and workers revolted in May and vividly reminded Roux of his disciples' failure to convert their children and the apparent failure of his prophecy that the movement would grow. On Christmas Day, 1979, apostles announced that the last judgment would not occur on January 1, 1980. Rather, disciples could become immortal spirits and creative artists through concentration on the church's hymns and refraining from listening to any other form of music. Tension, paradox, and opposition were overcome and transcended through ritual techniques, implying subtle alterations of physiology. Purification rules differentiate members from outsiders and construct a hierarchy within the group. But they are not the only criteria, and there are glaring exceptions to ranking by these rules. For example, disciples knew that Roux did not always adhere to the special diet, and yet they did not cease to regard him as the Messiah.

Douglas (1963b:246–247) is not sufficiently concerned with the deeper origins of the taboos that guide a prophetic movement. These origins might be best exemplified in Lele mythology, but Douglas tells us nothing about this; much less does she provide a theory of myth. This severely limits her project for awakening metaphysical consciousness in anthropology. And it probably expresses a deeper resistance. For myth projects people beyond what Douglas implies are the inevitable boundaries of life. More serious still, in her account of Lele witch cleansing, she implies that the rules of purity, which are the center of orientation for her entire work, do not have the great solidity and determinateness she so often attributes to them. She briefly notes that any member of the movement could come forward as a prophet inspired by dreams to make new rules of purity (Douglas 1963b:246–247).

Given the imperfections of mundane life, it is hardly surprising, then, that even after numerous prophetic "failures," movements spring up again, craving new hopes like the succession of cargo cults in Melanesia (Burridge 1960, 1969). Movements succeed insofar as they provide a new, higher measure for the person. For Burridge, the center of the movement is the prophet's magnetism.

The fixed point from which Festinger and Douglas view the prophecy or the movement as a failure is, for Burridge, external to the center of the movement. For Festinger, whether prophecy is confirmed or denied must be considered strictly in terms of external events, mechanical time, and the chronological moment for which fulfillment is predicted. Douglas adopts a similar two-element (prophecy and external events) position for quite different, nonpsychological reasons. Although chronological time is not central to her, she regards the prophetic movement as a failure, since it unintentionally destroys significant social relationships that it has promised to perfect. She and Festinger impute natural, inherent tendencies toward consistency and balance. Burridge sees the mind, emotions, and myth-dream of the prophet and his or her disciples as being obscure and profound. Even if the prophecy can be made to seem explicit, for him it is, if not from its very inception at least in the end, more of a dream interpretation, locating a sphere of interest. For Burridge, like Hegel, history seems triumphantly marching toward an open-ended, limitless world that bears little resemblance to the finite and ordered cosmos desired by Douglas.

In Burridge's sense, even the Seekers were a success (at least for a time). But when we contemplate why they were less of a success than the Rouxists, we come to the kernel of Burridge's contribution to our inquiry. Festinger and Douglas present prophetic movements as essentially egalitarian—there are no major distinctions between the prophet and his or her disciples. And yet Festinger reports some intriguing information. After prophecies failed, the Seekers searched aimlessly for some person to tell them what to do next (Festinger et al. 1956:180). They went to the extreme of identifying strangers as spacemen, most frequently in the form of a plea for orders and messages (1956:215). And the prophet compared herself to Jesus for the first time after her prophecies failed and after the five young men whom she had proclaimed to be spacemen launched a vigorous attack against the Seekers' ideology and prophecies (1956:151). But the prophet was neither magnetic nor effective in convincing her disciples of her divine identity. In fact, her identity never seemed particularly important to most disciples. Their interest was focused on the prophecy as empirical prediction and probably contributed to the movement's dispersion after prophetic failure—all members going their separate ways and not one following the prophet. If Festinger had not branded incidents such as the leadership struggle between the prophet and her rival medium as irrelevant to his main thesis (1956:110), he might have faced the issue of the relations between the prophet and disciples more creatively.

From this I conclude that when there are holes and gaps left between events, the prophet (if the movement is to survive) must enlarge his/her identity and the context of his/her mission to make the events consistent within himself/herself. I hypothesize that such a credible expansion of identity will help to contain the disruption of a significant prophetic failure. After it was apparent that Roux had failed to heal himself, he announced in 1950 that he was no longer a healer but a teacher and source of all healing. After his disciples privately reported their healing failures, he proclaimed in 1951 that he was Christ. He asserted that he was a spirit and refused all visitors immediately after the failure of a millennial prophecy on August 15, 1954. And after the children's deaths and more apocalyptic prophetic failures, he returned as God in 1955. With the movement shrinking in membership and the May 1968 students/workers revolt reminding him of the disciples' failure to convert their own children, he proclaimed in 1968 that they were unworthy of meeting him and that henceforth he would be an alien God. On Christmas, 1979, when his apostles announced that the Last Judgment would not occur on January 1, 1980, Roux declared that he was the paramount "new spirit" (l'Esprit), this phrase denoting the new supreme level.

Hierarchy

Festinger and Douglas treat movements as fundamentally egalitarian, and Burridge chooses to regard the prophet more as exemplar than leader. All ignore subtle gradations of ranking, and none adequately considers the disciple.

Douglas mistakenly supposes that the prophetic movement's attack on the limitations of a particular hierarchy is directed at hierarchy itself. By failing to see the hierarchy of the prophetic movement, she implies that each member is inspired by overreaching hubris rather than by a recognition of personal limitation within a stratified order. Even with the millennial movement's prophesied paradise, as in Roux's City of God, there may be grades. The goal of a movement such as Roux's is not equality but a just hierarchy, where each will be content because his place is proportionate to his qualities.

For Douglas and Burridge, the member's goal is to save himself and his community. For me, the prophet's and the disciple's aim is not so extreme: each strives to adapt himself closely to what is expected within the movement's legitimate and apparently inevitable order of inequality. For me, the basis of the prophetic movement might be very loosely called the totem (the classification and hierarchy of predicted norms of social action) and not so much Douglas's taboo and Burridge's charisma (which is more a prelude to forming the role of prophet than an enduring gift). Burridge and Douglas see prophetic movements as parts of an encompassing society and culture. But they fail to perceive the movement as a self-contained universe created by the hierarchical articulations of prophets and disciples, as a coordinated system and not merely a name given to an aggregate of associated individuals from the wider society.

The impetus of the prophetic movement is toward a universe in which it is no longer encompassed by a deficient traditional society but one that makes society over in its image and encompasses it. The prophecy represents a revolutionary promise of a universe that cannot be contained in the actual society. Hence the goal of the movement is revolutionary (even more radical than Burridge allows) and is not primarily futile (as for Festinger) or destructive (as for Douglas), although it may be these as well. It is revolutionary in tending toward an absolute view, upholding the ideal of a rigorous order that is demanded in the criticism of actuality. Roux's movement is analogous to an expanded family, and the revolutionary ideal it proposes is an intensely paternalistic society, where disciples express undying loyalty and enthusiasm for patronizing social relationships. No sympathy is felt for the extenuating circumstances that make that goal difficult to attain. The uncompromising demand and severity of outlook are hardly hinted at by Burridge, just as the rigorous order that is demanded is underplayed by Douglas.

A recurring paradox is how the movement can claim to represent and control the cosmos as a whole and yet remain a small minority group. These claims are most crystallized in its prophecies, and its paradoxes become most excruciating when prophecies fail. My central point is that the hierarchy of classification of people and ideas must be reordered after prophetic failure if the movement is to survive. With this change the movement produces a new revolutionary message—a new concept of ethics, epistemology, time, and space. Since the prophetic movement regards its social order as an integral part of the divine cosmic order, the realm of prophetic failure or the movement's inability to control history is the area from which the sense of precariousness, once aroused, will expand to the cosmos as a whole. A severe crisis will shake faith in the stability of the cosmic and social hierarchy, since its compact mode of symbolization cannot do justice to the differentiated structures of reality the members suddenly feel. The rhythm of the movement is disturbed and all activities within its total complex hierarchy are modified. It is out of balance. History attacks cosmos or, as Rouxists say, meaningless duration (*existence*) opposes being (*être*).

We must distinguish between specific and cosmic prophecies. For Festinger, the movement centers around the specific prophecy. For Douglas, specific prophecies and their failures accumulate to discredit the movement. For Burridge, the cosmic prophecy may generate specific predictions but is so metaphysical and sweeping that it is immune to contradiction at a pragmatic level. For me, the cosmic prophecy is defined by the movement's social hierarchy (or lack of it) as a model for the social structure of the redeemed world. The failure of specific prophecies may destroy a movement if it has little social hierarchy or an accepted basis for forming one (as among the Seekers). The failure of prophecy arises from the recognition of an insufficiency in the movement's grandeur, rather than from the simple nonappearance of something expected (as Festinger believes), a destruction of coherence (as Douglas postulates), or a sudden loss or termination of the movement's or the prophet's magnetic attraction (as Burridge perceives), although all these may be involved.

In its most general and programmatic form, my hypothesis is that to survive the failure of an important specific prophecy, a movement must become more hierarchical. It must demote the unreliable and consign nonbelievers to insignificance. But most important, it must elevate the prophet and his most trusted and original apostles and disciples by introducing new roles and statuses near the summit of the hierarchy. One of the central functions of these alterations is to contain contradictions by altering ethical, epistemological, historical, and spatial awareness.

Let me illustrate. In 1950 and 1951 Roux created a movement in which he was the "Master," second only to God, reordering relationships and status within his family and creating the categories of healing apostles *(apôtres)*, followers *(suivants)*, and prospects *(enseignes)* to be opposed to nonmembers *(étrangers)* and "enemies" *(ennemis)*. From 1953 to 1954 two followers who received spirit messages became powerful apostles. Members who criticized spirit communication were labeled Judases, and Roux later admitted killing one of them. Followers whose children died for want of medical care were demoted to "sympathizers" *(sympathisants)* or accused of betraying Roux. Apocalyptic threats against "enemies" increased in number and ferocity. Roux refused personal contact or even written communication even with disciples after the failure of the August 15, 1954, millennial prophecy. But in January 1955 he announced that he was God, and spirits preeminently represented by his daughters were recognized as more authoritative than any apostle. By 1968 all but one of the apostles belonged to Roux's family, the others having died, abandoned the faith, or been demoted. Throughout the process, from 1955 to 1979, Roux's daughter Jacqueline in Avignon became increasingly his representative in the world. Roux (as the paramount of the divine cosmic and social order) became ever more a spirit and less a distinct person whom one could encounter, feel, or converse with. As Roux was elevated ever higher over disciples and common humanity, he came to see himself as permitted to violate rules (such as those of diet) that were binding on other members. On Christmas Day, 1979, when apostles announced that the Last Judgment would not occur on January 1, 1980, apostles were elevated more clearly above followers. All members were promoted to an immortality denied to nonmembers. And Jacqueline's husband, René van Geringe, in Paris became the chief public representative of Roux's "new spirit" *(l'Esprit)*, a new supreme level of hierarchy. The growing hierarchy was increasingly based on the degree to which a person, group, or category was supposed to experience Roux's underlying, intangible embrace, thus realizing opportunities for healing power, spiritual happiness, immortality, and artistic creation.

These statuses and roles within the hierarchy, like taboos and institutionalized charisma, were the petrified and ritualized by-products of the energetic relations between prophet, apostles, followers, and involved outsiders, processes of give and take, rejection, selection, and amalgamation. Roux and his apostles controlled the movement's organization and communication, absorbed, threatened, or expelled challengers, and legitimated only ideas and activities that furthered their objectives. Since they shaped the entire structure, Roux's and his apostles' actions are the predominant features of the movement. This does not exclude considering followers, sympathizers, prospects, or involved outsiders, but only insofar as they influenced or impinged upon Roux and his apostles, that is, when they affected the movement as a whole. Webs of association crystallized into roles, statuses, and hierarchical structures that gained autonomy and permanency and confronted involved individuals as alien powers. The breaking out of roles solidified by ritual repetition occurred almost exclusively in crises after prophetic failures when new hierarchies, ritual rules, and roles were established. The amplified hierarchy resolved conflicts between prophecy and verisimilitude. On one hand, it raised Roux's (and hence the members') potential claims and conceivable powers of action. Conversely, when measured against Roux, members (even when rising within an ever-greater hierarchy) realized the limitations of their own experiences and reaffirmed their growing subordination to him.

The movement (insofar as it remained prophetic) survived to the extent that it was creative and did not surrender to the ordinary waking consciousness of the surrounding culture. Each amplification of hierarchy corresponded to a deepening critique of the authenticity of immediate conventional consciousness and a growing sense of an initiated group aware of a real meaning behind deceptive appearances, a group proclaiming the advent of new powers within themselves corresponding to this revelational age.

The surviving prophetic movement tended toward an autonomous universe, another world related to the conventional world by hierarchical analogy, or what Dumont (1970) calls encompassment, but not by imitation of the conventional world. The movement always attempted to be a self-enclosed system that entered into relationships with other systems, always on its own terms. Within an integrated and unified hierarchy, followers imitated apostles and members imitated Roux, but they did not imitate nonmembers.

It was after prophetic failure, when this hierarchy was jeopardized, that the confrontation with the conventional world became most crucial. Although there may be a universal structure to resolving prophetic failures through accentuating hierarchy, any study of a prophetic movement must refer to collective representations establishing canons of probability in that culture. This is true even in relatively familiar Western societies, since here understandings of the human condition have been shifting away from hierarchy, holism (Dumont 1970, 1977), and charismatic heroism (Wilson 1975) as meaningful solutions, making resolutions of conflicts through these more suspect. Rouxists' resolutions often corresponded to the most religious elements of common French collective representations and thereby seemed more plausible while at the same time never surrendering their superiority to the conventional world.

The central concern of the church's hierarchy changed over time (although all themes were present to some degree in any one stage). During the first stage, a hierarchy was formed in the early years of the movement and it acquired a specifically moral dimension (van Fossen 1984). Disciples desperately searched for ways to transcend illness, public attacks, fears of hideous apocalyptic death, self-castigation, and the encompassing problem of evil. In the second period, from October 1953 to January 1955, an ever-increasing membership used proselytism not so much to transform nonmembers as to express how disciples had, through spirit communication, risen above the mundane knowledge available to the unconverted. As the children died and millennial prophecies failed, the hierarchy was interpreted more epistemologically, with greater gaps between successive levels of hierarchy and a yawning cleavage between member and nonmember, each of whom thought the other to be the victim of the most dangerous illusions.

In the third stage, the hierarchy became identified with time and sexual desire in a way that encouraged disciples to repress unpleasant memories of prophetic failures (van Fossen 1980). In the fourth phase a new stratification of space emerged, where a supreme level of hierarchy was oriented around Paris, which encompassed Avignon and represented a new unattained goal for almost all disciples at the very moment their leaders told them that the City of God would not arrive on January 1, 1980.

Implications

This increasing hierarchy of person categories shows no sign of the compromise with conventionality and respectability that would make the movement a routinized "established sect" or denomination (Wallace 1956; Wilson 1959:10, 14 and 1970:51; Yinger 1970:264–273). It shows no appreciable tendencies toward bureaucracy and professionalism, and it continues to indicate the total transformation of the world order. Denominationalism is unlikely in a nation where the Catholic Church so dominates religious life and where the state is often hostile to religion. Bureaucracy and professionalism are unlikely in a small group whose vast majority of members are first-generation disciples attracted to apocalypticism. The Rouxists' lack of bureaucracy and professionalism may continue to hinder them in the competition with newly introduced American religions such as the Mormons, Seventh-Day Adventists, and Jehovah's Witnesses, which have employed modes of organization and communication utilized by successful commercial organizations. Rouxists express disgust at the large membership increases of these groups in France since 1950 and scoff at them as manifestations of the American penchant for advertising, which most French still regard as a means through which dubious businessmen lure and defraud the gullible (Zeldin 1977:512, 516–517).

Rouxism has not surrendered to the outside society. How, then, has it survived? Wilson and many others have implied that, apart from a military revolt doomed to defeat, the alternative to surrender is withdrawal, so as to avoid contact with the outside world so that the "sect" may maintain its purity. Since the Millennium does not come and magic does not work (Wilson 1973:488, 500), the prophetic movement may become "introversionist" (Wilson 1970:118–140; 1973:384–449). There is a sense in which this is true of Rouxism, in that it established an ever more enchanted, imaginative, and satisfying autonomous universe. But there is an equally important sense in which it is not true at all, and in which Wilson's model seriously distorts the manner in which Rouxism and probably other movements overcome failures of prophecy.

Rouxism is more active than passive, and it has influenced conventional French life more than it has been compromised by it. Rouxists see themselves as avant-garde, having presaged current popular interest in nonmedical healing, health foods, parapsychology, and apocalypticism. And now they view themselves as harbingers of a future popular neoromantic aestheticism. Rouxists are a proselytizing elite who have transformed those with whom they have come into contact by posing a radical alternative to mundane conventionality. They see even the most violent opposition to them as a sign of their influence and their self-definition as a successful radical movement; the revolution, the full success, will only be a matter of time. The surrounding society is not encompassing but is increasingly encompassed. And (even to an outside skeptical observer) it would appear that the Rouxists, in their extremity, have altered the French sense of what is possible to the extent that they represent a social reality with a power dispro-portionate to their numbers. Their attribution of ever-greater power to them-selves is not as strange as it might first appear.

But besides the internal relation of the members of a prophetic movement to its hierarchical structure and to the surrounding society (the issue with which most of this paper has been concerned), there is a more external relation between the prophetic movement and its academic interpreter that greatly affects the manner in which it is presented to the reader. I shall relate the Rouxist hierarchy of person categories to the interpretations of prophetic movements offered by Festinger, Douglas, Burridge, and myself, and I shall draw conclusions about the proper study of prophetic movements in general. The attitude implicit in these remarks is that the interpretation of a prophetic movement is not only a product of examining it in a detached manner as an objective artifact but also a process of constituting it from a certain point of view in line with the interpreter's men-tal priorities. These are not irreconcilable aspects, and the interpreter's subjective involvement will be read in terms of the objective position which he or she assumes.

In short, Festinger takes the position of the enemy; Douglas, that of the non-member; Burridge, that of the prophet; and I, that of the prospect. That locat-ing interpreters of prophetism of the Rouxist hierarchy may seem whimsical, amusing, or unscientific to some indicates a deep problem in many accounts of prophetism and with what passes for the "objective" investigation that "sects" are said to resist (Wallis 1973, 1979:196, 215; Wilson 1970:13). I do not deny that it is difficult to study people with whom one disagrees or that there are religious groups that are hostile to commentary upon them by outsiders. But I insist that social scientists have often posed as something else (e.g., Catton 1957:526ff; Festinger et al. 1956; Wallis 1979:194, 196) and have written accounts that emphasize the self-closure, delusion, and authoritarianism of members without penetrating the inner logic of their view of the world. Too many accounts of "sects" in Western societies are similar in tone to the tales of the prelogical men-tality and curious customs of "savages," and they betray the same lack of imagi-native understanding. The most sympathetic accounts have often selected the factors of class and social status. But very few have followed Burridge in sus-pending disbelief and tackling the far deeper problem of mythology, of how the members' behavior is affected by the structure of their ideas. Whether or not the anthropologist's suspension of disbelief about prophetic movements and "sects" and his postulation of the members' rationality are due to the "contemporary self-hatred of intellectuals" (Wilson 1973:500), it is through this suspension (and not some ringing affirmation of a largely unquestioned contemporary conventional rationality) that sociological insight will emerge.

Festinger looks down on members of a prophetic movement as inferior in knowledge, power, or intelligence to himself and his readers, and this is most characteristically the attitude of the enemies of Rouxists. The movement and its prophecies were false because they did not correspond to conventional reality. This was the attitude of psychiatrists whose disparaging diagnoses of Rouxists were published and it was the attitude of most journalists who found them ridiculous, mentally deficient, primitive, or fascist.

Douglas's view of the prophetic movement is similar to that which Rouxists think circumambient nonmembers have of them. Members are seen as people of more or less average power and intelligence who pretend or try to be something more than they are, who fail, and who are prone to violate standards of intellectual clarity and social order to maintain exaggerated notions of their importance. Her view is in many respects similar to that of the least unsympathetic journalists such as Bédarieux (1954), the nonmember who wrote the most extensive account of Rouxism before my studies. What promised to be attractive is revealed to be self-deceiving, dangerous, and even dreadful, but scarcely absurd or ridiculous. Yet this is still an outside view, and a surviving prophetic movement such as Rouxism is an increasingly self-contained texture to be approached from within its own frame of reference and interlocking levels of hierarchy.

Burridge presents a model of the prophetic movement similar to that which Roux maintains about his own church. Like Roux, Burridge does not sufficiently recognize the disciples' crucial influence upon the prophet, and their relations with him and with one another remain mysterious.

Rouxists continue to consider me a prospect or student *(enseigne)* as well as an ethnologist writing about their church. For the prospective member, the hierarchy of the Rouxist movement is defined particularly by the inner consistency of its aggregated texts, or actions treated as texts (Ricoeur 1971), produced chiefly by the apostles. The apostles were the prime social and ritual leaders, actors, counselors, preachers, and masters of decorum, and they were the ones whom prospective members and followers confronted personally as their teachers.

As a rule, followers' contributions were excluded from the sacred tribunes, and the hierarchy was defined primarily in terms of one's ability to write or willingness to read Rouxist publications. Disciples read and reread them—thoroughly absorbing Roux's and the apostles' vocabulary, often using their very words, and assimilating an attitude that was romantic, imposing, and superior to the mundane world. Even in proselytizing on the streets of Avignon, disciples closed their eyes to impersonate spirits who recited "lines" contained in the publications they sold. The often astonished or bemused passerby would (if they stopped) be more likely to hear a text than engage in a conversation that might lead to doubt or defection.

By adopting the point of view of the student *(enseigne)*, the anthropologist is able to realize the central importance of texts in Rouxism and places the prime producers of the texts, the apostles, at the center, so that the movement may be grasped most holistically. By contrast, the texts of any other level of the hierarchy seem fragmented, discontinuous, and episodic. Any prejudice against written texts, such as that expressed by Glazer (1980:648), discourages vitally important long-term studies of prophetic movements and prevents seeing them as historical wholes unfolding in time. The most complete accounts of new religions (e.g., those of Dohrman 1958; Lofland 1966; Wilson 1961:7) have emerged from the combination of participant observations and written records.

A final question suggests itself: Why was Rouxism able to survive by elaborating its hierarchy of person categories while the movements studied intensively by Festinger, Douglas, and Burridge were not? Rouxism, like the Seekers, started in a cultic milieu, so this is not a sufficient condition for explaining the movement's demise, as Wallis (1979:44–50) suggests somewhat equivocally. The John Frum movement on the island of Tanna has met prophetic failures by enlarging and solidifying its hierarchy of person categories, as a careful reading of Guiart (1951, 1956) will reveal. So there is no evident reason why a hierarchical and more or less permanent prophetic movement may not arise in what was traditionally a relatively egalitarian horticultural ranking society or elementary chiefdom, contrary to Wilson (1975:34–36, 89, 112), who suggests that such persistence is highly unlikely to be long sustained and who cites the Frum movement as an example!

NOTE

1. A prophetic movement is an organization oriented around an utterance that is supposed to have originated directly from a sacred source, is concerned with the immediate and ultimate future of the people meant to hear it, and is confirmed as decisively important by the earnestness of its bearer(s) (see Trompf 1977:1). The millennial movement is a prophetic movement specifying imminent paradise for its adherents and punishment for unbelievers. The messianic movement is a prophetic movement proclaiming its leader to be God in human human form, or at least to be guided directly by God. Logically, all millennial and messianic movements are prophetic movements, but not vice versa. Empirically, almost all messianic movements are millennial, but not vice versa.

REFERENCES

Alliez, J., M. Baudry, and R. Pujol. 1955. "Un nouveau messie: note sur Georges Roux, de Montfavet, à propos du comportement pathologique de ses adeptes." *Encephale* 44:155–169.

Bédarieux, P. 1954. *La secte tragique des Temoins du Christ.* Paris: Arabesque.

Burridge, K. 1960. *Mambu.* New York: Harper.

———. 1969. *New Heaven, New Earth.* New York: Schocken.

Catton, W. R. 1957. "What Kind of People Does a Religious Cult Attract?" *American Sociological Review* 22:561–565.

Dohrman, H. T. 1958. *California Cult.* Boston: Beacon.

Douglas, M. 1963a. "Techniques of Sorcery Control in Central Africa," in *Witchcraft and Sorcery in East Africa,* edited by J. Middleton and E. H. Winter. London: Routledge and Kegan Paul.

————. 1963b. *The Lele of the Kasai.* London: Oxford University Press.

————. 1966. *Purity and Danger.* London: Routledge and Kegan Paul.

————. 1973. *Natural Symbols.* London: Barrie & Jenkins.

Dumont, L. 1970. *Homo Hierarchicus.* Chicago: University of Chicago Press.

————. 1977. *From Mandeville to Marx.* Chicago: University of Chicago Press.

Festinger, L., H. W. Riecken, and S. Schachter. 1956. *When Prophecy Fails.* Minneapolis: University of Minnesota Press.

Glazer, S. D. 1980. "Review of Bainbridge, *Satan's Power.*" *American Anthropologist* 82: 647–648.

Guiart, J. 1951. "John Frum movement in Tanna." *Oceania* 22:165–175.

————. 1956. "Culture Contact and the 'John Frum' Movement on Tanna, New Hebrides." *Southwest Journal of Anthropology* 12:105–115.

Hughes, E. C. 1958. "Review of Festinger et al." *American Journal of Sociology* 63:437–438.

Lofland, J. 1966. *Doomsday Cult.* Englewood Cliffs, NJ: Prentice-Hall.

Ricoeur, P. 1971. "The Model of the Text: Meaningful Action Considered as a Text." *Social Research* 38:3.

Trompf, G. 1977. "Introduction," in *Prophets of Melanesia,* edited by G. Trompf. Port Moresby: Institute of Papua New Guinea Studies.

van Fossen, A. B. 1980. "Oral Tradition, Myth, and Social Structure: Historical Perception in a French Messianic Movement." *Social Analysis* 4:38–50.

————. 1984. "Prophetic Failure and Moral Hierarchy: The Origins of a Contemporary French Messianic Movement," in *Under the Shade of a Coolibah Tree: Australian Studies in Consciousness,* edited by R. A. Hutch and P. G. Fenner. New York: University Press of America.

Wallace, A.F.C. 1956. "Revitalization Movements." *American Anthropologist* 58:264–281.

Wallis, R. 1973. "Religious Sects and the Fear of Publicity." *New Sociologist* 24:554–557.

————. 1979. *Salvation and Protest.* London: Frances Pinter.

Wilson, B. R. 1959. "An Analysis of Sect Development." *American Sociological Review* 24: 3–15.

————. 1961. *Sects and Society.* London: Heinemann.

————. 1970. *Religious Sects.* New York: McGraw-Hill.

————. 1973. *Magic and the Millennium.* London: Heinemann.

————. 1975. *The Noble Savages.* Berkeley: University of California Press.

Yinger, J. M. 1970. *The Scientific Study of Religion.* New York: Macmillan.

Zeldin, T. 1977. *France 1848–1945: Intellect, Taste and Anxiety,* vol. 3. Oxford, UK: Clarendon.

"It Separated the Wheat from the Chaff"

The "1975" Prophecy and Its Impact among Dutch Jehovah's Witnesses

Richard Singelenberg

In 1966, the Watchtower Bible and Tract Society, the organization of Jehovah's Witnesses, published a book, *Life Everlasting—In Freedom of the Sons of God,* which said on pages 28 and 29:

> According to . . . trustworthy Bible chronology six thousand years from man's creation will end in 1975, and the seventh period of a thousand years of human history will begin in the fall of 1975 [C.E.]. So six thousand years of man's existence on earth will soon be up, yes, within this generation.

It was the first of a sequence of statements in the Society's literature on the importance of 1975: would that year herald the beginning of Christ's millennial reign, implicating doom for the nonbelievers?

Let it be clear from the outset that the Society in its literature *never* proclaimed flat out that 1975 would be the definite end of this world and its population. Nevertheless, the formulations from 1966 onward on what *might* happen in that year, the sense of urgency on a *probable* apocalyptic event, later followed by a *possibility* of a cataclysm, had a startling impact on the proselytizing activities of the Jehovah's Witnesses.

As Festinger and his colleagues hypothesized, nonmaterialization of a religious movement's prophecy will result in increased proselytizing in order to reduce cognitive dissonance (Festinger et al. 1964:25). However, up to now the theory has been tested only among relatively small, isolated groups with a distinctive ideology, not being part of an umbrella organization (see, for example, Hardyck and Braden 1962; Balch et al. 1983).

In contrast, what were the effects among approximately 30,000 Jehovah's Witnesses in Holland when the ambiguous prophecy did not occur?

The ambivalence of the prophecy poses the problem as to the applicability of the theory, since one of the conditions Festinger states is that "the belief must be sufficiently specific." As will be shown below, this requirement is hardly met.

Based on quantitative data of the proselytizing activities of Dutch Jehovah's Witnesses during the period 1961 to 1987, an attempt will be made to explain the rise and decline of the missionary zeal of the adherents.

The Prophecy

According to the Watchtower Society's doctrine, man was created in the autumn of 4026 B.C.E. So, in the fall of 1975, the first 6,000 years of human existence would come to an end. The crucial question—if this period corresponded with God's "rest day," to be followed by the seventh millennium of God's reign, as stated in the Book of Revelation—was the essence of the prophecy, for this transition had to be marked by the final Battle of Armageddon, implicating worldwide doom. From 1966 through 1975, this theme was a recurring topic in the Society's literature.

Analysis of these articles reveals three characteristics. First, contrary to the Society's marked uncompromising ideological jargon, the prophecy contains a definite "uncertainty" clause. The following example is illustrative:

> It [*Life Everlasting*], shows that 6000 years of human experience will end in 1975, about nine years from now. What does that mean? Does it mean that God's rest day began in 4026 [B.C.E.]? It could have. The . . . book does not say it did not. . . . You can accept it or reject it. . . . Does it mean that Armageddon is going to be finished . . . by 1975? It could! It could! All things are possible with God. Does it mean that Babylon the Great is going to go down by 1975? It could. . . . But we are not saying. (Frederick Franz, the then vice-president of the Society, during a speech, quoted in *The Watchtower* [hereafter *WT*], Oct. 15, 1966)

Secondly, the degree of uncertainty in the prophecy's formulations increases as 1975 draws nearer. Whereas the chances of Armageddon were initially considered as "feasible," "apparent," or "appropriate," from the end of 1968 onward it becomes a mere "possibility" (*WT,* Oct. 15, 1966; May 1, 1968; *Awake!* [hereafter *Aw*], Oct. 8, 1966; Oct. 8, 1968; *WT,* Aug. 15, 1968). So, in 1968, the Society considers its chronological calculations as "reasonably accurate (but admittedly not infallible)," while two years earlier they were "trustworthy" (*WT,* Aug. 15, 1968; *Life Everlasting*).

The basis of this gradual retraction was caused by Adam and Eve: what was the elapsed time between their dates of creation? The Society advanced the theory that they were created in the same year, after which God's rest day began, thus legitimizing the parallelism dogma (*WT,* May 1, 1968; Aug. 15, 1968; *Aw,* Oct. 8, 1966; Oct. 8, 1968). Interestingly, after mentioning this event, the writer of the 1968 *Awake!* article refers via a footnote to some pages in a 1963 publication in which the topic is dismissed: "No, for the creation of Adam does not correspond with the beginning of Jehovah's rest day. . . . It does no good to use Bible chronology for speculating on dates that are still future in the stream of time.

Matt. 24:36."[1] The October 8, 1968, issue of *Awake!* was the last publication which highlighted 1975 in a theological context. Subsequent editions did mention the "end of 6000 years of human history" to be imminent (in 1969 this event was described as "aproximately six years left," *WT,* May 1), but mainly non-Society, "Club of Rome Project"–like sources were quoted as support of a gloomy near future.[2] Actually, the October 8, 1971, issue of *Awake!* implicitly dismisses 1975 as a possible year of doom. In a diagram, 1975 is marked as an estimated date for worldwide famine and ecological collapse, but there is more to come: from 1980 onward, the earth will be scourged by environmental pollution, to be followed in 1985 by oxygen deficiency. Also, a book published in 1973 is rather noncommittal on 1975: "the end of 6000 years of man's existence and the beginning of the seventh millennium will be reached many years prior to the year 2000."[3]

If the premises of the prophecy contained a definite *rational* character, *emotional* arguments completed the package. Probably to neutralize the indefinite feature of the prediction, utterances of excitement, hope, and urgency can be marked as the third distinction. "The end is imminent" are key words intended to overrule possible doubts among the readers of the Society's literature. "What a time of big turmoil is ahead of us! A climax in man's history is imminent!" and similar expressions accompany the (usually) cogent exegetic assertions. In some cases, this leads to a remarkable view on certain Biblical passages. Consider the way, for example, the Society tossed around the crucial Markan and Matthian verses that "concerning that day and hour nobody knows but only the Father":

> This is not the time to be toying with the words of Jesus [then follows Matt. 24:36]. To the contrary, it is a time when one should be keenly aware that the end of this system of things is rapidly coming to its violent end (*WT,* Aug. 15, 1968);

> versus,

> How close we may exactly be to the end of the present divisive system of things cannot be predicted, as Jesus reported that even he did not know the day or the hour . . . (Matt. 24:36). (*WT,* May 1, 1970)

The monthly bulletin *Our Kingdom Ministry* (*KM*), distributed to Jehovah's Witnesses only, used considerably less cautious language. As this periodical mainly contains proselytizing strategies, adherents were encouraged to increase their preaching activities, because time was running out rapidly: "Less than a hundred months separate us from the end of 6000 years of man's history. What can YOU do in that time?" (*KM,* Feb. 1968; similar announcements appeared in the Sept. 1968, Mar. 1969, and Mar. 1972 Dutch editions). Incentives for greater commitment were put on the stage, like an eighty-seven-year-old Witness in New Zealand who sold his business in 1914 in anticipation of the then-prophesied cataclysm, "so that he could enjoy a few months of 'colportage' pioneer service." This person encourages young people to act in a similar way (*WT,*

Feb. 15, 1967). Obviously, the Society considers this a policy worth following: "Reports are heard of brothers selling their homes and property and planning to finish out the rest of their days in this old system in the pioneer service. Certainly this is a fine way to spend the short time remaining before the wicked world's end" (*KM,* May 1974, English ed.; Dec. 1974, Dutch ed.). In sum, in the written sources of the Society, the 1975 expectation emerges as an amalgam of a rational exegetic construction and an emotional millennial prerogative of urgency, hope, and actions. As the year draws nearer, the Biblical framework is less emphasized because of an uncertain variable, and the emotional argument, mainly fed by relevant, external references, is more accentuated.

The Society's literature was one channel to disseminate the prophecy; the other was made up of lectures in congregations and during assemblies. The scanty data on what the Witnesses were told also reveal a considerably less sophisticated view of the 1975 events. During an assembly in 1974, the Dutch branch overseer tells the audience:

> The youth has a bright future. Many of us suffered from misery, sickness and death. You don't have to experience that any more. The new order is near. . . . There will be a very special Service Meeting [a weekly congregational gathering] in the week of 8 September 1975. Invite everybody. And what will then happen? Well, we don't tell. You think that if Jehovah makes such an appeal, that there's nothing unusual behind it? Yes? . . . Well, sell your house, sell everything you own and say oh boy, how long can I carry on with my private means. That long? Get rid of things! Pioneer! [more or less full-time proselytizing]. Plan to shower people with magazines during these last months of this dying system of things! Everybody you meet! (from: tape-recording, of *Divine Purpose District Assembly*, Utrecht, Holland, Aug. 1974; also cf. Penton 1985:327, n9)

The October 1, 1975, edition of *The Watchtower* explains why the Final Battle has not taken place. Sure enough, the time lapse between the creation of Adam and Eve proved to be the weak link in the prophecy. The Society, convinced in earlier publications that this period would be "weeks or months, not years," had now substituted the word "or" for "not," thus concluding that any speculation on that date does no good. Apparently, many Witnesses were not satisfied with the way the prophecy, or rather the correction, had been proclaimed (cf. Penton 1985:100). So the July 15, 1976, *Watchtower* came back to the issue and repeated the argument. Much more important, however, was the way in which the Society distanced itself from its earlier highly suggestive recommendations to part with one's possessions. The Witnesses themselves were to blame for their carelessness, for they had misread the Bible. Since the Scriptures do not reveal a specific date, "it was not the word of God that failed or deceived him [the Witness] and brought disappointment, but . . . his own understanding was based on wrong premises." It took the leading members of the Society four years before they decided to acknowledge their error in the initial formulation of the prophecy

(Franz 1985:209). During the summer assemblies of 1979, the Society accepted the responsibility for a part of the disappointment among the adherents who felt victimized by the prophecy's disconfirmation. The final word on the topic was stated in the March 15, 1980, edition of *WT* in which utterances regarding 1975 were regretted. The case was closed.

In January and February 1987, the Dutch branch of the Society offered a bargain package of nine publications, which were an average of twenty years old. Witnesses were encouraged to distribute them as a "special book offer" during their house-to-house calls. Included was the book *Life Everlasting—In Freedom of the Sons of God,* the first source of the prophecy.

Methodology

The major indication of a Jehovah's Witness's commitment to his faith is his proselytizing activity. The Watchtower Society keeps extremely detailed records of the missionary efforts of its adherents, publishing them annually and monthly. Generally, this information is considered reliable (Wilson 1978:183; Rogerson 1969:73).

The data presented here have been obtained from the annual editions of the *Yearbook of Jehovah's Witnesses* and the monthly bulletin *Our Kingdom Ministry.*[4] The *Yearbook* contains a quantitative overview, indicating the Witnesses' preaching activities in each country in which they are allowed to operate. It states, for example, the average number of "publishers," that is, those Witnesses who proselytize; growth or decline percentages of publishers compared to the previous year; number of baptisms; average number of "pioneers," that is, those Witnesses spending at least sixty or ninety hours preaching monthly; the total number of hours spent on proselytizing, and so on. *Our Kingdom Ministry* holds information on nationwide proselytizing activity in terms of average individual monthly activity. Besides the numbers of publishers and pioneers in a particular month, it states the average number of preached hours per individual; the "back-calls,"that is, return visits to someone paying initial interest in the publisher's message by purchasing a publication; the average number of "Bible studies," which can be considered as introductory courses for candidate members; the average amount of distributed magazines, and the like.[5]

The number of publishers, the pioneer-publisher ratio, hours spent on proselytizing, back-calls, and magazine sales are applied as commitment indicators, both at the individual and collective level. The first three indicators are essentially independent of public reception, while back-calls and magazine sales are more contingent on interactional processes: a house dweller can refuse to purchase *Awake!;* the time it takes the Witness to persuade him to accept it and to get the message over is part of the proselytizing package. The output of these efforts is reflected in the baptismal figures.

The results are graphically represented in Figures 1 and 2. Figure 1 is self-explanatory. Figure 2 shows the indicators *per individual* publisher. It is important to stress the fact that the Watchtower Society in its statistics shows proselytizing Witnesses only. Those who, for whatever reason, do not participate in preaching activities are omitted in the data. Figures showing a decrease in publishers may indicate marginalization, exclusion, or defection. However, in view of the Society's own definition of "Jehovah's Witnesses," which includes the clause "those who actively witness," the term "defection" will be applied to indicate declining membership.[6] Based on baptismal figures and number of publishers, it is possible to estimate the magnitude of defection and, more specifically, a "defection/recruitment ratio," hereafter D/R-ratio. For example: in 1975, an average of 28,097 Witnesses were reported active. In the period 1976 to 1979, a total of 3,807 were baptized. Adding this amount to the 1975 figure and reducing it by the annual Dutch mortality rate (averaging 0.66 percent), 1979 should count 31,050 adherents. In fact, 26,040 were reported, giving a "shortage" of 5,010. So it is assumed that 16.1 percent dropped out, resulting in an average annual defection of 4 percent. Consequently, the D/R-ratio is 5010/3807, which equals 1.3.

Because of the effect of the 1975 prophecy on proselytizing activities and membership quantities, it is important to distinguish four phases in the period 1961 to 1987. As will be shown, each of them is characterized by specific activities and distinctive growth and decline patterns. As the main sources for this analysis consist of the Society's quantitative overviews, the derived conclusions are highly tentative. Additional qualitative research, such as in-depth interviewing of (former) Witnesses, is in progress. Also, comparative data from other regions will no doubt shed more light on this phenomenon.

Proselytizing Activities 1961–1987

The Pre-prophecy Phase: 1961–1966

As Figure 1A shows, this period is characterized by a moderate increase of adherents. The annual average growth of active Witnesses amounts to 2.8 percent. The other commitment indicators are more or less stable: each Witness spends an average of 130 hours yearly on preaching, distributes approximately 110 magazines, and makes forty-seven back-calls; almost 2.3 percent are active as pioneers. Also, the baptismal figures do not show significant fluctuations: an average of almost 750 converts dedicate themselves yearly. The annual average defections amount to 1.5 percent; the D/R-ratio is 0.29.

The Prophecy Phase: 1967–1975

Highly significant is the rapid increase of all indicators from 1966 onward. Top scores in growth rates of active Witnesses are made in 1968, 1971, 1973, and 1974, with 10.7 percent, 10.4 percent, 12.4 percent, and 10.6 percent respectively.

The thus-far unmatched number of 29,723 Witnesses is reached in November 1975. In this possible autumn of doom, exactly 6000 years after the postulated creation of Adam, the active following has more than doubled in less than ten years.

Figure 1

Active Witnesses, Baptisms, and Pioneers

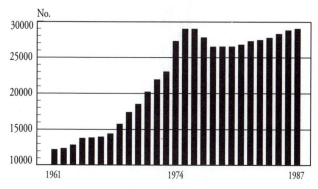

Fig. 1A. **Active Jehovah's Witnesses**

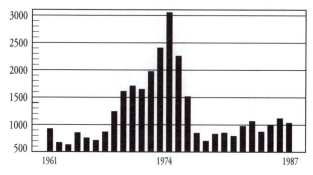

Fig. 1B. **Persons Baptized**

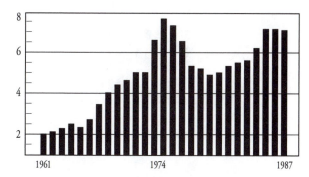

Fig. 1C. **Percentage of Pioneers**

Figure 2
Individual Proselytizing Activities

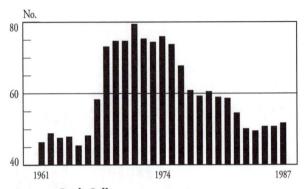

Fig. 2A. **Back-Calls**

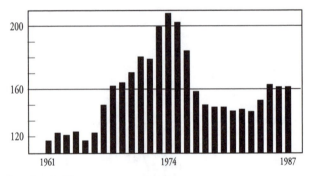

Fig. 2B. **Hours**

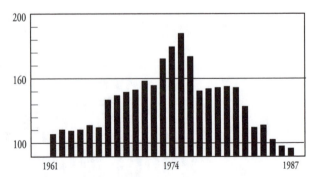

Fig. 2C. **Magazines Distributed**

Figure 3
Monthly Activities July 1974–September 1976

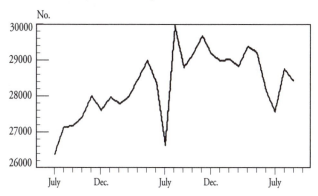

Of special interest as far as prophecy expectancy is concerned is the summer period of 1975 (see Figure 3). According to the Society's *Yearbook* 1976, the maximum number of active Witnesses in Holland during 1975 amounted to 29,723. These were registered in November. In the monthly bulletin, however, a high point of 30,000 Witnesses was noted during the month of August (*KM*, Nov. 1975; Feb. 1976, Dutch ed.). Upon my query of this discrepancy, the Dutch branch office answered that this was due to late reception of data from congregations. The number stated in the *Yearbook* was correct, not the one from the bulletin. It is interesting to speculate on this "late reception." Procedure prescribes that publishers should file their activities on specially designed forms through their congregations at the end of each month. As the graph for July 1975 indicates, there is either a strikingly low activity in that month, or activities were not reported. The first possibility seems unlikely, in view of the urgency of the epoch and the significant difference in activity between July and August. In this case the difference was an ample 12 percent, whereas the average amounted to 5 percent. But why this late filing, as asserted by the Society? Could it be that a more than average number of Witnesses were absent, so they were unable to file their reports? Did they perceive this was a last opportunity to enjoy a vacation within the secular institutions before Armageddon, which would temporarily discontinue this pleasure?

In the previous month more records are set: some 687,000 copies of *The Watchtower* and *Awake!* are distributed, and almost 715,000 hours are spent in preaching. But these high points are not the result of the growing number of adherents only. The individual activity increases simultaneously, as Figure 2 shows. The indicators of back-calls and hours reach their maxima earlier than 1975. It is unclear what the cause of these "premature" commitment maxima is, but it might be that there exists a proselytizing "ceiling": after all, there is a physical limit to door-to-door preaching.

Undoubtedly, the Society's 1914 doctrine contributed to its growth during this period. This still-current teaching assumes, among other things, that "before the last persons of the generation alive in 1914 will pass away, . . . this present wicked world will come to its end."[7] In view of the elapsed time, many new converts and dormant members must have considered this an extra impulse to join the Society's ranks (Botting and Botting 1984:63).

According to the Society's branch office in Holland, the introduction in 1968 of a new study aid for potential converts was another major contribution to the increment. This book, called *The Truth that Leads to Eternal Life*, was used as an introductory course during home Bible studies among those showing interest in the Society's ideology. Important, however, was the Society's advice on this issue. After six months, the potential convert should have visited the Kingdom Hall. If not, the study should be discontinued and conducted among those "who really want to know 'The Truth' and are willing to make progress."[8]

Defection in this period is low. Some 1.8 percent leave the Watchtower Society, while the D/R-ratio is extremely high in favor of recruitment: 0.09. Strictly quantitatively speaking, this is not surprising in view of the baptismal figures: in this period 16,660 new Witnesses join the Society, amounting to an average of 1,851 annually.

The Disconfirmation Phase: 1976–1979

Obviously, many Witnesses believed that Armageddon might be postponed for a short while (the Society was rather explicit on this possibility), therefore 1976 doesn't show a significant decrease in the number of active members. Other commitment indicators, however, leveled off earlier. A definite diminution of the Society's following started in the summer of 1976, a process that would continue until 1980. It is estimated that in Holland approximately 5,000 Witnesses either left the movement, were excluded, or became marginal members, which amounts to a 4 percent annual defection rate and a D/R-ratio of 1.32.

The annual average baptismal figure drops to 952. This combination of baptisms and defectors may partially answer a question by Wilson, who, after mentioning the stagnation in growth of the Society's global following in 1976, wonders if this is caused by a decrease of recruitment or by defection (Wilson 1978:184). The Dutch case clearly points to both phenomena.

Illustrative of the total decline of proselytizing activities are the figures in Table 1. It is clear that all proselytizing aspects suffered severe drawbacks, both at the individual and collective level.

The Post-prophecy Phase: 1980–1987

The 1980s might be best characterized as a recovery from the traumatic disconfirmation phase. However, it seems that the more public-dependent indicators, such as magazine distribution and back-calls, experience a continuation of their decline. The negative publicity in the Dutch media in 1982 and 1983 may have caused adverse societal susceptibility to the Society's ideology, whereas the other indicators show a gradual increase. Still, individual commitment is remote from 1975. Comparing October 1975 and 1985, there is only 3 percent less active membership, but the preached hours and pioneer/publisher ratios show a decrease of 28 percent and 30 percent respectively. The defections amount to 1.7 percent annually; the D/R-ratio over the period is 0.49.[9] This means that of every two Witnesses being baptized, one is not actively engaged in proselytizing.

Table 1
**Collective and Individual Proselytizing Activity
of Dutch Jehovah's Witnesses, 1975 versus 1979**

Year	Number	Hours	Pio	Magazines	Back-Calls
1975	28,643	5,749,100	2,093	5,328,366	2,079,464
1979	26,103	3,853,324	1,294	3,730,059	1,542,817
decrease	-9%	-33%	-38%	-30%	-26%
1975	per individual	200.7		186.0	72.6
1979	per individual	147.6		142.9	59.1
decrease	-26.5%			-23.2%	-18.6

Note: On the collective level, the data refer to total yearly amounts.
Source: *Kingdom Ministry*, Dutch eds., 1975, 1979.

Summarizing, it is obvious that the reaction of the Dutch Witnesses to the 1975 prophecy is one of initial hope, expectancy, and tension. This is reflected in growing commitment in terms of time invested in proselytizing activities: "the more imminent Armageddon is conceived to be, the more urgent recruitment becomes" (Assimeng 1970:107). However, being committed is one thing; a house dweller accepting the message is another. Undoubtedly, the prophecy had a social breeding ground. Via its literature, the Society jumped on the bandwagon of the Club of Rome, which predicted a gloomy situation for the mid-seventies. Also, airplane hijackings and the Watergate scandal were perceived as definite omens.[10] Beside, the amalgam of sociocultural changes in the Dutch society of the late sixties and early seventies must have had a pessimistic impact on certain segments of the population concerning their perception of the unfolding of the near future. Adverse novel phenomena, such as drug abuse and emerging unemployment, plus the Society's traditional topics, such as war, crime, and other misery, made them susceptible to the prophecy and, gradually, to the complete ideological package.

Also, the Society operated in a highly competitive religious "market" (cf. Wallis 1987). To be sure, the essentials of the apocalyptic message were more or less the same as those propagated by many of the so-called New Religious Movements (NRMs); a significant part of the doctrinal system, however, was diametrically opposed to the countercultural ideas of the novel faiths. Though the growth of both the NRMs and the Society functioned as a religious Dow Jones Index of social change, it may be hypothesized that the Society's increase can be partly attributed to the NRMs: if the latter catered to the needs of a "seeking youth" resisting petrified societal values, the former offered the "concerned citizen" ample ideological justification for his anxiety caused by the confrontation with deviant belief systems (cf. Bromley and Shupe 1979:85).

After 1975 the picture totally reversed: decreasing activities, low recruitment, and high defection. As far as this last is concerned, it is interesting to note that other scholars publishing on the Watchtower Society have neglected to relate defection to the prevailing doctrinal climate. Thus Beckford estimates 19 percent defection in England during the period 1963 to 1971 (Beckford 1975:65); Penton uses 20 percent for the world from 1967 through 1983 (Penton 1985:294). Franz's calculation adds up to a defection of "four out of ten persons baptized" in the period 1970 to 1979 (Franz 1985:31). Also, Beckford's remarks on the growing drop-out rate of British publishers since World War II and the recruitment/drop-out ratio of 3:1 can probably be more differentiated if phase-specific analysis is applied (Beckford 1977:22, 1975:65). One might argue that many religious movements reached their peak in this period. However, in Holland the decline in membership of the NRMs did not start until the early eighties, thus eliminating this general trend as a variable causing the decrease of the Society's missionary zeal right after 1975.

Discussion

" 'Do you know why nothing happened in 1975?' Then, pointing at his audience, he shouted: 'It was because YOU expected something to happen' " (Penton 1985:100). Thus said the Watchtower Society's president to Canadian Witnesses during a speech held in 1976. This attitude of nonresponsibility of the leading members towards the Witnesses' frustrations caused by the prophecy failure was also exhibited in the Society's initial publications. As distinct from the probability of a coalescence of the first 6,000 years' termination of man's history with the beginning of the Millennium, this expectation was now flatly denied. Doctrinal changes were called for. It turned out that Eve's creation was the weak link in the prophecy's starting point: the 6,000 years should have been counted from that date on. The Scriptures, however, were not decisive on when that event took place, as opposed to the 1966 results of the Society's exegetic research. So it was impossible to construct a specific apocalyptic calendar. Failure had been expounded.

The majority of the authors commenting on the Society's prophecy failures agree that the organization's ability to reinterpret retrospectively foreseen events is one of its most powerful means of survival (Beckford 1975; Brose 1982; Curry 1980; Penton 1985; Rogerson 1969; Whalen 1962; Zygmunt 1981). Nineteen hundred and seventy-five was not the first time: 1874, 1878, 1881, 1914, 1918, and 1925 had also been predestined for important events (see Curry 1980:ch.5); and every time there was an occurrence of rise, fall, and recovery. Often, the prediction was later said to have been fulfilled in the "invisible" world. Still, followers became disappointed and left the movement each time. White (1967:399) notes that the Society had become careful about mentioning another specific date after the considerable defections of the early twenties. Stevenson (1967:87) speculates on the fact that the Society's top leadership was concerned about the growing apathy of the Witnesses and thus the prophecy might "rekindle zeal and devotion." The Bottings believe it used intentional manipulation to increase membership (Botting and Botting 1984:156), while Zygmunt (1981:204) considers prophecy revelation a revitalization strategy. Franz (1985:208), a former member of the Society's Brooklyn elite, is not very clear on this issue. He mentions only the then-vice-president as being the one most convinced of the teaching.

Also, it has been observed that the 1975 prophecy was consciously formulated rather ambiguously in order to prevent massive falling away in case of disconfirmations (Beckford 1975:220; Penton 1985:95). However, the ambiguity may have been important not only *after* the disconfirmation date, but also *during* the prophecy phase. Consider, for example, the remarks of the anthropologist Schwartz, who, as a result of his study of Melanesian cargo cults, notes that the function of proselytizing is *not* the *reduction* of dissonance, but instead that dissonance is *required* in order to maintain missionary activities: "The function of much cult behavior is not necessarily to lessen dissonance or to overcome ambivalence. Rather it is to assure a certain level of persisting ambivalence that sustains cult excitement and activity, which becomes an end in itself" (1976:189). Following Schwartz, one may assert that the mere formulation of the 1975 prophecy may have caused considerable awkwardness among the Witnesses, since it was (and is) far beyond the Society's doctrinal stance to disseminate diffuse exegesis. Doctrines used to be inflexible and legalistic (which, to be sure, could be modified at a later date), so no confusion among the adherents could arise as to how to interpret "The Truth." But, this rigidity was absent as far as the prophecy was concerned: the Society's literature didn't give an absolute hold, let alone what was said by some of the Society's high-ranking officials, so it is likely that dissonance arousal occurred prior to disconfirmation, contributing to the increase of missionary activities.

The indicators of the preaching activities of the Dutch Jehovah's Witnesses after 1975 seem to depart from Festinger's original hypothesis that increased proselytizing would occur following disconfirmation of a prediction (Festinger 1964:25). A review of the reaction of the adherents does raise some questions as to whether cognitive dissonance theorizing is applicable in this specific situation. A recovery of preaching activities takes place in 1980, but only as far as the numbers of publishers and pioneers are concerned. Commitment in terms of time investment continues to decline until 1984.

Though several scholars writing on the Watchtower movement seem, to a greater or lesser degree, to adhere to Festinger's theory, since prophetic failure reactions are described in general terms as "initial shocks followed by resumption and increase of proselytism," it is questionable whether this is due to renewed activity of "old" adherents (see, e.g., Curry 1980:182; Zygmunt 1981:202, 216). There is an equal case to be made that the increase in numbers of newly baptized from 1979 onward caused this revitalization; the more so because defection in the beginning of the eighties, as well as in 1987, remained high.

The fact that the empirical evidence seems to contradict cognitive dissonance theorizing evokes alternative approaches. First, it is important to consider whether the conditions under which increased proselytizing occurs are fulfilled (Festinger 1964:4):

1. A belief must be held with deep conviction and it must have some relevance to action, that is, to what the believer does or how he behaves.
2. The person holding the belief must have committed himself to it; that is, for the sake of his belief he must have taken some important action that is difficult to undo.
3. The belief must be sufficiently specific and sufficiently concerned with the real world so that events may unequivocally refute the belief.
4. Such undeniable disconfirmatory evidence must occur and must be recognized by the individual holding the belief. . . .
5. The individual believer must have social support. It is unlikely that one isolated believer could withstand the kind of disconfirming evidence specified.

A first glance at these conditions already results in a rather uneasy feeling. After all, how many Witnesses were "deeply convinced" of the prophecy? How many "have committed themselves" to it, in spite of Aronson's remark that commitment is not a necessary condition for dissonance arousal (Aronson 1968:446)? What were the actions taken by Witnesses that were "difficult to undo"? And, most of all, how "sufficiently specific" was the prophecy? These questions cast doubt on the applicability of Festinger's theory, though there were Witnesses conforming to the conditions. Some reports, mainly based on the situation in the United States, mention the giving up of jobs, suspension of medical treatment, postponement of marriages, and selling of property, but the magnitude of these actions is unknown (Brose 1982:157; Franz 1985:206; Penton 1985:95; Zygmunt 1977:56). Analysis of letters of former Witnesses, sent to a Dutch organization of disgruntled ex-adherents, reveals hardly any frustration directly related to 1975 except for some isolated cases of people who borrowed large amounts of money in 1974, convinced that the apocalypse would salvage them from repayment. Considerably less dramatic was to abandon wallpapering the house, as one Witness was advised.

Most likely, the belief in the prophecy can best be represented like the bell-shaped curve of a normal distribution: at one extremity, the nonbelievers, convinced that nothing would occur; at the other side, the true believers, who had no doubt. In between, the bulk of adherents presented themselves; they were not sure, but hedged their bets just in case. Because the analysis is aimed at the majority of the Witnesses, who do not conform to the conditions of Festinger's theory, further references to the hypothesis do not seem productive. However, an exception will be made for the fifth condition, isolating it from its context and emphasizing the in-group characteristics on the congregational level during the prophecy phase.

A significant revision of cognitive dissonance theory put forward by Hardyck and Braden focuses on in-group cohesion and outsiders' reaction:

the more social support an individual receives above the minimum he needs to maintain his belief, the less he will have to proselytize, . . . if a group is receiving considerable ridicule from nonmembers, one way of reducing dissonance that would be apparent to them would be to convince these "unbelievers" that the group is right. (Hardyck and Braden 1962:140; see also Carroll 1979:95; Gager 1975:47)

Starting with the second condition, there is no indication that the Dutch Witnesses were met with considerable outside ridicule after 1975. In any case, nothing was mentioned in the calvinistically oriented Dutch Reformed press, the movement's most prominent ideological adversary. According to my informants, some scornful remarks have been made during the door-to-door preaching, but this was a marginal phenomenon.

The first condition mentioned by Hardyck and Braden is much more significant. Being a Jehovah's Witness is more than being a follower of a religious movement. It often means a way of life confined within the microcosm of the congregation among fellow believers. Social relationships have endogamous features, not in the least as a result of an indifferent or hostile environment.

The Society is aware of the immense importance of group cohesion for the continuity of its operation. This message in the organization's monthly bulletin expresses the danger of isolation:

Removal can sometimes attend a big loss of contact with the congregation. Cases are known of brothers and sisters and persons showing interest, who got out of the routine completely after a removal and who lost their spiritual conviction almost completely. (*KM,* June 1976, Dutch ed.)

Group cohesion is also being reinforced by excluding members who challenge the Society's ideological statements. At the end of the seventies many Witnesses were disfellowshipped, being accused of apostasy. Even the Society's headquarters in New York turned out not to be immune to dissent (Botting and Botting 1984:ch.7; Penton 1985:ch.4, 295ff.; Franz 1985:ch.9; *Yearbook* 1979:23 and 1980:11). No doubt post-prophecy frustrations contributed to these insubordinate reactions of the Witnesses. Elimination of these elements is one of the organizational readjustments "if the causes of prophetic failures are identified as internal to the movement itself" (Zygmunt 1972:261).

In-group socialization of new adherents entails both cognitive mastering of the Society's ideology and affective incorporation into a new community. This situation is conceivable in circumstances of a nonstirring doctrinal climate, implying a more or less stable amount of congregation members; however, during the four-year period from 1972 to 1975, almost 10,000 new adherents joined the organization in Holland, increasing the total amount by approximately 50 percent, while at the same time the number of congregations increased by only 15 percent. Apart from this quantitative momentum, which must have been a barrier for thorough enculturation, there is also a qualitative dimension: 1975 as the main motive for joining the movement.

According to the Witnesses, this would have been an inadequate attitude towards "The Truth." After all, there is a rather complicated ideology to be absorbed, of which, no doubt, the eschatological component is the most significant; and it is highly questionable whether the newly baptized were completely familiar with the remainder of the Society's teachings. So it seems unlikely that the main part of the new members were fully integrated in the movement's congregations, because of the numbers involved versus the capacity of the organization to absorb them within a relatively short time, and the neophytes' focused ideological orientation.

When disconfirmation occurred, the committed were able to revert to the basic teachings of the Society, also supported by the group, which functioned as a defensive shield for the individual arousal of dissonance (Beckford 1975:221). It is likely that for the newly baptized those possibilities were lacking. Brose, quoting her informants, notes:

> . . . those who left . . . were really opportunists. . . . [T]hey had postponed joining until a more convenient time. When the end appeared imminent . . . [t]hey became afraid and joined the group. When disconfirmation occurred, they had little investment in the group and found it easy to leave. (Brose 1982:159, 160; cf. Wilson 1978:184)

The doctrinal aspect was clearly articulated by an elder who, upon being asked who left after 1975, answered:

> Those who left were the ones who were afraid of 1975. But they never were really in "The Truth." Regarding this, it was good that Armageddon did not take place: "it separated the wheat from the chaff." (fieldwork notes)

Besides the interesting phenomenon of the trial function of prophecy disconfirmation, as stipulated by the elder, these remarks confirm the observations of other scholars. So Balch and his colleagues, in their paper on a millennial Baha'i splinter faction, note the ability of the committed to readjust their beliefs to the basic issues of the Baha'i teachings, away from a prophecy failure (Balch et al. 1983:153). In their monograph on the Unification Church, Bromley and Shupe conclude similarly: "[A]s long as the basic metaphor remains intact and a strong network of reinforcing social relationships is maintained, . . . changes in ideology do not necessarily pose a threat to the movement" (1979:107). Finally Gager, commenting on the missionary attempts of the first Christians, notes: "[T]he fact that the identity of individuals with the group as well as their breaking of old loyalties had long been established suggests that the prophecy was less important to the members than the existence of the group itself" (Gager 1975:47; see also Carroll 1979:95).

Conclusion

It may be argued that the increase in proselytizing activities of the Dutch Jehovah's Witnesses during the prophecy phase in the period 1966 to 1975 was caused by three factors: first, there was a favorable sociocultural climate in which a millennial, conservative message constituted a counterbalance against incipient and already progressed societal changes as well as pessimistic expectations for the near future. Second, the adherents, according to both the Society's literature and verbal statements of its officials, were continuously needled to intensify their preaching efforts, legitimized by the possibility of salvation in 1975. Third, the phraseology of the prophecy departed from the traditional rigid terminology, in the sense that the prophecy contained an uncertainty clause. This phenomenon may have caused a certain amount of dissonance among long-standing members, used as they were to the noncompromising language of the Society, resulting in increased missionary efforts.

It is hardly fruitful to apply Festinger's cognitive dissonance theory to the events after 1975, because the preconditions accompanying the hypothesis are barely met. Preaching activities declined sharply and continued to do so in the eighties. The organization's ideological and infrastructural resources prevented significant losses on a macro-level, while on a micro-level group cohesion was an effective barrier against dissonance arousal among the long-term adherents. Also, this category was able to revert to the basic issues of the Society's teachings. Most probably, those forming part of the recruitment bulge during the prophecy phase left the movement because of a lack of proper sectarian resocialization, both socially and religiously.

The recovery from 1980 onward does not seem related to Festinger's theory. Individual time investment in preaching activities continued to decline through 1983. Those who left the movement after 1975 have been replaced by a new generation, most of them not aware of the 1975 events, and it is assumed that this group is mainly responsible for the slight revitalization of the preaching activities. Also, no firm empirical evidence has so far been presented to establish a causal relationship between declining economic conditions and the Society's recovery in the eighties, as suggested by Botting and Botting (1984:184).

Whatever the reasons people join the ranks of the Watchtower Society, the element of salvation from a world approaching unavoidable doom is still its most distinctive ideological feature, and the Society is committed to another prophecy: the generation of 1914 will witness the end of this worldly system. Taking Schwartz's cue, one may suggest that dissonance is maintained in order to activate proselytizing. Exactly how the 1914 generation and "the end" will be defined in the future will become evident within one or two decades—perhaps in the way Whalen foresees: "By the year 2000 The *Watchtower* may be speaking about the invisible Armageddon that took place years before" (1962:228). Whatever the outcome, "prophecies cannot and do not fail for the committed" (Weiser 1974:20).

NOTES

1. *All Scripture Is Inspired of God and Beneficial.* WBTS, New York, 1963; Dutch ed., 1966, p. 285. So at the same time, two opposite dogmas were current. Note the time gap between the publication of the English and Dutch editions. In this period, the Dutch *Watchtower,* the Society's main channel to disseminate doctrinal matters, appeared three months after the English edition, while *Awake!,* more accessible to nonmembers, was published six months later. Probably to prevent an ideological lead for the English-reading public, *The Watchtower* has been published simultaneously in approximately twenty languages since 1985.

2. Frequent references were made to a book called *Famine 1975!* in which worldwide catastrophe was predicted for the mid-seventies. For a critical review on the Society's quotation policy regarding secular sources, see Jonsson and Herbst 1987.

3. *God's Kingdom of a Thousand Years Has Approached.* WBTS, New York, 1973; Dutch ed., p. 12.

4. The Society presents its annual statistics over the period September through August. With the exception of the baptismal figures, the data presented in this text are based on calendar years, derived from the monthly statistics in *Kingdom Ministry.*

5. By multiplying the average individual number by the number of Witnesses, the total number has been obtained.

6. *Reasoning From the Scriptures.* WBTS, New York, 1985; Dutch ed., p. 216.

7. *Reasoning From the Scriptures.* Dutch ed., p. 89.

8. "The Truth" is Witnesses' jargon, meaning the Society's belief system; see *KM,* Nov. 1968, Dutch ed.; and Penton 1985:95.

9. This figure gains greater relief if the annual ratios are given: 1980: 0.65, 1981: 0.63, 1982: 0.47, 1983: 0.49, 1984: 0.48, 1985: 0.34, 1986: 0.28, 1987: 0.68.

10. As stated by several high-ranking officials of the Dutch branch in newspaper interviews.

REFERENCES

Aronson, E. 1968. "Discussion: Commitments about Commitments," pp. 464–66 in *Theories of Cognitive Consistency: A Sourcebook,* edited by R. P. Abelson et al. Chicago: Rand McNally.

Assimeng, J. M. 1970. "Sectarian Allegiance and Political Authority: The Watch Tower Society in Zambia, 1907–1935." *Journal of Modern African Studies* 8:97–112.

Balch, R. W., et al. 1983. "When the Bombs Drop: Reactions to Disconfirmed Prophecy in a Millennial Sect." *Sociological Perspectives* 26:137–158.

Beckford, J. A. 1975. *The Trumpet of Prophecy: A Sociological Study of Jehovah's Witnesses.* London: Basil Blackwell.

———. 1977. "The Watchtower Movement World-Wide." *Social Compass* 24:5–31.

Botting, H., and G. Botting. 1984. *The Orwellian World of Jehovah's Witnesses.* Toronto: University of Toronto Press.

Bromley, D. G., and A. D. Shupe. 1979. *"Moonies" in America.* Beverly Hills, CA: Sage.

Brose, A. J. 1982. "Jehovah's Witnesses: Recruitment and Enculturation in a Millennial Sect." Ph.D. dissertation, University of California. Ann Arbor, MI: University Microfilms International.

Carroll, R. P. 1979. *When Prophecy Failed: Reactions and Responses to Failure in the Old Testament Prophetic Traditions.* London: SCM.

Curry, M.D. 1980. "Jehovah's Witnesses: The Effects of Millenarianism on the Maintenance of a Religious Sect." Ph.D. dissertation, Florida State University. Ann Arbor, MI: University Microfilms International.

Festinger, L., et al. 1964 [1956]. *When Prophecy Fails.* New York: Harper & Row.

Franz, R. 1985. *Crises of Conscience.* Atlanta: Commentary Press.

Gager, J. G. 1975. *Kingdom and Community: The Social World of Early Christianity.* Englewood Cliffs, NJ: Prentice-Hall.

Hardyck, J. A., and M. Braden. 1962. "Prophecy Fails Again: A Report of a Failure to Replicate." *Journal of Abnormal and Social Psychology* 65:136–141.

Jonsson, C. A., and W. Herbst. 1987. *The "Sign" of the Last Days—When?* Atlanta: Commentary Press.

Penton, M. J. 1985. *Apocalypse Delayed: The Story of Jehovah's Witnesses.* Toronto: University of Toronto Press.

Rogerson, A. T. 1969. *Millions Now Living Will Never Die.* London: Constable.

Schwartz, T. 1976. "The Cargo-Cult: A Melanesian Type Response to Change," pp. 157–206 in *Responses to Change: Society, Culture and Personality,* edited by G. A. De Vos. New York: Van Nostrand.

Stevenson, W. C. 1967. *Year of Doom, 1975: The Story of Jehovah's Witnesses.* London: Hutchinson (also published as: *The Inside Story of Jehovah's Witnesses.* New York: Hart Publishing, 1968).

Wallis, R. 1987. "New Religions and the Potential for World Re-Enchantment: Religion as Way of Life, Preference and Commodity," pp. 87–98 in *Secularization and Religion: The Persisting Tension* (Acts of the XIXth CISR). Lausanne: CISR.

Weiser, N. 1974. "The Effects of Prophetic Disconfirmation of the Committed." *Review of Religious Research* 16:19–30.

Whalen, W. J. 1962. *Armageddon around the Corner.* New York: Day.

White, T. 1967. *A People for His Name: A History of Jehovah's Witnesses and an Evaluation.* New York: Vantage Press.

Wilson, B. 1978. "When Prophecy Failed." *New Society* 43 (January 26):183–184.

Zygmunt, J. F. 1972. "When Prophecies Fail." *American Behavioral Scientist* 16:245–267.

———. 1977. "Jehovah's Witnesses in the USA: 1942–1976," *Social Compass* 24:45–47.

———. 1981. "Prophetic Failure and Chiliastic Identity: The Case of Jehovah's Witnesses," pp. 195–220 in *Religieuze Bewegingen,* edited by L. G. Jansma and P. Schulten. The Hague: Mouton [orig. in *American Journal of Sociology* 76 (1970):926–948].

Coping with Apocalypse in Canada
Experiences of Endtime in La Mission de l'Esprit Saint and the Institute of Applied Metaphysics

Susan J. Palmer and Natalie Finn

In 1973, Emmanuel Robitaille, Head Servant of La Mission de l'Esprit Saint (MES), announced to members gathered in their Montreal Hall that he had received a warning of the end of the world from his dead father, Gustav, who had appeared to him in a dream. Members of the congregation were advised to store food, diapers and clothing, and to wait for further instructions, but not to return to the Hall or they would "be in Hell." Meanwhile, the core group began to construct an underground bunker in Oka to prepare for the end of the world in 1975.

One year later, another Canadian cult waited for world's end. On June 7, 1976, Winifred (Win) Barton, founder of the Ottawa-based Institute of Applied Metaphysics (IAM), announced during a radio interview that "the end of the world as we know it" would occur on June 13. Her students were instructed to gather at three rural "campuses" in Quebec, Ontario, and Saskatchewan, and to bring money, fuel, and food. Approximately 400 people, including students' families and complete strangers who were impressed by the radio announcement, spent the weekend in highly organized activities including farmwork, housework, singing, and circle dancing. Then, on Sunday the 13th, they sat in meditation waiting for the world to end.

The outcome of apocalypse in these two New Religious Movements (NRMs) was quite different. What outsiders would perceive in both cases to be a non-event was variously interpreted by insiders as a tragic fiasco (in Robitaille's group) and as an unmitigated triumph (in Barton's group). When 1975 passed uneventfully, Emmanuel Robitaille defected to the Jehovah's Witnesses, taking over 1200 members with him. The remaining five hundred-odd members split into three sects, each rejecting Gustav Robitaille as a "false prophet." Winifred Barton's organization, initially advertised as a course in "Psychic Development," transformed within three months of "World's End" into a utopian, postmillennialist commune. Around 200 students accepted Win's invitation to become "Citizens of the Kingdom of Heaven on Earth." This involved liquidating one's assets and donating the proceeds to IAM, moving into rural communes, marrying one's "Yin-Yang" partner, and—for a hundred-odd men—undergoing vasectomies. These communes lasted from 1976 until 1984.

The mystery which this study will attempt to solve is the following: Why did the experience of "Endtime" cause one group to disintegrate and the other group to thrive?

John Gager, in his study of early Christianity, argues that certain aspects of millenarian movements suggest that "they may indeed reach the millennium in other, less obvious, ways." This success is primarily manifested in "the undeniable continuity of the group and its individual members." While failure of prophecy "always produces some defections . . . the remarkable fact that the majority remains should prompt us to ask whether the millennium has in some sense come to life in the experience of the community as a whole" (1975:49).

Barton's millennium did come to life and, according to Gager's criteria, was "successful." This raises the question of whether there is a list of ingredients or set of conditions under which a "successful" apocalypse can be experienced. If so, what are they?

A survey of the literature on millenarian movements suggests a cognitive bias in scholars' treatments of this phenomenon. Many of the groups studied—medieval apocalyptic heresies (Cohn 1970) and Melanesian cargo cults (Worsley 1975)—are both chronologically and geographically distant so that their beliefs have been recorded but their rituals have not. The classic studies by anthropologists and historians (Burridge 1971; Talmon 1970) assume that millenarian movements fail because they do not achieve their goal—the millennium. From the outsider's point of view, of course, this would appear to be common sense, but from the insider's standpoint, experiences of Endtime might vary considerably. Why, for example, should participants in apocalypse as staged by Mrs. Keech (Festinger et al. 1956) and by Mrs. Shepard (Hardyck and Braden 1962) return home convinced, in the words of one IAM informant, that "something spiritual had just happened," while members of BUPC (Balch et al. 1983) and MES fall into apostasy and schism?

Most studies of contemporary millenarian movements refer to Festinger's and his colleagues' five conditions. Festinger focuses on the enigma of belief and its durability in the face of contradictory external events. He argues that members of apocalyptic groups who have made strong commitments or long-term investments in their beliefs, and are inevitably confronted with "cognitive dissonance" when external events fail to conform to their leader's prophecy, will zealously embark on missionary activity in the effort to reassure themselves that their beliefs are valid. Subsequent studies by Hardyck and Braden and by Balch and his colleagues have found evidence that contradicts the Festinger hypothesis, even though the cults chosen appear to fulfill Festinger's five conditions adequately. These authors elaborate upon Festinger's fifth condition—*social support;* Hardyck and Braden contend that a strong community could reduce dissonance to the point where converting outsiders becomes unnecessary, and Balch proposes that during those first ambiguous moments following disconfirmation, such facts as decisive action on the part of the leader, adequate communication among believers, and the attitude of the public play a critical role in determining future evangelical action.

Out of the three groups studied which experienced "cognitive dissonance," we find three distinctly different responses:

1. A group survives and begins to proselytize (Festinger et al. 1956).
2. A group survives but does not proselytize (Hardyck and Braden 1962).
3. A group neither survives nor proselytizes (Balch et al. 1983).

The two NRMs in this study correspond to responses 2 and 3. Neither group attempted to win converts after the world's "end," nor did they fulfill Festinger's five conditions. It would be a fruitless effort, therefore, to pursue the "dissonance theory." A more intriguing phenomenon than post-apocalyptic evangelism is the successful navigation through the clashing rocks of sacred Time and Greenwich time whereby some groups reach a consensus that all those present are witnesses to some form of marriage between "Heaven and Earth." A study of the transformations occurring in these groups in their post-apocalyptic phase might perhaps tell us something about the function of millenarian activity.

This study follows in the footsteps of Balch and his colleagues and Hardyck and Braden in focusing on the social context in which "disconfirmation" occurs and in attempting to explore the inner logic of millenarianism—not as a set of beliefs, but as a collective process. First, a comparison of the two case histories in our study strongly suggests that the age of a movement (with the accompanying factors of older members, settled patterns of family life, the routinization of charisma, and so on) is an important variable affecting the doctrinal and emotional flexibility of a group's response to a prophetic failure. Second, it is postulated that the ritual context in which "disconfirmation" takes place is at least as important in determining the future success or failure of the movement as is the commitment to belief and the social context. Moreover, it is observed (rather than postulated, because this appears self-evident) that the prophet plays a crucial role in this ritual. His or her skill and flexibility in facilitating groups, reinterpreting doctrines, and "orchestrating" ritual appear to be essential for bringing about a "successful" apocalypse—an event which might well be considered the *magnum opus* in a charismatic cult leader's career. Finally, the founder of a movement appears to hold a distinct advantage over a second- or third-generation prophet (a mere priestly authority) who undertakes to revitalize religion by stirring up chiliastic excitement. The latter is contending with a codified body of doctrines and a more settled, family-oriented congregation for whom the investment of money and labor in Endtime holds a greater potential for disappointment and tragedy than for younger, first-generation followers. This argument challenges at least three assumptions on which Festinger's theory rests: that millenarian activity is the outcome of a set of beliefs, "deeply felt" and rigidly adhered to; that beyond the final moment of prophetic expectation lurks a crisis of beliefs, or "cognitive dissonance"; and that this crisis is both inevitable and monolithic.

Data Collection

Unfortunately neither researcher was invited to attend either "End of the World" in the mid-seventies, and therefore we have had to rely on interviews with former members who participated in these events.

The main difficulty in obtaining information on MES and IAM lies in the fact that both communities were disbanded. Emmanuel Robitaille abdicated from his position as Head Servant in 1976, when he joined the Jehovah's Witnesses. Winifred Barton was deposed by her husband, Pierre, in 1984, and core group members had been defecting from the commune since 1981. By 1985, only seven commune residents (and Pierre's six dobermans) were left (Morris 1986).

Palmer first became aware of IAM through a conversation with a librarian at her college, who had been one of the "Four Beasts" in IAM. The librarian put her in contact with two other former "Citizens of the Universe" (including one other "Beast"), who were interviewed. The Beasts gave Palmer books published by the organization in the 1970s and also Madeline Morris's senior essay, "IAM: A Group Portrait" (1986). Morris had been a member of IAM for nine years, and five years after leaving the commune wrote her essay while studying with Rosabeth Moss Kanter at Yale University. Two news reports were discovered on the "End of the World" in the Ottawa *Citizen* and the Ottawa *Journal* (June 14, 1976).

Natalie Finn first established contact with a former member of MES through meeting (and subsequently interviewing) her friend's mother, who is the widow of one of the sons of Gustav Robitaille, "Le Prince." Another female apostate permitted us to read her study of MES, written for the sociology class of Jean Guy Vaillancourt. More information became available through the Centre de l'Information des Nouvelles Religions (CINR) in Montreal, where *Les Documents* (1976—the collected letters of the founder, Eugène Richer "Dit Lafleche") and notes on MES's history by anonymous researchers, "G.W.L." and "M.B.," and by Dr. James Penton are filed. Palmer was assisted in her endeavors to translate Lafleche's extraordinary revelations by Louis B. Pariseau of the University of Ottawa who was in the process of writing a *fiche descriptive* and had organized the CINR material under headings. Palmer also paid a visit to the original Hall, which still bears the sign *La Mission de l'Esprit Saint* over the door and, according to an article in *La Presse* (February 15, 1984), is still a meeting place for "quelques douzaines de personnes" who venerate Richer as l'Esprit Saint, but reject the Robitailles. There she found the windows barred but, after ringing the bell several times, managed to carry on a conversation through an antique, crackling intercom with an invisible person whom she assumed was the wife of the current Servant. After Palmer had explained her interest, the intercom replied, "Va t'en! Il n'y a personne ici!"

La Mission de l'Esprit Saint

MES was founded in 1913 in the province of Quebec by Eugène Richer "Dit Lafleche," who claimed to be the Third Person in the Trinity, the living Incarnation of the Holy Spirit. Richer first recognized his mission when visiting the Eglise de Notre Dame du St-Saveur in Montreal, on which occasion the Virgin Mary appeared holding baby Jesus and told him in front of two witnesses that it was 2000 years since the Angel Gabriel had blessed her, and now it was Richer's mission to regenerate humanity through "la sein de la mère."

The MES was a close-knit sect composed of large French Canadian families from the working class. Only one member (the architect who later designed "Le Troue") had received over a fifth-grade education. The largest congregation was in Montreal and numbered between 2000 and 3000 members (or 150 families, according to another source). These figures probably include the children who were God's Chosen People or "Enfants de Dieu." In order to be born a Child of God, conceived miraculously through the Holy Spirit, one's mother's womb had to be blessed by Richer, and the same ritual, a laying on of hands, was performed by his successor, Gustav Robitaille, and after the latter's death, by the twenty-nine Servants. The members met several times a week in their meeting hall in Montreal. Women were heavily pressured to give birth every year, and the average family size was nine children. Fire, smoke, burnt cooking, and rainy weather were blamed on the secret sexual sins of women, who were encouraged to make public confessions. Alcoholic drinks, dancing, swimming, and taking vacations were forbidden, but oddly enough, men and women in the movement "smoked like chimneys." Children attended a special Mission school and wore Salvation Army clothes.

Richer lived from 1871 to 1925 and displayed his charisma through control of rainfall, the teleportation of women about to be run over, and reviving the dead. One of the current Servants is the grandson of Simon Breault, "Le Vieillard," who met Richer when he first arrived in Montreal off the boat from Quebec City. Breault brought him home, where Richer amazed the family by greeting each of the seventeen children at first sight by their proper Christian names.

When Richer died he transferred his powers to Gustav Robitaille, who had broken away from his Catholic family and Jesuit Seminary in 1920 to become Richer's disciple. Robitaille was called "Le Prince" and was also believed to be the Holy Spirit incarnate. He was described by Finn's informant as a "fat man" and a fine musician who played the organ during the service, but humbly mopped the Hall floor after meetings. In 1940 he caused a schism in the Mission by publically denouncing his wife as a "baby murderer," accusing her of secret abortions, and went to live with a Mlle. Hachey, against whom he leveled similar accusations. He then remarried, to a seventeen-year-old girl, and became the father of fifteen children. He died in 1965, leaving the leadership in the hands of twenty-nine Servants, many of whom were his sons. Through the *Imposition des Mains,* the Servants held the power to bless the wombs of women to receive the Holy Spirit and generate Children of God.

Beliefs

The doctrines of La Mission de l'Esprit Saint combine ideas from spiritualism, Mormonism, and adventism. The Mormon concept of three worlds—the Celestial, Terrestrial, and Telestial, through which the soul journeys in the course of its moral evolution—is combined with the (Theosophical) doctrine of reincarnation. Rebirth occurs three or four times on Earth, and Mission members expect to be reincarnated in the bodies of their own great-great grandchildren, when they will achieve moral perfection, immortality, and psychic powers. Evildoers are reborn as butterflies, whereas pigs and cows are considered to be a benign rebirth because of their abundant fertility.

In the alternative cosmology of the sect, Earth is pear-shaped, the smaller bump being the location of Hell. The sky is a glass sphere in which the stars and planets are merely the reflections of Hellfire. Time commences with the birthdate of Lafleche (1871) and will end with the Third World War between the white and yellow races who will destroy each other with gas, leaving only the Children of God to replenish the Earth.

Prophecy and Preparations for the End

In 1973 Emmanuel Robitaille, the Head Servant, received a dream in which his father, "Le Prince," warned him that the Battle of Armageddon would be waged in 1975 and that a modern Noah's Ark must be constructed to protect the members. In an ensuing series of nightmares, Emmanuel was told of forthcoming political events, the death of two Servants, and of various sexual improprieties occurring among Mission women and teenagers. The Servants announced the news to the congregation in the next meeting. Our informant recalls them saying that Emmanuel had seen the number "1975, in red, flashing, flashing!" Women were warned that their salvation was in doubt unless they happened to be pregnant when the Battle of Armageddon commenced. The Servants advised all the families to store canned food, diapers, and warm clothing over the next two years, and announced: "For no reason should anyone ever go back to the Hall again. If you do, you will be put in Hell!" Members were forbidden to try to contact the Servants but were to wait for instructions when the End arrived.

The doors of the Hall were locked, and no one dared to return until one year after the prophecy was proved false.

The Servants and a few of the wealthier brothers began to construct three shelters. The largest of these was "Le Troue," an underground bunker in Oka, Quebec. This was located in the middle of a large apple orchard on a farm owned by a Mission family who kept watch over the path leading to it from their farm-house window. Our informant, whose husband had invested $30,000 in his share and spent every Sunday working on it, states five or six families were involved, each bringing between nine and twelve children. Women were to be kept in ignorance, and the wives would bring picnic baskets and checkered cloths to Oka on Sundays and play with their children while the men worked. Our informant descended into "Le Troue" with her husband on one occasion and described it as follows:

> We lifted up a piece of turf by a leather strap and climbed down a ladder. There was a washer and dryer, an air purifier, and a water purifier in the first room. Then there was a large kitchen and beyond that a room with many bunks and canned food and clothing.

The other two shelters were in the Laurentians; these were cottages rendered gas-proof and stocked with food under a twenty-four-hour guard. (One of these burned down during the critical year.)

Emmanuel had offered no details concerning the forthcoming disaster, but our informant said she had understood it to be the prophesied Third World War. She also assumed that when the End came the lower echelons of La Mission would be left behind, since no provisions were being made for them.

Responses to Prophetic Failure

When 1975 ended uneventfully, members were scattered and in confusion because they were forbidden to congregate at the Hall. Many fathers had invested all their savings in stored food or in building Le Troue and had quit their jobs, while even more women were pregnant than usual, hoping to guarantee their own salvation. The Servants kept telling them to wait ("We'll get in touch with you."), while Emmanuel was meeting with his brothers and fellow-Servants to relate the nightmares he was receiving about the End of the World. He then vis-ited some Jehovah's Witnesses with the intention of converting them, but instead became a convert himself. At that point he began to contact Mission members and invite them to the Jehovah's Witnesses meetings. A year later, over 1200 MES members were baptized as JWs.

Unfortunately, there is no record of the careers of these apostates within the Jehovah's Witnesses. Since the JWs also faced prophetic disconfirmation in 1975, it would be interesting to study the process whereby MES members came to accept the larger sect's reinterpretation of prophecy.

Richer Robitaille, Gustav's oldest son, appeared to suffer a severe case of "cognitive dissonance," according to his widow:

> My husband, Richer, seriously doubted after the prophecy proved false. His father had told him, "Richer, I was there when this young boy sat in the lap of the Master and the Master said, 'I will not live to see the end, but you, you will live to see the end.' " The boy grew up to be a man, he had children, and his children told my husband that this man had died. So, that prophecy did not come true. The man died, and it was not the end of the world. And that's why he didn't believe it. . . . I suspect that was the beginning of my husband's illness, that breakup . . . because that had been his whole life from birth. When someone comes and tells you that everything . . . everything is fake about your family. . . . He felt he'd been lied to all his life, and half of those people said that Gustav Robitaille was a false prophet. He'd be praying all the time. . . . He'd pray to the Holy Spirit (that's his father). At one point he threw the Bible into the fireplace. He went through a very bad stage. He went . . . crazy. . . . This Bible, he treasured it all his life. Things were written in it. He got very sick—physically sick and then mentally sick. There were so many problems.

Unfortunately, we have no other accounts of members' reactions to prophetic disconfirmation. The remaining 500-odd members who did not join the Jehovah's Witnesses either dropped out or followed one of the three Servants who organized their own schismatic sects, each rejecting Robitaille but continuing to venerate Eugène Richer as the Holy Spirit and blessing the wombs of women to bring forth a superior race.

The Institute of Applied Metaphysics

IAM was founded in 1963 by Winifred G. Barton (b. 1919), an Ottawa housewife and mother of four sons, after an encounter with her spirit guide, Loliad R. Kahn, in the basement of her suburban home. Loliad described himself as a metaphysician from Lost Atlantis, now reincarnated as an insectlike alien on the planet Vringg, but she recognized him as the "Ringmaster" of her shamanic dream-visions, experienced throughout her childhood in Britain. Under his inspiration, Barton set up classes in metaphysics in her basement. By 1965 she had established a small following with local branches across Canada and was publicizing her courses. IAM was granted the status of a nonprofit, charitable organization in 1967, and proceeded to purchase three residential schools or "campuses," in Madoc, Ontario (1972), Nominingue, Quebec (1973), and Gravelbourg, Saskatchewan (1974). Loliad's revelations were written down by Win in a series of ten books which explore an eclectic range of topics such as dreams, astral travel, auras, psychic phenomena, ghosts, UFOs, and Lost Atlantis. Christian doctrines and symbols are superimposed upon theosophical and spiritualist themes, and her richly mythologized Universe is ruled over by a patriarchal "Master."

IAM was presented in Open Houses and in a conference series across Canada as offering courses in which the student could realize her or his full human potential through meditation, dream analysis, keeping journals, and exploring the esoteric meaning of world religions. This training laid the foundation for the "Applied Metaphysics" course during which, it was understood, students would directly experience the spiritual realm and be reborn into it.

In 1973, Win began to predict a "Psychic Explosion" through confidential memos sent to senior students. In September of the same year, during the two-week Applied Metaphysics course at Madoc, Ontario, students reported experiencing intense feelings of love and ecstasy which were explained as a major breakthrough of spiritual energy on the planet (Morris 1986). During the Psychic Explosion, Win fell in love with Pierre Levesque, a handsome twenty-two year-old IAM student, thirty-two years her junior. Soon afterwards she left her aged husband, Ernest, and announced to her students that she and Pierre were two halves of the same soul, reunited after aeons of separation into a "Yin-Yang unit."

Barton's next revelation was that the true identity of Pierre was Loliad, the Cosmic Lord in charge of planet Earth. This meant that she and Pierre were now claiming to be the Messianic Couple, or the spiritual Queen and King of the Planet.

Between 1974 and 1975, students were strongly encouraged to form Yin-Yang units, to be formalized in bucolic group weddings during the summer. Hippie couples legalized "living together," and singles were assigned to work teams with a member of the opposite sex and told approvingly that they "looked alike" or "worked so well together." At least eight couples resembled Win and Pierre in that the woman was over twenty years older than her husband, and these couples were praised in the literature as ideal Yin-Yang units, forming the vanguard of Win's "Angels of Armageddon." The organization of IAM was restructured in a hierarchical fashion, with the Messianic Couple ruling over a "theocracy," and four couples titled the "Four Beasts" placed in charge of four quadrants or departments: administration, teaching, domestic work, and marketing. The Yin-Yang units who worked in the four departments were separated into colors: the yellow, green, blue, and red couples.

Win began to hold seminars in hotels across Canada featuring herself and different speakers on ecological and New Age issues. Our informant, "Cora," described a change in her during this period:

> I think at this time there was a striking change in Win. When I first met her, she was a dowdy, sloppy sort of looking lady. You know, she'd wear stretch pants and a shapeless sweater, and she'd smoke. . . . Then, all of a sudden . . . she's lost weight, she's got nice clothes, she's taking on this new look and, of course, she loves it. . . . She's met Pierre Levesque at this

point . . . I don't know what happened, but all of a sudden you start to see him with Winifred. I remember at one seminar, her changing clothes three times a day, and coming out in these new outfits and looking quite ravishing.

Barton was attending the United Nations Habitat Conference in Vancouver when she announced during an interview broadcast over the radio on June 7, 1976, that the world "as we know it" would end as of 6:00 P.M., on June 13. She added that there would be a landing of extraterrestrials at that time. Morris (1986:15–16) describes the End-of-the-World experience as follows:

The weekend of the "End of the World" was a very special and touching experience. Approximately three hundred members gathered at the three residential school locations to witness the end of the world and the birth of the millennium. Throughout Thursday and Friday people arrived usually bringing whatever relatives and close friends they could persuade to come. Hundreds of pounds of food, gallons of fuel, and various kinds of emergency supplies were brought in so that the group would be ready for anything. On Saturday night, in each of the three locations, as all those present gathered to sing together, each participant felt what they described as a composite or collective mystical experience—a feeling of being in the presence of, and at one with, God. Later that night, Winifred phoned each of the three locations and said that "it" had happened—one day earlier than expected. This statement came as no surprise since all who were present felt already that some very special spiritual event had occurred. Winifred maintained, after that weekend was over, that the world as we knew it (and now the stress was on the phrase "as we knew it") had, in fact, come to an end. This ending, she said, would become apparent in time and would manifest physically within a maximum of three and a half years.

Our informant, "Cora," presented a slightly different version of the weekend:

Anyway, we all decided to go to the country campuses for the weekend. There were about one hundred and fifty of us gathered at the centre in Nominingue. Winifred's warning was broadcast on the HAM radio, and people were calling in to ask about it, but nobody knew what was going on. There were no details about how it was going to end. The police came looking for Win because the radio stations were calling her and doing interviews and there was a big panic—there was a big reaction. The faith in her was quite something. On Sunday morning it was coming up to the deadline. Is something going to happen? At ten o'clock suddenly Win arrives. She just came in and went to the front and started meditating. There was music playing and we all meditated. An hour passed, then suddenly it was twelve o'clock. We were still here. What had happened? Then I heard people around me saying, "Wow! Did you feel that?" A lot of people definitely felt something, that something spiritual had happened. Certainly, nothing physical had. It's lucky that Win always tacked on that phrase, "as we know it."

Another informant who attended the Gravelbourg, Saskatchewan, event describes it as follows:

> But on the eight hour drive to Gravelbourg I felt panicky. When I arrived around one hundred people were there. . . . My job was to welcome them as they arrived. There were piles of food brought in. I sat in the front entrance, took their money and put it in envelopes with their names on them. I told them, "We don't know exactly what is going to happen. If you want to leave you can get your money back." I had a few thousand dollars by the end. I assigned them to different rooms and duties. We had a work weekend. Most of the people there were students and their families. I didn't feel it end. . . . Win would call us and ask to speak to certain people and check to see how things were going. She'd say, "Keep calm. Keep up the Vibe." Anyway, we had a great weekend. There was spiritual music piped in while we worked, cooked, fed the animals . . . and we danced in the evening: polkas, circle dances. We would dance to "Loliad's Prayer" to the Master of the Universe. And you know, the Vibes were high. Maybe we did have a mystical experience. At times there was a very spiritual atmosphere. So, when the moment arrived we played "Loliad's Prayer," put our minds together and then. . . . We looked at each other. Some said, "I feel a change." But I didn't feel a change. Some people came to us privately and said, "I feel bad. I didn't feel anything. What's wrong with me?" I'd say to them, "Don't worry. It's very subtle. It happened on different levels. I didn't feel much either." People packed up and left. Some took their money, some left their money, but there was a division. It was a definite turning point. We lost the students who were just hanging on. The people who stayed were those who felt, "Yes! This is where I want to be—what I want to give my life to."

There are some puzzling discrepancies in these different accounts concerning *when* the end occurred: Saturday in Madoc, Sunday at noon in Nominingue, and 3:00 P.M. Sunday in Saskatchewan; and yet all three informants note there was communication and consensus between the centers. Second, no one pointed out the failure of the aliens to materialize. In a similar fashion, three and a half years later, members apparently forgot about the physical manifestation of the world's end.

Within the next four months the structure of the organization changed dramatically, from an urban institute offering courses which attracted a large but transitory body of students, to three postmillennialist communes in the countryside composed of a small but stable population of couples. Win and Pierre followed up the apocalyptic weekend by inviting members to become "Citizens of the Kingdom of Heaven on Earth." This required students to marry their "Yin-Yang unit," sign over all their assets to the Institute, and live communally in one of the three rural locations. Citizens were also required to sever the "Genetic Link" by writing to their parents informing them that they would not be in contact again, since they were devoting their lives to God. Husbands had vasectomies and wives were told to surrender to the "male Vibe" by manifesting obedience and servitude toward their husbands. Morris (1986:17) writes, "Once citizenship was instituted, the total number of citizens quickly reached, and then stabilized at, around two hundred."

Having described these two examples of "prophetic disconfirmation," in order to account for their different responses to this phenomenon, it is necessary to explore at least four aspects of prophecy:

1. its place within the larger body of belief or religious "thought-world" of the group;
2. its social context and social support systems;
3. its improvisational and ritual aspect;
4. the role of the leader in the midst of this ritual innovation as shaman or midwife.

The Doctrinal Context of Prophecy

The doctrinal context within which prophecy is "disconfirmed" cannot be dismissed as negligible. Melton (1985:202) challenges the frequent assumption of "media representatives, nonmillennial religious rivals and scholars" that "prophecy is the organizing or determining principle for millennial groups," and he emphasizes the weight of the larger belief structure and the "unfalsifiable beliefs out of which religious thought-worlds are constructed." Within this larger doctrinal context, believers "can engage in a reaffirmation of basic faith and make a reappraisal of their predicament." Zygmunt (1972) traces the various routes whereby believers can integrate overly-specified prophecies into the group's broader theological framework and return to a mood of expectancy. The vagueness of Barton's announcement appears to have given her an advantage over Robitaille, whose anticipated gas-wielding Japanese warriors became conspicuous by their absence. A comparison of the two groups' belief systems prior to the announcements suggest that the flexibility and the extent to which the founders' ideas were codified and institutionalized might, under the severe stress of disconfirmation, become important variables in determining their success in redefining prophecy.

MES is an example of an NRM with strong and well-defined millenarian beliefs, neatly codified in *Les Documents*. Eugène Richer, the original founder, had warned his people of the imminent—but undated—Battle of Armageddon involving "Le Japonais." The self-concept of the community resided in the conviction that they were God's Chosen People, His children, a new race who would survive the holocaust and inhabit the Millennium. Emmanuel's message was consistent with this relatively long-established creed, but his predictions were overly specific—and hence unwieldy when the time came to recast them.

It has already been established that the belief system in IAM was vague, eclectic, and inconsistent. On the basis of interview data, it appears that Barton's prophecy was not rooted in a preestablished apocalyptic ideology nor a coherent cosmology, but arrived like the proverbial bolt from the blue. Her followers were given a mere six days to invest in doom, so there was not much committed activity "difficult to undo" surrounding the "belief." Moreover, Barton said very little about the form that World's End would take: "Winifred's warning was broadcast on the HAM radio and people were calling in to ask about it, but nobody knew what was going on. There were no details about how it was going to end. . . . We didn't know what it meant at all!" The response to her prediction among her students appears to have been quite varied. All sources agree that it was unexpected:

> I remember I went to lunch that day . . . and when we got back to the center we were met by one of the girls. She had a paper in her hand and she said, "Winifred announced the End of the World today at twelve o'clock noon in Vancouver." And I thought, "Where does this come from? No one was expecting this!" I thought we were going to find more people to take courses and would go on having fun, and all of a sudden this end of the world thing comes up!

Even Win's Yin-Yang partner appears to have been taken by surprise: "I saw Pierre's face when he heard it, and even *he* looked shocked!" Some members responded with ridicule: "There were about twenty people there and we laughed." Others responded with disbelief or doubt. A core member stated: "We didn't know what to make of it. I mean, Eric was at work, so do I call and say, 'Come home right now, the End of the World is at hand!' Do I believe this? I remember not knowing what to think. . . . I mean, are you kidding?"

Other IAM members responded with faith: "So we get together with some of the people and they really had a big reaction to this. They really thought that was it. Their faith in Win was quite something!"

The Social Context

A significant variable between IAM and MES is found in the ages of the respective movements. IAM was in its twelfth year when its charismatic founder began to wax apocalyptic. The MES community had flourished for sixty-one years and was in its third generation of leadership and in its fourth generation of family life (due to pubescent marriages) when its dormant millenarian expectations were stimulated. Another variable, closely related to the movements' respective ages, was their social organization. Many MES members had been born into the sect; their religious, familial, and social lives were confined within its boundaries, whereas most IAM students had invested little more than a few weeks of course work in Barton's organization. Therefore, it was not difficult for nonbelievers to walk away from Barton's Endtime—puzzled, amused, and perhaps even faintly inspired. For Mission members, however, the failure of prophecy presented a serious problem. They had invested all their savings in emergency preparations, they had waited for two years without access to their meeting place, and their social fabric had been eroded during this period. The congregation was deprived of guidance due to the secrecy of the Servants, who were preoccupied with saving their own families and the upper echelons of the Mission. Women were excluded from their husbands' confidences, and resorted to exchanging rumors. Men were unemployed, their savings misspent; many more wives were pregnant, according to our second informant (although it is difficult to see how this was possible). After two years of enormous suspense and investment, and considering the lack of social support, it is not surprising that prophetic disconfirmation posed a serious threat to the Mission's collective identity and led to wholesale apostasy and schism.

Given the striking differences in the social organization of these two groups, it seems reasonable to suggest that waiting for the End served a different function in each case. In Barton's group, it erected walls between the cult and the larger society, facilitating a mystical study group's transformation into a commune. MES, which fits the organizational type of a sect (Ellwood 1973), also appeared to embark on the millenarian adventure with the intention of shutting out "the world." Our informant's account suggests that, in their expectant mood, members were looking forward to living a communal life: "It was their dream to have a commune, their most fervent dream. Every single person in the Mission would work and they would have a cafeteria open 24 hours a day, there'd be people working and coming and eating at anytime. That was their dream in the New World." As it turned out, the failure of prophecy actually achieved the opposite effect—of dissolving the boundaries between the sect and the outside world. For those members who adopted the Jehovah's Witnesses' authoritative and sophisticated postmillennialism, the cramping boundaries of a tiny, local sect were exchanged for the expanded margins of a large, international one. For the three family-based congregations who remain faithful to the vision of Eugène Richer, their millenarian expectations are projected into an unspecified future, and in the interim, they have adopted a more accommodating relationship with Quebec society.

Apocalypse as Improvised Ritual

Millenarian expectations may take different forms. In those cases, however, where the prophet has assigned a specific time-frame for world destruction or for supernatural spectacle, the tendency among scholars is to treat this phenomenon as a *crisis of belief*. One of the impediments to approaching Millerite-style adventism as ritual is that it is a one-time event. It lacks what Bird (1979) has identified as two essential characteristics of rituals: that they are "stereotyped" and "repeated." Paradoxically, the ritual of apocalypse has the unique characteristic of being newly-forged and improvised, although its creator might refer to a transcendent authority from the past (like Nostradamus or Lost Atlantis).

Sometimes a traditional ritual might be coopted and its meaning altered (like Jim Jones's "White Nights"). Nevertheless, waiting for world's end is a symbolic act—"stylized," "intrinsically valued," and "authoritatively designated" like other rituals— and requires the presence of ritual actors and the organization of sacred time and sacred space.

But, what kind of ritual is it? It is difficult to categorize because its social function has never been clearly established. While it could be argued that the "rite of apocalypse" requires an independent category, it could also be observed that it combines elements from all three types of ritual behavior observed by Bird in NRMs. It is a ritual of *initiation* in that it formalizes a new and more intense relationship between master and disciple, and implies a rebirth into a new identity. It can be a ritual of *meditation* in that it often employs techniques to induce altered states of consciousness, such as ecstatic singing and dancing. It could be argued that the expectation of world destruction in one minute could propel even the laziest Zen student into alert mindfulness. It is a ritual of *purification,* for the participants expect to shed their morality, or to become purged of sin or Satan's blood, or to clone themselves on other planets, or to "metamorphose" into androgyny, and to rest among the chosen few out of the great threshing of humanity. In its complexity and richness, the well-staged apocalyptic event can involve an operatic integration of art forms and should inspire "pity and terror," inducing an emotional catharsis (and perhaps even a religious experience) in its ritual actors.

While it is not our intention to trivialize millenarian movements nor, having studied several examples of contemporary apocalypticism, to write a sort of "hostess manual" for doomsday prophets offering advice on how to stage a "successful" Endtime, the evidence suggests that for a millenarian movement to survive, its members must initially or eventually act out their beliefs within a microcosm of sacred space and time. The beliefs, no matter how frequently reinterpreted, deeply felt or highly elaborated, are not in themselves sufficient to fuel a movement. Some groups realize the Millennium by providing the occasion for ongoing testimonials bearing witness to the meeting of Heaven and Earth. The Shakers, for example, "labored for a gift" from dead prophets and Indian chiefs who, they believed, were among them in their gatherings. Those movements, however, which expect the Millennium to become manifest in a one-time event and which successfully weather the storm of "cognitive dissonance," appear to possess the following ingredients:

An Ordeal of Sacred Time or Terror

There must be a specific moment in time when the elect gather to witness, hoping to survive—and perhaps even to avert—world destruction. This moment of shared and appalled expectation creates close bonds between the participants. Turner (1969:154) defines this moment as "one of the chief ingredients in the production of existential communitas," and observes that "[communitas] movements are by no means always associated with visions or theories of world catastrophe . . . but we very often do find that the concept of threat or danger to the group . . . is importantly present."

Sacred Space: A Haven of Safety

Apocalypse must occur while the group is huddled in a safe haven or sacred territory, symbolically separated from the world of the unchosen. Tunnels and underground bunkers are a common form, from the Rappite secret passages to Sheela's underground bunker in Rajneeshpuram. Even Turner's tribesmen begin their rite of passage at the entrance to an animal's burrow.

A Technique of Ecstasy

The experience of "prophetic confirmation" appears to be reinforced by involvement in a collective ritual through which means the expectant millenarian can achieve enstatic or ecstatic states of consciousness. Lucy DuPertuis's theory (1986:113) of charisma as an "active, conscious social process involving the confirmation of belief through noncognitive methods of altering perception" is relevant to understanding this process. She defines charisma as a dynamic social relationship, as Worsley (1968) has emphasized, rather than as a set of qualities attributed to the leader. Moreover, she postulates that the recognition of charisma involves the integration of both cognitive and noncognitive methods which are taught and applied so that charisma might be recognized and experienced as residing not only in the leader, but also in the self and in the community. Millenarians, therefore, are not necessarily the gullible, passive creatures of Festinger's study. Waiting for the world's end can be an active, conscious, and social process during which initiates strive for an inner physiological and emotional catharsis equivalent to Carlos Castaneda's "stopping the world" or Ann Lee's "turning, turning we come round right" (Shaker hymn). This is quite different from the Monty Pythonesque situation of nervously checking one's watch before Endtime. While some millenarians might strike a skeptical audience as "sitting ducks" for cognitive dissonance, others might be more correctly perceived as actively seeking "noncognitive consonance."

The Prophet's Role in the Ritual

The prophet's presence should be felt throughout the ordeal. His or her presence is critical to assist in the "birth pangs of a new order" (Burridge 1969). Foster (1981:9) compares millenarian prophets to Turner's ritual elders, claiming the former have a more difficult task. Prophets must "begin to create a new way of life and status relationships at the very same time that they are trying to initiate individuals into those not yet established roles. In short, the end point is often unclear, or else is in the process of being created."

Prophets often demand from their disciples the renunciation of social roles and the symbolic death of their former identity, and may reduce them, through the ordeal of terror, to a psychological state not unlike that of an initiate in a puberty rite of a primitive tribe, as eloquently described by Prince (1974:226):

> The essential task is a psychological metamorphosis . . . the freeing of the initiate from his childish attitudes . . . through a regression induced by fear and clothed and interpreted by symbols of infancy. The initiate's ego is . . . reduced to a kind of primal ego-plasm by terror at the hands of the masqueraders wielding circumcision knives. Then the adult identity can be imprinted like a seal in wax.

For the prophet to remain silent or inaccessible, having reduced his initiate to a "primal ego-plasm," and then to fail to imprint the new identity would understandably be interpreted as a loss of charisma or failure of prophecy. If each initiate is left to his or her own devices to struggle into a new, self-determined identity, it is not surprising that the cohesion and survival of the group is threatened. The process of rationalization-reinterpretation, however, must commence immediately within the first few moments following prophetic disconfirmation, as part of the ritual. The necessity for promptness is that reinterpretation must occur within the ritual process, that is, before sacred time fades into profane time.

From this perspective, the outcome of the two prophecies begins to "make sense." Barton provided a satisfying ritual experience for her followers; Robitaille did not.

Although Barton could be described as a minimalist as regards prophetic utterances, her apocalyptic ritual was well-organized and complex, occurring within a sacred time and space. The entire weekend was described by participants as an intensely emotional and therapeutic experience which provided students with a vision of her future utopia. Techniques of ecstasy, such as circle dancing and embracing, were used, and as doomsday approached, the group meditated to "Loliad's Prayer." Finally, Win's presence remained strong throughout the entire crisis. She kept phoning all three centers, reminding them to "Keep up the Vibe." She staged a dramatic entrance at Nominingue two hours before world's end, and at noon, when her meditating students lifted their eyes to her (like Lorenz's baby geese), she was ready to reinterpret. As Balch and his colleagues (1983:154) observe, "It is hard to imagine a more ambiguous situation than the first uneasy moments after disconfirmation." Win quickly averted ambiguity by reinterpreting World's End as an inner experience as opposed to an external event. The good news was immediately broadcast to group leaders in Madoc and Gravelbourg.

A testimonial to the power of Win's apocalyptic ritual is offered by this account of the conversion of a man who was previously quite unfamiliar with IAM's beliefs:

> I remember there was one guy I'd never seen before. His brother had taken a course with us and he'd met a girl in Europe the previous summer.

When he heard the news he thought, "If I had to be a witness to the end of the world, she'd be the one I'd want to do it with." So he drove up to her house in Alberta and convinced her to come with him to this weekend. It's amazing she agreed, because they hardly knew each other—and her parents weren't too crazy about the idea—but they ended up living with us in the Domes [the commune], and I hear they're still together.

Emmanuel Robitaille's prophecy, however, was never consummated in ritual. The community shared no sacred moment. A sacred space was created, but only for the more financially advantaged members. "Le Troue" was never occupied. The majority of members were abandoned, bereft of their meeting place, and kept waiting for further instructions that never came. While it would be facile to embark upon a *post facto* analysis of this prophet's failure as a privation of charisma, it is undeniable that Emmanuel Robitaille's presence was weak in December 1975, and that he made no effort to reinterpret his prophecy but turned to the Jehovah's Witnesses to accomplish this task for him.

It has already been established that prophecy can be understood as a charisma-building strategy (Wallis 1982), or as a test of loyalty (Foster 1981). Winifred Barton's career suggests that apocalyptic ritual can also function as an initiatory ordeal whereby the leader undergoes a symbolic death and rebirth into a new phase or style of leadership.

A close study of Barton's career demonstrates she had been steadily building charisma in preparation for her metamorphosis of 1976. The back cover of an IAM publication (Barton 1968) features a sketch of Barton as an energetic writer-lecturer-broadcaster-teacher who is also a devoted wife-mother-gardener:

> With several thousand students within the Society, she is in constant demand as a teacher for seminar and immersion courses, as well as giving seminars to businessmen; . . . She is currently writing a twenty-book series on various aspects of metaphysics. . . . She is married, has four sons, two grandchildren, a home she maintains herself, a huge garden and a boundless enthusiasm and zest for life. She is a perfect example of her metaphysical teaching—that metaphysics can enable you to be a happier, fulfilled and loving individual.

At this phase, Barton conformed to Weber's model of the exemplary prophet, or to Bird's typology (1979) of a "teacher of techniques" who presides over the apprentice-type NRM in which the aim is power and well-being. By 1977, however, Barton conformed to the ethical prophet or Bird's devotee-type "God in Flesh" who demands total surrender. Four events since 1973—the Psychic Explosion, the Barton-Levesque "Yin-Yang" wedding, the revelation that Pierre was Loliad the Cosmic Lord, and the creation of an inner circle of "Angels of Armageddon"—were steps leading up to her shamanic descent to the underworld and protean metamorphosis into a charismatic duo.

Robitaille's announcement, however, was made during a phase of declining charisma in MES's leadership. Unlike his father and the founder Richer,

Emmanuel was not considered to be the Holy Spirit Incarnate. He shared with twenty-eight other Servants a mere priestly authority, a charisma of office. Even his dream-vision was not his own, but was putatively sent by his father, Le Prince. It is unfortunate that no account of the internal political relationships between the Servants exists, so that the possibilities might be explored of his dream and subsequent behavior reflecting the sibling rivalry between the sons of Le Prince. These ideas, however, must remain in the world of the subjunctive.

Conclusion

Kenelm Burridge (1971) has characterized millenarian activity as "the birth pangs of a new order." Victor Turner (1969:111) sees such movements as "essentially a phenomenon of transition." These scholars emphasize the social upheavals of certain historical periods that are reflected or dramatized in their apocalyptic cults. Millenarians are the "dispossessed," the "disinherited," or even the voluntary poor bereft of social status, like the Beguines of the "Free Spirit" who were spinsters from the rising middle class of Renaissance Europe (Cohn 1970). Turner expresses this view convincingly: "Mostly such movements occur during phases of history that are in many respects 'homologous' to the liminal periods of important rituals in stable and repetitive societies when major groups or social categories in those societies are passing from one cultural state to another."

A study of contemporary spiritual movements suggests that millenarian activities can also arise from tensions experienced within the group itself, having very little relevance to the problems or changes occurring in the larger society. Leaders in the second or third generation might claim dream messages from the original founder in a strategic effort to coopt charisma and deinstitutionalize the organization—as, for example, initiating gurus in ISKCON who aspired to inheriting the mantle of guruhood from the late Swami Prabhupada (Rochford 1985). Spiritual politics might be the motivating force behind NRMs of the "world affirming" variety (Wallis 1984) suddenly preparing for doomsday. Other examples of this phenomenon besides IAM are the Rajneesh movement (Gordon 1987), The Process (Bainbridge 1978), and the "spiritual schools" of E. J. Gold (Palmer 1976). These groups, like IAM, do not fit the "protorevolutionary" or "dispossessed" mold, inhabited as they are by affluent middle- to upper-class ex-college students, and offering (as they initially did) techniques to empower the individual in secular life.

How can these tentative and experimental forays into apocalypticism be understood? When contemporary spiritual groups unexpectedly embark on the millenarian adventure, the leader appears to be responding to conflicts or "growing pains" within her or his community that require a radical reorganization—or a rebirth. In such cases, the rite of apocalypse, ostensibly aimed at destroying the old order of planet Earth, actually functions to bring about a new order within the cult or sect. When examined within the framework of the charismatic career of the leader-founder, or the group's changing relationship with its host society, the "acting out" of Endtime often appears to function as a collective rite of passage into a new group identity. When a loosely knit group begins to band together in a commune, the apocalyptic ritual could be compared to Kanter's (1968) six commitment mechanisms all operating simultaneously in full force. It could also, perhaps, be explained in Bainbridge's terms (1978) as an extreme example of "social implosion." Alternatively, when a tightly-knit sect that is hostile toward its host society and in its third generation of leadership undertakes to revitalize its community through the charisma of prophecy, a "successful" Endtime might fulfill a positive function; it might reinforce social bonds, enhance the self-identity of elect Peoples, and redefine the boundaries insulating youthful members from a corrupt outside world.

In some cases, apocalyptic rituals appear to facilitate an abrupt *volte-face* in the direction of a movement or to hasten its transformation from one type of religious organization to another. Of the millenarian movements that survive their passage through apocalypse (and many emerge stillborn), some might unfurl their wings as if from a cocoon into extravagant new forms: as militant revolutionary movements, as evangelical sects, or as communal utopias.

REFERENCES

Bainbridge, W. S. 1978. *Satan's Power*. Berkeley: University of California Press.

Balch, R. W., G. Farnsworth, and S. Wilkins. 1983. "When the Bombs Drop." *Sociological Perspectives* 6:137–158.

Barton, W. G. 1968. *Loliad R. Kahn*. Ottawa: PSI Science Productions.

Bird, F. 1979. "The Pursuit of Innocence: New Religious Movements and Moral Accountability." *Sociological Analysis* 40:335–346.

Burridge, K. 1969. *New Heaven, New Earth: A Study of Millenarian Activities*. New York: Blackwell.

Cohn, N. 1970. *The Pursuit of the Millennium*. New York: Oxford University Press.

DuPertuis, L. 1986. "How People Recognize Charisma: The Case of Darshan in Rahasoami and Divine Light Mission." *Sociological Analysis* 47:111–124.

Ellwood, R. S. 1973. *Religious and Spiritual Groups in Modern America*. Englewood Cliffs, NJ: Prentice-Hall.

Festinger, L., et al. 1956. *When Prophecy Fails*. Minneapolis: University of Minnesota Press.

Foster, L. 1981. *Religion and Sexuality*. New York: Oxford University Press.

Gager, J. G. 1975. *Kingdom and Community: The Social World of Early Christianity*. Englewood Cliffs, NJ: Prentice-Hall.

Gordon, J. S. 1987. *The Golden Guru*, Lexington, MA: The Stephen Greene Press.

Hardyck, J. A., and M. Braden. 1962. "Prophecy Fails Again: A Report of a Failure to Replicate." *Journal of Abnormal and Social Psychology* 65:136–141.

Kanter, R. M. 1968. "Commitment and Social Organization: A Study of Commitment Mechanisms in Utopian Communities." *American Sociological Review* 33:499–517.

Lofland, J. 1977. *Doomsday Cult: A Study of Conversion, Proselytization and Maintenance of Faith*. New York: Irvington.

Morris, M. 1986. "IAM: A Group Portrait." Senior essay, Yale University.

Palmer, S. J. 1976. "Shakti!:The Spiritual Science of DNA." M.A. Thesis, Concordia University, Montreal.

———. 1988. "Charisma and Abdication." *Sociological Analysis* 49:119–135.

Penton, M. J. 1985. *Apocalypse Delayed: The Story of Jehovah's Witnesses.* Toronto: University of Toronto Press.

Prince, R. 1974. "Cocoon Work: An Interpretation of the Concern of Contemporary Youth with the Mystical," pp. 264–275 in *Religious Movements in Contemporary America*, edited by I. Zaretsky and M. P. Leone. Princeton: NJ: Princeton University Press.

Rochford, E. B. 1985. *Hare Krishna in America.* New Brunswick, NJ: Rutgers University Press.

Talmon, Y. 1970. "Pursuit of the millennium," pp. 103–137 in *Millennial Dreams in Action*, edited by S. Thrupp. New York: Schocken.

Turner, V. W. 1969. *The Ritual Process: Structure and Anti-Structure.* Chicago: University of Chicago Press.

Wallis, R. 1977. *The Road to Total Freedom: A Sociological Analysis of Scientology.* New York: Columbia University Press.

———.1982. *Millennialism and Charisma.* Belfast: Queen's University.

———. 1984. *The Elementary Forms of the New Religious Life.* London: Routledge & Kegan Paul.

Worsley, P. 1968. *The Trumpet Shall Sound: A Study of "Cargo" Cults in Melanesia.* New York: Schocken.

Zygmunt, J. F. 1972. "When Prophecies Fail." American Behavioral Scientist 16:245–267.

When Festinger Fails
Prophecy and the Watchtower

Mathew N. Schmalz

Few homeowners have failed to see a Jehovah's Witness at their front door. Well trained in their Theocratic Ministry Schools, Witnesses calmly announce that God's Kingdom will soon rule the earth. If pressed about the specific date for the Millennium's arrival, they often reply that only Jehovah God knows the precise time but that the end will surely come within the lifetime of the generation which witnessed the events of 1914. Yet it was 1914 that was originally to see the glorious New Order, according to the Watchtower's founder Charles Taze Russell. Indeed, within their history Jehovah's Witnesses have often set specific dates for the coming of the Apocalypse. Far from destroying the movement, the disconfirmation of these prophecies revealed the distinctive strength of the Watchtower to withstand fundamental challenges to its faith. While their growth far exceeds that of mainline American churches, Jehovah's Witnesses have not attracted the widespread public or scholarly attention that many less dynamic denominations receive. Yet their responses to failed predictions are intriguing, for they depart not only from conventional wisdom but from widely held academic theories concerning reactions to disconfirmed prophecy.

Any discussion of prophecy and disconfirmation must inevitably confront Leon Festinger's classic study, *When Prophecy Fails*.[1] An American academic specializing in social psychology, Festinger argues that when committed individuals adhere to a specific prophecy, they will maintain that belief in spite of unequivocal refutation. Believers will then proselytize to persuade others that the belief was correct. Although almost forty years old, Festinger's theory still exists as a crucial referent for any discussion of cognitive dissonance and the failure of prophecy.[2] Even the studies that challenge his theory have nonetheless followed Festinger's lead by focusing upon single instances of disconfirmation.[3] The Watchtower, however, offers a distinctive example of a single religious group that has a long history of proclaiming the imminent fulfilment of its millennial hopes, and then facing the disappointment that the postponement of those hopes brings. The experience of Jehovah's Witnesses with prophetic speculation thus allows us not only to view distinct moments of prophetic failure, but also to compare these responses to disconfirmation over the course of the Watchtower's long wait for Armageddon.

This paper will focus upon two moments in the history of the Watchtower to examine Festinger's hypothesis. After reviewing the five conditions Festinger establishes for the testing of his theory, we will delve into the origins of the Watchtower and observe the response of the organization when the Millennium failed to arrive in 1914. While Festinger's model initially helps us to understand the movement's development, the reaction of the Watchtower to disconfirmation also departs from his hypothesis. We will then examine another prediction: 1975 as the year of the Apocalypse. The response to the continuing existence of the present system after that date brought denial and purge rather than the increased proselytism required by Festinger's model. After discussing the organizational and ideological elements of the Watchtower movement which enable such a response, we will return to Festinger's model and attempt to revise it in relation to the attitude of Jehovah's Witnesses to prophetic speculation. I will argue that Festinger's model fails to recognize how complex organizations and systems of belief shape responses to disconfirmed prophecy. Indeed, the history of Jehovah's Witnesses demonstrates that organizational structure and ideology constitute crucial variables for any analysis of reaction to prophetic failure. It is the power of the Watchtower as a millenarian movement that allows not only the rationalization of disconfirmation but also retrospective denial of the prophecy itself.

When Prophecy Fails: The Model of Leon Festinger

In a study conducted in the early 1950s, the psychologist Leon Festinger and a group of research assistants penetrated a movement that had predicted the destruction of the world. A Mrs. Marian Keech had been receiving messages from outer space forecasting the end of civilization in a great flood. A small group eventually formed around her, eagerly awaiting the words of their extraterrestrial "Guardians" which Mrs. Keech would record in her notebook. The group began to proselytize after Sananda, one of the Guardians from the planet Losolo, set a date for the flood and promised that they would all be rescued before the deluge. Surprisingly, the disconfirmation of this prophecy and the others that followed led only to increased fervor and proselytism. Mrs. Keech called newspapers, and the group began to issue pamphlets detailing the prophecy. Members also sought confirmation of elements of the prophecy, and Mrs. Keech revealed more predictions. Even after successive all-night vigils waiting for flying saucers that never came, some explanation was put forth to explain the disconfirmations: they were interpreted either as a test or as a postponement of the cataclysm. In each case, the believers maintained the validity of the prophecy to conform with their experience. It was only after a rapid series of disconfirmations and increasing hostility from their neighbors and local authorities that the group finally disbanded.

Festinger's research supported his overall theory of cognitive dissonance, which states that when an individual's strong belief encounters unequivocal refutation, that person will defend the position with increased fervor. Festinger qualifies this analysis by positing five requirements for this particular response to disconfirmation.[4] First, a belief must be held with conviction and have some relevance to action. Second, the person holding the belief must have taken some action that is difficult to undo. Third, the belief must be specific and sufficiently connected with the real world that events may refute it. Fourth, the disconfirmatory evidence must occur and be recognized by the believer. Fifth, if there is sufficient social support, the belief will be maintained and believers will attempt to persuade others that the belief was correct. This final condition becomes especially important for Festinger's analysis, since it is doubtful that any individual could maintain a disconfirmed prediction without the aid of a surrounding community.

Festinger makes expansive claims for his model, citing both the Sabbatai Zevi phenomenon and the Millerite movement to buttress his case. According to Festinger, it was only after Sabbatai Zevi proclaimed himself the Messiah and the era of Redemption did not arrive in 1648 that he and his followers began to proselytize.[5] The prophecy of William Miller that the Second Coming of Christ would occur in 1843 also survived successive disconfirmations.[6] His chronology was first slightly changed to mean the "Jewish Year" which extended the date to March 21, 1844. Yet when this date passed, October 22, 1844, was set as the coming of the Apocalypse. After this disconfirmation, however, the Millerites finally disbanded. For Festinger, these movements reflect the same pattern: when people commit themselves to a belief and a related course of action, disconfirming evidence leads to deepened conviction and increased proselytism. Although there exists a point beyond which belief cannot endure, Festinger argues that dedicated members will continue to maintain validity of their belief system and prophecy. We will now apply his model to the history of the Watchtower movement.

Prophecy Disconfirmed and Prophecy Revised: The Beginnings of the Watchtower Movement

The story of Jehovah's Witnesses and their bold interpretations of Biblical prophecy begins with Charles Taze Russell. He was born on February 16, 1852, into a strict Presbyterian home near Pittsburgh.[7] Long searching to understand the divine will, Russell's views about the nature of God began to crystallize when he attended a gathering of Seventh-Day Adventists in 1870.[8] Attracted by their confident exposition of doctrine, Russell became a regular member of their meetings. After attending one service, Russell is reported to have thought "Is it possible that the handful of people who meet here have something more sensible to offer than the creeds of the great churches?"[9] Russell, together with a small group of followers, then returned to the Bible to understand the true message of God.

Russell's study of the Bible produced a millennial chronology that predicted 1914 as the end of Gentile times and the beginning of Christ's thousand-year reign on earth. Understanding the Bible as a cypher containing God's plan for humankind, Russell believed that the time of redemption was at hand. He argued that Christ had secretly arrived in 1874 and that the terrestrial Kingdom of God would be established in 1914 to be ruled by Christ and "translated saints" who had been immediately resurrected to heaven.[10] Based upon his study of the Bible and the Great Pyramid, Russell included a bewildering number of dates in his calculations to support his overall claim.[11] He remarked that altering the prophecy by even one year would destroy the perfect symmetry of this Biblical chronology.

With the proclamation of the Millennium's arrival in 1914, Russell's movement expanded rapidly. In 1880, he consolidated the movement as Zion's Watchtower Tract Society and appointed colporteurs to sell Watchtower literature.[12] To accommodate increasing numbers of converts, Russell allowed local meetings in rented halls, moving them away from Curry Hall in Pittsburgh.[13] Overseas evangelism began with a branch office opened in England in 1881, and Russell himself visited promising areas for conversion yearly, his travels culminating with a world tour in 1912.[14] By this time, the Watchtower had moved to Brooklyn with an enlarged printing facility and the Bethel House living quarters for workers. The movement, on the eve of the Millennium, numbered over 15,000 members.

With this background, we may now return to Festinger's conditions for reaction to disconfirmed prophecy. The first and second requirements, demanding deep commitment to a belief that finds expression in irrevocable action, seem fulfilled by the actions of Russell and his followers. The progressive development of Russell's views about the Millennium led the organization to commit enormous amounts of capital to the proclamation of his message through literature and photo-dramas.[15] The publication of his massive *Studies in the Scriptures* precipitated the increased growth of the movement by explicitly identifying the year 1914 as the end of Gentile times and the beginning of Christ's millennial reign. The decisions made by Russellites to move to Bethel or work in proselytism became publicly associated with this widely disseminated prophecy. All of them expected the immediate "translation of saints" to rule with the revealed Christ in 1914. This belief was unequivocal, satisfied only upon the establishment of an earthly paradise. Thus the third condition of Festinger's model is met as well, for now deep belief becomes attached to a prediction of an empirically verifiable event.

The year 1914 came and went without the millennial dawn that Russell had so ardently expected. Faced with such a disconfirmation, Russell drew upon cautionary pronouncements he had made several years earlier. In 1912 he wrote that, while the prophecy remains valid, the power of the Gentiles could end either in October 1914 or in October 1915.[16] In November 1914, one month after his prophecy had failed, he remarked that the period of transition could run a "good many years."[17] Russell himself recognized his miscalculation, thus fulfilling the fourth condition of Festinger's hypothesis. Yet he did not encourage his followers to proselytize for the belief, deciding instead to place the organization in a prophetic limbo.

Instead of vigorously supporting his original position as Festinger's fifth condition would demand, Russell paved the way for revising the entire chronology. When 1914 did not see "the revealment in flaming fire," Russell encouraged his followers to wait patiently, stating that God's Kingdom on Earth would be established gradually. After Russell died in 1916, with the time of transition continuing, the movement codified his rationalizations to preserve its strength. Posthumous editions of Russell's *Studies in the Scriptures* refer to 1914 as "the beginning of the end of Gentile times," with entire sections rewritten in light of this revised interpretation of Biblical prophecy.[18] With the rise of Russell's successor, Joseph Franklin Rutherford, the movement first suggested new dates for the Apocalypse and then rested with the belief that the Millennium would come within the generation who saw the events of 1914.[19] Eighteen seventy-four and other significant dates in Russell's millennial chronology were then progressively abandoned.[20] It is crucial to recognize that no increase in proselytism occurred until three to four years after disconfirmation.[21] In fact, it was only after recognition of a continuing increase in membership that extensive evangelical activities resumed.[22] Such a tentative reaction to disconfirmation becomes understandable in light of the massive reorientation that Watchtower chronology required after 1914. Many Bible Students simply did not know upon what basis the coming of the Millennium could be proclaimed. By announcing an undefined time of transition, Russell had shrewdly offered his movement a way out of the restrictions of prophecy. Today the Watchtower simply acknowledges that "something must have been miscalculated."[23]

Russell's successful postponement of Armageddon initially depended upon the authoritarian organization of the Watchtower. As membership increased, Russell tentatively allowed the formation of local study groups headed by "elders" who were elected by the congregation. Yet he soon realized that he courted subversion of his authority with such division of responsibilities. Moving swiftly to establish his preeminence, Russell brought the elders under his control by substituting the use of his own "Berean" pamphlets in study.[24] To maintain doctrinal conformity, he purged Watchtower offices that deviated from his teachings and often despatched elite "pilgrims," his specially trained ministers, to oversee congregational activity.[25] These actions not only strengthened Russell's control of information but ensured that Watchtower administrators would be responsive to his directives. Since Russell's followers were distributed worldwide, all communication in the society went vertically to him rather than horizontally to other congregations.[26] Russell could thus isolate threats to his authority, and Watchtower members could never consolidate to affirm the 1914 prophecy, had they chosen to do so.

In spite of the institutional controls at his disposal, it is doubtful that Russell could have preserved his movement without the legitimating power of charisma. It is therefore not surprising that his actions were those of a charismatic leader in a classically Weberian sense.[27] He claimed a divine purpose for his mission through his interpretation of Biblical prophecy and considered himself Ezekiel's "man with an inkhorn, marking the foreheads of people."[28] In order to emphasize the distinctiveness of their calling, he and his followers stood outside the world and waited for it to die, scrupulously maintaining a strict neutrality in all political affairs and devoting themselves to proselytism. He demanded recognition of his mission through the vows all members made to obey him, and many responded by coming to live with Russell at Bethel. Yet, because of his status as an anointed leader, Russell had to prove himself worthy of his station. Thus when his prophecy failed, he reminded his followers that even if the Millennium did not arrive, they were still a blessed and happy people.[29] Indeed, it was the very nature of the Watchtower as a charismatic community with an efficient organizational structure that allowed the movement to continue and prosper.

While the actions of Russell and his followers after 1914 initially seem to depart from Festinger's model, the central premise of his hypothesis remains untouched. The Watchtower movement did continue to maintain its belief in the Millennium, although in an empirically unverifiable form. In contrast, Mrs. Keech and her followers, a much more limited group, continued to affirm the truth of disconfirmed prophecies through a variety of rationalizations. The Millerites, however, altered their chronology slightly and sustained a high degree of evangelical activity for a year after the failure of their initial prediction. The Watchtower was able to revise its interpretation of Biblical prophecy much more comprehensively by reinterpreting the significance of 1914 and gradually denying other significant events in its schedule for Armageddon. Thus specific beliefs in prophetic dates were sacrificed or changed in order to salvage the general millennial orientation of the group.

While Festinger's overall hypothesis seems confirmed, the ability of Jehovah's Witnesses to reinterpret and deny elements of the 1914 prophecy suggests a more complex system of belief than his model assumes. What we see in the Watchtower's reaction to disconfirmed prophecy is an initial attempt to reduce dissonance on the part of the leadership by altering or disassociating themselves from a particular prophetic formulation through doctrinal change and denial. Rank-and-file members then reciprocally move to conform to these adaptations in order to reestablish group cohesion. Only after these two responses succeed do we see a resumption of proselytism which, in the case of Jehovah's Witnesses, comes years after the original disconfirmation.

Festinger would perhaps respond that Russell's rationalizations and their later elaboration are but variations on a single theme, since they did not constitute a complete rejection of the particular prophecy. Festinger might then point to World War I and the persecution of Jehovah's Witnesses throughout the world as sufficient explanation for the absence of any increase in evangelical activity. In order to revise or augment Festinger's model, it is therefore necessary to examine another instance of disconfirmation to see what pattern it displays. Accordingly, we turn to the Watchtower prophecy of the beginning of the Millennium in 1975.

Prophecy and Purge: Armageddon 1975

By 1966, Jehovah's Witnesses had become a worldwide organization with approximately one million publishers and almost twice that number attending meetings and the annual memorial service.[30] As former Witnesses Gary and Heather Botting recount, many Witnesses expected something significant in June of that year because of the association of the date 6/66 with 666, the mark of the beast in Revelation 13:18.[31] It was in this month that the Watchtower Bible and Tract Society published *Life Everlasting in Freedom of the Sons of God*. The work contains a chronological chart which identifies 1975 as the "end of the sixth thousand year day of man's existence."[32] The accompanying text calmly observes "how appropriate it would be for Jehovah God to make of this coming period of a thousand years a Sabbath period of rest and release."[33] Articles in the society's chief publications, *Watchtower* and *Awake!*, reinforced the millennial interpretation of the date and its attendant schedule.[34] Speakers at Watchtower assemblies also encouraged Witnesses to look forward to the autumn of 1975,[35] a hope expressed in the saying "make do till '72, stay alive till '75."[36] This prophecy galvanized the movement and proselytism increased substantially. On the eve of the Millennium in 1974, the number of publishers rose by 13.5 percent worldwide, and many Witnesses were actively preparing for the dawn of the New Order.[37]

Once again we may apply the first three requirements of Festinger's model to Watchtower prophecy. Not only was the prediction of the end of the "sixth thousand year day of man's existence" published in organizational literature, it was also used as a basis for proselytism. The prediction, therefore, required deep commitment and possessed a relevance to action. In addition to proclaiming this belief to a largely incredulous world, some Jehovah's Witnesses sold their possessions, postponed surgery, or cashed in their insurance policies to prepare for Christ's millennial reign.[38] As Festinger would describe it, these actions were certainly difficult to undo. While the Watchtower attached various caveats to the prophecy, the date was nonetheless specific and the existence of qualifications did little to dampen the enthusiastic proselytism of 1974.[39] Indeed, ex-Witness M. James Penton states that refusal to become outwardly excited about society's schedule for Armageddon "was looked upon as somewhat heretical and therefore spiritually dangerous for the highly disciplined community of Jehovah's Witnesses."[40] This state of affairs led a former Witness to write, in a book entitled *Year of Doom 1975*, "either 1975 will mark the end of the world or of Jehovah's Witnesses."[41]

In spite of dissent and counter-prophecies predicting the end of the Watchtower, the organization finally gained a pyrrhic victory in the face of disconfirmation. The first evidence of dissatisfaction came in 1976 when proselytism began to decline, with the next two years seeing an unprecedented decrease in the number of publishers.[42] Initially Watchtower President Frederick Franz attempted to revise the prophecy by stating that the time of man's existence should be dated from the creation of Eve rather than that of Adam.[43] While this fulfills the fourth requirement of Festinger's model by recognizing disconfirmation, it did not stop hundreds of thousands of Witnesses from leaving the movement.[44] Faced with such a crisis, the leadership turned to more severe measures to preserve the organization.

Instead of maintaining the prophetic significance of 1975, the Watchtower leadership embarked upon a five-year period of denial and purge. *Watchtower* articles and speeches given by members of the governing body blamed rank-and-file Witnesses for misreading the organization's interpretation of 1975.[45] The leadership drew attention away from disconfirmation by requiring an even greater loyalty from its members, a demand enforced with the expulsion of nearly 30,000 Witnesses in 1978 alone.[46] This insistence upon doctrinal orthodoxy even reached the highest levels of the organization in 1980, with many in the writing committee dismissed and disfellowshipped.[47] While the organization accepted some responsibility for contributing to the excitement surrounding 1975,[48] it assigned no different interpretation to the date and demanded that its members recognize that there was never such an explicit prophecy. No schismatic sects formed, and the organization recovered its normal growth. Indeed, Witnesses who left the movement recount how quickly remaining members "rearranged" their memories to deny that there had ever been a prophecy.[49] The prophetic beacon of 1975 thus darkened as the movement extended its wait for the Apocalypse.

Festinger's fifth condition, requiring that believers maintain a prophecy after disconfirmation and proselytize to reduce dissonance, does not adequately explain the reaction of the Watchtower to the failure of its 1975 prophecy. Proselytism did not increase beyond its normal rate. In fact, for two years following disconfirmation evangelical activity declined, according to the organization's own statistics. After the failure of the prophecy, the full ideological and organizational apparatus of the movement became focused upon denying the prediction; the chronology was ignored and many were expelled from the theocratic community. Intense pressures were exerted to make members adhere to an even stricter orthodoxy which demanded absolute fealty to the organization and its governing body.

It is important to recognize that Festinger never mentions an instance in which a prophecy was denied. In his analysis, he emphasizes an almost Pavlovian response to disconfirmation, with rationalizations put forward to justify the prophecy and to increase proselytism. Within this framework, he makes few distinctions between core and peripheral beliefs and does not seem to recognize differences in organizational structures which allow for the exercise of power to maintain ideological conformity and sustain social cohesion within a movement. Mrs. Keech's group, the Millerites, and the Sabbataian movement possessed only rudimentary organization and were more localized phenomena compared to the Watchtower movement of 1914 or 1975. Their reactions to disconfirmed prophecy were based upon group consensus rather than upon mandates from a hierarchical leadership. Yet to rework Festinger's hypothesis to include these observations, we must once again examine why the Watchtower's response proved so persuasive.

Theocracy and Power

When the Watchtower succeeded in denying the specificity of its 1975 prophecy, it departed not only from the pattern outlined by Festinger but from the precedent set by its founder Charles Taze Russell. In its transition from a community centered around a charismatic leader to a theocratic organization, the Watchtower was able to refine its organizational controls and further expand the ideology that legitimates its leadership. While these elements enabled the movement to survive the 1975 crisis, it is the powerful identity of the Watchtower as a millenarian movement with privileged knowledge that continues to attract members.

As in Russell's time, the Watchtower leadership of 1975 had a powerful organization that allowed it to control information and enforce conformity. The contemporary president heads a governing board that supervises committees devoted to specific aspects of the organization's work: writing, teaching, service, publishing, and personnel. All writings must receive governing board approval before publication. While this demonstrates that *Life Everlasting* could not have been released without the leadership's consent, it paradoxically also shows how the hierarchy could retrospectively revise or deny prophetic pronouncements. Because its control of published information is so total, the governing board does not face the prospect of immediate dissent when its prophecies fail. This gives the leadership crucial time to rationalize or deny its failed predictions. Yet, when dissatisfaction over the 1975 prophecy could no longer be ignored, the leadership could exert its power in a descending line of authority through Branch and Circuit offices to the congregational level. Witnesses in these crucial positions are absolutely dedicated to the organization, since they have been effectively screened through a rigidly sequential process of promotion.[50] Disfellowshipping then becomes a powerful means of enforcing conformity by expelling deviant members from the theocratic community. The overall organization of the movement thus ensures that members are responsive to the hierarchy's directives.

The pronouncements and actions of the governing board assume a great significance because only they possess charismatic authority as representatives of Jehovah God. While the Watchtower of 1914 derived its strength from Russell's personal magnetism, the personal qualities of the present-day president receive no special attention. The governing board as a collective entity, however, is always represented as the earthly extension of Jehovah's theocracy. But unlike other religious groups, the Watchtower does not have charisma distributed throughout every level of the organization. Instead, middle level officials, like managers in a corporation, decide how best to meet the leadership's objectives, and individual Witnesses have an instrumental function to carry out their orders.[51] Even organizational literature carries no attribution of individual authorship and is simply marked with the theocratic imprimatur of the Watchtower Bible and Tract Society. As James Beckford has observed, the distance between the governing board and rank-and-file Witnesses cloaks the hierarchy in a veneer of mystery while allowing subordinates to be blamed for organizational failures.[52] Thus after the 1975 prophecy, members of the writing committee were disfellowshipped and others throughout the organization were made scapegoats. Because Witnesses below the governing board do not have any charismatically legitimated authority, it would be extremely difficult for them to counter effectively the hierarchy's pronouncements. Such a combination of power and charisma lends a tremendous credibility to assertions made by the leadership that failed prophecies were due not to an error of the theocracy but to the mistakes of individuals.

The Watchtower's ability to enforce such strict discipline gains strength from a powerful ideology emphasizing self-denial and the dangers of independent thought. The most prominent exemplar of the self-denial that the Watchtower demands is Christ. Jesus, identified as the archangel Michael in Watchtower theology, became God's unquestioning servant as he went to death,[53] a potent symbol for Jehovah's Witnesses, who describe themselves as "God's faithful and discreet slaves."[54] Disobedience then becomes literally a mortal sin, since it was Adam and Eve who brought death to humankind by disobeying Jehovah God.[55] Indeed, before Jehovah restores his gift of immortality, he will test those faithful to him, and all Witnesses must therefore display unquestioning devotion to God and His organization. The presence of these themes and symbols constantly reminds Witnesses that independent thought is fraught with peril and that any apparent fault within the organization lies with them. The rigorous structures of five meetings a week, devoted to Bible or *Watchtower* study, allows Witnesses little public expression beyond the parameters set by the organization. Themes and practices emphasizing self-denial thus constitute an ideological largesse which the leadership draws upon to insist that members of the organization conform to its pronouncements, even though they may contradict previous assertions. Thus an article in 1979, referring to disfellowshippings in the wake of the 1975 prophecy, emphasizes total obedience in addition to the danger of lukewarmness in proclaiming God's Truth.[56] Not only do Witnesses have little authority to question the Watchtower, it is in fact their duty not to question at all.

Although some view the power of the Watchtower as oppressive, for many rank-and-file Witnesses it is the very ideological and organizational cohesion of the movement that gives meaning and identity to their lives. The fundamental chiliastic orientation of the movement has only deepened since Russell's time. The world remains in the grip of Satan, who lures people away from God's truth through the machinations of government, big business and the organized churches of "Christendom." The righteous will be redeemed in the Battle of Armageddon when Jehovah will lay low this wicked system of things and cleanse the earth. For many, this vision is not only comforting but empowering. The pervasive use of scriptural citations to buttress all theological assertions emphasizes the Watchtower's claim to a privileged insight which is nonetheless accessible to committed members of the community. The organizational structure provides a well-articulated division of responsibilities that remains invariant within the wide geographical boundaries of the movement. Each Witness thus has a clear identity within the organization and possesses a common bond with other members throughout the world. It is the rigid enforcement of doctrinal conformity and constant pressure to proselytize that paradoxically both force members to leave and allow the movement to endure the worldly trials that accompany its wait for the Apocalypse.

If the strength of Jehovah's Witnesses comes from their cohesive identity, we can understand the role of proselytism within the movement from a perspective different from Festinger's vantage point. Many authors have identified aggressive evangelism as a characteristic of religious groups who believe in the absolute truth of their belief system.[57] Embedded within this is the desire to have matters of great conviction confirmed by others to achieve personal balance. This is indeed a response to dissonance, but the initial point of conflict does not necessarily involve disconfirmation of prophecy. For Jehovah's Witnesses, who have recorded their highest rates of growth in years during which no prophetic date had been set, the locus of conflict is between them and a world they believe is completely evil. If others can be persuaded to join, their original separation from modern social institutions is justified. This helps explain the presence of high degrees of proselytism before the disconfirmation of the 1914 prophecy and the substantial growth of the movement before the publication of the chronology identifying 1975 as Armageddon.[58] Proselytism thus becomes empowering, for Witnesses can lay claim to a special knowledge and an identity which find increasing social affirmation with the thousands who enter the movement every year.

Prophecy then represents the ultimate claim to certainty and special identity by the Watchtower movement. When one walks into a Kingdom Hall, one finds members discussing Watchtower exegetical works, citing Scripture and planning for the day's proselytism. There is little or no ritual, no claims of charismatic gifts, no personal confessions, and no emotionalism of any kind. James Beckford reports that Watchtower converts rarely report experiencing heightened emotions such as joy or love upon entering the movement.[59] Instead, Witnesses describe their conversion as "coming into the Truth" and use images of darkness and light to contrast their previous lives to their present membership in the Watchtower.[60] What is central to the Watchtower movement is its identity as a calm and rational community. Jehovah's Witnesses continually inveigh against other religious groups who base their activities upon unbounded emotion and refuse to acknowledge the Watchtower's reasoned interpretation of Scripture. While the leadership is often careful to qualify some of its boldest prophetic pronouncements, the fact that such specific predictions can be made is entirely consistent with the overall attitude of the organization. Prophecy is a claim to a rationality so precise that it can pinpoint exact dates within a maze of Biblical passages. Yet, as we have seen, it is a malleable rationality which the leadership may adapt to changing or unforeseen events. Thus the 1914 prophecy was reinterpreted to mean "the beginning of the End of Gentile times" and World War I taken to be its confirmation. No such pivot could be found in 1975, and needs dictated that the prophecy be denied. One would expect such a variety of responses for what the Watchtower must maintain is a particular cognitive stance that rejects the world in favor of the theocracy. It is a cool identity of reason and certainty waiting for the fires of the Apocalypse.

When Festinger Fails

Festinger's model provides an initially valuable tool for understanding the development of the Watchtower movement. His first condition for reaction to disconfirmation, that a belief must be held deeply and possess relevance to action, allows us to understand the context that the millenarianism of Charles Taze Russell set for his organization and for present-day Jehovah's Witnesses. Festinger's second condition, linking belief to individual actions which are difficult to undo, reveals the extreme dedication Witnesses have made to the imminence of the Apocalypse and to the prophecies which have heralded its arrival. The third condition, stating that the belief must be specific and open to empirical refutation, focuses analysis upon disconfirmation as a crucial moment for understanding a prophetic movement.

It is when we reach the fourth and fifth conditions of Festinger's hypothesis that we begin to leave the parameters of his model. He states that undeniable disconfirmatory evidence must occur and be recognized by the individual holding the belief. With Jehovah's Witnesses, the only way to determine this is through the official publications of the organization, which themselves often do not admit the unqualified nature of the original prediction. As for individual Witnesses, we could perhaps speculate that some who left the organization did so because of disconfirmation, but those who remain in the movement will often deny that any specific prophecy was made. The question then becomes whether large religious groups like the Watchtower can ever fully conform to the carefully controlled conditions of Festinger's hypothesis.

On a broader level, however, Festinger's conception of belief contained in his fifth condition is uncharacteristically ambiguous. Recall that he argues that if an individual has social support, the belief will be maintained and members will attempt to persuade others that "the belief" was correct. Yet he also states that members will reduce dissonance by defending the overall "system of belief," leaving us to wonder whether the specific prophecy or the overarching stance of the group will be advanced in the face of disconfirmation.

This distinction between belief in a specific prophecy and the belief system as a whole becomes crucial when we address the Watchtower's attitude toward Biblical prophecy. For Mrs. Keech's group, faith in a specific prophecy constituted virtually the entire belief system. It is for this very reason that the reaction of the Watchtower to 1914 generally corresponds to Festinger's hypothesis, since belief in the imminence of the Millennium oriented the entirety of Russell's theology. In contrast, when the Watchtower set 1975 as the date for the Apocalypse, two levels of prophetic speculation emerged in a complex organizational and ideological system. There existed a primary prophecy which expected the Millennium during the generation who saw the events of 1914. Within this framework, 1975 constituted a secondary prophecy, representing a likely time for the fulfillment of the group's millennial hopes. Thus, when disconfirmation came, the Watchtower could successfully separate its secondary prophecy from its overall belief system through a rigorous application of organizational controls. While Festinger's hypothesis certainly survives these observations, we find Jehovah's Witnesses able to jettison beliefs which they had previously advanced precisely because the interrelationship between the beliefs they hold is shaped by the organizational and ideological structure of the Watchtower.

This question of how the prophetic beliefs of a group relate to its overall organization and ideology leads us to consider two crucial variables that Festinger does not address. First, differing organizational structures of religious groups may alter reactions to disconfirmed prophecy. Mrs. Keech's followers and Sabbatai Zevi's movement, groups which depended upon an almost unmediated relationship with a charismatic leader, maintained the validity of their original prophecies despite disconfirmation. The Millerites, who developed a publishing apparatus to spread their beliefs, were able to alter their chronology slightly but nonetheless were not able to endure for more than two years after the first disconfirmation. The Watchtower, which had a complex organizational structure even in Russell's time, was successful not only in totally reinterpreting prophecies but in retrospectively denying their very specificity. Based upon these comparisons, we could perhaps relate the complexity of organizational structures to responses to disconfirmed prophecies. Small, geographically localized groups, which depend upon consensus, might support the validity of the original prophecy. Complex groups, with distinct divisions of labor and hierarchical structure, might rationalize or deny the prediction and enforce such decisions by emphasizing organizational discipline and its legitimating ideology. Denial would be especially likely in organizations in which only the highest levels possess decision-making power and charismatic legitimation. In organizations that have charisma distributed throughout the hierarchy, we might include schism as a possible reaction to disconfirmation.

Denial, however, cannot succeed unless ideology supports it. This is the second variable that Festinger ignores. Mrs. Keech's group did not possess anything approaching a theodicy, although her position as the appointed communicator between Earth and Losolo was legitimated by the belief that she was the reincarnation of the Virgin Mary. Watchtower ideology is radically millenarian with a theodicy that allows suffering to be understood within the context of Jehovah's desire to test humankind before the Apocalypse. Thus denial becomes a plausible response not only because Witnesses have so totally immersed themselves in the organization but because their ideology demands total obedience to the theocracy as proof of their dedication to Jehovah. This context loosens Festinger's linkage of proselytism with disconfirmation, as the Watchtower was always an evangelical movement. While it seems relatively clear that, for Mrs. Keech, the Millerites, and Sabbatai Zevi, proselytism was connected to dissonance caused by disconfirmation, with Jehovah's Witnesses the source of proselytism is different. By persuading others to join the movement, Witnesses find confirmation of their rejection of the world and power in their claim to privileged knowledge. Thus when disconfirmation comes, energy must be directed inward to maintain the coherence of group identity as opposed to increasing the external expression of proselytism. Watchtower reactions to disconfirmation seem primarily directed toward reestablishing group cohesion through revision, denial, and purge. Proselytism increases markedly when a specific date is set but levels off or declines for several years after disconfirmation. Such a complex interplay of reactions suggests that the failure of prophecy elicits a greater variety of responses than Festinger's model can encompass.

Conclusion

The Watchtower's experience with prophetic speculation highlights some of the crucial issues that have arisen in the debate surrounding Festinger's hypothesis.[61] Joseph F. Zygmunt, himself an expert on Jehovah's Witnesses, argued in 1972 that global treatments of prophetic disconfirmation under the rubric of cognitive dissonance often divert scholarly attention from the variety of collective and interactional dimensions that shape the responses of religious communities to such challenges.[62] He specifically remarks that what remain crucial are the ideological, organizational, and cultic means for the revitalization of group solidarity.[63] Reactions to disconfirmation, in turn, may include moderate measures such as rationalization or more radical responses such as denial, assignment of blame, and purge.[64] The example of Jehovah's Witnesses amplifies and extends Zygmunt's broad theoretical observations by revealing the specific organizational and ideological elements that enable extreme reactions to disconfirmation. The Watchtower hierarchy's exclusive possession of charisma, its control of power and information within the organization, and its expansive legitimating ideology allow distinctive responses to prophetic failure that move far beyond the simple rationalizations required by Festinger's model. Any analysis that seeks to understand movements like the Watchtower must then focus upon how organizational and ideological structures set the context for millennial expectation.

We can conclude this discussion of prophecy and the Watchtower with the final caveat that the responses of particular individuals to disconfirmation will always vary in relation to their social surroundings. In a study of a millennial Baha'i sect, Robert Balch has argued that psychological forces are less important than the social circumstances existing at the time of disconfirmation.[65] In spite of their vigorous efforts to proselytize nonbelievers, Jehovah's Witnesses have little sustained social contact with those outside the organization. Thus, when disconfirmation comes, it becomes essential to maintain a coherent group identity. Because the Watchtower proclaims itself as Jehovah's theocratic government, there exists a tremendous amount of pressure to conform obediently to this defining element of social interaction within the organization. Nevertheless, for Jehovah's Witnesses who are ridiculed for their beliefs, or for those less integrated within the movement, prophetic failure may raise quite different challenges and options.[66] If the generation who witnessed the events of 1914 does not see the dawn of the New Order, many Jehovah's Witnesses will soon find their beliefs tested once again.

It is tempting to consider the Watchtower nothing but a landmark on the lunatic fringe of American religiosity. Yet the movement's power receives eloquent and painful testimony from the numerous monographs written by those who have left its confines. In the few academic studies of the movement we find detailed analyses of the Watchtower's organizational structure, its evangelical methods, and its use of prophecy. What is difficult to capture, however, is the intense appeal of the movement which preserves it through seemingly unendurable crises. Festinger's hypothesis thus has a beguiling simplicity because it does not consider the complex intellectual and social forces that allow a prophetic movement like the Watchtower to prosper. Yet these are precisely the elements we must understand if we are to gain any insight into how disconfirmed prophecies may be advanced, revised, or denied. It is not that Festinger's elegantly controlled hypothesis fails to account for the phenomena he chooses to discuss but that it fails to illuminate other significant structures that shape the contours of prophecy and proselytism. But Jehovah's Witnesses certainly do not invite such examination, so it is perhaps not surprising that their relative neglect in the academic study of religion should mirror their own rejection of society as a whole.

NOTES

1. Leon Festinger, Henry W. Riecken, and Stanley Schachter, *When Prophecy Fails* (Minneapolis: University of Minnesota Press, 1956).

2. For a broad comparative survey of prophetic failure among a variety of religious groups, see Neil Weiser, "The Effects of Prophetic Disconfirmation of the Committed," *Review of Religious Research* 16 (1974):19–30. Weiser argues that Festinger's theory may be used to explain the behavior of both modern and "primitive" cult believers when they are faced with the disconfirmation of a particular prophecy.

3. Studies that have specifically challenged Festinger's theory include: Robert W. Balch, Gwen Farnsworth, and Sue Wilkins, "When the Bombs Drop: Reactions to Disconfirmed Prophecy in a Millennial Sect," *Sociological Perspectives* 26 (1983): 137–158, and Jane Allyn Hardyck and Marcia Braden, "Prophecy Fails Again: A Report of a Failure to Replicate," *Journal of Abnormal and Social Psychology*, 65 (1962): 136–141.

4. Leon Festinger, *A Theory of Cognitive Dissonance* (New York: Row, Peterson and Co., 1957): 246–259.

5. Festinger, Riecken, and Schachter 1956, pp. 9–12.

6. *Ibid.*, pp. 16–23.

7. Barbara Grizutti Harrison, *Visions of Glory: A History and a Memory of Jehovah's Witnesses* (New York: Simon and Schuster, 1978), p. 44.

8. *Ibid.*, pp. 45–46.

9. Allan Rogerson, *Millions Now Living Will Never Die* (London: The Anchor Press 1969), p. 6.

10. Charles Taze Russell, *Thy Kingdom Come*, vol. 3 of *Studies in the Scriptures* (Pittsburgh: The Watchtower Bible and Tract Society, 1891), pp. 305–306, 364.

11. Significant among these dates was 1799, interpreted as beginning of the Time of the End and marked by the ending of 1260 years of papal power and the rise of Napoleon. 1844, the year of the Millerite prophecy, saw the beginning of true prophetic understanding, and 1874 and then 1881 were perhaps to witness the translation of the saints to heaven.

12. James A. Beckford, *The Trumpet of Prophecy: A Sociological Study of Jehovah's Witnesses* (Oxford: Basil Blackwell, 1975), p. 7. Beckford's study of the Watchtower in England remains the definitive work on the Witnesses with an exceptionally fine analysis of Watchtower organizational structure.

13. *Ibid.*, p. 7.

14. Timothy A. White, *A People for His Name: A History of Jehovah's Witnesses and an Evaluation* (New York: Vantage Press, 1967), p. 54.

15. *Ibid.*, p. 46.

16. *The Watchtower* (1912), p. 377.

17. *The Watchtower* (1914), p. 327.

18. Milton Stacey Czatt, *The International Bible Students: Jehovah's Witnesses* (Scottdale, PA: Mennonite Press, 1933), pp. 8–9. Czatt contrasts parallel passages from 1910 and 1923 editions of *Studies in the Scriptures* to show revisions of crucial parts of Russell's chronology.

19. For a detailed account and interpretation of these changes see Joseph F. Zygmunt, "Prophetic Failure and Chiliastic Identity: The Case of Jehovah's Witnesses," *American Journal of Sociology* 75 (1970):926–948.

20. White, p. 82.

21. Beckford, p. 20.

22. *Ibid.*, pp. 19–20.

23. For the Watchtower's present interpretation of the events surrounding 1914, see *God's Kingdom of a Thousand Years Has Approached* (New York: Watchtower Bible and Tract Society, 1973), pp. 186–191.

24. Beckford, p. 15.

25. *Ibid.*, p. 15.

26. *Ibid.*, p. 20.

27. For Weber's discussion of the qualities of a charismatic leader, see Max Weber, *Max Weber on Charisma and Institute Building: Selected Papers*, S. N. Eisenstadt, ed. (Chicago: The University of Chicago Press, 1968), pp. 18–22.

28. Grizutti Harrison, p. 171.

29. *The Watchtower* (1914), p. 327.

30. A publisher is a Witness who devotes at least one hour a month to proselytizing.

31. Heather and Gary Botting, *The Orwellian World of Jehovah's Witnesses* (Toronto: The University of Toronto Press, 1984), p. 44.

32. *Life Everlasting in Freedom of the Sons of God* (New York: Watchtower Bible and Tract Society, 1966), p. 35.

33. *Ibid.*, pp. 29–30.

34. See especially "Why Are You Looking Forward to 1975?" *The Watchtower* (1968), p. 499. This article states that Armageddon could stray from the current timetable only by months, not by years.

35. Botting and Botting, p. 46.

36. James M. Penton, *Apocalypse Delayed* (Toronto: The University of Toronto Press, 1985), p. 95. This saying was used among "Pioneers," an elite group among Jehovah's Witnesses who devote at least ninety hours a month to proselytizing.

37. *1975 Yearbook of Jehovah's Witnesses* (New York: Watchtower Bible and Tract Society, 1975), p. 30.

38. Raymond Franz, *In Search of Christian Freedom* (Atlanta: Commentary Press, 1991), p. 567. The organization praised Witnesses who sold their homes to become full-time evangelists in *Kingdom Ministry* (1974), p. 3.

39. These qualifications were usually phrases such as "it could" or "perhaps." It does seem clear, however, that there was enormous psychological pressure to proselytize for this belief, especially on the circuit and congregational levels. Richard Singelenberg, in his study of the reaction of Dutch Witnesses to this prophecy, observes that as 1975 drew closer, the Biblical chronology was less emphasized and the emotional appeal to proselytize accentuated; see Richard Singelenberg, "It Separated the Wheat from the Chaff: The 1975 Prophecy and Its Impact among Dutch Jehovah's Witnesses," *Sociological Analysis* 50 (1988):23–40.

40. Penton, p. 95.

41. W. C. Stevenson, *Year of Doom 1975* (London: Hutchinson, 1967), p. 3.

42. *1979 Yearbook of Jehovah's Witnesses* (New York: Watchtower Bible and Tract Society, 1979), p. 30.

43. Botting and Botting, pp. 46–47.

44. Penton, p. 8.

45. See *The Watchtower* (1976), p. 441. See also Penton, p. 100.

46. Botting and Botting, p. 48. Excommunication is called "disfellowshipping" in Watchtower parlance.

47. *Ibid.*, p. 49.

48. *The Watchtower* (1980), p. 17. This "apology" began the purge of 1980; see Botting and Botting, p. 49.

49. Botting and Botting, p. 50; Penton, p. 100.

50. Beckford, p. 79.

51. *Ibid.*, pp. 85–86. Beckford argues that the Watchtower constitutes an utilitarian organization resembling a modern bureaucratic corporation; for the typology upon which he bases his analysis, see Amitai Etzioni, *A Comparative Analysis of Complex Organizations* (New York: The Free Press, 1961), pp. 4–5, 214–218.

52. Beckford, p. 83.

53. See *Babylon the Great Has Fallen! God's Kingdom Rules!* (New York: The Watchtower Bible and Tract Society, 1963), p. 235.

54. For a discussion of "the discreet slave class" see *God's Kingdom of a Thousand Years Has Approached*, pp. 342–63.

55. See *The Truth that Leads to Eternal Life* (New York: Watchtower Bible and Tract Society, 1968), pp. 27–33.

56. *1979 Yearbook of Jehovah's Witnesses* (Watchtower Bible and Tract Society, 1979), pp. 30–31.

57. Newton H. Maloney, "The Psychology of Proselytism," in Martin Marty, ed., *Pushing the Faith* (New York: Crossroad, 1988), p. 133.

58. Richard Singelenberg (see note 39) suggests that, among Dutch Witnesses, dissonance surrounding the 1975 prophecy itself may have contributed to increased evangelism. While he suggests an interesting line of inquiry, since Jehovah's Witnesses achieved over 20 percent growth in the late forties and early fifties when no specific prophetic date had been set, we perhaps need to look beyond the dissonance created by prophecy to explain Watchtower evangelism.

59. Beckford, p. 191.

60. *Ibid.*, p. 192.

61. For an overview of the development of cognitive dissonance theory since Festinger, see Anthony G. Greenwald and David L. Ronis, "Twenty Years of Cognitive Dissonance: Case Study of the Evolution of a Theory," *Psychological Review* 85 (1978): 53–57. Greenwald and Ronis argue that in the twenty years since the publication of Festinger's theory, the focus of the study of reactions to disconfirmation has shifted from an emphasis upon maintaining logical consistency among cognitions to the preservation of self-esteem. They also argue, quite interestingly, that the development of cognitive dissonance theory itself reflects some of the same characteristics that Festinger identifies in his theory.

62. Joseph F. Zygmunt, "When Prophecies Fail: A Theoretical Perspective on the Comparative Evidence," *American Behavioral Scientist* 16 (1972): 246. Although this article does not discuss specific examples in any detail, it remains an excellent theoretical overview of the wide range of possible responses to disconfirmation.

63. *Ibid.*, p. 250.

64. *Ibid.*, p. 261.

65. Balch, Farnsworth, and Wilkins, p. 137.

66. Hardyck and Braden (see note 3) make the point that proselytism is likely to increase when believers receive ridicule from the outside world.

When Prophecy Is Not Validated

Explaining the Unexpected in a Messianic Campaign

William Shaffir

In earlier articles, I have written about the campaign of the Lubavitch (Habad)[1] movement to popularize their conviction that the arrival of the Jewish Messiah was imminent.[2] Faithful believers asserted that it was their present Rebbe, the charismatic Rabbi Menachem Mendel Schneerson, who was the long-awaited Messiah, and some of them begged him to "reveal" himself. Advertisements appeared in the *New York Times* as well as in other newspapers, listing the events which were seen as harbingers of the Redemption, and announcing: "The Era of Moshiach is upon us."[3] That campaign had been given a dramatic momentum in April 1991, when the Lubavitch Rebbe delivered a memorable speech—later to be much quoted and analyzed—in the course of which he had declared that he had done all that he could to spur Jews to work actively for the Messianic Redemption and that his followers must do the rest; he urged them: "Now do everything you can to bring Moshiach, here and now, immediately." Such a forceful command from their revered leader caused the Lubavitcher to begin at once an extensive and intensive campaign.

As that campaign was gaining in momentum, nearly a year later, in March 1992, the Rebbe suffered a stroke while he was visiting the grave of his predecessor and father-in-law; that was to be the first of a series of ailments which eventually deprived the Rebbe of his power of speech and caused him at the end to lapse into total loss of consciousness. The faithful had to endure "cognitive dissonance": the simultaneous presence of two inconsistent happenings, which can be expected to cause great stress. When events challenge belief, the response can be a reinterpretation of the basis of belief; the Rebbe was devoutly believed to be the Messiah, but he was very seriously incapacitated by his stroke and could communicate with any degree of certainty only by vague gestures of one hand, difficult to interpret with any assurance. That situation continued for two years. In my last article on the subject, published in June 1994, I commented that if the Rebbe failed to regain his health and to reveal himself as the Jewish Messiah, and died, his followers would be shaken as if by an earthquake, and added:

> ... if all attempts to prolong the Rebbe's life fail and he is given a tradi-
> tional Jewish burial, those followers who have resolutely maintained that
> their leader was undoubtedly the Messiah-in-waiting will then try to
> explain that the blame for the failure of the Rebbe to reveal himself as the
> true Messiah was precisely the result of those doubting Jews, who by
> being creatures of little faith, did not show enough commitment to pro-
> vide the final impetus for the advent of the Redemption—so that the
> Rebbe had to die in despair.[4]

(While the article was in press, the news came that he had in fact died and been
buried and that was added in bold type at the end of that page.)

The Rebbe died in a New York hospital in the early hours of June 12, 1994,
which was the third day (Gimmel in Hebrew) of the month of Tammuz in the
Hebrew calendar; he was buried before the end of that day. The prophecy that
he had indeed been the Messiah had clearly not been confirmed, so far.

Ever since the Lubavitch Moshiach campaign had gained momentum,
when the Rebbe was already in his nineties, there was much speculation about
what would happen to the movement when he died. He was childless, there
was therefore no prospective dynastic successor, and no one seemed to know
whether he had decided upon the man who would replace him as leader. The
Lubavitcher's answer was that there would be no need for a successor, since the
Rebbe would initiate the Redemption. However, he did die, there was obviously no Redemption, and he had been buried according to traditional
Orthodox Jewish rites. In New York, in the expectation of the hysteria which
might well follow the announcement of his death, there had been a special
plan devised during the last period of his illness. It was code-named Operation
Demise, and police, social workers, and psychiatrists were ready to go to the
Crown Heights neighborhood; the Lubavitch epicenter was at 770 Eastern
Parkway. Everything was in place to provide counselling akin to that offered in
a disaster zone.[5] Two days after his death, the opinion of a psychologist of religion was quoted in the *New York Times*: "It's clear that the rebbe's death has
created a crisis, but it's not an insurmountable one. Some people will expect
a resurrection, but most will develop all kinds of rationalizations. . . . the
majority of people are capable of accepting the explanations." Another psychologist commented: "It does seem to make some sense psychologically, if what
one is doing is drowning the dissonance with increased emphasis on one of the
cognitions."[6]

Leon Festinger and his colleagues published a study in 1956 entitled *When
Prophecy Fails*.[7] A small apocalyptic group in the American Midwest, with a sci-
ence-fiction eschatology, that claimed to be in communication with beings from
Outer Space, had believed a prediction that on a specific day a flood would inundate much of the Western hemisphere; some members had gathered in a vigil,
waiting for a flying saucer which they were confident would raise them and carry
them to safety before the flood. But there was no flying saucer and no flood. The
members of the group then concluded that they had been saved by God, and

went on to spread their particular gospel. Festinger and his coauthors concluded that the strong ties uniting the members of that group had helped them to overcome their shock at the failure of their predicted events to materialize. Those who were not very closely linked to their fellow members, however, lost their faith, this in contrast to those who proceeded to renew their efforts at proselytization with great enthusiasm while enjoying a considerable amount of social support from the other believers. A. D. Shupe, referring to that study and to other research into religious movements, concluded: "It is not unfulfilled prophecy *per se* that irrevocably disillusions believers, but rather it is the social conditions in which such disconfirmations are received that determine their ultimate impact on faith."[8] J. G. Melton, in a later analysis of the reactions to a failure of prophecy, argued that it was a common error to suppose that millennial movements would be expected to disintegrate after a prediction had failed to materialize, since predictions are typically made within the context of a wider belief system. As a result, if a prediction fails, the members of the group do not abandon the movement but aim to resolve the dissonance while relying on the "unfalsifiable beliefs out of which religious thought-worlds are constructed [and] within that context believers can engage in a reaffirmation of basic faith and make a reappraisal of their predicament."[9] In that way, the members are reassured that the prophecy had not failed but had merely been misunderstood.

In the present paper, I focus on the attempt by Lubavitcher to reconstruct and reinterpret the events surrounding the Rebbe's illness and death in order to deal with the reality of that death and of the failure of the prediction of imminent Redemption. I have gathered data from a number of sources: about fifty interviews, all in the English language, with Lubavitcher Hasidim, including officials of the movement at various levels of the organizational hierarchy; the publications of the Lubavitcher literature about the Moshiach and the Moshiach campaign; and video and audio cassette tapes. Most of the interviews were carried out in Canada—in Toronto and Montreal—and in Israel; and I also spent brief but intensive periods at Lubavitch headquarters at 770 Eastern Parkway, in the Brooklyn district of Crown Heights, observing proceedings and chatting informally with the members whom I met there.

The Rebbe Dies

One despairing Hassid told me soon after the Rebbe's death was announced: "What happened was not only unexpected, it's much worse. This thing that we didn't believe would happen, happened. We really didn't believe it. I can tell you that I'm a broken man and Lubavitch is broken." Other followers expressed the same sorrow and shock; they had known that the Rebbe was very seriously ill and that his condition had been deteriorating rapidly but they devoutly believed that as a result of divine intercession, a miracle would restore him to health and vigor and he would continue to lead them in their Messianic campaign. Some of them even convinced themselves that he would soon be resurrected. His death

death had received front-page coverage in the *New York Times* and the article, fram-ing a photograph of the Lubavitcher surrounding the coffin, stated:

> Within hours of his death at 1:50 A.M., thousands of his followers began gathering on the streets around Lubavitch World Headquarters . . . to mourn a teacher and scholar that most of them had hoped would reveal himself to be the Messiah before he died.
>
> But when his plain pine coffin was borne out of the headquarters building into a light rain yesterday afternoon, a huge cry of grief shook the crowd of mourners jammed into Eastern Parkway which the Emergency Medical Service estimated at 12,000. The coffin, draped with the black coat of the Grand Rabbi, or Rebbe, as he was universally known, was supported by about 20 men, and it seemed in danger of top-pling to the ground as Hasidim desperate with grief reached to touch it with their fingers or umbrellas. . . .
>
> From the rooftops it appeared that a huge wave of black was cascad-ing down the parkway, following the Rebbe's motorcade. Thousands of people ran until they could run no further, some collapsing into sobs.[10]

The *Jerusalem Post* reported that in Israel many hundreds clamored for plane tickets at Ben Gurion airport, some of them standing on countertops trying to get tickets, while others rushed in all directions when rumors spread that tickets were available in a particular area of the airport.[11] In Toronto, a charter flight left within hours of the announcement of the Rebbe's death on June 12, carrying a planeload of mourners.

Many believed the Rebbe to be immortal and could not be reconciled to the fact that he had indeed died: The *Forward*, an English weekly newspaper pub-lished in New York, reported a few days after the burial that a group asserted that their leader's resurrection was imminent and they were sleeping close to the Rebbe's grave, hoping to be the first to see their Messiah rise from the tomb.[12] The resurrection theme was to become within days the subject of public sermons within the movement. On the day of the funeral, moreover, a small group were dancing and singing outside the Lubavitch headquarters, which unnerved the vast majority of the mourners. Allan Nadler described the scene immediately before the funeral cortège set out of the building:

> Still, many of his faithful refuse to be deterred by so small a matter as Schneerson's mortality. When I arrived in Crown Heights that Sunday morning . . . I was amazed to see young Lubavitcher singing, dancing and drinking vodka directly across the street from 770 Eastern Parkway, the Lubavitch World Headquarters where the body of their beloved rebbe was lying . . . in shrouds on a wooden floor. Even more stunning was a small group of women encouraging the men with tambourines.[13]

These individuals were convinced at the time that the Rebbe's death signalled the onset of the Redemption, and one person was quoted as saying, ". . . any minute now the rebbe will rise up to take us all to Israel."[14] The same was true of another group of adherents in Kfar Habad, the movement's stronghold in Israel: some Hasidim refused to believe that their Rebbe had died, while others asserted that if he had died, it would be only to cause him to rise to redeem the Jews. A driver employed by Habad was quoted in the *Jerusalem Post* issue of June 13, the day after the death and burial, as stating: "This is a happy day, because this is the last day of exile," and with the chant of "Moshiach, Moshiach, Moshiach" blaring from his van's loudspeakers, he added: "We came here to cheer people up, to tell them this is the last day of exile."[15]

The tragic news of the Rebbe's final deterioration in health spread quickly, only to be followed at first with the announcement that his heartbeat had stabilized; but soon after came a message on the beepers that it was urgently requested that *Tehillim* (Psalms) be recited, and a few minutes later there came the shattering words "Borukh Dayan Ha'emes" ("blessed is the true judge")[16]— the formula which broadcast the fact that the unthinkable had occurred, that the Rebbe had ceased to live. Then sirens were heard, arousing the Crown Heights residents and informing them of the calamity. At 3:25 A.M., a police helicopter hovered over No. 770, and to the blaring sound of sirens, an ambulance arrived, a stretcher was carried out and taken into the building surrounded by members of the *hevra kadisha* (the burial society whose duty it is to prepare the body for interment), and the door of the building was quickly closed. Half an hour later, the followers were told that they would be permitted to enter the Rebbe's room and file through while reciting psalms. The funeral was to take place at 4 P.M. that afternoon.

At the cemetery, the Rebbe's grave had been dug to the immediate left of his predecessor's tomb in the mausoleum; the male mourners filed past one entrance and the females through another gate, and the *kriya* ceremony proceeded, the tearing of a garment worn by the mourner.[17] Meanwhile, at No. 770 the synagogue was filled with mourners sitting on the floor or on low stools, in the prescribed manner for *shiva*, the seven days of intense mourning. A Hassid described the scene in his diary; it was printed in one of the publications of the movement:

> The sound of weeping and lamentation has replaced yesterday's shock and stupor. Wherever you look in Crown Heights you see chasidim, alone and in small groups, standing and crying to themselves. . . . The front lawn of 770 is covered with people. . . . The benches along the parkway are packed with mourners, some of whom are nodding off after having been awake for almost two full days.
>
> Seven-seventy is packed with people. A steady stream of mourners continues to flow, coming and going. Men, women and children all try to come to terms with what has happened, but they cannot make peace with the new situation.
>
> They cannot understand what has happened. . . .[18]

The majority of those with whom I had conversations in Toronto and in Montreal said that they had learnt the news of the Rebbe's death by a telephone call from a friend or relative in the early hours of the morning. They already knew that the life of their Rebbe was despaired of by the physicians. One follower commented: "I knew what that phone call meant. No one calls for social reasons at three o'clock in the morning." Many of the women could tell that the Rebbe had died when they saw the faces of their husbands when they returned from the synagogue. One woman told me: "As soon as I saw him, I knew. The look on his face said everything." Another commented that no words were necessary when her husband came home; she just went to rouse their children to prepare them for the journey to Crown Heights: "We were on the road in twenty minutes," she added.

The Rebbe had been well known as a Biblical scholar in both Jewish and non-Jewish informed circles, and the activities of the Lubavitch were often reported in the press of various countries. Condolences were received from the President and the Vice-President of the United States, from the Chief Rabbi of the United Hebrew Congregations in London, from the Canadian Prime Minister, from a United States senator, the governor and the mayor of New York, and many other prominent persons.[19] He was hailed as "a great leader," as one of the world's "great moral and religious leaders," as a "towering religious figure," while Jewish eulogies contained tributes to the Rebbe's efforts to combat assimilation and out-marriage. Such praise not only provided solace to the Lubavitcher in their grief but also confirmed the eminence of their revered leader and reflected the respect with which his scholarship and dedication were viewed by eminent individuals in many countries.

Since the Lubavitch had pursued with vigor their Moshiach campaign for several years, especially in the early 1990s, it was inevitable that comparisons would be drawn with other Messianic groups in Jewish history. The most widely known, of course, was the case of Sabbatai Zevi who in the seventeenth century had attracted a wide following in Turkey, Italy, and Poland after he had proclaimed himself to be the Jewish Messiah. He proved to be a false messiah, he was eventually converted to Islam, and his followers were engulfed in despair and bitterness, causing a proportion of them to abandon Judaism. In 1994, there was great concern over the fact that the Rebbe had died, been buried, and not risen from the grave and shown himself to be the Messiah, lest that tragedy of unfulfilled promises of Redemption would result in very large defections from the Lubavitch movement.

There had been fierce condemnations of the Messianic campaign in the Rebbe's lifetime, and his death only served to reinforce the case of the movement's critics. The *Forward* was still on the attack several months after the Rebbe's death; it stated that those who believed that ". . . the rebbe had misled his people during his lifetime, are now perturbed by the fact that a cluster of his most fanatic entourage is perpetuating what the critics see as the false and dangerous notion of Rabbi Schneerson as a super-mortal being"[20]—referring to those who supported the prediction that the Rebbe would without much delay rise from the grave. The paper went on to state that an eminent rabbi who was also a scholar had come to the conclusion that the Rebbe's followers were still deluded, that they failed "to realize they have been duped by a charlatan who masqueraded as a saint."[21]

Two weeks later, in December 1994, the *Forward* printed a front-page story with the headline: "Rabbis Blast Lubavitcher Messianism"; the opening paragraph stated:

> The Lubavitcher Chasidim of Crown Heights are alarming Jewish theologians with their growing fervor of their belief in the imminent "resurrection" of Menachem Mendel Schneerson as the "Messiah," and some critics are warning that eerie parallels to Christianity are flickering inside the Lubavitch movement.[22]

The article was set around a photograph of Sabbatai Zevi, with the caption "False Messiah," and referred to the continuing belief by followers of the Rebbe that he was indeed the real Jewish Messiah and that he would return to earth. Paradoxically, such attacks only seem to reinforce the commitment of the faithful to that belief.

The *Forward* also claimed that, several months after the Rebbe's death, ". . . some of his followers are in the throes of despair, and others are deeply disillusioned" and that his leadership might "be to blame for the angst of the Jews of Crown Heights."[23] In fact, the movement has experienced neither mass suicide nor even a minimal exodus from the Crown Heights area. While Lubavitcher with whom I had frequent conversations admitted freely that they were still shaken by the Rebbe's death, they insisted that they were still committed to their movement's style of Judaism. One of them told me:

> Generally speaking, if I tell you it didn't affect anyone, I'd be lying to you. But I don't know anybody who lost their faith or converted out of Yiddishkayt. No one shaved their beard, stopped putting *tefillin* [phylacteries], or took off their *shytl* [wig]. . . . To say that there aren't problems that people have to deal with, *bin eech kein mentsh nit* [I am not human]. We're not pure *neshomo* [soul].

There has been much soul-searching about the unfulfilled Messianic prophecy with the death of the Rebbe. The adherents had been aware for months and years that the Rebbe's health was failing, since they were kept informed by daily reports of his condition, but they had still expected nothing less than a miraculous recovery and the realization of the Messianic prophecy. They had found reassurance in the fact (according to them) that the Rebbe had never been proved wrong in any of his advice or predictions, and only a few days before his death a Lubavitch publication stated:

> As this newsletter goes to press, our beloved guide and mentor, . . . the Lubavitcher Rebbe. . . lies grievously ill. . . . It is now many weeks that

the Rebbe lies unconscious. . . . Medically the situation seems hopeless. Naturally, rationally—it would seem appropriate to prepare for the "inevitable." . . . the reaction of this Jew at a time when everything seems so hopeless, is one of unbridled hope in totally supernatural salvation. Even at this time, and perhaps precisely because of it, we remember that the same Rebbe who accurately predicted the safety of Israel during the Gulf War, in spite of countless indications to the contrary, has prophesied that the "time of your Redemption has arrived"—a prophecy in which we must continue to have absolute faith.[24]

Techniques of Neutralization

We must now consider the techniques, the vocabulary of motives,[25] which the Lubavitcher commonly employed in order to neutralize any dissonant feelings and to reinforce their faith in the imminent Redemption by their King Messiah, their Rebbe. In order to minimize the disjuncture between their expectations and the obvious reality, they drew upon a series of explanations which would not only preserve but enhance their commitment to the Messianic prophecy.

No single explanation is uniformly advanced by all the followers, but they all adhere to the belief in Divine Providence, *hashgocheh protees*, a belief which provides them with the underlying foundation on which they rest their interpretations of the events preceding and following the Rebbe's death. For them, the hand of Divine Providence must be seen in all that occurs, but God's intentions may be difficult to grasp with our finite intelligence. An article in a Lubavitch publication stated three months after his death: "Even with all the explanations which have been advanced, the bottom line is that we don't understand the ways of Hashem"[26] (the Name: that is, God); and, "Hashem has taken the Rebbe from our physical presence for reasons only He understands."[27] Variations on this basic theme were consistently advanced during my conversations with the faithful. For example, a woman did not deny that the Rebbe's death had come as an enormous shock, but she remained firmly dedicated to the cause: "If you believe that Hashem guides us in everything, then you accept what happens as for the good. Who knows why the Rebbe died? Only one thing is clear: it's part of Hashem's master plan."

For an observant and pious believer, it is inconceivable that God could have erred in his judgment: the Rebbe's statements on Redemption had the seal of prophetic utterance and must therefore not be considered as false assertions. If the prophecy must remain unchallenged, the Rebbe's statements had to be reinterpreted to conform to the present reality. One follower explained to me:

> We haven't been wrong [in identifying the Rebbe as the Messiah]. We have only been wrong in assuming that this is going to happen in the Rebbe's lifetime. . . . So we were wrong in the calculation of the timing . . . but not in terms of theology. To me nothing has changed except the Rebbe's presence.

I had a conversation with two Lubavitch women, in the course of which they stressed that the movement in general, and they in particular, had failed to comprehend adequately the Rebbe's views on Redemption; the fault for the misinterpretation was theirs alone. As one said:

> By now we have learned to realize that the only sure things are things we heard straight from the Rebbe. . . . The things the Rebbe said clearly in the last four years are things that always always happened. So the way we understood there would not be a period of no life [that is, the Rebbe would not die], on these things we were wrong. But those were our own views. As long as we are going on the words of the Rebbe, those things can't go wrong.

She concluded by saying that the followers were reexamining the statements of the Rebbe: "Now, there are many things that people are finding in the words of the Rebbe." The Rebbe's behavior immediately before his first stroke in 1992 was carefully being reconsidered, as it now seemed that there was evidence to show that he was fully aware that he was on the verge of death: "Truthfully, on his own, for a half a year the Rebbe was preparing his staff, and the Rebbe was preparing all of us [for his death]," asserted a Lubavitcher. The Rebbe was able therefore to decide on the path to be taken after he had ceased to live. He could have ushered in the Redemption if he had chosen to do so, but he had taken another course. A Lubavitch publication claimed: "Our Rebbe . . . was just about ready to cross the finish line when he decided at the last second to give the baton . . . to us, and said, 'It is now in your hands to bring Moshiach.' "[28]

The accusation that Lubavitcher failed to foresee (and therefore to be prepared for) the Rebbe's death was countered by the argument that the disappointment about the hopes for Redemption had occurred precisely because the present generation had failed to deserve Divine Redemption. A woman told me: "Moshiach would have come, but we didn't merit it. . . . if we merited it, things would have worked out differently," and another follower had come to the same conclusion: "If it didn't happen, this means we were not worthy of it." There was some discussion of the various natural and supernatural sequences leading to the coming of the Jewish Messiah; I was told: "We blew it. Obviously, whatever we have done is not enough;" and by another follower: "Obviously we didn't do everything right, or not enough. . . . Otherwise we wouldn't be discussing it now. We'd be sitting in the *Bays Hamikdosh* [the Holy Temple] and enjoying Moshiach and the Rebbe."

Immediately after the Rebbe's death, there circulated a printed statement on a single page from the Chairman of the International Campaign to Bring Moshiach; it included the following words:

> The Rebbe's instructions are clear. It is up to us to respond. The campaign . . . urges all Jews to continue to carry out, with renewed vigor, the Rebbe's directive to study the sections of the Torah which discuss the Redemption and the coming of Moshiach and to do more acts of goodness and kindness. . . .[29]

The Rebbe, as we noted above, died and was buried on Sunday, June 12, 1994; and on the Sunday following the week-long traditional *shiva*, a Moshiach Day was convened in Crown Heights. An afternoon teach-in lasted into early evening and was attended by several hundred members who were assured by a panel of rabbis that the Rebbe's prophecy remained as relevant after his death as it had been in his lifetime. All the speakers stressed that the Rebbe's guidance remained valid, reiterating what the chairman had stated in his opening statement to the gathering: "As far as what we are supposed to do, we have to listen to what the Rebbe tells us. . . . There's no doubt that we will find in the Rebbe's words all that we need for every step of the way." Indeed, on that day, that was the core theme of the various speakers. One declared:

> And . . . he clearly gave us a program which is so meticulous. . . . He took us from step to step. Our work has been defined very very clearly. . . . And even though we may not be able to see him [the Rebbe] with our eyes . . . he's here with us today telling us what he told us for forty-four years. Nothing is missing in his instruction.

The Lubavitcher were told that in spite of suffering overwhelming grief in mourning for their revered leader, they had to take immediate action to obey the Rebbe's directives, and the Rebbe's emissaries, the *shluchim*, who had gathered in Crown Heights for the funeral, were urged to pursue their activities as zealously as before. The report of a meeting of these emissaries contains the following passage:

> "We will continue!" was the sentiment of all the shluchim assembled in the room. Rabbi Shmuel Kaplan . . . chaired the event and said: ". . . we all know what the Rebbe wants of us, and each one of us knows his responsibility."
> Rabbi Moishe Kotlarsky spoke in the same vein. "None of us knows what should be *said* at such a bitter time. No one knows what to say, but we all know what to *do*."
> . . . All participants spoke about the special mission and obligation of *shluchim* at this critical hour. . . .[30]

A Lubavitch woman affirmed this decision when she told me in the course of an interview: "The Rebbe told us what to do. The job the Rebbe gave us to do we must continue." The followers also recalled the advice and comfort which Rabbi Schneerson had given when his predecessor had died, and they read and reread a letter he had written at the time of their bereavement. He had stated that "salvation lies not in mourning, and that despair and sorrow do not lead towards light,"[31] and he had then asserted as a second principal guideline that a true bonding with the Rebbe is derived from the study of his discourses and by fulfilling his requests. A Lubavitch publication commented on the first point, and an excerpt reads (*Gimmel Tammuz* refers to the day and the month on which the Rebbe had died):

> We have lost a limb. If we look at the events of *Gimmel Tammuz* with

fleishige oigen—physical eyes—we lost our head . . . and our heart. Now we could walk around feeling totally handicapped, with little ability to overcome this shock to our lives. . . . The Rebbe never allowed us to look at anything in life negatively—how much more so in a situation like this.[32]

One of the Rebbe's secretaries urged the members of the movement to remember that the Rebbe's presence must continue to dominate every aspect of their life (thus reiterating the Rebbe's own recommendation when his predecessor had died):

> The Alter Rebbe [the first Lubavitcher Rebbe] in Tanya [the first Lubavitcher Rebbe's work outlining the philosophy of Habad] . . . quotes the Zohar, "A Tzaddik who departs from this world, is present in all the worlds more than he was during his lifetime." And the Alter Rebbe explains that the Zohar also means to say that the Tzaddik is present in this physical world more than during his life on this world. He also tells us that after the departure of the Neshomo [the soul] from this world, the Neshomo of the Tzaddik generates more strength and more Koach [power] to his devoted disciples.[33]

In that context, a Lubavitcher commented: "The leader remains a leader even now and even though not seen physically still remains a leader," then he cited sacred texts in support of that statement: "It's also a principle in the Torah, the Zohar, and the Talmud that a *tzaddik* [righteous person] even after his death, his presence can be felt more than even before, not being limited by the physical body." Another said: "The Rebbe is here. We feel and sense this," and then gave several examples of the Rebbe's miraculous powers which were being manifested now, after his death. A third follower was convinced of the Rebbe's continued presence and support:

> I'd venture to say that I'm stronger now than before. Now I can't slow down because he [the Rebbe] sees me 24 hours a day. And I know that he sees me. If I can function today, it's only because he sees me. It is only because he gives me strength. . . .

The Rebbe had given a talk several months after his predecessor's death in 1950, and some of his advice contained in the record of that talk was repeatedly cited by the Lubavitcher to derive comfort in their mourning and grief several decades later:

> . . . Even when we find ourselves in a low, fallen state, we should not feel removed from the Rebbe after his passing. We should know, that now too, the Rebbe answers and responds to questions . . . as before. . . . The Rebbe is here with us as before.[34]

An editorial in a Lubavitch publication declared: "The Rebbe remains our Rebbe, and we remain his chasidim,"[35] adding that his death had been "the most forceful event that has so dramatically changed our world. . . . We know that the 'faithful shepherd does not abandon his flock' and he continues to watch over us and guide us."[36] The Rebbe's secretary asserted in another article: "And just as the Rebbe served his flock before his departure, so is he continuing to serve them now, but with an increase both qualitatively and quantitatively."[37]

Lubavitcher had to accept the fact that the Rebbe was no longer alive and they now came to believe that the unexpected tragedy of his demise might have been expected. Sources were being identified and interpreted to show that the Jewish Messiah would in fact die: this meant that the Rebbe's death was *not* a proof that he had been only a false Messiah. However, some followers did not immediately grasp that vindication; a woman commented: "Everyone's confused and everyone doesn't know how to interpret this and how to understand it. . . . it forced a lot of people to go to the sources . . . and to find some consolation from this." That reliance upon sources, or that use of the sources, was expressed again and again during the conversations I had. When I asked a Lubavitcher, whom I had known before the Rebbe's death, how he reconciled the fact that he had previously asserted that the Rebbe would not die with the reality that he had indeed died and been buried, he invoked the sources:

> There's also things which are written, which are predicted and which talk about this possibility. The Talmud talks about it, the Zohar says it in no uncertain terms, the Kabbalists speak about it. Moshiach will go through that period. There will be a period of Moshiach dying and reviving.

Some Lubavitcher with whom I had conversations after the Rebbe's death were clearly not familiar with the texts of the sources, but they did not doubt their validity: "There are several sources but I'm not exactly sure where"; but others demonstrated a measure of expert knowledge:

> We can talk about specific sources in the Talmud, in the Zohar specifically . . . that speak about Moshiach's passing away. There are contradictory statements in the Talmud about Moshiach's arrival and they all boil down to two things: miraculous and natural . . . and within this miraculous and natural there are many stages. There can be sickness, natural recovery, severe sickness, miraculous recovery. . . . Different sources point to different possibilities. . . .

According to that follower, the scenario in the most extreme case was that the advent of the Messiah would be miraculous and would therefore involve the Rebbe's complete recovery. Sadly, he had to admit that clearly the miracle had not taken place; the Rebbe had not recovered, he had died. There had been several possibilities, according to the sources, for the Rebbe to have been restored to health and to have revealed himself as the Messiah but, he admitted, "It didn't go that way."

Although familiarity with the relevant sources had become more widespread after the Rebbe's death, their contents had been known also during his lifetime but had not been publicized. There were two reasons: first, no one dared to entertain the thought that the Rebbe might indeed die, especially as there were what they believed to be many signals to the contrary—he had successfully recovered from severe illnesses following his first stroke, to the amazement of qualified medical specialists. They were familiar with a particular religious tenet that the Messiah might manifest himself from either the living or the dead, but the indications at the time were that a living man would declare himself as the Messiah. The second reason was that the various sources dealing with the advent of the Messiah, in Biblical commentaries on the subject, were not derived from the actual texts of the Halakha, of Orthodox Jewish law. The important point to bear in mind was that predictions of that kind should not be expected inevitably to occur, to be realized literally. One of the speakers at the teach-in previously mentioned stressed that all that is stated in the Midrash (the exposition and commentaries on the Hebrew Bible) does not constitute a legal ruling, is not embodied in the Halakha. "It doesn't have to be fulfilled . . ." argued the speaker, adding that you cannot base Jewish law on the commentaries, which do not have the same legitimacy; but one must still heed the words of the Midrash, a competent religious exposition, although "it doesn't mean that it's the way it's going to happen, but it's definitely a possibility," when it comes to predictions in the Midrash.

Such techniques of rationalization were not used by all the Lubavitcher, or not generally known to all, but they were a spur for the active members to encourage them in their Messianic proselytization and even in some cases to enhance their enthusiasm. The Lubavitcher retained their belief in the Rebbe's assurance that the redemptive process had begun; it was now their task to see that the necessary further steps were taken to fulfill the Messianic prophecy. A Lubavitch woman declared: "The Rebbe said that the process has begun and everything that needs to be done to bring Moshiach has been done. The reservoir is filled, so it's filled. The Rebbe promised in the words of prophecy." Another follower concurred: "To me, nothing has changed except the Rebbe's presence. So I still look forward to the Rebbe's prediction. I believe it'll happen in our generation simply going by the Rebbe's track record." It was that deep-seated confidence in the Rebbe's wisdom and in his knowledge of the Divine purpose that strengthened their devotion to him and to his teachings even after he had died and not risen from his grave. One woman supported her steadfast commitment with the use of the following analogy:

> So they stood there in front of the sea and Moishe [Moses] said "Go." Did anyone of them, in their wildest imagination, know they were going to cross the sea? Did anyone of them imagine the sea would split? A moment before it happened, nobody knew how they were going to cross the sea. So, in a way, we're standing in front of the sea and we know we are going to cross it. How it's going to happen, we'll see.

Conclusion

A Lubavitcher elaborated on the subject of the profound conviction of his fellow members that the Messiah's advent would assuredly take place. He illustrated their adherence to that belief with the following tale:

> I'm not sure at which airport it was. . . . A plane . . . full of hasidic Jews and they're waiting at the conveyer belt for their suitcases. There this Lubavitch man found himself standing between two Gerer Hassidim. About one hundred suitcases passed and it just so happened that they happened to be standing right at the beginning where the valises start coming out. And they're standing for fifteen minutes watching suitcases falling out and being sure that the next one is his. . . . So he [the Lubavitcher] turns around to them and says, "You know, it's an amazing thing. The three of us are focused here on this opening and although hundreds of suitcases have passed, we're convinced that the next suitcase will be ours. And if another hundred suitcases are going to pass by, until the last suitcase, we are still going to be convinced that our suitcase is coming at any minute. And although a long time has passed, it doesn't diminish my ultimate belief that my suitcase is coming." It's the same story with Moshiach. We've had two thousand years of suitcases travelling and flowing. . . . Nevertheless, I'm convinced that the next suitcase, the next moment, Moshiach is coming. . . . There's no question in my mind, and I can talk for every Hassid.

There is great variation in the manner in which different religious groups deal with their disillusionment or shock that the predictions of their leaders, which they had wholeheartedly believed, failed to materialize. In some cases, the reaction has been to persist in the commitment to their particular religious tenets, to find or manufacture explanations for the failure of the promised events, and to continue with their efforts to recruit more adherents; the overwhelming majority in the Lubavitch movement reacted in that way. An article, marking the conclusion of the thirty-day mourning period after the death and burial, stated in an English-language Lubavitch magazine:

> Some antagonists had initially predicted a diminishing of Chabad activity after the Rebbe's passing, or even a complete breakdown and collapse of Lubavitch. Thank G-d, the doomsayers were proven false, and their bad predictions did not materialize. On the contrary, we are witnessing a worldwide spur of new activities, projects and institutions established in the Rebbe's honor.[38]

That statement was indeed true: the December 1994 issue of *World of Lubavitch* listed ninety-three institutions which have been established since the Rebbe's death.[39] A journalist commented: "If Chabad has managed to outwit despair, that is partly because hasidim believe the rebbe continues to guide and protect them; he has simply exchanged a physical for a spiritual body."[40] That was also my own experience when hearing again and again the Lubavitcher say to me as if intoning a refrain: "The Rebbe remains the Rebbe." The most common theme in the prolific Lubavitch literature which was published after the Rebbe's death was that of the enduring value of his teachings and the validity of the belief that a Messianic Redemption would come to pass, while the arguments to refute critics and doubters were advanced with force.

But such faithfulness and determination does not characterize all the members of the movement. In the matter of interpreting the last will and testament of the Rebbe, which was dated February 14, 1988, and filed for probate immediately after his burial, there was concern that he had left his entire estate—valued at about $50,000—to the Lubavitch movement but had left no instructions about the procedure for appointing his successor. Much significance was attached to the fact that he had named as his sole executor one of his senior secretaries, a man who had long opposed the rising tide of Messianism in the movement, a man who was reportedly the most pragmatic and conservative of his principal assistants. The role of an executor of a modest estate is theoretically a minor one; but in this particular case, his selection gave him a status superior to that of other members of the Rebbe's secretariat and seemed to mark him as a man appointed by the revered Rebbe to exert considerable influence and authority to chart the movement's future along a conservative course.

It must be noted here that even in the Rebbe's lifetime, after his stroke had rendered him speechless and as his condition steadily deteriorated, there had been disagreements about the manner in which the Rebbe's teachings and advice were to be implemented. These disagreements had chiefly been voiced about the intensity of the Messianic proselytizing campaign as well as about the confident tone used to identify the Rebbe as the Jewish Messiah who was about to manifest himself. Since his death, there have been disputes about what the Rebbe would have sanctioned if he had been still alive: for example, a rabbi in Oxford who has been generally considered to be a follower of the Lubavitch movement was compelled to resign by the Lubavitch Foundation in Britain because it objected to the invitation he had extended to the prime minister of Israel to give a public lecture at Oxford University after he had been awarded the Nobel Prize for Peace. Since that prime minister had committed himself to surrendering some Holy Land territory during his peace negotiations with Palestinian leaders, it was argued that such an invitation was disrespectful to the Rebbe's memory:[41] the Rebbe had been firmly opposed to the surrender of Biblical Jewish land. The resulting conflict was publicized in the Jewish press in England and elsewhere, but the Lubavitcher have gone to some pains in cases such as these to describe such public disagreements as events of little significance.

The Rebbe's published works and the audio and video cassettes of his *farbrengens* [gatherings of his Hasidic followers] are readily available and enable the members of the movement to recall his extraordinary presence and the contents of his teachings. The vast organizational infrastructure which has shaped the movement provides it with a measure of momentum for the maintenance and the intensification of its activities. In this way, the Rebbe's death has failed to alter dramatically the movement's educational and religious endeavors.

Nevertheless, the faithful are now bereft of the living presence of their spiritual leader, and there will have to be a decision eventually to designate a successor. A rising star in the Lubavitch intellectual firmament has stated boldly in print: "Either our family gets closer, and the loss brings us together, or G-d forbid, the opposite."[42] Clearly, the Lubavitch movement is not immune from the bitter dissensions and factionalism which occur in other religious groups when a momentous event causes shock, reappraisal of policies, and rivalries between potential new leaders. There is evidence now that there is some turmoil among the Lubavitch senior officials, with various segments which are each considering mobilizing support for the claim to best represent the Rebbe's legacy. It will not be easy for a successor to follow into the late Rebbe's footsteps and to provide the guidance and care which so endeared him to his followers. He had earned their affection, respect, and reverence for decades and he was the central figure which provided the focus and unity of the movement.

NOTES

1. The terms Lubavitch and Habad are synonymous and refer to followers of the same Hasidic sect. Habad is an acronym for the Hebrew *hokhmah, binah,* and *da'at*—intelligence or wisdom, understanding, and knowledge. In Israel the term Habad is commonly used, while in North America the term Lubavitch or Lubavitcher is more popular.

2. See *The Jewish Journal of Sociology,* "Jewish Messianism Lubavitch-Style: An Interim Report," vol. 35, no. 2, December 1993, and "Interpreting Adversity: Dynamics of Commitment in a Messianic Redemption Campaign," vol. 36, no. 1, June 1994.

3. *New York Times,* August 22, 1991.

4. W. Shaffir, op. cit. in note 2 above, p. 52.

5. A New York congressman, who represents the Crown Heights district in the state assembly in Albany, remarked: "It's a community in some ways in denial. . . . People are going to feel immensely let down when something they believed in for so long, the expectation that he would return after death, doesn't happen"; see *Toronto Star,* June 13, 1994, p. A4.

6. *New York Times,* June 14, 1994, p. A11.

7. See Leon Festinger, Henry W. Riecken, and Stanley Schachter, *When Prophecy Fails* (Minneapolis, 1956).

8. See Anson D. Shupe, Jr., *Six Perspectives on New Religions: A Case Study Approach* (New York, 1981), p. 141.

9. J. G. Melton, "Spiritualization and Reaffirmation: What Really Happens When Prophecy Fails," *American Studies,* vol. 26, no. 2, 1985:20.

10. *New York Times,* op. cit. in note 3 above, p. 1.

11. *Jerusalem Post,* June 14, 1994, p. 1.

12. See *Forward,* June 17, 1994, p. 1.

13. Allan Nadler, "King of Kings County," *The New Republic,* July 11, 1994, pp. 16–17.

14. *Ibid.,* p. 17.

15. *Jerusalem Post,* June 13, 1994, p. 1.

16. The blessing which mourners recite after death.

17. *Kriya* is the rending of the garment of the mourner. The rent, at least four inches long, is made in the lapel of an outer garment before the funeral. For parents, the *kriya* is made on the left side; for other relatives, on the right.

18. See *Chabad* magazine, June 1994, p. 17.

19. *Ibid.*

20. See *Forward*, November 18, 1994, p. 13.

21. *Ibid.*

22. *Forward*, December 2, 1994, p. 1.

23. *Forward*, November 18, 1994, p. 13.

24. See *N'shei Chabad* newsletter, June 1994, p. 21.

25. C. Wright Mills, "Situated Actions and Vocabularies of Motive," in *American Sociological Review*, vol. 5, no. 5, 1940:904–913.

26. See *N'shei Chabad* newsletter, September 1994, p. 32.

27. *Ibid.*

28. *N'shei Chabad* newsletter, September 1994, p. 34.

29. "Moshiach and the Test of Faith," n.d.

30. *Chabad* magazine, June 18, 1994, p. 22.

31. *Ibid.*, p. 6.

32. *N'shei Chabad* newsletter, September 1994, p. 33.

33. *Ibid.*, p. 47.

34. *Chabad* magazine, June 1994, p. 6.

35. *Ibid.*, September 1994, p. 5.

36. *Ibid.*

37. *N'shei Chabad* newsletter, September 1994, p. 47.

38. *Chabad* magazine, August 1994, p. 47.

39. *World of Lubavitch*, December 1994, p. 4.

40. See *Jerusalem Report*, July 28, 1994, p. 22.

41. See *Forward*, October 21, 1994, and *Canadian Jewish News*, October 20, 1994.

42. *Chabad* magazine, August 1994, p. 78.

Fifteen Years of Failed Prophecy
Coping with Cognitive Dissonance in a Baha'i Sect

Robert W. Balch, John Domitrovitch, Barbara Lynn Mahnke, and Vanessa Morrison

On April 29, 1980, members of the Baha'is Under the Provisions of the Covenant (BUPC) entered fallout shelters to await a nuclear holocaust that they believed would fulfill the prophecies of Revelation. In the first hour, they expected a third of the world's population to perish, and they claimed that over the next twenty years, the planet would be ravaged by starvation, disease, revolutions, and natural disasters. They believed that by the year 2000 God's Kingdom would be established on earth and a thousand years of peace would ensue.

This prediction was only the first in a long series of failed prophecies that would test the faith of the BUPC. Between 1980 and 1995 the group's leader, Dr. Leland Jensen, set twenty dates for the Battle of Armageddon or lesser disasters that would lead up to the Apocalypse. In this paper we will examine the long-term effects of these failed prophecies on the BUPC.

Our analysis is based on the theory of cognitive dissonance, which Festinger, Riecken, and Schachter (1956) used to analyze reactions to failed prophecy in a millennial flying saucer cult. The group's leader, Marian Keech, was a medium who claimed an extraterrestrial being named Sananda had warned her that much of the Midwest would be inundated by a catastrophic flood on December 21, 1954.

Paradoxically, Festinger and his colleagues predicted that the failure of Mrs. Keech's prophecy would result in increased conviction and heightened efforts to recruit new believers. They argued that Mrs. Keech and her followers would experience severe cognitive dissonance when the prophecy failed, but that it would be extremely difficult for them to abandon their beliefs because they had made numerous public and private commitments to the prediction. To reduce the dissonance they would invent rationalizations to explain away the disconfirmation, and more importantly they would try to gain social support for their beliefs by increasing their efforts to recruit new believers.

The study by Festinger and his colleagues supported these hypotheses. Mrs. Keech responded to the failure of her prophecy by proclaiming that the catastrophe had been called off because her group "had spread so much light that God had saved the world from destruction" (1956:169). She eagerly granted interviews to reporters and invited curiosity seekers into her home to explain Sananda's latest revelation. Most of her followers were equally enthusiastic about publicizing Sananda's message, which was remarkable because the group had never shown much interest in proselytizing.

Festinger and his colleagues specified five conditions that must be met before prophetic failure will be followed by increased conviction and vigorous proselytizing:

1. Belief in the prediction must be held with deep conviction.
2. Members must have committed themselves to the prediction by engaging in important actions that are difficult to undo.
3. The prediction must be specific enough that it can be clearly disconfirmed.
4. There must be undeniable evidence that the prediction was wrong.
5. Members must have social support from fellow believers.

The BUPC clearly met these conditions in 1980, but less so when Jensen made his second prediction a few years later. By the 1990s, when Jensen made a flurry of predictions, hardly anyone in the BUPC except for Jensen and a few members of his inner circle met the first condition of deep conviction, and the commitments specified in the second condition were minimal compared to those that members had made in 1980. Our data suggest that the diminishing relevance of the Festinger theory reflects the emergence of an underground *culture of dissonance-reduction* consisting of disclaimers and *post facto* rationalizations that reduced the impact of the predictions and subsequent disconfirmations. This culture enabled members to dismiss the predictions and move on with their everyday lives while still claiming allegiance to Jensen and the Baha'i faith. The goal of preparing for the holocaust was ultimately displaced by more immediate, mundane concerns, despite the fact that the group's rhetoric remained as apocalyptic as ever.

Data Collection

Our data on the BUPC come from four participant-observer studies we conducted between 1980 and 1996. Besides taking part in numerous group activities, including potluck dinners, teaching sessions, and weekly meetings, we conducted forty-seven formal interviews with members, three group interviews with six ex-members, three individual interviews with high-ranking defectors who left in 1994 and 1996, and a lengthy interview with Jensen in 1980. Balch and two students also spent the night of April 29, 1980, in three BUPC fallout shelters. In addition, we have studied the group's press releases and BUPC newsletters pertaining to the predictions.[1]

An Overview of the BUPC

The BUPC is a small Baha'i sect based in Missoula, Montana. Its founder, a chiropractor named Leland Jensen, was expelled from the mainstream Baha'i religion in 1960. During a doctrinal dispute following the death of Shoghi Effendi, the Guardian of the Baha'i faith, Jensen aligned himself with a schismatic leader named Mason Remey who claimed to be the second Guardian. However, Remey died a few years later and his followers split into rival factions, each proclaiming a different Guardian. In 1964, after becoming disillusioned with the infighting, Jensen and his wife, Opal, moved to Missoula, where they opened a chiropractic clinic. Although Jensen had once been a highly acclaimed Baha'i missionary, he had stopped teaching the Faith by the time he got to Montana.

Then in 1969 Jensen was convicted of sexually molesting a fifteen-year-old patient. During the trial, several women testified against him, and he was sentenced to twenty years in the Montana State Prison. Shortly after his imprisonment, Jensen had a revelation: "I felt a presence only. I saw nobody. I saw no dove, no burning bush or anything of this nature. It talked to me—not in a physical voice but very vividly expressing to me that I was the Promised Joshua [prophesied in Zechariah 3]." After studying the Bible and Baha'i writings, Jensen understood that his mission was to establish the Baha'i Universal House of Justice after the world was cleansed of evil and apostasy by a nuclear holocaust.[2]

Jensen immediately began tying together diverse strands of Bible prophecies, Baha'i teachings, and pyramidology to substantiate his claims. He recruited many followers in prison, and after being paroled in 1973 he founded the BUPC in Missoula. By the end of the 1970s Jensen also had attracted followers in Wyoming, Colorado, and Arkansas.

Since 1980 membership in the BUPC has fluctuated considerably, but it probably has never exceeded 200 nationwide, despite Jensen's claims of having thousands of followers around the world. In 1994, the last year for which we have a membership list, there were only sixty-six members in Montana and fewer than twenty in other states. The Wyoming and Arkansas contingents disbanded after the 1980 disconfirmation, but new groups were formed in Minnesota and Wisconsin.

Over the years, about a third of the members have had college degrees, and the group has always stressed the importance of reading and research, so members tend to be exceptionally well informed about the Bible, Baha'i teachings, world religions, and international politics.

One of the most significant events in the history of the BUPC was the recruitment of Neal Chase, a spiritual seeker from Wisconsin who proved to be brilliant at synthesizing Jensen's teachings with other prophetic beliefs. Chase's most notable contribution was to bolster the "proofs" for Jensen's mission by incorporating the prophecies of George Williams, leader of an obscure nineteenth-century Mormon sect known as the Morrisites (Anderson 1988; Chase 1990). According to Chase, Williams predicted that Christ would return in Montana's Deer Lodge Valley where the Montana State Prison is located. The anticipated date of Christ's return, August 9, 1969, happened to be the first full day that Jensen spent in the prison, which Chase claims bears a striking resemblance to Ezekiel's temple described in the Bible.[3] By 1990, Jensen, then seventy-six, had turned much of the responsibility for interpreting the scriptures over to Chase.[4]

The Predictions

Between 1979 and 1995 Jensen and Chase made twenty specific predictions. The first time Jensen set a date for the Apocalypse was in 1979, when he proclaimed that a nuclear war would begin on April 29, 1980. Jensen's second prediction came in 1985, when he claimed that Halley's comet would crash into the earth the following year, triggering catastrophic upheavals that would culminate in the Battle of Armageddon. All eighteen predictions in the 1990s were made by Chase, although each had Jensen's approval. Unlike Jensen's two predictions in the 1980s, which foretold worldwide catastrophes, Chase's predictions pertained to small-scale disasters that he claimed would lead step by step toward the Apocalypse. Some of his predictions focused on upheavals caused by meteors, asteroids, and comets, but most pertained to the destruction of New York City by a nuclear bomb that would be planted by Middle Eastern terrorists.

Reactions to Prophecy Failure in the BUPC

Two predominant patterns emerged in response to the BUPC's failed prophecies. Jensen and Chase reacted in a manner that for the most part supports dissonance theory, whereas their followers generally did not. Therefore, it is important to treat these patterns separately.

The Reactions of Jensen and Chase

Before and after each prophesied date, Jensen and Chase behaved much like Marian Keech. Prior to every date they made strong public commitments by issuing strident press releases, and in the 1990s Chase made numerous unequivocal proclamations on the BUPC's public-access television show, "Baha'i Phone-In Live." Before the 1980 date, Jensen urged his followers to build fallout shelters and stock them with food, water, and survival gear, and he allowed his own shelter to be photographed for a front-page story in the local newspaper. Jensen also proclaimed in one of his books that any religion that cannot predict the exact moment of the Apocalypse "lacks Divine Guidance" (1979:61–62).

Jensen and Chase also reacted like Mrs. Keech when their predictions were disconfirmed. In light of the hypothesis that proselytizing should increase after disconfirmation, their most notable response was to heighten efforts to spread the BUPC message. After each failed prediction they quickly issued more press releases in which they insisted they had been right all along. These releases were sent as far away as the Vatican and the United Nations, and frequently they were hand-delivered to politicians and media executives. Jensen and Chase eagerly granted interviews to newspapers and radio talk shows, and they urged BUPC members to take advantage of each reprieve by renewing their efforts to recruit the 144,000 who would enter God's Kingdom.

Renewed proselytizing, however, required plausible explanations for each prophecy failure. Throughout the fifteen-year period, at least seven types of explanations were used: (1) the prediction was fulfilled spiritually rather than physically; (2) the prophecy was fulfilled physically, but not in the manner expected; (3) the date was off because of a miscalculation; (4) the date was a prediction, not a prophecy; (5) the leaders had a moral responsibility to warn the public despite the date's uncertainty; (6) God had given the world a reprieve; and (7) the predictions had been tests of members' faith.

(1) Jensen relied heavily on the notion of a *spiritual fulfillment* in 1980. He claimed that the seven-year Tribulation described in Revelation had commenced on April 29 and that the four winds of destruction (Revelation 7:1) were being held back until the 144,000 had been recruited. He offered a similar explanation in 1986 after Halley's comet failed to crash into the earth:

> The spiritual fulfillment [of the prophecy] did take place. A spiritual stone hit the earth. This stone is the message of the messiahship that only the [true] Baha'is understand. The spiritual stone crushes and destroys what the Christians claim, and what the covenant breakers [mainstream Baha'is] claim.

When a meteor collision and massive earthquakes failed to occur as predicted in 1991, Jensen claimed the prediction had been fulfilled by a "spiritual earthquake" caused by the defection of one of his most important followers. "Everything," he said, "happens on the spiritual plane before it manifests in the physical plane."

(2) More often, Jensen and Chase claimed their predictions were *physically fulfilled by other events* that happened on or around the dates or shortly thereafter. In 1980, Jensen cited numerous phone calls from reporters as far away as Australia to prove that he had fulfilled the prophecy that the Seventh Angel would pour his "bowl of wrath" into the air (Revelation 16:17–18). He claimed this referred to the worldwide media coverage his message received on April 29. When Mount St. Helens erupted nineteen days later, Jensen proclaimed that the volcanic ash that inundated Missoula was a warning of what would happen when Portland and Seattle were bombed.

A more recent instance of claiming a physical fulfillment occurred in 1994 after Chase made the following prediction about the bombing of New York City:

> On March 23, 1994, the veils will be rent asunder with the fiery holocaust of New York City's millions of inhabitants! Forty days later will come the Battle of Armageddon, in which one third of mankind will be

killed in one hour of thermonuclear war. (Press release, November 1, 1993)

In fact, on March 24, 1994, a gas pipeline exploded in Edison, New Jersey, across the Hudson River from New York. To buttress his claim that the prophecy had been fulfilled, Chase quoted an eyewitness who compared the explosion to a nuclear blast.

(3) Jensen and Chase frequently claimed to have made a *miscalculation* when they missed the mark. After the prophecy failure in 1980, Jensen immediately set a second date and then a third. Chase used this strategy continuously in the 1990s. For example, Chase's first prediction about New York was that the city would be bombed on November 29, 1992. Nothing happened until the World Trade Center was bombed three months later, although not with a nuclear weapon. Chase subsequently cited Daniel 7:12, which says, "their lives were prolonged for a season and a time," to prove that his prediction had been correct. Claiming that "a season" is three months, he announced that the November 29 date "plus the prophesied season of three months brought us to February 26, 1993, the day, the minute, the hour, the second that the World Trade Center was bombed" (press release, August 4, 1993).

(4) The admission of human error was rationalized by making a sharp distinction between a *prediction* and a *prophecy*. Prophecies came directly from God, whereas the BUPC's predictions were based on research and logic, which are subject to human fallibility. As Chase put it: "We can't be false prophets because we don't claim to be prophets. We simply *interpret* what is already there in the Bible." Jensen had always made this distinction, but it became increasingly important in the 1990s. According to this reasoning, Jensen and Chase were only human and they could make mistakes like everyone else.

(5) Despite the uncertainties caused by human failings, Jensen and Chase claimed they had a *moral responsibility* to warn the public because so many "signs" had suggested that catastrophes were imminent. The signs were synchronistic events that converged around a particular date. For instance, Chase claimed that numerous events had pointed to November 26, 1992, as the date for the bombing of New York:

1. Thousands of covenant-breaking Baha'is would be gathering on this date in New York, a city marked for destruction in the prophecies of Nostradamus.
2. Comet Swift-Tuttle, which supposedly heralded the founding of the Baha'i faith in 1863, would reach its closest distance to earth on December 18.
3. During a lunar eclipse on December 9, the moon would turn blood red, as foretold in Revelation 6:12 and Joel 2:31.

To ignore these signs would have been morally irresponsible because the BUPC had a "mandate from God to warn the people" about the Apocalypse. If New

York had been destroyed while they kept silent, because they only *suspected* something might happen, then "the blood of the people" would have been on their hands.

(6) With each disconfirmation, Jensen and Chase claimed that God had granted the BUPC a *reprieve*. After the 1980 prediction, Jensen claimed that God had given the BUPC more time to recruit the 144,000. The same explanation was offered in 1986. After both the Trade Center bombing and the Edison pipeline explosion in the 1990s, Chase claimed that God in his mercy had spared New York, but that the predictions were "wake-up" calls for the city's residents.

(7) Finally and most consistently, Jensen and Chase repeatedly claimed that the predictions were *tests*. After the 1980 prediction, Jensen pointed out that Matthew 24:37 says that the "coming of the Son of Man [Jensen] will repeat what happened in Noah's time," which according to Baha'i teachings is that Noah predicted the flood several times (Baha'u'llah 1931). Noah's first predictions separated the "sheep from the goats" so that when the flood finally happened only the pure of heart remained. By the 1990s, Jensen was referring to the 1980 prediction as "God's fire drill" and a "practice run."

The explanations offered by Jensen and Chase are examples of what Lyman and Scott (1968) call *accounts*. These are face-saving strategies intended to reduce embarrassment after a discrediting situation has occurred. In the BUPC these accounts enabled Jensen and Chase to claim they had been right all along: "We didn't make a mistake," Chase proclaimed after two failed attempts to predict the nuclear destruction of New York, "not even a teeny eeny one!" (Press release, November 1, 1993). Almost a year later, after five more failed prophecies, Chase claimed that the BUPC had "a 100 percent track record!" (Press release, October 9, 1994).

At first glance, the way Jensen and Chase reacted to the failure of their predictions seems to be entirely consistent with cognitive dissonance theory. However, the theory does not consider the effects of *repeated* prophecy failures.

Before the 1980 date, Jensen encouraged his followers to build fallout shelters and store food to prepare for the holocaust. Yet by the time of the second prediction in 1986, Jensen no longer emphasized physical preparedness, and the group's fallout shelters, including his own, had been dismantled. Instead he claimed that Missoula would be safe because of its remote mountainous location, as well as the fact that the "Promised One" lived there. In the event that shelters might be needed, Jensen said that the BUPC would be able to occupy an extensive network of tunnels under the university and city center, and he claimed his followers could stockpile all the provisions they would need in just three days.

By downplaying the need for building, stocking, and maintaining shelters, Jensen eliminated one of the most important commitments members had made in 1980. This is significant because, following the reasoning of Festinger and his colleagues, the fewer commitments members make before a prediction, the less the dissonance should be when a prophecy fails.

Perhaps more important are two changes that occurred in the 1990s. First, the nature of the predictions changed from apocalyptic global catastrophes to small-scale disasters heralding the nuclear conflagration. Chase explained that prophecy fulfillment is not a discrete event but a continuous, unfolding process. This had the effect of diffusing the impact of any particular prophecy failure.

Second, beginning in 1993, Jensen and Chase began making *disclaimers* before their predictions. Disclaimers are face-saving strategies that are used to head off *anticipated* embarrassment (Hewitt and Stokes 1975). For example, one of the dates for the bombing of New York was September 4, 1993, the third anniversary of Opal Jensen's death. Even before the day was over Jensen was speculating that the real date might be September 8, the anniversary of his wife's burial. Before the next date Chase clearly hedged his bets by saying: "I don't really care if the bombing is today, tomorrow, or next year. I only know that it is part of God's plan, and it *will* happen as prophesied. Nothing can alter the plan of God." Because severe dissonance is likely to occur only when a prediction is believed with deep conviction, the use of disclaimers should reduce the dissonance caused by prophecy failure. What is most interesting about these disclaimers, however, is that ordinary members had been using them for years before Jensen and Chase.

The Reactions of Ordinary Members

The responses of ordinary BUPC members to the failed predictions were considerably more complicated than those of Jensen and Chase. Not only were their reactions less consistent with the hypotheses proposed by Festinger and his colleagues, but their reactions changed considerably over time. By "ordinary members" we refer to everyone in the BUPC except Jensen and Chase. It will help to divide the fifteen-year period into three phases: 1980–1981, before and after the original prediction; 1986–1987, before and after the second prediction; and 1990–1995, when Chase made a flurry of predictions about lesser events that would culminate in Armageddon.

1980–1981

The first prediction provided the clearest test of dissonance theory because the BUPC met all the conditions specified by Festinger and his colleagues. (Balch, Farnsworth, and Wilkins 1983).

The prediction was specific down to the minute, and members had made substantial commitments based on their belief that it would come true. The most important commitment was the construction of fallout shelters, but members also wrote numerous pamphlets and books using Bible prophecies and pyramidology to prove the prediction was correct. Several members sent letters to the local paper warning people to prepare for the holocaust, and the BUPC organized a nuclear-preparedness group called SAFE (Safety and Fall-Out Education), which distributed thousands of leaflets urging Missoulians to prepare for nuclear war. The disconfirmation was painfully obvious to everyone, but, consistent with Festinger's fifth condition, members had the support of a close-knit community of fellow believers.

However, there was no increase in proselytizing after the date. In fact, prose-lytizing stopped altogether, which is significant because the BUPC had been heavily committed to teaching the Faith before April 29. During the first BUPC meeting after the prophecy failure, Jensen gave an emotional speech in which he exhorted his followers to capitalize on the reprieve: "Rise and Shine!" he shouted. "Establish the Kingdom! Teach as you never have before!" Although he had brought a large box of books for members to distribute, not one was taken. The BUPC were extremely confused and demoralized, and attendance at meetings dropped precipitously. These reactions clearly contradict dissonance theory.

On the other hand, it took six months before anyone openly defected, and when members left, their stated reasons usually had no direct connection to the failed prophecy. Instead their leaving was usually prompted by doctrinal disputes or interpersonal conflicts within the group. The prophecy failure may have con-tributed to their disillusionment, but it was not emphasized by any of our infor-mants. The members who stayed were able to sustain their faith by claiming that the prophecy was only a test which had given them more time to prepare. The Noah analogy was quickly adopted throughout the group. However, rather than redoubling their efforts to prepare for the holocaust, most members seemed burned out by the group's apocalyptic fervor. They claimed they had become so wrapped up in the prophecy that they had lost sight of the basic Baha'i teach-ings. As a member explained: "I think we all made a mistake. We got too caught up in the physical. We weren't ready for the war because spiritually none of us were strong enough."

1986–1987

Since Jensen claimed the seven-year Tribulation began on April 29, 1980, he had committed himself to a second prediction for 1987. Halley's comet, which was due to arrive in 1986, provided the rationale. Jensen predicted that on April 29, 1986, the comet would get pulled into an orbit around the earth and begin breaking up, pelting the planet with debris that would strike with the force of nuclear warheads. The gravitational pull of the comet would produce massive earthquakes and a convulsive shifting of the earth's crust. This would continue for one year until April 29, 1987, when the remainder of the comet would plum-met to earth, producing tidal waves thousands of feet high and earthquakes more devastating than any before.

The prediction rekindled the group's millennial enthusiasm. The comet dom-inated practically every meeting, as members eagerly discussed books, articles, TV documentaries, and biblical prophecies about comets. On March 22, 1986, the group finally went public with the prediction by issuing a press release proclaiming Halley's comet as the herald of the new kingdom.

However, the activities of the BUPC prior to the 1986 prediction differed from those in 1980 in two important ways. First, this time members made hardly any personal preparations to survive the coming destruction. Missoula presumably would be safe from the tidal waves and earthquakes that would devastate coastal cities.

The second difference was that members began hedging their bets with disclaimers before the 1986 date. The group's self-taught comet expert suggested that God might be using the comet to distract mankind from the real threat, which he speculated might be asteroids. Others speculated that God might be using the comet to test their faith, much as they had been tested in 1980. Still others claimed Jensen could be mistaken because, despite his identity as the "Promised One," he was "only a man" with failings like everyone else.

On the evening of April 28, 1986, the BUPC had a potluck dinner. Unlike a similar meeting the night before the 1980 date, when Jensen delivered a fiery speech and members had talked excitedly about the impending holocaust, Jensen did not address the group and nobody even mentioned the comet.

The morning after the disconfirmation, members quietly resumed their lives by going to work, attending school, or taking care of their children, as if it were just another day. As in 1980, there was no increase in proselytizing, and members offered accounts to explain the failed prophecy, the most common being the parallel with Noah's predictions. But unlike 1980, there was no apparent confusion or disillusionment, perhaps because members had not committed themselves to the same extent and because they already had prepared themselves for the prophecy failure. The expression "business as usual" is a good description of the aftermath of the disconfirmation. Although some members continued to profess belief that Armageddon would happen by April 29, 1987, others appeared to have lost interest in Jensen's date-setting.

By August of 1986, the emphasis had shifted away from the new date to being spiritually prepared for the end, whenever it might occur. Reports by ex-members indicate that the 1987 date was ignored by virtually everyone. Jensen began ridiculing the Tribulation as a misguided concept promoted by "the Christian sects," and his followers quickly followed suit.

1990–1995

Prior to the 1980 and 1986 predictions, members had sought confirming evidence to prove the accuracy of the prophecies, and that pattern continued in the 1990s. The evidence marshalled to support the predictions included Hopi prophecies, planetary conjunctions, dreams, numerological coincidences, the prophecies of Nostradamus, and predictions made by psychics and other religious leaders, such as Jeane Dixon and Elizabeth Clare Prophet.

However, as in 1986, the BUPC made few public commitments to the dates. The members who had weathered the disconfirmations of the 1980s were the least likely to take the predictions seriously. They made virtually no preparations. Some of the newer members attended Civil Defense workshops and stored survival gear, but these were isolated individual efforts. No maps of the city's Civil Defense tunnels were distributed to the BUPC, and members did not make an effort to warn the public as they had with SAFE in 1980. On two occasions members boxed up their possessions and camped in parks or their backyards when earthquakes were expected, but these commitments were minimal compared to those in the shelter-building days of 1979 and 1980.

Members also used disclaimers more often than ever before. Significantly, these face-saving strategies were extensions of the accounts that had been offered to explain past prophecy failures. Even members of Jensen's inner circle used these disclaimers. For example, one of Jensen's staunchest supporters started telling prospective members "not to lay any stock in the predictions Neal made [because] the real sign would be the entrance of the 144,000." She added that "the truth is that people would have really preferred for Neal to knock off his prophesying."

After each failed prediction, life for the BUPC continued on course. There were few traces of disillusionment among either new or old members. The BUPC provided the usual accounts in an offhanded manner: Jensen and Chase had to warn the public whether they were sure or not; God gave the BUPC more time because they were not ready yet; the prediction had been just another test. Some members did not even bother to offer accounts for the failed predictions. "I didn't get too concerned about these predictions," one said, "because a number of them had not materialized in the past." Proselytizing continued unabated, but few members stressed the predictions when teaching the Faith. Instead they focused more on Jensen's mission and the importance of being spiritually prepared when the prophecies of Revelation would ultimately be fulfilled. Even the World Trade Center bombing and Edison gas explosion failed to rekindle the group's apocalyptic enthusiasm.

Instead of focusing on Armageddon, members became increasingly absorbed by everyday life in the BUPC. In addition to the traditional round of weekly and monthly events, new group activities developed. These included a public-access television show, information tables at the university, Sunday church services, song writing and a choir, and demonstrations against the U.S. government's treatment of Iraq. The demonstrations are significant because prior to the 1990s the BUPC had never shown an interest in changing political events, only monitoring them for warning signs.

In 1991, Jensen established a twelve-person governing body called the Second International Baha'i Council (IBC) whose stated purpose was to lay the foundation for the Universal House of Justice, which Jensen expected to govern the world after the Apocalypse.[5] The IBC quickly came to dominate the lives of its members as its meetings steadily became longer and more frequent. IBC members engaged in endless wrangling over administrative details, writing projects, plans for establishing the world government, and discussions of other members' personal affairs, including marital problems, homosexuality, drug use, and gambling.

In contrast to the informality of previous years, the BUPC took on an increasingly bureaucratic character despite the fact that by 1990 the group probably had fewer than 100 members nationwide. The IBC elected officers passed numerous "laws" governing the conduct of BUPC members, and conducted its meetings according to Robert's Rules of Order. To deal with more mundane matters, local BUPC "councils" were formed in Montana, Colorado, and Wisconsin. City and county councils were established in Missoula, each with its own officers and formal responsibilities.

We found no evidence that these changes were prompted by the spate of failed prophecies in the 1990s. Instead, former IBC members attributed them to the death of Jensen's wife in 1990 and the growing irrelevance of the predictions. According to their first hypothesis, Opal Jensen's death compelled Jensen to consider his own mortality and the need for an administrative structure to carry on his mission after he died. The second hypothesis was that the new councils, offices, and activities were created to keep members motivated as the predictions lost their grip on the BUPC.

In addition to the structural changes that occurred in the BUPC, the defection rate accelerated in the 1990s. However, this too seems unrelated to the failed prophecies. Instead members were leaving because of doctrinal disputes[6] and resentment over the intrusion of the IBC into their private lives.

By 1996 we found only one member who still placed much emphasis on the predictions. He admitted to "feeling stupid" when they failed and he claimed he would leave if the nuclear war did not happen by the year 2000. For the others, the date-setting had become irrelevant, even though they continued to believe in Jensen's mission. The IBC's former vice president explained the general attitude this way:

> I think we're immune to it now. We've been desensitized. [The dates] come and they go and they come and they go and they come and they go. I think that's . . . why there isn't much preparedness. I think people mostly really don't believe them. I think mostly people would be really shocked [if a prediction came true].

Conclusion

When reviewing the reactions of the BUPC to repeated prophecy failures, two major patterns emerge: the behavior of the BUPC leaders generally supports the theory proposed by Festinger and his colleagues, but the responses of ordinary members do not. Jensen and Chase maintained their enthusiasm for the predictions and never seemed disheartened when their prophecies failed. This was not true for their followers. After the 1980 debacle, Jensen's followers became disillusioned and for a while they stopped proselytizing altogether. Over the next fifteen years, Jensen's predictions became less and less important for the average member. BUPC members made fewer preparations and they showed little disappointment when the prophecies failed. By the mid-1990s the predictions had become largely irrelevant.

The long-term responses of the ordinary members reflect the emergence of a *culture of dissonance-reduction* within the BUPC. The key ingredients of this culture are accounts and disclaimers that were disseminated in BUPC meetings, press releases, newsletters, and conversations among members. The origins of this culture can be traced to the accounts Jensen used to explain the 1980 failure. Following subsequent predictions, the ordinary members began turning these accounts into disclaimers to reduce the *possibility* of dissonance even before it could occur.

Eventually even Jensen and Chase began to conform to the culture of dissonance-reduction. Not only did they start using disclaimers themselves, but they reduced the magnitude of the dissonance caused by their failed prophecies by making predictions about relatively minor events instead of a global catastrophe. They also demanded fewer commitments to their predictions.

The trends between 1980 and 1995 illustrate the process of *goal displacement*. Goal displacement occurs when an organization's original goals are supplanted by more achievable ends. Group members "retreat from the initial program to a more moderate and conservative program in the interest of maintaining the strength of the organization" (Blau and Scott 1962:229). In goal displacement, the means of achieving organizational goals become ends in themselves as members focus their attention on mundane administrative jobs, and the group's original ideals become increasingly irrelevant to members' everyday lives.

The concept of goal displacement describes what happened in the BUPC. In 1980 the group's primary goal was preparing for the holocaust, but by the 1990s this objective had been supplanted by the more immediate goal of creating an administrative structure for ushering in God's Kingdom. The first hints of goal displacement occurred after the failed prophecy in 1980, when members began downplaying the importance of physical preparedness in favor of getting back to the basics of the Baha'i faith. The back-to-the-basics movement reemerged after the second disconfirmation in 1986. By 1995 the culture of dissonance-reduction had become so entrenched in the BUPC that hardly anyone was concerned about the imminence of the Apocalypse.

Our study of the BUPC, like all case studies, is more suggestive than conclusive. However, the data reveal two important weaknesses in Festinger's dissonance theory of prophecy failure. First, the theory ignores a fundamental structural distinction between leaders and followers: the leaders who make prophecies may respond to their failure quite differently from their followers. Second, the theory fails to address the long-range effects of prophecy failure. Our findings suggest that repeated failures cause a decline in both the fervor before the predictions and the disappointment afterward, until the goal of preparing for the Apocalypse is finally displaced by more ordinary and achievable objectives.

NOTES

1. Balch observed the BUPC over an eight-month period before and after the 1980 prediction. Mahnke (1987) spent eight months with the group in 1986 when members expected Halley's comet to collide with the earth. Domitrovich took part in BUPC activities between 1990 and 1995 when most of the failed prophecies occurred, and Morrison observed the group for almost twelve months in 1995 and 1996.

2. The development of the BUPC is a classic example of the psychopathological model of cult formation, in which religious founders assume a messianic role to compensate for a devastating collapse of their self-image and social world (Bainbridge and Stark 1979).

3. Leroy Anderson, the leading expert on the Morrisites (Anderson 1988), disputes Chase's claims about Williams's Deer Lodge prophecy. In a personal conversation, Anderson told Balch that Williams never specified August 9, 1969, as the date for the Second Coming of Christ. The date simply happened to be the day of the last annual Morrisite gathering.

4. Jensen died unexpectedly on August 6, 1996. Chase has taken the helm, and members seem to be taking the transition in stride. Neither the group's apocalyptic rhetoric nor its routine activities appear to have changed. However, Jensen's death is likely to have serious repercussions because Chase is disliked by some influential longtime members.

5. The first IBC was established by Shoghi Effendi, the Guardian of the Baha'i faith. The BUPC's IBC was an exact replica of the first.

6. These disputes usually revolved around the Guardianship. Ever since the 1970s, Jensen had claimed that Mason Remey's son, Pepe, was the Guardian, but Pepe steadfastly refused the title. After Pepe died in 1994, Jensen began hinting that Chase might be the next Guardian, but many members disagreed.

REFERENCES

Anderson, C. Leroy. 1988. *Joseph Morris and the Saga of the Morrisites*. Logan, UT: Utah State University Press.

Baha'u'llah. 1931. *The Book of Certitude*, translated by Shoghi Effendi. Willmette, IL: Baha'i Publishing Trust.

Bainbridge, William Sims, and Rodney Stark. 1979. "Cult Formation: Three Compatible Models." *Sociological Analysis* 40:283–295.

Balch, Robert W., Gwen Farnsworth, and Sue Wilkins. 1983. "When the Bombs Drop: Reactions to Disconfirmed Prophecy in a Millennial Sect." *Sociological Perspectives* 26:137–158.

Blau, Peter M., and W. Richard Scott. 1962. *Formal Organizations: A Comparative Approach*. San Francisco: Chandler.

Chase, Neal. 1990. *Ezekiel's Temple in Montana*. Private publication: Baha'i Center, 1830 South Avenue, Missoula, MT.

Festinger, Leon, Henry Riecken, and Stanley Schachter. 1956. *When Prophecy Fails*. Minneapolis: The University of Minnesota Press.

Hewitt, John P., and Randall Stokes. 1975. "Disclaimers." *American Sociological Review* 40:1–11.

Jensen, Leland. 1979. *The Most Mighty Document*. Private publication: Baha'i Center, 1830 South Avenue, Missoula, MT.

Lyman, Sanford M., and Marvin B. Scott. 1968. "Accounts." *American Sociological Review* 33:46–62.

Mahnke, Barbara Lynn. 1987. "Prophetic Failure: A Re-Testing of the Festinger, Riecken, and Schachter Study of Disconfirmed Prophecy in a Millennial Cult." Unpublished thesis. Missoula, MT: The University of Montana.

Sources

Leon Festinger, Henry W. Riecken, and Stanley Schachter, "Unfulfilled Prophecies and Disappointed Messiahs," from *When Prophecy Fails* (University of Minnesota Press, 1956), pp. 3–32.

Jane Allyn Hardyck and Marcia Braden, "Prophecy Fails Again: A Report of a Failure to Replicate," *Journal of Abnormal and Social Psychology*, 1962, Vol. 65, No. 2, pp. 136–141.

Joseph F. Zygmunt, "Prophetic Failure and Chiliastic Identity: The Case of Jehovah's Witnesses," *American Journal of Sociology*, May 1970, Vol. 75, No. 6.

Joseph F. Zygmunt, "When Prophecies Fail: A Theoretical Perspective on the Comparative Evidence" in *American Behavioral Scientist*, November/December 1972, Vol. 16, No. 2, pp. 245–268.

Neil Weiser, "The Effects of Prophetic Disconfirmation of the Committed," in *Review of Religious Research*, Fall 1974, No. 1, pp. 19–30.

Takaaki Sanada and Edward Norbeck, "Prophecy Continues to Fail: A Japanese Sect" *Journal of Cross-Cultural Psychology*, September 1975, Vol. 6, No. 3, pp. 331–345, © 1975 Washington State College.

Robert W. Balch, Gwen Farnsworth, and Sue Wilkins, "When the Bombs Drop: Reactions to Disconfirmed Prophecy in a Millennial Sect," *Sociological Perspectives*, April 1983, Vol. 26, No. 2, pp. 137–158, © 1983 Pacific Sociological Association.

J. Gordon Melton, "Spiritualization and Reaffirmation: What Really Happens When Prophecy Fails," *American Studies*, 1985, Vol. 26, No. 2, pp. 17–29.

Lawrence Foster, "Had Prophecy Failed?: Contrasting Perspectives of the Millerites and Shakers," from *The Disappointed: Millerism and Millenarianism in the Nineteenth Century*, edited by Ronald L. Numbers and Jonathon M. Butler, 1987, pp. 173–188.

Anthony B. van Fossen, "How Do Movements Survive Failures of Prophecy?," *Research in Social Movements, Conflicts and Change*, 1988, Vol. 10, pp. 193–212.

Richard Singelenberg, " 'It Separated the Wheat from the Chaff': The '1975'

Prophecy and Its Impact among Dutch Jehovah's Witnesses," *Sociological Analysis*, Spring 1989, Volume 50, No. 1, pp. 23–40.

Susan J. Palmer and Natalie Finn, "Coping with Apocalypse in Canada: Experiences of Endtime in La Mission de l'Esprit Saint and the Institute of Applied Metaphysics," *Sociological Analysis*, Winter 1992, Volume 53, No. 4, pp. 397–415.

Matthew N. Schmalz, "When Festinger Fails: Prophecy and the Watchtower," *Religion*, October 1994, Volume 24, No. 4, pp. 293–308.

William Shaffir, "When Prophecy Is Not Validated: Explaining the Unexpected in a Messianic Campaign," *The Jewish Journal of Sociology*, December 1995, Volume 37, No. 2, pp. 119–136.

Robert W. Balch, John Domitrovitch, Barbara Lynn Mahnke, and Vanessa Morrison, "Fifteen Years of Failed Prophecy: Coping with Cognitive Dissonance in a Baha'i Sect," from *Millennium, Messiahs, and Mayhem: Contemporary Apocalyptic Movements* (Routledge, 1997), ch. 4.